Effective awk Programming

Effective awk Programming

Third Edition

Arnold Robbins

O'REILLY®

Beijing · Cambridge · Farnham · Köln · Paris · Sebastopol · Taipei · Tokyo

Effective awk Programming, Third Edition
by Arnold Robbins

Printed in the United States of America.

Free Software Foundation, Inc., 59 Temple Place, Suite 330, Boston, MA 02111-1307, USA. Phone: (617) 542-5942, Fax: (617) 542-2652, Email: *gnu@gnu.org*, URL: *http://www.gnu.org*.

Published by O'Reilly & Associates, Inc., 101 Morris Street, Sebastopol, CA 95472.

This is Edition 3 of *Effective awk Programming: A User's Guide for GNU awk*, for the 3.1.0 (or later) version of the GNU implementation of awk.

Editor: Chuck Toporek

Production Editor: Jeffrey Holcomb

Cover Designer: Hanna Dyer

Printing History:

March 1996:	First Edition (published by Specialized Systems Consultants, Inc. and the Free Software Foundation, Inc. as *Effective AWK Programming: A User's Guide for GNU AWK*)
February 1997:	Second Edition (published by Specialized Systems Consultants, Inc. and the Free Software Foundation, Inc. as *Effective AWK Programming: A User's Guide*)
May 2001:	Third Edition (published by O'Reilly & Associates, Inc.)

ISBN: 0-596-00070-7

[M]

To Miriam, for making me complete.

To Chana, for the joy you bring us.

To Rivka, for the exponential increase.

To Nachum, for the added dimension.

To Malka, for the new beginning.

Table of Contents

Foreword

Arnold Robbins and I are good friends. We were introduced 11 years ago by circumstances—and our favorite programming language, *awk*. The circumstances started a couple of years earlier. I was working at a new job and noticed an unplugged Unix computer sitting in the corner. No one knew how to use it, and neither did I. However, a couple of days later it was running, and I was root and the one-and-only user. That day, I began the transition from statistician to Unix programmer.

On one of many trips to the library or bookstore in search of books on Unix, I found the gray *awk* book, a.k.a. Aho, Kernighan, and Weinberger, *The AWK Programming Language* (Addison Wesley, 1988). *awk*'s simple programming paradigm—find a pattern in the input and then perform an action—often reduced complex or tedious data manipulations to few lines of code. I was excited to try my hand at programming in *awk*.

Alas, the *awk* on my computer was a limited version of the language described in the *awk* book. I discovered that my computer had "old awk" and the *awk* book described "new awk." I learned that this was typical; the old version refused to step aside or relinquish its name. If a system had a new *awk*, it was invariably called *nawk*, and few systems had it. The best way to get a new *awk* was to *ftp* the source code for *gawk* from `prep.ai.mit.edu`. *gawk* was a version of new *awk* written by David Trueman and Arnold, and available under the GNU General Public License.

(Incidentally, it's no longer difficult to find a new *awk*. *gawk* ships with Linux, and you can download binaries or source code for almost any system; my wife uses *gawk* on her VMS box.)

My Unix system started out unplugged from the wall; it certainly was not plugged into a network. So, oblivious to the existence of *gawk* and the Unix community in general, and desiring a new *awk*, I wrote my own, called *mawk*. Before I was finished I knew about *gawk*, but it was too late to stop, so I eventually posted to a comp.sources newsgroup.

A few days after my posting, I got a friendly email from Arnold introducing himself. He suggested we share designs and algorithms and attached a draft of the POSIX standard so that I could update *mawk* to support language extensions added after publication of the *awk* book.

Frankly, if our roles had been reversed, I would not have been so open and we probably would have never met. I'm glad we did meet. He is an *awk* expert's *awk* expert and a genuinely nice person. Arnold contributes significant amounts of his expertise and time to the Free Software Foundation.

This book is the *gawk* reference manual, but at its core it is a book about *awk* programming that will appeal to a wide audience. It is a definitive reference to the *awk* language as defined by the 1987 Bell Labs release and codified in the 1992 POSIX Utilities standard.

On the other hand, the novice *awk* programmer can study a wealth of practical programs that emphasize the power of *awk*'s basic idioms: data driven control-flow, pattern matching with regular expressions, and associative arrays. Those looking for something new can try out *gawk*'s interface to network protocols via special */inet* files.

The programs in this book make clear that an *awk* program is typically much smaller and faster to develop than a counterpart written in C. Consequently, there is often a payoff to prototyping an algorithm or design in *awk* to get it running quickly and expose problems early. Often, the interpreted performance is adequate and the *awk* prototype becomes the product.

The new *pgawk* (profiling *gawk*) produces program execution counts. I recently experimented with an algorithm that for n lines of input exhibited $\sim Cn^2$ performance, while theory predicted $\sim Cn \log n$ behavior. A few minutes of poring over the *awkprof.out* profile pinpointed the problem to a single line of code. *pgawk* is a welcome addition to my programmer's toolbox.

Arnold has distilled over a decade of experience writing and using *awk* programs, and developing *gawk*, into this book. If you use awk or want to learn how, then read this book.

Michael Brennan
Author of *mawk*

Preface

Several kinds of tasks occur repeatedly when working with text files. You might want to extract certain lines and discard the rest. Or you may need to make changes wherever certain patterns appear, but leave the rest of the file alone. Writing single-use programs for these tasks in languages such as C, C++, or Pascal is time-consuming and inconvenient. Such jobs are often easier with *awk*. The *awk* utility interprets a special-purpose programming language that makes it easy to handle simple data-reformatting jobs.

The GNU implementation of *awk* is called *gawk*; it is fully compatible with the System V Release 4 version of *awk*. *gawk* is also compatible with the POSIX specification of the *awk* language. This means that all properly written *awk* programs should work with *gawk*. Thus, we usually don't distinguish between *gawk* and other *awk* implementations.

Using *awk* allows you to:

- Manage small, personal databases
- Generate reports
- Validate data
- Produce indexes and perform other document preparation tasks
- Experiment with algorithms that you can adapt later to other computer languages

In addition, *gawk* provides facilities that make it easy to:

- Extract bits and pieces of data for processing
- Sort data
- Perform simple network communications

This book teaches you about the *awk* language and how you can use it effectively. You should already be familiar with basic system commands, such as *cat* and *ls*,* as well as basic shell facilities, such as input/output (I/O) redirection and pipes.

Implementations of the *awk* language are available for many different computing environments. This book, while describing the *awk* language in general, also describes the particular implementation of *awk* called *gawk* (which stands for "GNU awk"). *gawk* runs on a broad range of Unix systems, ranging from 80386 PC-based computers up through large-scale systems, such as Crays. *gawk* has also been ported to Mac OS X, MS-DOS, Microsoft Windows (all versions) and OS/2 PCs, Atari and Amiga microcomputers, BeOS, Tandem D20, and VMS.

History of awk and gawk

The name *awk* comes from the initials of its designers: Alfred V. Aho, Peter J. Weinberger, and Brian W. Kernighan. The original version of *awk* was written in 1977 at AT&T Bell Laboratories. In 1985, a new version made the programming language more powerful, introducing user-defined functions, multiple input streams, and computed regular expressions. This new version became widely available with Unix System V Release 3.1 (SVR3.1). The version in SVR4 added some new features and cleaned up the behavior in some of the "dark corners" of the language. The specification for *awk* in the POSIX Command Language and Utilities standard further clarified the language. Both the *gawk* designers and the original Bell Laboratories *awk* designers provided feedback for the POSIX specification.

Paul Rubin wrote the GNU implementation, *gawk*, in 1986. Jay Fenlason completed it, with advice from Richard Stallman. John Woods contributed parts of the code as well. In 1988 and 1989, David Trueman, with help from me, thoroughly reworked *gawk* for compatibility with the newer *awk*. Circa 1995, I became the primary maintainer. Current development focuses on bug fixes, performance improvements, standards compliance, and occasionally, new features.

---

* These commands are available on POSIX-compliant systems, as well as on traditional Unix-based systems. If you are using some other operating system, you still need to be familiar with the ideas of I/O redirection and pipes.

In May of 1997, Jürgen Kahrs felt the need for network access from *awk*, and with a little help from me, set about adding features to do this for *gawk*. At that time, he also wrote the bulk of *TCP/IP Internetworking with gawk* (a separate document, available as part of the *gawk* distribution). Chapter 14, *Internetworking with gawk*, is condensed from that document. His code finally became part of the main *gawk* distribution with *gawk* Version 3.1.

See Appendix A, *The Evolution of the awk Language*, for a complete list of those who made important contributions to *gawk*.

A Rose by Any Other Name

The *awk* language has evolved over the years. Full details are provided in Appendix A. The language described in this book is often referred to as "new *awk*" (*nawk*).

Because of this, many systems have multiple versions of *awk*. Some systems have an *awk* utility that implements the original version of the *awk* language and a *nawk* utility for the new version.* Others have an *oawk* version for the "old *awk*" language and plain *awk* for the new one. Still others only have one version, which is usually the new one.†

All in all, this makes it difficult for you to know which version of *awk* you should run when writing your programs. The best advice I can give here is to check your local documentation. Look for *awk*, *oawk*, and *nawk*, as well as for *gawk*. It is likely that you already have some version of new *awk* on your system, which is what you should use when running your programs. (Of course, if you're reading this book, chances are good that you have *gawk*!)

Throughout this book, whenever we refer to a language feature that should be available in any complete implementation of POSIX *awk*, we simply use the term *awk*. When referring to a feature that is specific to the GNU implementation, we use the term *gawk*.

Using This Book

The term *awk* refers to a particular program as well as to the language you use to tell this program what to do. When we need to be careful, we call the language "the *awk* language," and the program "the *awk* utility." This book explains both the *awk* language and how to run the *awk* utility. The term *awk program* refers to a program written by you in the *awk* programming language.

---

* Of particular note is Sun's Solaris, where */usr/bin/awk* is, sadly, still the original version. Use */usr/xpg4/bin/awk* to get a POSIX-compliant version of *awk* on Solaris.

† Often, these systems use *gawk* for their *awk* implementation!

Primarily, this book explains the features of *awk*, as defined in the POSIX standard. It does so in the context of the *gawk* implementation. While doing so, it also attempts to describe important differences between *gawk* and other *awk* implementations.* Finally, any *gawk* features that are not in the POSIX standard for *awk* are noted.

This book has the difficult task of being both a tutorial and a reference. If you are a novice, feel free to skip over details that seem too complex. You should also ignore the many cross-references; they are for the expert user and for the online info version of the document.

There are sidebars scattered throughout the book. They add a more complete explanation of points that are relevant, but not likely to be of interest on first reading. All appear in the index, under the heading "advanced features."

Most of the time, the examples use complete *awk* programs. In some of the more advanced sections, only the part of the *awk* program that illustrates the concept currently being described is shown.

While this book is aimed principally at people who have not been exposed to *awk*, there is a lot of information here that even the *awk* expert should find useful. In particular, the description of POSIX *awk* and the example programs in Chapter 12, *A Library of awk Functions*, and in Chapter 13, *Practical awk Programs*, should be of interest.

Chapter 1, *Getting Started with awk*, provides the essentials you need to know to begin using *awk*.

Chapter 2, *Regular Expressions*, introduces regular expressions in general, and in particular the flavors supported by POSIX *awk* and *gawk*.

Chapter 3, *Reading Input Files*, describes how *awk* reads your data. It introduces the concepts of records and fields, as well as the `getline` command. I/O redirection is first described here.

Chapter 4, *Printing Output*, describes how *awk* programs can produce output with `print` and `printf`.

Chapter 5, *Expressions*, describes expressions, which are the basic building blocks for getting most things done in a program.

Chapter 6, *Patterns, Actions, and Variables*, describes how to write patterns for matching records, actions for doing something when a record is matched, and the built-in variables *awk* and *gawk* use.

---

* All such differences appear in the index under the entry "differences in *awk* and *gawk*."

Chapter 7, *Arrays in awk*, covers *awk*'s one-and-only data structure: associative arrays. Deleting array elements and whole arrays is also described, as well as sorting arrays in *gawk*.

Chapter 8, *Functions*, describes the built-in functions *awk* and *gawk* provide, as well as how to define your own functions.

Chapter 9, *Internationalization with gawk*, describes special features in *gawk* for translating program messages into different languages at runtime.

Chapter 10, *Advanced Features of gawk*, describes a number of *gawk*-specific advanced features. Of particular note are the abilities to have two-way communications with another process, perform TCP/IP networking, and profile your *awk* programs.

Chapter 11, *Running awk and gawk*, describes how to run *gawk*, the meaning of its command-line options, and how it finds *awk* program source files.

Chapter 12, *A Library of awk Functions*, and Chapter 13, *Practical awk Programs*, provide many sample *awk* programs. Reading them allows you to see *awk* solving real problems.

Chapter 14, *Internetworking with gawk*, provides an in-depth discussion and examples of how to use *gawk* for Internet programming.

Appendix A, *The Evolution of the awk Language*, describes how the *awk* language has evolved since first release to present. It also describes how *gawk* has acquired features over time.

Appendix B, *Installing gawk*, describes how to get *gawk*, how to compile it under Unix, and how to compile and use it on different PC operating systems. It also describes how to report bugs in *gawk* and where to get three other freely available implementations of *awk*.

Appendix C, *Implementation Notes*, describes how to disable *gawk*'s extensions, as well as how to contribute new code to *gawk*, how to write extension libraries, and some possible future directions for *gawk* development.

Appendix D, *Basic Programming Concepts*, provides some very cursory background material for those who are completely unfamiliar with computer programming. Also centralized there is a discussion of some of the issues surrounding floating-point numbers.

Appendix E, *GNU General Public License*, and Appendix F, *GNU Free Documentation License*, present the licenses that cover the *gawk* source code and this book, respectively.

The Glossary defines most, if not all, the significant terms used throughout the book. If you find terms that you aren't familiar with, try looking them up here.

Typographical Conventions

The following typographical conventions are used in this book:

Italic

Used to show generic arguments and options; these should be replaced with user-supplied values. Italic is also used to highlight comments in examples. In the text, italic indicates commands, filenames, options, and the first occurrences of important terms.

`Constant width`

Used for code examples, inline code fragments, and variable and function names.

`Constant width italic`

Used in syntax summaries and examples to show replaceable text; this text should be replaced with user-supplied values. It is also used in the text for the names of control keys.

`Constant width bold`

Used in code examples to show commands or other text that the user should type literally.

$, >

The $ indicates the standard shell's primary prompt. The > indicates the shell's secondary prompt, which is printed when a command is not yet complete.

[ ]   Surround optional elements in a description of syntax. (The brackets themselves should never be typed.)

When you see the owl icon, you know the text beside it is a note.

On the other hand, when you see the turkey icon, you know the text beside it is a warning.

Dark Corners

Until the POSIX standard (and *The Gawk Manual*), many features of *awk* were either poorly documented or not documented at all. Descriptions of such features (often called "dark corners") are noted in this book with "(d.c.)". They also appear in the index under the heading "dark corner."

Any coverage of dark corners is, by definition, something that is incomplete.

The GNU Project and This Book

The Free Software Foundation (FSF) is a nonprofit organization dedicated to the production and distribution of freely distributable software. It was founded by Richard M. Stallman, the author of the original Emacs editor. GNU Emacs is the most widely used version of Emacs today.

The GNU* Project is an ongoing effort on the part of the Free Software Foundation to create a complete, freely distributable, POSIX-compliant computing environment. The FSF uses the "GNU General Public License" (GPL) to ensure that their software's source code is always available to the end user. A copy of the GPL is included in this book for your reference (see Appendix E). The GPL applies to the C language source code for *gawk*. To find out more about the FSF and the GNU Project online, see the GNU Project's home page at *http://www.gnu.org*. This book may also be read from their documentation web site at *http://www.gnu.org/ manual/gawk/*.

Until the GNU operating system is more fully developed, you should consider using GNU/Linux, a freely distributable, Unix-like operating system for Intel 80386, DEC Alpha, Sun SPARC, IBM S/390, and other systems.† There are many books on GNU/Linux. One that is freely available is *Linux Installation and Getting Started* by Matt Welsh (Specialized Systems Consultants). Another good book is *Learning Debian GNU/Linux* by Bill McCarty (O'Reilly). Many GNU/Linux distributions are often available in computer stores or bundled on CD-ROMs with books about Linux. (There are three other freely available, Unix-like operating systems for 80386 and other systems: NetBSD, FreeBSD, and OpenBSD. All are based on the 4.4-Lite Berkeley Software Distribution, and they use recent versions of *gawk* for their versions of *awk*.)

The book you are reading is actually free—at least, the information in it is free to anyone. The machine-readable source code for the book comes with *gawk*; anyone may take this book to a copying machine and make as many copies as they like. (Take a moment to check the Free Documentation License in Appendix F.)

---

* GNU stands for "GNU's not Unix."

† The terminology "GNU/Linux" is explained in the Glossary.

Although you could just print it out yourself, bound books are much easier to read and use. Furthermore, part of the proceeds from sales of this book go back to the FSF to help fund development of more free software. In keeping with the GNU Free Documentation License, O'Reilly & Associates is making the DocBook version of this book available on their web site (*http://www.oreilly.com/catalog/awkprog3*). They also contributed significant editorial resources to the book, which were folded into the Texinfo version distributed with *gawk*.

The book itself has gone through a number of previous editions. Paul Rubin wrote the very first draft of *The GAWK Manual*; it was around 40 pages in size. Diane Close and Richard Stallman improved it, yielding a version that was around 90 pages long and barely described the original, "old" version of *awk*.

I started working with that version in the fall of 1988. As work on it progressed, the FSF published several preliminary versions (numbered 0.*x*). In 1996, Edition 1.0 was released with *gawk* 3.0.0. SSC published the first two editions of *Effective awk Programming*, and the FSF published the same two editions under the title *The GNU Awk User's Guide*.

This edition maintains the basic structure of Edition 1.0, but with significant additional material, reflecting the host of new features in *gawk* Version 3.1. Of particular note is the section "Sorting Array Values and Indices with gawk" in Chapter 7, as well as the section "Bit-Manipulation Functions of gawk" in Chapter 8, all of Chapter 9 and Chapter 10, and the section "Adding New Built-in Functions to gawk" in Appendix C.

Effective awk Programming will undoubtedly continue to evolve. An electronic version comes with the *gawk* distribution from the FSF. If you find an error in this book, please report it! See the section "Reporting Problems and Bugs" in Appendix B for information on submitting problem reports electronically, or write to me in care of the publisher.

How to Contribute

As the maintainer of GNU *awk*, I am starting a collection of publicly available *awk* programs. For more information, see *ftp://ftp.freefriends.org/arnold/Awkstuff*. If you have written an interesting *awk* program, or have written a *gawk* extension that you would like to share with the rest of the world, please contact me (*arnold@gnu.org*). Making things available on the Internet helps keep the *gawk* distribution down to manageable size.

Acknowledgments

The initial draft of *The GAWK Manual* had the following acknowledgments:

> Many people need to be thanked for their assistance in producing this manual. Jay Fenlason contributed many ideas and sample programs. Richard Mlynarik and Robert Chassell gave helpful comments on drafts of this manual. The paper *A Supplemental Document for awk*, by John W. Pierce of the Chemistry Department at UC San Diego, pinpointed several issues relevant both to *awk* implementation and to this manual, that would otherwise have escaped us.

I would like to acknowledge Richard M. Stallman, for his vision of a better world and for his courage in founding the FSF and starting the GNU Project.

The following people (in alphabetical order) provided helpful comments on various versions of this book, up to and including this edition. Rick Adams, Nelson H.F. Beebe, Karl Berry, Dr. Michael Brennan, Rich Burridge, Claire Cloutier, Diane Close, Scott Deifik, Christopher ("Topher") Eliot, Jeffrey Friedl, Dr. Darrel Hankerson, Michal Jaegermann, Dr. Richard J. LeBlanc, Michael Lijewski, Pat Rankin, Miriam Robbins, Mary Sheehan, and Chuck Toporek.

Robert J. Chassell provided much valuable advice on the use of Texinfo. Karl Berry helped significantly with the TEX part of Texinfo.

I would like to thank Marshall and Elaine Hartholz of Seattle and Dr. Bert and Rita Schreiber of Detroit for large amounts of quiet vacation time in their homes, which allowed me to make significant progress on this book and on *gawk* itself.

Phil Hughes of SSC contributed in a very important way by loaning me his laptop GNU/Linux system, not once, but twice, which allowed me to do a lot of work while away from home. I would also like to thank Phil for publishing the first two editions of this book, and for getting me started as a technical author.

David Trueman deserves special credit; he has done a yeoman job of evolving *gawk* so that it performs well and without bugs. Although he is no longer involved with *gawk*, working with him on this project was a significant pleasure.

The intrepid members of the GNITS mailing list, and most notably Ulrich Drepper, provided invaluable help and feedback for the design of the internationalization features.

Nelson Beebe, Martin Brown, Scott Deifik, Darrel Hankerson, Michal Jaegermann, Jürgen Kahrs, Pat Rankin, Kai Uwe Rommel, and Eli Zaretskii (in alphabetical order) are long-time members of the *gawk* "crack portability team." Without their hard work and help, *gawk* would not be nearly the fine program it is today. It has been and continues to be a pleasure working with this team of fine people.

David and I would like to thank Brian Kernighan of Bell Laboratories for invaluable assistance during the testing and debugging of *gawk*, and for help in clarifying numerous points about the language. We could not have done nearly as good a job on either *gawk* or its documentation without his help.

Michael Brennan, author of *mawk*, contributed the Foreword, for which I thank him. Perhaps one of the most rewarding aspects of my long-term work with *gawk* has been the friendships it has brought me, both with Michael and with Brian Kernighan.

A special thanks to Chuck Toporek of O'Reilly & Associates for thoroughly editing this book and shepherding the project through its various stages.

I must thank my wonderful wife, Miriam, for her patience through the many versions of this project, for her proofreading, and for sharing me with the computer. I would like to thank my parents for their love, and for the grace with which they raised and educated me. Finally, I also must acknowledge my gratitude to G-d, for the many opportunities He has sent my way, as well as for the gifts He has given me with which to take advantage of those opportunities.

Arnold Robbins
Nof Ayalon
ISRAEL
March, 2001

I

The awk Language and gawk

Part I describes the *awk* language and *gawk* program in detail. It starts with the basics and continues through all of the features of *awk* and *gawk*. This part contains the following chapters:

1

Getting Started with awk

The basic function of *awk* is to search files for lines (or other units of text) that contain certain patterns. When a line matches one of the patterns, *awk* performs specified actions on that line. *awk* keeps processing input lines in this way until it reaches the end of the input files.

Programs in *awk* are different from programs in most other languages, because *awk* programs are *data-driven*; that is, you describe the data you want to work with and then what to do when you find it. Most other languages are *procedural*; you have to describe, in great detail, every step the program is to take. When working with procedural languages, it is usually much harder to clearly describe the data your program will process. For this reason, *awk* programs are often refreshingly easy to read and write.

When you run *awk*, you specify an *awk program* that tells *awk* what to do. The program consists of a series of *rules*. (It may also contain *function definitions*, an advanced feature that we will ignore for now. See the section "User-Defined Functions" in Chapter 8, *Functions*.) Each rule specifies one pattern to search for and one action to perform upon finding the pattern.

Syntactically, a rule consists of a pattern followed by an action. The action is enclosed in curly braces to separate it from the pattern. Newlines usually separate rules. Therefore, an *awk* program looks like this:

```
pattern { action }
pattern { action }
...
```

How to Run awk Programs

There are several ways to run an *awk* program. If the program is short, it is easiest to include it in the command that runs *awk*, like this:

```
awk 'program' input-file1 input-file2 ...
```

When the program is long, it is usually more convenient to put it in a file and run it with a command like this:

```
awk -f program-file input-file1 input-file2 ...
```

This section discusses both mechanisms, along with several variations of each.

One-Shot Throwaway awk Programs

Once you are familiar with *awk*, you will often type in simple programs the moment you want to use them. Then you can write the program as the first argument of the *awk* command, like this:

```
awk 'program' input-file1 input-file2 ...
```

where *program* consists of a series of *patterns* and *actions*, as described earlier.

This command format instructs the *shell*, or command interpreter, to start *awk* and use the *program* to process records in the input file(s). There are single quotes around *program* so the shell won't interpret any *awk* characters as special shell characters. The quotes also cause the shell to treat all of *program* as a single argument for *awk*, and allow *program* to be more than one line long.

This format is also useful for running short or medium-sized *awk* programs from shell scripts, because it avoids the need for a separate file for the *awk* program. A self-contained shell script is more reliable because there are no other files to misplace.

The section "Some Simple Examples" later in this chapter presents several short, self-contained programs.

Running awk Without Input Files

You can also run *awk* without any input files. If you type the following command line:

```
awk 'program'
```

awk applies the *program* to the *standard input*, which usually means whatever you type on the terminal. This continues until you indicate end-of-file by typing Ctrl-d. (On other operating systems, the end-of-file character may be different. For example, on OS/2 and MS-DOS, it is Ctrl-z.)

As an example, the following program prints a friendly piece of advice (from Douglas Adams's *The Hitchhiker's Guide to the Galaxy*), to keep you from worrying about the complexities of computer programming (BEGIN is a feature we haven't discussed yet):

```
$ awk "BEGIN { print \"Don't Panic!\" }"
Don't Panic!
```

This program does not read any input. The \ before each of the inner double quotes is necessary because of the shell's quoting rules—in particular because it mixes both single quotes and double quotes.*

This next simple *awk* program emulates the *cat* utility; it copies whatever you type on the keyboard to its standard output (why this works is explained shortly):

```
$ awk '{ print }'
Now is the time for all good men
Now is the time for all good men
to come to the aid of their country.
to come to the aid of their country.
Four score and seven years ago, ...
Four score and seven years ago, ...
What, me worry?
What, me worry?
Ctrl-d
```

Running Long Programs

Sometimes your *awk* programs can be very long. In this case, it is more convenient to put the program into a separate file. In order to tell *awk* to use that file for its program, you type:

```
awk -f source-file input-file1 input-file2 ...
```

The *–f* instructs the *awk* utility to get the *awk* program from the file *source-file*. Any filename can be used for *source-file*. For example, you could put the program:

```
BEGIN { print "Don't Panic!" }
```

into the file *advice*. Then this command:

```
awk -f advice
```

does the same thing as this one:

```
awk "BEGIN { print \"Don't Panic!\" }"
```

---

* Although we generally recommend the use of single quotes around the program text, double quotes are needed here in order to put the single quote into the message.

This was explained earlier (see the previous section "Running awk Without Input Files)." Note that you don't usually need single quotes around the filename that you specify with *–f*, because most filenames don't contain any of the shell's special characters. Notice that in *advice*, the *awk* program did not have single quotes around it. The quotes are only needed for programs that are provided on the *awk* command line.

If you want to identify your *awk* program files clearly as such, you can add the extension *.awk* to the filename. This doesn't affect the execution of the *awk* program but it does make "housekeeping" easier.

Executable awk Programs

Once you have learned *awk*, you may want to write self-contained *awk* scripts, using the #! script mechanism. You can do this on many Unix systems* as well as on the GNU system. For example, you could update the file *advice* to look like this:

```
#! /bin/awk -f

BEGIN { print "Don't Panic!" }
```

After making this file executable (with the *chmod* utility), simply type advice at the shell and the system arranges to run *awk*† as if you had typed awk -f advice:

```
$ chmod +x advice
$ advice
Don't Panic!
```

Self-contained *awk* scripts are useful when you want to write a program that users can invoke without their having to know that the program is written in *awk*.

Comments in awk Programs

A *comment* is some text that is included in a program for the sake of human readers; it is not really an executable part of the program. Comments can explain what the program does and how it works. Nearly all programming languages have provisions for comments, as programs are typically hard to understand without them.

---

* The #! mechanism works on Linux systems, systems derived from the 4.4-Lite Berkeley Software Distribution, and most commercial Unix systems.

† The line beginning with #! lists the full filename of an interpreter to run and an optional initial command-line argument to pass to that interpreter. The operating system then runs the interpreter with the given argument and the full argument list of the executed program. The first argument in the list is the full filename of the *awk* program. The rest of the argument list contains either options to *awk*, or datafiles, or both.

> ## *Portability Issues with #!*
>
> Some systems limit the length of the interpreter name to 32 characters. Often, this can be dealt with by using a symbolic link.
>
> You should not put more than one argument on the #! line after the path to *awk*. It does not work. The operating system treats the rest of the line as a single argument and passes it to *awk*. Doing this leads to confusing behavior—most likely a usage diagnostic of some sort from *awk*.
>
> Finally, the value of ARGV[0] (see the section "Built-in Variables" in Chapter 6, *Patterns, Actions, and Variables*) varies depending upon your operating system. Some systems put awk there, some put the full pathname of *awk* (such as */bin/awk*), and some put the name of your script (advice). Don't rely on the value of ARGV[0] to provide your script name.

In the *awk* language, a comment starts with the sharp sign character (#) and continues to the end of the line. The # does not have to be the first character on the line. The *awk* language ignores the rest of a line following a sharp sign. For example, we could have put the following into *advice*:

```
# This program prints a nice friendly message. It helps
# keep novice users from being afraid of the computer.
BEGIN    { print "Don't Panic!" }
```

You can put comment lines into keyboard-composed throwaway *awk* programs, but this usually isn't very useful; the purpose of a comment is to help you or another person understand the program when reading it at a later time.

Shell-Quoting Issues

For short to medium length *awk* programs, it is most convenient to enter the program on the *awk* command line. This is best done by enclosing the entire program in single quotes. This is true whether you are entering the program interactively at the shell prompt or writing it as part of a larger shell script:

```
awk 'program text' input-file1 input-file2 ...
```

Once you are working with the shell, it is helpful to have a basic knowledge of shell-quoting rules. The following rules apply only to POSIX-compliant, Bourne-style shells (such as *bash*, the GNU Bourne-again shell). If you use *csh*, you're on your own:

As mentioned in the section "One-Shot Throwaway awk Programs" earlier in this chapter, you can enclose small- to medium-sized programs in single quotes, in order to keep your shell scripts self-contained. When doing so, *don't* put an apostrophe (i.e., a single quote) into a comment (or anywhere else in your program). The shell interprets the quote as the closing quote for the entire program. As a result, usually the shell prints a message about mismatched quotes, and if *awk* actually runs, it will probably print strange messages about syntax errors. For example, look at the following:

```
$ awk '{ print "hello" } # let's be cute'
>
```

The shell sees that the first two quotes match, and that a new quoted object begins at the end of the command line. It therefore prompts with the secondary prompt, waiting for more input. With Unix *awk*, closing the quoted string produces this result:

```
$ awk '{ print "hello" } # let's be cute'
> '
awk: can't open file be
 source line number 1
```

Putting a backslash before the single quote in `let's` wouldn't help, since backslashes are not special inside single quotes. The next section describes the shell's quoting rules.

- Quoted items can be concatenated with nonquoted items as well as with other quoted items. The shell turns everything into one argument for the command.

- Preceding any single character with a backslash (\) quotes that character. The shell removes the backslash and passes the quoted character on to the command.

- Single quotes protect everything between the opening and closing quotes. The shell does no interpretation of the quoted text, passing it on verbatim to the command. It is *impossible* to embed a single quote inside single-quoted text. Refer back to the section "Comments in awk Programs" earlier in this chapter for an example of what happens if you try.

- Double quotes protect most things between the opening and closing quotes. The shell does at least variable and command substitution on the quoted text. Different shells may do additional kinds of processing on double-quoted text. Since certain characters within double-quoted text are processed by the shell, they must be *escaped* within the text. Of note are the characters $, `, \, and ", all of which must be preceded by a backslash within double-quoted text if they are to be passed on literally to the program. (The leading backslash is stripped first.) Thus, the example seen previously in the section "Running awk Without Input Files" is applicable:

```
$ awk "BEGIN { print \"Don't Panic!\" }"
Don't Panic!
```

Note that the single quote is not special within double quotes.

- Null strings are removed when they occur as part of a non-null command-line argument, while explicit nonnull objects are kept. For example, to specify that the field separator FS should be set to the null string, use:

```
awk -F "" 'program' files # correct
```

Don't use this:

```
awk -F"" 'program' files  # wrong!
```

In the second case, *awk* will attempt to use the text of the program as the value of FS, and the first filename as the text of the program! This results in syntax errors at best, and confusing behavior at worst.

Mixing single and double quotes is difficult. You have to resort to shell quoting tricks, like this:

```
$ awk 'BEGIN { print "Here is a single quote <'"'"'>" }'
Here is a single quote <'>
```

This program consists of three concatenated quoted strings. The first and the third are single-quoted, the second is double-quoted.

This can be "simplified" to:

```
$ awk 'BEGIN { print "Here is a single quote <'\''>" }'
Here is a single quote <'>
```

Judge for yourself which of these two is the more readable.

Another option is to use double quotes, escaping the embedded, *awk*-level double quotes:

```
$ awk "BEGIN { print \"Here is a single quote <'>\" }"
Here is a single quote <'>
```

This option is also painful, because double quotes, backslashes, and dollar signs are very common in *awk* programs.

If you really need both single and double quotes in your *awk* program, it is probably best to move it into a separate file, where the shell won't be part of the picture, and you can say what you mean.

Datafiles for the Examples

Many of the examples in this book take their input from two sample datafiles. The first, *BBS-list*, represents a list of computer bulletin-board systems together with information about those systems. The second datafile, called *inventory-shipped*, contains information about monthly shipments. In both files, each line is considered to be one *record*.

In the datafile *BBS-list*, each record contains the name of a computer bulletin board, its phone number, the board's baud rate(s), and a code for the number of hours it is operational. An A in the last column means the board operates 24 hours a day. A B in the last column means the board operates only on evening and weekend hours. A C means the board operates only on weekends:

```
aardvark      555-5553      1200/300           B
alpo-net      555-3412      2400/1200/300      A
barfly        555-7685      1200/300           A
bites         555-1675      2400/1200/300      A
camelot       555-0542      300                C
core          555-2912      1200/300           C
fooey         555-1234      2400/1200/300      B
foot          555-6699      1200/300           B
macfoo        555-6480      1200/300           A
sdace         555-3430      2400/1200/300      A
sabafoo       555-2127      1200/300           C
```

The datafile *inventory-shipped* represents information about shipments during the year. Each record contains the month, the number of green crates shipped, the number of red boxes shipped, the number of orange bags shipped, and the number of blue packages shipped, respectively. There are 16 entries, covering the 12 months of last year and the first 4 months of the current year:

```
Jan  13  25  15 115
Feb  15  32  24 226
Mar  15  24  34 228
Apr  31  52  63 420
May  16  34  29 208
Jun  31  42  75 492
Jul  24  34  67 436
Aug  15  34  47 316
Sep  13  55  37 277
Oct  29  54  68 525
Nov  20  87  82 577
Dec  17  35  61 401

Jan  21  36  64 620
Feb  26  58  80 652
Mar  24  75  70 495
Apr  21  70  74 514
```

Some Simple Examples

The following command runs a simple *awk* program that searches the input file *BBS-list* for the character string foo (a grouping of characters is usually called a *string*; the term *string* is based on similar usage in English, such as "a string of pearls," or "a string of cars in a train"):

```
awk '/foo/ { print $0 }' BBS-list
```

When lines containing foo are found, they are printed because print $0 means print the current line. (Just print by itself means the same thing, so we could have written that instead.)

You will notice that slashes (/) surround the string foo in the *awk* program. The slashes indicate that foo is the pattern to search for. This type of pattern is called a *regular expression,* which is covered in more detail later (see Chapter 2, *Regular Expressions*). The pattern is allowed to match parts of words. There are single quotes around the *awk* program so that the shell won't interpret any of it as special shell characters.

Here is what this program prints:

```
$ awk '/foo/ { print $0 }' BBS-list
fooey       555-1234     2400/1200/300    B
foot        555-6699     1200/300         B
macfoo      555-6480     1200/300         A
sabafoo     555-2127     1200/300         C
```

In an *awk* rule, either the pattern or the action can be omitted, but not both. If the pattern is omitted, then the action is performed for *every* input line. If the action is omitted, the default action is to print all lines that match the pattern.

Thus, we could leave out the action (the print statement and the curly braces) in the previous example and the result would be the same: all lines matching the pattern foo are printed. By comparison, omitting the print statement but retaining the curly braces makes an empty action that does nothing (i.e., no lines are printed).

Many practical *awk* programs are just a line or two. Following is a collection of useful, short programs to get you started. Some of these programs contain constructs that haven't been covered yet. (The description of the program will give you a good idea of what is going on, but please read the rest of the book to become an *awk* expert!) Most of the examples use a datafile named *data*. This is just a placeholder; if you use these programs yourself, substitute your own filenames for *data*. For future reference, note that there is often more than one way to do things in *awk*. At some point, you may want to look back at these examples and see if you can come up with different ways to do the same things shown here:

- Print the length of the longest input line:

```
awk '{ if (length($0) > max) max = length($0) }
     END { print max }' data
```

- Print every line that is longer than 80 characters:

```
awk 'length($0) > 80' data
```

The sole rule has a relational expression as its pattern and it has no action—
so the default action, printing the record, is used.

- Print the length of the longest line in *data*:

```
expand data | awk '{ if (x < length()) x = length() }
                   END { print "maximum line length is " x }'
```

The input is processed by the *expand* utility to change tabs into spaces, so the
widths compared are actually the right-margin columns.

- Print every line that has at least one field:

```
awk 'NF > 0' data
```

This is an easy way to delete blank lines from a file (or rather, to create a new
file similar to the old file but from which the blank lines have been removed).

- Print seven random numbers from 0 to 100, inclusive:

```
awk 'BEGIN { for (i = 1; i <= 7; i++)
             print int(101 * rand()) }'
```

- Print the total number of bytes used by *files*:

```
ls -l files | awk '{ x += $5 } ; END { print "total bytes: " x }'
```

- Print the total number of kilobytes used by *files*:

```
ls -l files | awk '{ x += $5 }
                   END { print "total K-bytes: " (x + 1023)/1024 }'
```

- Print a sorted list of the login names of all users:

```
awk -F: '{ print $1 }' /etc/passwd | sort
```

- Count the lines in a file:

```
awk 'END { print NR }' data
```

- Print the even-numbered lines in the datafile:

```
awk 'NR % 2 == 0' data
```

If you use the expression NR % 2 == 1 instead, the program would print the
odd-numbered lines.

An Example with Two Rules

The *awk* utility reads the input files one line at a time. For each line, *awk* tries the patterns of each of the rules. If several patterns match, then several actions are run in the order in which they appear in the *awk* program. If no patterns match, then no actions are run.

After processing all the rules that match the line (and perhaps there are none), *awk* reads the next line. (However, see the section "The next Statement" and also see the section "Using gawk's nextfile Statement" in Chapter 6). This continues until the program reaches the end of the file. For example, the following *awk* program contains two rules:

```
/12/  { print $0 }
/21/  { print $0 }
```

The first rule has the string 12 as the pattern and print $0 as the action. The second rule has the string 21 as the pattern and also has print $0 as the action. Each rule's action is enclosed in its own pair of braces.

This program prints every line that contains the string 12 *or* the string 21. If a line contains both strings, it is printed twice, once by each rule.

This is what happens if we run this program on our two sample datafiles, *BBS-list* and *inventory-shipped*:

```
$ awk '/12/ { print $0 }
>       /21/ { print $0 }' BBS-list inventory-shipped
aardvark     555-5553    1200/300          B
alpo-net     555-3412    2400/1200/300     A
barfly       555-7685    1200/300          A
bites        555-1675    2400/1200/300     A
core         555-2912    1200/300          C
fooey        555-1234    2400/1200/300     B
foot         555-6699    1200/300          B
macfoo       555-6480    1200/300          A
sdace        555-3430    2400/1200/300     A
sabafoo      555-2127    1200/300          C
sabafoo      555-2127    1200/300          C
Jan   21   36  64 620
Apr   21   70  74 514
```

Note how the line beginning with sabafoo in *BBS-list* was printed twice, once for each rule.

A More Complex Example

Now that we've mastered some simple tasks, let's look at what typical *awk* programs do. This example shows how *awk* can be used to summarize, select, and rearrange the output of another utility. It uses features that haven't been covered yet, so don't worry if you don't understand all the details:

```
ls -l | awk '$6 == "Nov" { sum += $5 }
             END { print sum }'
```

This command prints the total number of bytes in all the files in the current directory that were last modified in November (of any year).* The `ls -l` part of this example is a system command that gives you a listing of the files in a directory, including each file's size and the date the file was last modified. Its output looks like this:

```
-rw-r--r-- 1 arnold    user     1933 Nov  7 13:05 Makefile
-rw-r--r-- 1 arnold    user    10809 Nov  7 13:03 awk.h
-rw-r--r-- 1 arnold    user      983 Apr 13 12:14 awk.tab.h
-rw-r--r-- 1 arnold    user    31869 Jun 15 12:20 awk.y
-rw-r--r-- 1 arnold    user    22414 Nov  7 13:03 awk1.c
-rw-r--r-- 1 arnold    user    37455 Nov  7 13:03 awk2.c
-rw-r--r-- 1 arnold    user    27511 Dec  9 13:07 awk3.c
-rw-r--r-- 1 arnold    user     7989 Nov  7 13:03 awk4.c
```

The first field contains read-write permissions, the second field contains the number of links to the file, and the third field identifies the owner of the file. The fourth field identifies the group of the file. The fifth field contains the size of the file in bytes. The sixth, seventh, and eighth fields contain the month, day, and time, respectively, that the file was last modified. Finally, the ninth field contains the name of the file.†

The `$6 == "Nov"` in our *awk* program is an expression that tests whether the sixth field of the output from `ls -l` matches the string `Nov`. Each time a line has the string `Nov` for its sixth field, the action `sum += $5` is performed. This adds the fifth field (the file's size) to the variable `sum`. As a result, when *awk* has finished reading all the input lines, `sum` is the total of the sizes of the files whose lines matched the pattern. (This works because *awk* variables are automatically initialized to zero.)

After the last line of output from *ls* has been processed, the `END` rule executes and prints the value of `sum`. In this example, the value of `sum` is 140963.

---

* In the C shell (*csh*), you need to type a semicolon and then a backslash at the end of the first line; see the section "awk Statements Versus Lines" later in this chapter for an explanation. In a POSIX-compliant shell, such as the Bourne shell or *bash*, you can type the example as shown. If the command `echo $path` produces an empty output line, you are most likely using a POSIX-compliant shell. Otherwise, you are probably using the C shell or a shell derived from it.

† On some very old systems, you may need to use `ls -lg` to get this output.

These more advanced *awk* techniques are covered in later sections (see the section "Actions" in Chapter 6). Before you can move on to more advanced *awk* programming, you have to know how *awk* interprets your input and displays your output. By manipulating fields and using print statements, you can produce some very useful and impressive-looking reports.

awk Statements Versus Lines

Most often, each line in an *awk* program is a separate statement or separate rule, like this:

```
awk '/12/  { print $0 }
     /21/  { print $0 }' BBS-list inventory-shipped
```

However, *gawk* ignores newlines after any of the following symbols and keywords:

```
,    {    ?    :    ||    &&    do    else
```

A newline at any other point is considered the end of the statement.*

If you would like to split a single statement into two lines at a point where a newline would terminate it, you can *continue* it by ending the first line with a backslash character (\). The backslash must be the final character on the line in order to be recognized as a continuation character. A backslash is allowed anywhere in the statement, even in the middle of a string or regular expression. For example:

```
awk '/This regular expression is too long, so continue it\
 on the next line/ { print $1 }'
```

We have generally not used backslash continuation in the sample programs in this book. In *gawk*, there is no limit on the length of a line, so backslash continuation is never strictly necessary; it just makes programs more readable. For this same reason, as well as for clarity, we have kept most statements short in the sample programs presented throughout the book. Backslash continuation is most useful when your *awk* program is in a separate source file instead of entered from the command line. You should also note that many *awk* implementations are more particular about where you may use backslash continuation. For example, they may not allow you to split a string constant using backslash continuation. Thus, for maximum portability of your *awk* programs, it is best not to split your lines in the middle of a regular expression or a string.

---

* The ? and : referred to here is the three-operand conditional expression described in the section "Conditional Expressions" in Chapter 5, *Expressions*. Splitting lines after ? and : is a minor *gawk* extension; if *--posix* is specified (see the section "Command-Line Options" in Chapter 11, *Running awk and gawk*), then this extension is disabled.

Backslash continuation does not work as described with the C shell. It works for *awk* programs in files and for one-shot programs, provided you are using a POSIX-compliant shell, such as the Unix Bourne shell or *bash*. But the C shell behaves differently! There, you must use two backslashes in a row, followed by a newline. Note also that when using the C shell, *every* newline in your *awk* program must be escaped with a backslash. To illustrate:

```
% awk 'BEGIN { \
?   print \\
?        "hello, world" \
? }'
hello, world
```

Here, the % and ? are the C shell's primary and secondary prompts, analogous to the standard shell's $ and >.

Compare the previous example to how it is done with a POSIX-compliant shell:

```
$ awk 'BEGIN {
>   print \
>        "hello, world"
> }'
hello, world
```

awk is a line-oriented language. Each rule's action has to begin on the same line as the pattern. To have the pattern and action on separate lines, you *must* use backslash continuation; there is no other option.

Another thing to keep in mind is that backslash continuation and comments do not mix. As soon as *awk* sees the # that starts a comment, it ignores *everything* on the rest of the line. For example:

```
$ gawk 'BEGIN { print "dont panic" # a friendly \
>                               BEGIN rule
> }'
gawk: cmd. line:2:              BEGIN rule
gawk: cmd. line:2:              ^ parse error
```

In this case, it looks like the backslash would continue the comment onto the next line. However, the backslash-newline combination is never even noticed because it is "hidden" inside the comment. Thus, the BEGIN is noted as a syntax error.

When *awk* statements within one rule are short, you might want to put more than one of them on a line. This is accomplished by separating the statements with a semicolon (;). This also applies to the rules themselves. Thus, the program shown at the start of this section could also be written this way:

```
/12/ { print $0 } ; /21/ { print $0 }
```

 The requirement that states that rules on the same line must be separated with a semicolon was not in the original *awk* language; it was added for consistency with the treatment of statements within an action.

Other Features of awk

The *awk* language provides a number of predefined, or *built-in*, variables that your programs can use to get information from *awk*. There are other variables your program can set as well to control how *awk* processes your data.

In addition, *awk* provides a number of built-in functions for doing common computational and string-related operations. *gawk* provides built-in functions for working with timestamps, performing bit manipulation, and for runtime string translation.

As we develop our presentation of the *awk* language, we introduce most of the variables and many of the functions. They are defined systematically in the section "Built-in Variables" in Chapter 6 and the section "Built-in Functions" in Chapter 8.

When to Use awk

Now that you've seen some of what *awk* can do, you might wonder how *awk* could be useful for you. By using utility programs, advanced patterns, field separators, arithmetic statements, and other selection criteria, you can produce much more complex output. The *awk* language is very useful for producing reports from large amounts of raw data, such as summarizing information from the output of other utility programs like *ls*. (See the section "A More Complex Example" earlier in this chapter.)

Programs written with *awk* are usually much smaller than they would be in other languages. This makes *awk* programs easy to compose and use. Often, *awk* programs can be quickly composed at your terminal, used once, and thrown away. Because *awk* programs are interpreted, you can avoid the (usually lengthy) compilation part of the typical edit-compile-test-debug cycle of software development.

Complex programs have been written in *awk*, including a complete retargetable assembler for eight-bit microprocessors (see the Glossary" for more information), and a microcode assembler for a special-purpose Prolog computer. However, *awk*'s capabilities are strained by tasks of such complexity.

If you find yourself writing *awk* scripts of more than, say, a few hundred lines, you might consider using a different programming language. Emacs Lisp is a good choice if you need sophisticated string or pattern matching capabilities. The shell is also good at string and pattern matching; in addition, it allows powerful use of the system utilities. More conventional languages, such as C, C++, and Java, offer better facilities for system programming and for managing the complexity of large programs. Programs in these languages may require more lines of source code than the equivalent *awk* programs, but they are easier to maintain and usually run more efficiently.

2

Regular Expressions

A *regular expression*, or *regexp*, is a way of describing a set of strings. Because regular expressions are such a fundamental part of *awk* programming, their format and use deserve a separate chapter.

A regular expression enclosed in slashes (/) is an *awk* pattern that matches every input record whose text belongs to that set. The simplest regular expression is a sequence of letters, numbers, or both. Such a regexp matches any string that contains that sequence. Thus, the regexp foo matches any string containing foo. Therefore, the pattern /foo/ matches any input record containing the three characters foo *anywhere* in the record. Other kinds of regexps let you specify more complicated classes of strings.

Initially, the examples in this chapter are simple. As we explain more about how regular expressions work, we will present more complicated instances.

How to Use Regular Expressions

A regular expression can be used as a pattern by enclosing it in slashes. Then the regular expression is tested against the entire text of each record. (Normally, it only needs to match some part of the text in order to succeed.) For example, the following prints the second field of each record that contains the string foo anywhere in it:

```
$ awk '/foo/ { print $2 }' BBS-list
555-1234
555-6699
555-6480
555-2127
```

Regular expressions can also be used in matching expressions. These expressions allow you to specify the string to match against; it need not be the entire current input record. The two operators ~ and !~ perform regular expression comparisons. Expressions using these operators can be used as patterns, or in if, while, for, and do statements. (See the section "Control Statements in Actions" in Chapter 6, *Patterns, Actions, and Variables.*) For example:

```
exp ~ /regexp/
```

is true if the expression *exp* (taken as a string) matches *regexp*. The following example matches, or selects, all input records with the uppercase letter J somewhere in the first field:

```
$ awk '$1 ~ /J/' inventory-shipped
Jan   13   25   15 115
Jun   31   42   75 492
Jul   24   34   67 436
Jan   21   36   64 620
```

So does this:

```
awk '{ if ($1 ~ /J/) print }' inventory-shipped
```

This next example is true if the expression *exp* (taken as a character string) does *not* match *regexp*:

```
exp !~ /regexp/
```

The following example matches, or selects, all input records whose first field *does not* contain the uppercase letter J:

```
$ awk '$1 !~ /J/' inventory-shipped
Feb   15   32   24 226
Mar   15   24   34 228
Apr   31   52   63 420
May   16   34   29 208
...
```

When a regexp is enclosed in slashes, such as /foo/, we call it a *regexp constant*, much like 5.27 is a numeric constant and "foo" is a string constant.

Escape Sequences

Some characters cannot be included literally in string constants ("foo") or regexp constants (/foo/). Instead, they should be represented with *escape sequences*, which are character sequences beginning with a backslash (\). One use of an escape sequence is to include a double-quote character in a string constant. Because a plain double quote ends the string, you must use \" to represent an actual double-quote character as a part of the string. For example:

```
$ awk 'BEGIN { print "He said \"hi!\" to her." }'
He said "hi!" to her.
```

The backslash character itself is another character that cannot be included normally; you must write \\ to put one backslash in the string or regexp. Thus, the string whose contents are the two characters " and \ must be written "\"\\".

Backslash also represents unprintable characters such as tab or newline. While there is nothing to stop you from entering most unprintable characters directly in a string constant or regexp constant, they may look ugly.

The following list describes all the escape sequences used in *awk* and what they represent. Unless noted otherwise, all these escape sequences apply to both string constants and regexp constants:

\\   A literal backslash, \.

\a   The "alert" character, Ctrl-g, ASCII code 7 (BEL). (This usually makes some sort of audible noise.)

\b   Backspace, Ctrl-h, ASCII code 8 (BS).

\f   Formfeed, Ctrl-l, ASCII code 12 (FF).

\n   Newline, Ctrl-j, ASCII code 10 (LF).

\r   Carriage return, Ctrl-m, ASCII code 13 (CR).

\t   Horizontal tab, Ctrl-i, ASCII code 9 (HT).

\v   Vertical tab, Ctrl-k, ASCII code 11 (VT).

nnn

The octal value *nnn*, where *nnn* stands for 1 to 3 digits between 0 and 7. For example, the code for the ASCII ESC (escape) character is \033.

\x*hh*...

The hexadecimal value *hh*, where *hh* stands for a sequence of hexadecimal digits (0–9, and either A–F or a–f). Like the same construct in ISO C, the escape sequence continues until the first nonhexadecimal digit is seen. However, using more than two hexadecimal digits produces undefined results. (The \x escape sequence is not allowed in POSIX *awk*.)

\/   A literal slash (necessary for regexp constants only). This expression is used when you want to write a regexp constant that contains a slash. Because the regexp is delimited by slashes, you need to escape the slash that is part of the pattern, in order to tell *awk* to keep processing the rest of the regexp.

\"   A literal double quote (necessary for string constants only). This expression is used when you want to write a string constant that contains a double quote. Because the string is delimited by double quotes, you need to escape the quote that is part of the string, in order to tell *awk* to keep processing the rest of the string.

In *gawk*, a number of additional two-character sequences that begin with a backslash have special meaning in regexps. See the section "gawk-Specific Regexp Operators" later in this chapter.

In a regexp, a backslash before any character that is not in the previous list and not listed in the section "gawk-Specific Regexp Operators" later in this chapter means that the next character should be taken literally, even if it would normally be a regexp operator. For example, /a\+b/ matches the three characters a+b.

For complete portability, do not use a backslash before any character not shown in the previous list.

Backslash Before Regular Characters

If you place a backslash in a string constant before something that is not one of the characters previously listed, POSIX *awk* purposely leaves what happens as undefined. There are two choices:

Strip the backslash out
>   This is what Unix *awk* and *gawk* both do. For example, "a\qc" is the same as "aqc". (Because this is such an easy bug both to introduce and to miss, *gawk* warns you about it.) Consider FS = "[\t]+\|[\t]+" to use vertical bars surrounded by whitespace as the field separator. There should be two backslashes in the string FS = "[\t]+\\|[\t]+".

Leave the backslash alone
>   Some other *awk* implementations do this. In such implementations, typing "a\qc" is the same as typing "a\\qc".

Escape Sequences for Metacharacters

Suppose you use an octal or hexadecimal escape to represent a regexp metacharacter. (See the section "Regular Expression Operators" later in this chapter.) Does *awk* treat the character as a literal character or as a regexp operator?

Historically, such characters were taken literally. (d.c.) However, the POSIX standard indicates that they should be treated as real metacharacters, which is what *gawk* does. In compatibility mode (see the section "Command-Line Options" in Chapter 11, *Running awk and gawk*), *gawk* treats the characters represented by octal and hexadecimal escape sequences literally when used in regexp constants. Thus, /a\52b/ is equivalent to /a*b/.

Regular Expression Operators

You can combine regular expressions with special characters, called *regular expression operators* or *metacharacters*, to increase the power and versatility of regular expressions.

The escape sequences described in the previous section "Escape Sequences" are valid inside a regexp. They are introduced by a \ and are recognized and converted into corresponding real characters as the first step in processing regexps.

Here is a list of metacharacters. All characters that are not escape sequences and that are not listed here stand for themselves:

\   This is used to suppress the special meaning of a character when matching. For example, \$ matches the character $.

^   This matches the beginning of a string. For example, `^@chapter` matches `@chapter` at the beginning of a string and can be used to identify chapter beginnings in Texinfo source files. The ^ is known as an *anchor*, because it anchors the pattern to match only at the beginning of the string.

It is important to realize that ^ does not match the beginning of a line embedded in a string. The condition is not true in the following example:

```
if ("line1\nLINE 2" ~ /^L/) ...
```

$ This is similar to ^, but it matches only at the end of a string. For example, p$ matches a record that ends with a p. The $ is an anchor and does not match the end of a line embedded in a string. The condition is not true as follows:

```
if ("line1\nLINE 2" ~ /1$/) ...
```

. (A period, or "dot.") This matches any single character, *including* the newline character. For example, .P matches any single character followed by a P in a string. Using concatenation, we can make a regular expression such as U.A, which matches any three-character sequence that begins with U and ends with A.

In strict POSIX mode (see the section "Command-Line Options" in Chapter 11), the dot does not match the NUL character, which is a character with all bits equal to zero. Otherwise, NUL is just another character. Other versions of *awk* may not be able to match the NUL character.

[...]

This is called a *character list.*[*] It matches any *one* of the characters that are enclosed in the square brackets. For example, [MVX] matches any one of the characters M, V, or X in a string. A full discussion of what can be inside the square brackets of a character list is given in the section "Using Character Lists" later in this chapter.

[^ ...]

This is a *complemented character list.* The first character after the [*must* be a ^. It matches any characters *except* those in the square brackets. For example, [^awk] matches any character that is not an a, w, or k.

| This is the *alternation operator* and it is used to specify alternatives. The | has the lowest precedence of all the regular expression operators. For example, ^P|[[:digit:]] matches any string that matches either ^P or [[:digit:]]. This means it matches any string that starts with P or contains a digit.

The alternation applies to the largest possible regexps on either side.

(...)

Parentheses are used for grouping in regular expressions, as in arithmetic. They can be used to concatenate regular expressions containing the alternation operator, |. For example, @(samp|code)\{[^}]+\} matches both @code{foo} and @samp{bar}.

* This symbol means that the preceding regular expression should be repeated as many times as necessary to find a match. For example, ph* applies the * symbol to the preceding h and looks for matches of one p followed by any number of hs. This also matches just p if no hs are present.

The * repeats the *smallest* possible preceding expression. (Use parentheses if you want to repeat a larger expression.) It finds as many repetitions as possible. For example, awk '/\(c[ad][ad]*r x\)/ { print }' sample prints every

---

[*] In other literature, you may see a character list referred to as either a *character set*, a *character class*, or a *bracket expression*.

record in *sample* containing a string of the form (car x), (cdr x), (cadr x), and so on. Notice the escaping of the parentheses by preceding them with backslashes.

+ This symbol is similar to *, except that the preceding expression must be matched at least once. This means that wh+y would match why and whhy, but not wy, whereas wh*y would match all three of these strings. The following is a simpler way of writing the last * example:

```
awk '/\(c[ad]+r x\)/ { print }' sample
```

? This symbol is similar to *, except that the preceding expression can be matched either once or not at all. For example, fe?d matches fed and fd, but nothing else.

{n}, {n,}, {n,m}
One or two numbers inside braces denote an *interval expression*. If there is one number in the braces, the preceding regexp is repeated *n* times. If there are two numbers separated by a comma, the preceding regexp is repeated *n* to *m* times. If there is one number followed by a comma, then the preceding regexp is repeated at least *n* times:

wh{3}y
Matches whhhy, but not why or whhhhy.

wh{3,5}y
Matches whhhy, whhhhy, or whhhhhy, only.

wh{2,}y
Matches whhy or whhhy, and so on.

Interval expressions were not traditionally available in *awk*. They were added as part of the POSIX standard to make *awk* and *egrep* consistent with each other.

However, because old programs may use { and } in regexp constants, by default *gawk* does *not* match interval expressions in regexps. If either *--posix* or *--re-interval* are specified (see the section "Command-Line Options" in Chapter 11), then interval expressions are allowed in regexps.

For new programs that use { and } in regexp constants, it is good practice to always escape them with a backslash. Then the regexp constants are valid and work the way you want them to, using any version of *awk*.[*]

In regular expressions, the *, +, and ? operators, as well as the braces { and }, have the highest precedence, followed by concatenation, and finally by |. As in arithmetic, parentheses can change how operators are grouped.

---

[*] Use two backslashes if you're using a string constant with a regexp operator or function.

In POSIX *awk* and *gawk*, the *, +, and ? operators stand for themselves when there is nothing in the regexp that precedes them. For example, /+/ matches a literal plus sign. However, many other versions of *awk* treat such a usage as a syntax error.

If *gawk* is in compatibility mode (see the section "Command-Line Options" in Chapter 11), POSIX character classes and interval expressions are not available in regular expressions.

Using Character Lists

Within a character list, a *range expression* consists of two characters separated by a hyphen. It matches any single character that sorts between the two characters, using the locale's collating sequence and character set. For example, in the default C locale, [a-dx-z] is equivalent to [abcdxyz]. Many locales sort characters in dictionary order, and in these locales, [a-dx-z] is typically not equivalent to [abcdxyz]; instead it might be equivalent to [aBbCcDdxXyYz], for example. To obtain the traditional interpretation of bracket expressions, you can use the C locale by setting the LC_ALL environment variable to the value c.

To include one of the characters \,], -, or ^ in a character list, put a \ in front of it. For example:

    [d\]]

matches either d or].

This treatment of \ in character lists is compatible with other *awk* implementations and is also mandated by POSIX. The regular expressions in *awk* are a superset of the POSIX specification for Extended Regular Expressions (EREs). POSIX EREs are based on the regular expressions accepted by the traditional *egrep* utility.

Character classes are a new feature introduced in the POSIX standard. A character class is a special notation for describing lists of characters that have a specific attribute, but the actual characters can vary from country to country and/or from character set to character set. For example, the notion of what is an alphabetic character differs between the United States and France.

A character class is only valid in a regexp *inside* the brackets of a character list. Character classes consist of [:, a keyword denoting the class, and :]. Table 2-1 lists the character classes defined by the POSIX standard.

Table 2-1. POSIX Character Classes

Class	Meaning
[:alnum:]	Alphanumeric characters.
[:alpha:]	Alphabetic characters.
[:blank:]	Space and tab characters.
[:cntrl:]	Control characters.
[:digit:]	Numeric characters.
[:graph:]	Characters that are both printable and visible. (A space is printable but not visible, whereas an a is both.)
[:lower:]	Lowercase alphabetic characters.
[:print:]	Printable characters (characters that are not control characters).
[:punct:]	Punctuation characters (characters that are not letters, digits, control characters, or space characters).
[:space:]	Space characters (such as space, tab, and formfeed, to name a few).
[:upper:]	Uppercase alphabetic characters.
[:xdigit:]	Characters that are hexadecimal digits.

For example, before the POSIX standard, you had to write /[A-Za-z0-9]/ to match alphanumeric characters. If your character set had other alphabetic characters in it, this would not match them, and if your character set collated differently from ASCII, this might not even match the ASCII alphanumeric characters. With the POSIX character classes, you can write /[[:alnum:]]/ to match the alphabetic and numeric characters in your character set.

Two additional special sequences can appear in character lists. These apply to non-ASCII character sets, which can have single symbols (called *collating elements*) that are represented with more than one character. They can also have several characters equivalent for *collating*, or sorting, purposes. (For example, in French, a plain "e" and a grave-accented "è" are equivalent.) These sequences are:

Collating symbols

Multicharacter collating elements enclosed between [. and .]. For example, if ch is a collating element, then [[.ch.]] is a regexp that matches this collating element, whereas [ch] is a regexp that matches either c or h.

Equivalence classes

Locale-specific names for lists of characters that are equal. The name is enclosed between [= and =]. For example, the name e might be used to represent all of "e," "è," and "é." In this case, [[=e=]] is a regexp that matches any of e, é, or è.

These features are very valuable in non-English-speaking locales.

The library functions that *gawk* uses for regular expression matching currently recognize only POSIX character classes; they do not recognize collating symbols or equivalence classes.

gawk-Specific Regexp Operators

GNU software that deals with regular expressions provides a number of additional regexp operators. These operators are described in this section and are specific to *gawk*; they are not available in other *awk* implementations. Most of the additional operators deal with word matching. For our purposes, a *word* is a sequence of one or more letters, digits, or underscores (_):

\w   Matches any word-constituent character—that is, it matches any letter, digit, or underscore. Think of it as short-hand for `[[:alnum:]_]`.

\W   Matches any character that is not word-constituent. Think of it as shorthand for `[^[:alnum:]_]`.

\\<   Matches the empty string at the beginning of a word. For example, `/\<away/` matches away but not stowaway.

\\>   Matches the empty string at the end of a word. For example, `/stow\>/` matches stow but not stowaway.

\y   Matches the empty string at either the beginning or the end of a word (i.e., the word boundary). For example, `\yballs?\y` matches either ball or balls, as a separate word.

\B   Matches the empty string that occurs between two word-constituent characters. For example, `/\Brat\B/` matches crate but it does not match dirty rat. \B is essentially the opposite of \y.

There are two other operators that work on buffers. In Emacs, a *buffer* is, naturally, an Emacs buffer. For other programs, *gawk*'s regexp library routines consider the entire string to match as the buffer. The operators are:

\`   Matches the empty string at the beginning of a buffer (string).

\'   Matches the empty string at the end of a buffer (string).

Because ^ and $ always work in terms of the beginning and end of strings, these operators don't add any new capabilities for *awk*. They are provided for compatibility with other GNU software.

In other GNU software, the word-boundary operator is \b. However, that conflicts with the *awk* language's definition of \b as backspace, so *gawk* uses a different letter. An alternative method would have been to require two backslashes in the GNU operators, but this was deemed too confusing. The current method of using \y for the GNU \b appears to be the lesser of two evils.

The various command-line options (see the section "Command-Line Options" in Chapter 11) control how *gawk* interprets characters in regexps:

No options
> In the default case, *gawk* provides all the facilities of POSIX regexps and the previously described GNU regexp operators. However, interval expressions are not supported.

--posix
> Only POSIX regexps are supported; the GNU operators are not special (e.g., \w matches a literal *w*). Interval expressions are allowed.

--traditional
> Traditional Unix *awk* regexps are matched. The GNU operators are not special, interval expressions are not available, nor are the POSIX character classes ([[:alnum:]], etc.). Characters described by octal and hexadecimal escape sequences are treated literally, even if they represent regexp metacharacters.

--re-interval
> Allow interval expressions in regexps, even if *--traditional* has been provided.

Case Sensitivity in Matching

Case is normally significant in regular expressions, both when matching ordinary characters (i.e., not metacharacters) and inside character sets. Thus, a w in a regular expression matches only a lowercase w and not an uppercase W.

The simplest way to do a case-independent match is to use a character list—for example, [Ww]. However, this can be cumbersome if you need to use it often, and it can make the regular expressions harder to read. There are two alternatives that you might prefer.

One way to perform a case-insensitive match at a particular point in the program is to convert the data to a single case, using the tolower or toupper built-in string functions (which we haven't discussed yet; see the section "String-Manipulation Functions" in Chapter 8, *Functions*). For example:

```
tolower($1) ~ /foo/  { ... }
```

converts the first field to lowercase before matching against it. This works in any POSIX-compliant *awk*.

Another method, specific to *gawk*, is to set the variable IGNORECASE to a nonzero value (see the section "Built-in Variables" in Chapter 6). When IGNORECASE is not zero, *all* regexp and string operations ignore case. Changing the value of IGNORE-CASE dynamically controls the case-sensitivity of the program as it runs. Case is significant by default because IGNORECASE (like most variables) is initialized to zero:

```
x = "aB"
if (x ~ /ab/) ...    # this test will fail

IGNORECASE = 1
if (x ~ /ab/) ...    # now it will succeed
```

In general, you cannot use IGNORECASE to make certain rules case-insensitive and other rules case-sensitive, because there is no straightforward way to set IGNORE-CASE just for the pattern of a particular rule.* To do this, use either character lists or tolower. However, one thing you can do with IGNORECASE only is dynamically turn case-sensitivity on or off for all the rules at once.

IGNORECASE can be set on the command line or in a BEGIN rule (see the section "Other Command-Line Arguments" in Chapter 11; also see the section "Startup and cleanup actions" in Chapter 6). Setting IGNORECASE from the command line is a way to make a program case-insensitive without having to edit it.

Prior to *gawk* 3.0, the value of IGNORECASE affected regexp operations only. It did not affect string comparison with ==, !=, and so on. Beginning with Version 3.0, both regexp and string comparison operations are also affected by IGNORECASE.

Beginning with *gawk* 3.0, the equivalences between upper- and lowercase characters are based on the ISO-8859-1 (ISO Latin-1) character set. This character set is a superset of the traditional 128 ASCII characters, which also provides a number of characters suitable for use with European languages.

The value of IGNORECASE has no effect if *gawk* is in compatibility mode (see the section "Command-Line Options" in Chapter 11). Case is always significant in compatibility mode.

---

* Experienced C and C++ programmers will note that it is possible, using something like IGNORECASE = 1 && /foObAr/ { ... } and IGNORECASE = 0 || /foobar/ { ... }. However, this is somewhat obscure and we don't recommend it.

How Much Text Matches?

Consider the following:

```
echo aaaabcd | awk '{ sub(/a+/, "<A>"); print }'
```

This example uses the sub function (which we haven't discussed yet; see the section "String-Manipulation Functions" in Chapter 8) to make a change to the input record. Here, the regexp /a+/ indicates "one or more a characters," and the replacement text is <A>.

The input contains four a characters. *awk* (and POSIX) regular expressions always match the leftmost, *longest* sequence of input characters that can match. Thus, all four a characters are replaced with <A> in this example:

```
$ echo aaaabcd | awk '{ sub(/a+/, "<A>"); print }'
<A>bcd
```

For simple match/no-match tests, this is not so important. But when doing text matching and substitutions with the match, sub, gsub, and gensub functions, it is very important. Understanding this principle is also important for regexp-based record and field splitting (see the section "How Input Is Split into Records" and the section "Specifying How Fields Are Separated" in Chapter 3, *Reading Input Files*).

Using Dynamic Regexps

The righthand side of a ~ or !~ operator need not be a regexp constant (i.e., a string of characters between slashes). It may be any expression. The expression is evaluated and converted to a string if necessary; the contents of the string are used as the regexp. A regexp that is computed in this way is called a *dynamic regexp*:

```
BEGIN { digits_regexp = "[[:digit:]]+" }
$0 ~ digits_regexp    { print }
```

This sets digits_regexp to a regexp that describes one or more digits, and tests whether the input record matches this regexp.

When using the ~ and !~ operators, there is a difference between a regexp constant enclosed in slashes and a string constant enclosed in double quotes. If you are going to use a string constant, you have to understand that the string is, in essence, scanned *twice*: the first time when *awk* reads your program, and the second time when it goes to match the string on the lefthand side of the operator with the pattern on the right. This is true of any string-valued expression (such as digits_regexp, shown previously), not just string constants.

What difference does it make if the string is scanned twice? The answer has to do with escape sequences, and particularly with backslashes. To get a backslash into a regular expression inside a string, you have to type two backslashes.

For example, /*/ is a regexp constant for a literal *. Only one backslash is needed. To do the same thing with a string, you have to type "*". The first backslash escapes the second one so that the string actually contains the two characters \ and *.

Given that you can use both regexp and string constants to describe regular expressions, which should you use? The answer is "regexp constants," for several reasons:

- String constants are more complicated to write and more difficult to read. Using regexp constants makes your programs less error-prone. Not understanding the difference between the two kinds of constants is a common source of errors.

- It is more efficient to use regexp constants. *awk* can note that you have supplied a regexp and store it internally in a form that makes pattern matching more efficient. When using a string constant, *awk* must first convert the string into this internal form and then perform the pattern matching.

- Using regexp constants is better form; it shows clearly that you intend a regexp match.

Using \n in Character Lists of Dynamic Regexps

Some commercial versions of *awk* do not allow the newline character to be used inside a character list for a dynamic regexp:

```
$ awk '$0 ~ "[ \t\n]"'
awk: newline in character class [
]...
 source line number 1
 context is
         >>> <<<
```

But a newline in a regexp constant works with no problem:

```
$ awk '$0 ~ /[ \t\n]/'
here is a sample line
here is a sample line
Control-d
```

gawk does not have this problem, and it isn't likely to occur often in practice, but it's worth noting for future reference.

3

Reading Input Files

In the typical *awk* program, all input is read either from the standard input (by default, this is the keyboard, but often it is a pipe from another command) or from files whose names you specify on the *awk* command line. If you specify input files, *awk* reads them in order, processing all the data from one before going on to the next. The name of the current input file can be found in the built-in variable FILENAME (see the section "Built-in Variables" in Chapter 6, *Patterns, Actions, and Variables*).

The input is read in units called *records*, and is processed by the rules of your program one record at a time. By default, each record is one line. Each record is automatically split into chunks called *fields*. This makes it more convenient for programs to work on the parts of a record.

On rare occasions, you may need to use the getline command. The getline command is valuable, both because it can do explicit input from any number of files, and because the files used with it do not have to be named on the *awk* command line (see the section "Explicit Input with getline" later in this chapter).

How Input Is Split into Records

The *awk* utility divides the input for your *awk* program into records and fields. *awk* keeps track of the number of records that have been read from the current input file. This value is stored in a built-in variable called FNR. It is reset to zero when a new file is started. Another built-in variable, NR, is the total number of input records read so far from all datafiles. It starts at zero, but is never automatically reset to zero.

Records are separated by a character called the *record separator*. By default, the record separator is the newline character. This is why records are, by default, single lines. A different character can be used for the record separator by assigning the character to the built-in variable RS.

Like any other variable, the value of RS can be changed in the *awk* program with the assignment operator, = (see the section "Assignment Expressions" in Chapter 5, *Expressions*). The new record-separator character should be enclosed in quotation marks, which indicate a string constant. Often the right time to do this is at the beginning of execution, before any input is processed, so that the very first record is read with the proper separator. To do this, use the special BEGIN pattern (see the section "The BEGIN and END Special Patterns" in Chapter 6). For example:

```
awk 'BEGIN { RS = "/" }
     { print $0 }' BBS-list
```

changes the value of RS to "/", before reading any input. This is a string whose first character is a slash; as a result, records are separated by slashes. Then the input file is read, and the second rule in the *awk* program (the action with no pattern) prints each record. Because each print statement adds a newline at the end of its output, this *awk* program copies the input with each slash changed to a newline. Here are the results of running the program on *BBS-list*:

```
$ awk 'BEGIN { RS = "/" }
>        { print $0 }' BBS-list
aardvark        555-5553        1200
300             B
alpo-net        555-3412        2400
1200
300     A
barfly          555-7685        1200
300             A
bites           555-1675        2400
1200
300     A
camelot         555-0542        300             C
core            555-2912        1200
300             C
fooey           555-1234        2400
1200
300     B
foot            555-6699        1200
300             B
macfoo          555-6480        1200
300             A
sdace           555-3430        2400
1200
300     A
sabafoo         555-2127        1200
300             C

$
```

Note that the entry for the `camelot` BBS is not split. In the original datafile (see the section "Datafiles for the Examples" in Chapter 1, *Getting Started with awk*), the line looks like this:

```
camelot     555-0542    300         C
```

It has one baud rate only, so there are no slashes in the record, unlike the others that have two or more baud rates. In fact, this record is treated as part of the record for the `core` BBS; the newline separating them in the output is the original newline in the datafile, not the one added by *awk* when it printed the record!

Another way to change the record separator is on the command line, using the variable-assignment feature (see the section "Other Command-Line Arguments" in Chapter 11, *Running awk and gawk*):

```
awk '{ print $0 }' RS="/" BBS-list
```

This sets RS to / before processing *BBS-list*.

Using an unusual character such as / for the record separator produces correct behavior in the vast majority of cases. However, the following (extreme) pipeline prints a surprising 1:

```
$ echo | awk 'BEGIN { RS = "a" } ; { print NF }'
1
```

There is one field, consisting of a newline. The value of the built-in variable NF is the number of fields in the current record.

Reaching the end of an input file terminates the current input record, even if the last character in the file is not the character in RS. (d.c.)

The empty string `""` (a string without any characters) has a special meaning as the value of RS. It means that records are separated by one or more blank lines and nothing else. See the section "Multiple-Line Records" later in this chapter for more details.

If you change the value of RS in the middle of an *awk* run, the new value is used to delimit subsequent records, but the record currently being processed, as well as records already processed, are not affected.

After the end of the record has been determined, *gawk* sets the variable RT to the text in the input that matched RS. When using *gawk*, the value of RS is not limited to a one-character string. It can be any regular expression (see Chapter 2, *Regular Expressions*). In general, each record ends at the next string that matches the regular expression; the next record starts at the end of the matching string. This general rule is actually at work in the usual case, where RS contains just a newline: a record ends at the beginning of the next matching string (the next newline in the input), and the following record starts just after the end of this string (at the first character of the following line). The newline, because it matches RS, is not part of either record.

When RS is a single character, RT contains the same single character. However, when RS is a regular expression, RT contains the actual input text that matched the regular expression.

The following example illustrates both of these features. It sets RS equal to a regular expression that matches either a newline or a series of one or more uppercase letters with optional leading and/or trailing whitespace:

```
$ echo record 1 AAAA record 2 BBBB record 3 |
> gawk 'BEGIN { RS = "\n|( *[[:upper:]]+ *)" }
>               { print "Record =", $0, "and RT =", RT }'
Record = record 1 and RT =  AAAA
Record = record 2 and RT =  BBBB
Record = record 3 and RT =

$
```

The final line of output has an extra blank line. This is because the value of RT is a newline, and the print statement supplies its own terminating newline. See the section "A Simple Stream Editor" in Chapter 13, *Practical awk Programs*, for a more useful example of RS as a regexp and RT.

The use of RS as a regular expression and the RT variable are *gawk* extensions; they are not available in compatibility mode (see the section "Command-Line Options" in Chapter 11). In compatibility mode, only the first character of the value of RS is used to determine the end of the record.

Examining Fields

When *awk* reads an input record, the record is automatically *parsed* or separated by the interpreter into chunks called *fields*. By default, fields are separated by *whitespace*, like words in a line. Whitespace in *awk* means any string of one or more spaces, tabs, or newlines;* other characters, such as formfeed, vertical tab, etc. that are considered whitespace by other languages, are *not* considered whitespace by *awk*.

The purpose of fields is to make it more convenient for you to refer to these pieces of the record. You don't have to use them—you can operate on the whole record if you want—but fields are what make simple *awk* programs so powerful.

---

* In POSIX *awk*, newlines are not considered whitespace for separating fields.

RS = "\0" Is Not Portable

There are times when you might want to treat an entire datafile as a single record. The only way to make this happen is to give RS a value that you know doesn't occur in the input file. This is hard to do in a general way, such that a program always works for arbitrary input files.

You might think that for text files, the NUL character, which consists of a character with all bits equal to zero, is a good value to use for RS in this case:

```
BEGIN { RS = "\0" }  # whole file becomes one record?
```

gawk in fact accepts this, and uses the NUL character for the record separator. However, this usage is *not* portable to other *awk* implementations.

All other *awk* implementations* store strings internally as C-style strings. C strings use the NUL character as the string terminator. In effect, this means that RS = "\0" is the same as RS = "". (d.c.)

The best way to treat a whole file as a single record is to simply read the file in, one record at a time, concatenating each record onto the end of the previous ones.

A dollar-sign ($) is used to refer to a field in an *awk* program, followed by the number of the field you want. Thus, $1 refers to the first field, $2 to the second, and so on. (Unlike the Unix shells, the field numbers are not limited to single digits. $127 is the one hundred twenty-seventh field in the record.) For example, suppose the following is a line of input:

```
This seems like a pretty nice example.
```

Here the first field, or $1, is This, the second field, or $2, is seems, and so on. Note that the last field, $7, is example.. Because there is no space between the e and the ., the period is considered part of the seventh field.

NF is a built-in variable whose value is the number of fields in the current record. *awk* automatically updates the value of NF each time it reads a record. No matter how many fields there are, the last field in a record can be represented by $NF. So, $NF is the same as $7, which is example.. If you try to reference a field beyond the last one (such as $8 when the record has only seven fields), you get the empty string. (If used in a numeric operation, you get zero.)

---

* At least that we know about.

The use of $0, which looks like a reference to the "zero-th" field, is a special case: it represents the whole input record when you are not interested in specific fields. Here are some more examples:

```
$ awk '$1 ~ /foo/ { print $0 }' BBS-list
fooey       555-1234    2400/1200/300    B
foot        555-6699    1200/300         B
macfoo      555-6480    1200/300         A
sabafoo     555-2127    1200/300         C
```

This example prints each record in the file *BBS-list* whose first field contains the string foo. The operator ~ is called a *matching operator* (see the section "How to Use Regular Expressions" in Chapter 2); it tests whether a string (here, the field $1) matches a given regular expression.

By contrast, the following example looks for foo in *the entire record* and prints the first field and the last field for each matching input record:

```
$ awk '/foo/ { print $1, $NF }' BBS-list
fooey B
foot B
macfoo A
sabafoo C
```

Non-constant Field Numbers

The number of a field does not need to be a constant. Any expression in the *awk* language can be used after a $ to refer to a field. The value of the expression specifies the field number. If the value is a string, rather than a number, it is converted to a number. Consider this example:

```
awk '{ print $NR }'
```

Recall that NR is the number of records read so far: one in the first record, two in the second, etc. So this example prints the first field of the first record, the second field of the second record, and so on. For the twentieth record, field number 20 is printed; most likely, the record has fewer than 20 fields, so this prints a blank line. Here is another example of using expressions as field numbers:

```
awk '{ print $(2*2) }' BBS-list
```

awk evaluates the expression (2*2) and uses its value as the number of the field to print. The * sign represents multiplication, so the expression 2*2 evaluates to four. The parentheses are used so that the multiplication is done before the $ operation; they are necessary whenever there is a binary operator in the field-number expression. This example, then, prints the hours of operation (the fourth field) for every line of the file *BBS-list*. (All of the *awk* operators are listed, in order of decreasing precedence, in the section "Operator Precedence (How Operators Nest)" in Chapter 5.)

If the field number you compute is zero, you get the entire record. Thus, $(2-2) has the same value as $0. Negative field numbers are not allowed; trying to reference one usually terminates the program. (The POSIX standard does not define what happens when you reference a negative field number. *gawk* notices this and terminates your program. Other *awk* implementations may behave differently.)

As mentioned earlier in the section "Examining Fields," *awk* stores the current record's number of fields in the built-in variable NF (also see the section "Built-in Variables" in Chapter 6). The expression $NF is not a special feature—it is the direct consequence of evaluating NF and using its value as a field number.

Changing the Contents of a Field

The contents of a field, as seen by *awk*, can be changed within an *awk* program; this changes what *awk* perceives as the current input record. (The actual input is untouched; *awk* never modifies the input file.) Consider the following example and its output:

```
$ awk '{ nboxes = $3 ; $3 = $3 - 10
>         print nboxes, $3 }' inventory-shipped
13 3
15 5
15 5
...
```

The program first saves the original value of field three in the variable nboxes. The – sign represents subtraction, so this program reassigns field three, $3, as the original value of field three minus ten: $3 - 10. (See the section "Arithmetic Operators" in Chapter 5.) Then it prints the original and new values for field three. (Someone in the warehouse made a consistent mistake while inventorying the red boxes.)

For this to work, the text in field $2 must make sense as a number; the string of characters must be converted to a number for the computer to do arithmetic on it. The number resulting from the subtraction is converted back to a string of characters that then becomes field three. See the section "Conversion of Strings and Numbers" in Chapter 5.

When the value of a field is changed (as perceived by *awk*), the text of the input record is recalculated to contain the new field where the old one was. In other words, $0 changes to reflect the altered field. Thus, this program prints a copy of the input file, with 10 subtracted from the second field of each line:

```
$ awk '{ $2 = $2 - 10; print $0 }' inventory-shipped
Jan 3 25 15 115
Feb 5 32 24 226
Mar 5 24 34 228
...
```

It is also possible to also assign contents to fields that are out of range. For example:

```
$ awk '{ $6 = ($5 + $4 + $3 + $2)
>          print $6 }' inventory-shipped
168
297
301
...
```

We've just created $6, whose value is the sum of fields $2, $3, $4, and $5. The + sign represents addition. For the file *inventory-shipped*, $6 represents the total number of parcels shipped for a particular month.

Creating a new field changes *awk*'s internal copy of the current input record, which is the value of $0. Thus, if you do print $0 after adding a field, the record printed includes the new field, with the appropriate number of field separators between it and the previously existing fields.

This recomputation affects and is affected by NF (the number of fields; see the section "Examining Fields" earlier in this chapter). It is also affected by a feature that has not been discussed yet: the *output field separator*, OFS, used to separate the fields (see the section "Output Separators" in Chapter 4, *Printing Output*). For example, the value of NF is set to the number of the highest field you create.

Note, however, that merely *referencing* an out-of-range field does *not* change the value of either $0 or NF. Referencing an out-of-range field only produces an empty string. For example:

```
if ($(NF+1) != "")
    print "can't happen"
else
    print "everything is normal"
```

should print everything is normal, because NF+1 is certain to be out of range. (See the section "The if-else Statement" in Chapter 6 for more information about *awk*'s if-else statements. See the section "Variable Typing and Comparison Expressions" in Chapter 5 for more information about the != operator.)

It is important to note that making an assignment to an existing field changes the value of $0 but does not change the value of NF, even when you assign the empty string to a field. For example:

```
$ echo a b c d | awk '{ OFS = ":"; $2 = ""
>                        print $0; print NF }'
a::c:d
4
```

The field is still there; it just has an empty value, denoted by the two colons between a and c. This example shows what happens if you create a new field:

```
$ echo a b c d | awk '{ OFS = ":"; $2 = ""; $6 = "new"
>                       print $0; print NF }'
a::c:d::new
6
```

The intervening field, $5, is created with an empty value (indicated by the second pair of adjacent colons), and NF is updated with the value six.

Decrementing NF throws away the values of the fields after the new value of NF and recomputes $0. (d.c.) Here is an example:

```
$ echo a b c d e f | awk '{ print "NF =", NF;
>                           NF = 3; print $0 }'
NF = 6
a b c
```

Some versions of *awk* don't rebuild $0 when NF is decremented. Caveat emptor.

Specifying How Fields Are Separated

The *field separator*, which is either a single character or a regular expression, controls the way *awk* splits an input record into fields. *awk* scans the input record for character sequences that match the separator; the fields themselves are the text between the matches.

In the examples that follow, we use the small box (□) to represent spaces in the output. If the field separator is oo, then the following line:

```
moo goo gai pan
```

is split into three fields: m, □g, and □gai□pan. Note the leading spaces in the values of the second and third fields.

The field separator is represented by the built-in variable FS. Shell programmers take note: *awk* does *not* use the name IFS that is used by the POSIX-compliant shells (such as the Unix Bourne shell, *sh*, or *bash*).

The value of FS can be changed in the *awk* program with the assignment operator, = (see the section "Assignment Expressions" in Chapter 5). Often the right time to do this is at the beginning of execution before any input has been processed, so that the very first record is read with the proper separator. To do this, use the special BEGIN pattern (see the section "The BEGIN and END Special Patterns" in Chapter 6). For example, here we set the value of FS to the string ",":

```
awk 'BEGIN { FS = "," } ; { print $2 }'
```

Given the input line:

```
John Q. Smith, 29 Oak St., Walamazoo, MI 42139
```

this *awk* program extracts and prints the string ⊔29⊔Oak⊔St..

Sometimes the input data contains separator characters that don't separate fields the way you thought they would. For instance, the person's name in the example we just used might have a title or suffix attached, such as:

```
John Q. Smith, LXIX, 29 Oak St., Walamazoo, MI 42139
```

The same program would extract ⊔LXIX, instead of ⊔29⊔Oak⊔St.. If you were expecting the program to print the address, you would be surprised. The moral is to choose your data layout and separator characters carefully to prevent such problems. (If the data is not in a form that is easy to process, perhaps you can massage it first with a separate *awk* program.)

Fields are normally separated by whitespace sequences (spaces, tabs, and newlines), not by single spaces. Two spaces in a row do not delimit an empty field. The default value of the field separator FS is a string containing a single space, " ". If *awk* interpreted this value in the usual way, each space character would separate fields, so two spaces in a row would make an empty field between them. The reason this does not happen is that a single space as the value of FS is a special case—it is taken to specify the default manner of delimiting fields.

If FS is any other single character, such as ",", then each occurrence of that character separates two fields. Two consecutive occurrences delimit an empty field. If the character occurs at the beginning or the end of the line, that too delimits an empty field. The space character is the only single character that does not follow these rules.

Using Regular Expressions to Separate Fields

The previous section discussed the use of single characters or simple strings as the value of FS. More generally, the value of FS may be a string containing any regular expression. In this case, each match in the record for the regular expression separates fields. For example, the assignment:

```
FS = ", \t"
```

makes every area of an input line that consists of a comma followed by a space and a tab into a field separator.

For a less trivial example of a regular expression, try using single spaces to separate fields the way single commas are used. FS can be set to "[ ]" (left bracket, space, right bracket). This regular expression matches a single space and nothing else (see Chapter 2).

There is an important difference between the two cases of FS = " " (a single space) and FS = "[\t\n]+" (a regular expression matching one or more spaces, tabs, or newlines). For both values of FS, fields are separated by *runs* (multiple adjacent occurrences) of spaces, tabs, and/or newlines. However, when the value of FS is " ", *awk* first strips leading and trailing whitespace from the record and then decides where the fields are. For example, the following pipeline prints b:

```
$ echo ' a b c d ' | awk '{ print $2 }'
b
```

However, this pipeline prints a (note the extra spaces around each letter):

```
$ echo ' a   b   c   d ' | awk 'BEGIN { FS = "[ \t\n]+" }
>                              { print $2 }'
a
```

In this case, the first field is *null* or empty.

The stripping of leading and trailing whitespace also comes into play whenever $0 is recomputed. For instance, study this pipeline:

```
$ echo '    a b c d' | awk '{ print; $2 = $2; print }'
   a b c d
a b c d
```

The first print statement prints the record as it was read, with leading whitespace intact. The assignment to $2 rebuilds $0 by concatenating $1 through $NF together, separated by the value of OFS. Because the leading whitespace was ignored when finding $1, it is not part of the new $0. Finally, the last print statement prints the new $0.

Making Each Character a Separate Field

There are times when you may want to examine each character of a record separately. This can be done in *gawk* by simply assigning the null string ("") to FS. In this case, each individual character in the record becomes a separate field. For example:

```
$ echo a b | gawk 'BEGIN { FS = "" }
>                        {
```

```
   >                              for (i = 1; i <= NF; i = i + 1)
   >                                print "Field", i, "is", $i
   >                  }'
   Field 1 is a
   Field 2 is
   Field 3 is b
```

Traditionally, the behavior of FS equal to "" was not defined. In this case, most versions of Unix *awk* simply treat the entire record as only having one field. (d.c.) In compatibility mode (see the section "Command-Line Options" in Chapter 11), if FS is the null string, then *gawk* also behaves this way.

Setting FS from the Command Line

FS can be set on the command line. Use the *–F* option to do so. For example:

```
   awk -F, 'program' input-files
```

sets FS to the , character. Notice that the option uses an uppercase *–F* instead of a lowercase *–f*, which specifies a file containing an *awk* program. Case is significant in command-line options: the *–F* and *–f* options have nothing to do with each other. You can use both options at the same time to set the FS variable *and* get an *awk* program from a file.

The value used for the argument to *–F* is processed in exactly the same way as assignments to the built-in variable FS. Any special characters in the field separator must be escaped appropriately. For example, to use a \ as the field separator on the command line, you would have to type:

```
   # same as FS = "\\"
   awk -F\\\\ '...' files ...
```

Because \ is used for quoting in the shell, *awk* sees -F\\. Then *awk* processes the \\ for escape characters (see the section "Escape Sequences" in Chapter 2), finally yielding a single \ to use for the field separator.

As a special case, in compatibility mode (see the section "Command-Line Options" in Chapter 11) if the argument to *–F* is t, then FS is set to the tab character. If you type -F\t at the shell, without any quotes, the \ gets deleted, so *awk* figures that you really want your fields to be separated with tabs and not ts. Use -v FS="t" or -F"[t]" on the command line if you really do want to separate your fields with ts.

For example, let's use an *awk* program file called *baud.awk* that contains the pattern /300/ and the action print $1:

```
   /300/    { print $1 }
```

Let's also set FS to be the - character and run the program on the file *BBS-list*. The following command prints a list of the names of the bulletin boards that operate at 300 baud and the first three digits of their phone numbers:

```
$ awk -F- -f baud.awk BBS-list
aardvark     555
alpo
barfly       555
bites        555
camelot      555
core         555
fooey        555
foot         555
macfoo       555
sdace        555
sabafoo      555
```

Note the second line of output. The second line in the original file looked like this:

```
alpo-net     555-3412     2400/1200/300     A
```

The – as part of the system's name was used as the field separator, instead of the – in the phone number that was originally intended. This demonstrates why you have to be careful in choosing your field and record separators.

Perhaps the most common use of a single character as the field separator occurs when processing the Unix system password file. On many Unix systems, each user has a separate entry in the system password file, one line per user. The information in these lines is separated by colons. The first field is the user's logon name and the second is the user's (encrypted or shadow) password. A password file entry might look like this:

```
arnold:xyzzy:2076:10:Arnold Robbins:/home/arnold:/bin/bash
```

The following program searches the system password file and prints the entries for users who have no password:

```
awk -F: '$2 == ""' /etc/passwd
```

Field-Splitting Summary

The following list summarizes how fields are split, based on the value of FS (== means "is equal to"):

FS == " "
: Fields are separated by runs of whitespace. Leading and trailing whitespace are ignored. This is the default.

FS == *any other single character*
: Fields are separated by each occurrence of the character. Multiple successive occurrences delimit empty fields, as do leading and trailing occurrences. The character can even be a regexp metacharacter; it does not need to be escaped.

`FS == ` *`regexp`*

> Fields are separated by occurrences of characters that match *regexp*. Leading and trailing matches of *regexp* delimit empty fields.

`FS == ""`

> Each individual character in the record becomes a separate field. (This is a *gawk* extension; it is not specified by the POSIX standard.)

Changing FS Does Not Affect the Fields

According to the POSIX standard, *awk* is supposed to behave as if each record is split into fields at the time it is read. In particular, this means that if you change the value of FS after a record is read, the value of the fields (i.e., how they were split) should reflect the old value of FS, not the new one.

However, many implementations of *awk* do not work this way. Instead, they defer splitting the fields until a field is actually referenced. The fields are split using the *current* value of FS! (d.c.) This behavior can be difficult to diagnose. The following example illustrates the difference between the two methods (the *sed** command prints just the first line of */etc/passwd*):

```
sed 1q /etc/passwd | awk '{ FS = ":" ; print $1 }'
```

which usually prints:

```
root
```

on an incorrect implementation of *awk*, while *gawk* prints something like:

```
root:nSijPlPhZZwgE:0:0:Root:/:
```

Reading Fixed-Width Data

This section discusses an advanced feature of *gawk*. If you are a novice *awk* user, you might want to skip it on the first reading.

gawk Version 2.13 introduced a facility for dealing with fixed-width fields with no distinctive field separator. For example, data of this nature arises in the input for old Fortran programs where numbers are run together, or in the output of programs that did not anticipate the use of their output as input for other programs.

An example of the latter is a table where all the columns are lined up by the use of a variable number of spaces and *empty fields are just spaces*. Clearly, *awk*'s

---

* The *sed* utility is a "stream editor." Its behavior is also defined by the POSIX standard.

normal field splitting based on FS does not work well in this case. Although a portable *awk* program can use a series of substr calls on $0 (see the section "String-Manipulation Functions" in Chapter 8, *Functions*), this is awkward and inefficient for a large number of fields.

The splitting of an input record into fixed-width fields is specified by assigning a string containing space-separated numbers to the built-in variable FIELDWIDTHS. Each number specifies the width of the field, *including* columns between fields. If you want to ignore the columns between fields, you can specify the width as a separate field that is subsequently ignored. It is a fatal error to supply a field width that is not a positive number. The following data is the output of the Unix *w* utility. It is useful to illustrate the use of FIELDWIDTHS:

```
10:06pm  up 21 days, 14:04,   23 users
User     tty        login idle  JCPU  PCPU  what
hzuo     ttyV0     8:58pm          9     5  vi p24.tex
hzang    ttyV3     6:37pm   50              -csh
eklye    ttyV5     9:53pm    .     7     1  em thes.tex
dportein ttyV6     8:17pm 1:47              -csh
gierd    ttyD3    10:00pm    1              elm
dave     ttyD4     9:47pm          4     4  w
brent    ttyp0    26Jun91 4:46  26:46  4:41  bash
dave     ttyq4    26Jun9115days    46    46  wnewmail
```

The following program takes the above input, converts the idle time to number of seconds, and prints out the first two fields and the calculated idle time:

 This program uses a number of *awk* features that haven't been introduced yet.

```
BEGIN  { FIELDWIDTHS = "9 6 10 6 7 7 35" }
NR > 2 {
    idle = $4
    sub(/^ */, "", idle)    # strip leading spaces
    if (idle == "")
        idle = 0
    if (idle ~ /:/) {
        split(idle, t, ":")
        idle = t[1] * 60 + t[2]
    }
    if (idle ~ /days/)
        idle *= 24 * 60 * 60

    print $1, $2, idle
}
```

Running the program on the data produces the following results:

```
hzuo       ttyV0   0
hzang      ttyV3   50
eklye      ttyV5   0
dportein   ttyV6   107
gierd      ttyD3   1
dave       ttyD4   0
brent      ttyp0   286
dave       ttyq4   1296000
```

Another (possibly more practical) example of fixed-width input data is the input from a deck of balloting cards. In some parts of the United States, voters mark their choices by punching holes in computer cards. These cards are then processed to count the votes for any particular candidate or on any particular issue. Because a voter may choose not to vote on some issue, any column on the card may be empty. An *awk* program for processing such data could use the FIELD-WIDTHS feature to simplify reading the data. (Of course, getting *gawk* to run on a system with card readers is another story!)

Assigning a value to FS causes *gawk* to use FS for field splitting again. Use FS = FS to make this happen, without having to know the current value of FS. In order to tell which kind of field splitting is in effect, use PROCINFO["FS"] (see the section "Built-in Variables That Convey Information" in Chapter 6). The value is "FS" if regular field splitting is being used, or it is "FIELDWIDTHS" if fixed-width field splitting is being used:

```
if (PROCINFO["FS"] == "FS")
    regular field splitting ...
else
    fixed-width field splitting ...
```

This information is useful when writing a function that needs to temporarily change FS or FIELDWIDTHS, read some records, and then restore the original settings (see the section "Reading the User Database" in Chapter 12, *A Library of awk Functions*, for an example of such a function).

Multiple-Line Records

In some databases, a single line cannot conveniently hold all the information in one entry. In such cases, you can use multiline records. The first step in doing this is to choose your data format.

One technique is to use an unusual character or string to separate records. For example, you could use the formfeed character (written \f in *awk*, as in C) to separate them, making each record a page of the file. To do this, just set the variable RS to "\f" (a string containing the formfeed character). Any other character·could equally well be used, as long as it won't be part of the data in a record.

Another technique is to have blank lines separate records. By a special dispensation, an empty string as the value of RS indicates that records are separated by one or more blank lines. When RS is set to the empty string, each record always ends at the first blank line encountered. The next record doesn't start until the first non-blank line that follows. No matter how many blank lines appear in a row, they all act as one record separator. (Blank lines must be completely empty; lines that contain only whitespace do not count.)

You can achieve the same effect as RS = "" by assigning the string "\n\n+" to RS. This regexp matches the newline at the end of the record and one or more blank lines after the record. In addition, a regular expression always matches the longest possible sequence when there is a choice (see the section "How Much Text Matches?" in Chapter 2). So the next record doesn't start until the first nonblank line that follows—no matter how many blank lines appear in a row, they are considered one record separator.

There is an important difference between RS = "" and RS = "\n\n+". In the first case, leading newlines in the input datafile are ignored, and if a file ends without extra blank lines after the last record, the final newline is removed from the record. In the second case, this special processing is not done. (d.c.)

Now that the input is separated into records, the second step is to separate the fields in the record. One way to do this is to divide each of the lines into fields in the normal manner. This happens by default as the result of a special feature. When RS is set to the empty string, the newline character *always* acts as a field separator. This is in addition to whatever field separations result from FS.

The original motivation for this special exception was probably to provide useful behavior in the default case (i.e., FS is equal to " "). This feature can be a problem if you really don't want the newline character to separate fields, because there is no way to prevent it. However, you can work around this by using the split function to break up the record manually (see the section "String-Manipulation Functions" in Chapter 8).

Another way to separate fields is to put each field on a separate line: to do this, just set the variable FS to the string "\n". (This simple regular expression matches a single newline.) A practical example of a datafile organized this way might be a mailing list, where each entry is separated by blank lines. Consider a mailing list in a file named *addresses*, which looks like this:

```
Jane Doe
123 Main Street
Anywhere, SE 12345-6789
```

```
John Smith
456 Tree-lined Avenue
Smallville, MW 98765-4321
...
```

A simple program to process this file is as follows:

```
# addrs.awk --- simple mailing list program

# Records are separated by blank lines.
# Each line is one field.
BEGIN { RS = "" ; FS = "\n" }

{
    print "Name is:", $1
    print "Address is:", $2
    print "City and State are:", $3
    print ""
}
```

Running the program produces the following output:

```
$ awk -f addrs.awk addresses
Name is: Jane Doe
Address is: 123 Main Street
City and State are: Anywhere, SE 12345-6789

Name is: John Smith
Address is: 456 Tree-lined Avenue
City and State are: Smallville, MW 98765-4321

...
```

See the section "Printing Mailing Labels" in Chapter 13 for a more realistic program that deals with address lists. The following list summarizes how records are split, based on the value of RS:

RS == "\n"

Records are separated by the newline character (\n). In effect, every line in the datafile is a separate record, including blank lines. This is the default.

RS == *any single character*

Records are separated by each occurrence of the character. Multiple successive occurrences delimit empty records.

RS == ""

Records are separated by runs of blank lines. The newline character always serves as a field separator, in addition to whatever value FS may have. Leading and trailing newlines in a file are ignored.

RS == *regexp*

>   Records are separated by occurrences of characters that match *regexp*. Leading
>   and trailing matches of *regexp* delimit empty records. (This is a *gawk* exten-
>   sion it is not specified by the POSIX standard.)

In all cases, *gawk* sets RT to the input text that matched the value specified by RS.

Explicit Input with getline

So far we have been getting our input data from *awk*'s main input stream—either
the standard input (usually your terminal, sometimes the output from another program) or from the files specified on the command line. The *awk* language has a
special built-in command called getline that can be used to read input under your
explicit control.

The getline command is used in several different ways and should *not* be used
by beginners. The examples that follow the explanation of the getline command
include material that has not been covered yet. Therefore, come back and study
the getline command *after* you have reviewed the rest of this book and have a
good knowledge of how *awk* works.

The getline command returns one if it finds a record and zero if it encounters the
end of the file. If there is some error in getting a record, such as a file that cannot
be opened, then getline returns –1. In this case, *gawk* sets the variable ERRNO to a
string describing the error that occurred.

In the following examples, command stands for a string value that represents a shell
command.

Using getline with No Arguments

The getline command can be used without arguments to read input from the current input file. All it does in this case is read the next input record and split it up
into fields. This is useful if you've finished processing the current record, but want
to do some special processing on the next record *right now*. For example:

```
{
    if ((t = index($0, "/*")) != 0) {
        # value of 'tmp' will be "" if t is 1
        tmp = substr($0, 1, t - 1)
        u = index(substr($0, t + 2), "*/")
        while (u == 0) {
            if (getline <= 0) {
                m = "unexpected EOF or error"
                m = (m ": " ERRNO)
                print m > "/dev/stderr"
                exit
```

```
                }
                t = -1
                u = index($0, "*/")
            }
            # substr expression will be "" if */
            # occurred at end of line
            $0 = tmp substr($0, u + 2)
        }
    print $0
}
```

This *awk* program deletes all C-style comments (/* ... */) from the input. By replacing the print $0 with other statements, you could perform more complicated processing on the decommented input, such as searching for matches of a regular expression. (This program has a subtle problem—it does not work if one comment ends and another begins on the same line.)

This form of the getline command sets NF, NR, FNR, and the value of $0.

> The new value of $0 is used to test the patterns of any subsequent rules. The original value of $0 that triggered the rule that executed getline is lost. By contrast, the **next** statement reads a new record but immediately begins processing it normally, starting with the first rule in the program. See the section "The next Statement" in Chapter 6.

Using getline into a Variable

You can use getline *var* to read the next record from *awk*'s input into the variable *var*. No other processing is done. For example, suppose the next line is a comment or a special string, and you want to read it without triggering any rules. This form of getline allows you to read that line and store it in a variable so that the main read-a-line-and-check-each-rule loop of *awk* never sees it. The following example swaps every two lines of input:

```
{
    if ((getline tmp) > 0) {
        print tmp
        print $0
    } else
        print $0
}
```

It takes the following list:

```
wan
tew
free
phore
```

and produces these results:

```
tew
wan
phore
free
```

The `getline` command used in this way sets only the variables `NR` and `FNR` (and of course, *var*). The record is not split into fields, so the values of the fields (including `$0`) and the value of `NF` do not change.

Using getline from a File

Use `getline < `*file* to read the next record from *file*. Here *file* is a string-valued expression that specifies the filename. `< `*file* is called a *redirection* because it directs input to come from a different place. For example, the following program reads its input record from the file *secondary.input* when it encounters a first field with a value equal to 10 in the current input file:

```
{
    if ($1 == 10) {
        getline < "secondary.input"
        print
    } else
        print
}
```

Because the main input stream is not used, the values of `NR` and `FNR` are not changed. However, the record it reads is split into fields in the normal manner, so the values of `$0` and the other fields are changed, resulting in a new value of `NF`.

According to POSIX, `getline < `*expression* is ambiguous if *expression* contains unparenthesized operators other than `$`; for example, `getline < dir "/" file` is ambiguous because the concatenation operator is not parenthesized. You should write it as `getline < (dir "/" file)` if you want your program to be portable to other *awk* implementations. (It happens that *gawk* gets it right, but you should not rely on this. Parentheses make it easier to read.)

Using getline into a Variable from a File

Use getline *var* < *file* to read input from the file *file*, and put it in the variable *var*. As above, *file* is a string-valued expression that specifies the file from which to read.

In this version of getline, none of the built-in variables are changed and the record is not split into fields. The only variable changed is *var*. For example, the following program copies all the input files to the output, except for records that say @include *filename*. Such a record is replaced by the contents of the file *filename*:

```
{
    if (NF == 2 && $1 == "@include") {
        while ((getline line < $2) > 0)
            print line
        close($2)
    } else
        print
}
```

Note here how the name of the extra input file is not built into the program; it is taken directly from the data, specifically from the second field on the @include line.

The close function is called to ensure that if two identical @include lines appear in the input, the entire specified file is included twice. See the section "Closing Input and Output Redirections" in Chapter 4.

One deficiency of this program is that it does not process nested @include statements (i.e., @include statements in included files) the way a true macro preprocessor would. See the section "An Easy Way to Use Library Functions" in Chapter 13 for a program that does handle nested @include statements.

Using getline from a Pipe

The output of a command can also be piped into getline, using *command* | getline. In this case, the string *command* is run as a shell command and its output is piped into *awk* to be used as input. This form of getline reads one record at a time from the pipe. For example, the following program copies its input to its output, except for lines that begin with @execute, which are replaced by the output produced by running the rest of the line as a shell command:

```
{
    if ($1 == "@execute") {
        tmp = substr($0, 10)
        while ((tmp | getline) > 0)
            print
```

```
              close(tmp)
      } else
          print
   }
```

The `close` function is called to ensure that if two identical `@execute` lines appear in the input, the command is run for each one. See the section "Closing Input and Output Redirections" in Chapter 4. Given the input:

```
foo
bar
baz
@execute who
bletch
```

the program might produce:

```
foo
bar
baz
arnold     ttyv0   Jul 13 14:22
miriam     ttyp0   Jul 13 14:23      (murphy:0)
bill       ttyp1   Jul 13 14:23      (murphy:0)
bletch
```

Notice that this program ran the command *who* and printed the previous result. (If you try this program yourself, you will of course get different results, depending upon who is logged in on your system.)

This variation of `getline` splits the record into fields, sets the value of NF, and recomputes the value of $0. The values of NR and FNR are not changed.

According to POSIX, *expression* | `getline` is ambiguous if *expression* contains unparenthesized operators other than $—for example, `"echo " "date" | getline` is ambiguous because the concatenation operator is not parenthesized. You should write it as `("echo " "date") | getline` if you want your program to be portable to other *awk* implementations.

Using getline into a Variable from a Pipe

When you use *command* | `getline var`, the output of *command* is sent through a pipe to `getline` and into the variable *var*. For example, the following program reads the current date and time into the variable current_time, using the *date* utility, and then prints it:

```
BEGIN {
    "date" | getline current_time
    close("date")
    print "Report printed on " current_time
}
```

In this version of getline, none of the built-in variables are changed and the record is not split into fields.

Using getline from a Coprocess

Input into getline from a pipe is a one-way operation. The command that is started with command | getline only sends data *to* your *awk* program.

On occasion, you might want to send data to another program for processing and then read the results back. *gawk* allows you start a *coprocess*, with which two-way communications are possible. This is done with the |& operator. Typically, you write data to the coprocess first and then read results back, as shown in the following:

```
print "some query" |& "db_server"
"db_server" |& getline
```

which sends a query to *db_server* and then reads the results.

The values of NR and FNR are not changed, because the main input stream is not used. However, the record is split into fields in the normal manner, thus changing the values of $0, of the other fields, and of NF.

Coprocesses are an advanced feature. They are discussed here only because this is the section on getline. See the section "Two-Way Communications with Another Process" in Chapter 10, *Advanced Features of gawk*, where coprocesses are discussed in more detail.

Using getline into a Variable from a Coprocess

When you use command |& getline var, the output from the coprocess *command* is sent through a two-way pipe to getline and into the variable *var*.

In this version of getline, none of the built-in variables are changed and the record is not split into fields. The only variable changed is *var*.

Points to Remember About getline

Here are some miscellaneous points about getline that you should bear in mind:

- When getline changes the value of $0 and NF, *awk* does *not* automatically jump to the start of the program and start testing the new record against every pattern. However, the new record is tested against any subsequent rules.

- Many *awk* implementations limit the number of pipelines that an *awk* program may have open to just one. In *gawk*, there is no such limit. You can open as many pipelines (and coprocesses) as the underlying operating system permits.

- An interesting side effect occurs if you use `getline` without a redirection inside a BEGIN rule. Because an unredirected `getline` reads from the command-line datafiles, the first `getline` command causes *awk* to set the value of FILENAME. Normally, FILENAME does not have a value inside BEGIN rules, because you have not yet started to process the command-line datafiles. (d.c.) (See the section "The BEGIN and END Special Patterns" in Chapter 6; also see the section "Built-in Variables That Convey Information" in Chapter 6.)

Summary of getline Variants

Table 3-1 summarizes the eight variants of `getline`, listing which built-in variables are set by each one.

Table 3-1. getline Variants and What They Set

Variant	Effect
`getline`	Sets $0, NF, FNR, and NR
`getline var`	Sets *var*, FNR, and NR
`getline < file`	Sets $0 and NF
`getline var < file`	Sets *var*
`command	getline`	Sets $0 and NF
`command	getline var`	Sets *var*
`command |& getline`	Sets $0 and NF[a]
`command |& getline var`	Sets *var*[a]

[a] This is a *gawk* extension.

4

Printing Output

One of the most common programming actions is to *print*, or output, some or all of the input. Use the `print` statement for simple output, and the `printf` statement for fancier formatting. The `print` statement is not limited when computing *which* values to print. However, with two exceptions, you cannot specify *how* to print them—how many columns, whether to use exponential notation or not, and so on. (For the exceptions, see the section "Output Separators" and the section "Controlling Numeric Output with print" later in this chapter.) For printing with specifications, you need the `printf` statement (see the section "Using printf Statements for Fancier Printing" later in this chapter).

Besides basic and formatted printing, this chapter also covers I/O redirections to files and pipes, introduces the special filenames that *gawk* processes internally, and discusses the `close` built-in function.

The print Statement

The `print` statement is used to produce output with simple, standardized formatting. Specify only the strings or numbers to print, in a list separated by commas. They are output, separated by single spaces, followed by a newline. The statement looks like this:

```
print item1, item2, ...
```

The entire list of items may be optionally enclosed in parentheses. The parentheses are necessary if any of the item expressions uses the > relational operator;

otherwise, it could be confused with a redirection (see the section "Redirecting Output of print and printf" later in this chapter).

The items to print can be constant strings or numbers, fields of the current record (such as $1), variables, or any *awk* expression. Numeric values are converted to strings and then printed.

The simple statement print with no items is equivalent to print $0: it prints the entire current record. To print a blank line, use print "", where "" is the empty string. To print a fixed piece of text, use a string constant, such as "Don't Panic", as one item. If you forget to use the double-quote characters, your text is taken as an *awk* expression, and you will probably get an error. Keep in mind that a space is printed between any two items.

Examples of print Statements

Each print statement makes at least one line of output. However, it isn't limited to only one line. If an item value is a string that contains a newline, the newline is output along with the rest of the string. A single print statement can make any number of lines this way.

The following is an example of printing a string that contains embedded newlines (the \n is an escape sequence, used to represent the newline character; see the section "Escape Sequences" in Chapter 2, *Regular Expressions*):

```
$ awk 'BEGIN { print "line one\nline two\nline three" }'
line one
line two
line three
```

The next example, which is run on the *inventory-shipped* file, prints the first two fields of each input record, with a space between them:

```
$ awk '{ print $1, $2 }' inventory-shipped
Jan 13
Feb 15
Mar 15
...
```

A common mistake in using the print statement is to omit the comma between two items. This often has the effect of making the items run together in the output, with no space. The reason for this is that juxtaposing two string expressions in *awk* means to concatenate them. Here is the same program, without the comma:

```
$ awk '{ print $1 $2 }' inventory-shipped
Jan13
Feb15
Mar15
...
```

To someone unfamiliar with the *inventory-shipped* file, neither example's output makes much sense. A heading line at the beginning would make it clearer. Let's add some headings to our table of months ($1) and green crates shipped ($2). We do this using the BEGIN pattern (see the section "The BEGIN and END Special Patterns" in Chapter 6, *Patterns, Actions, and Variables*) so that the headings are only printed once:

```
awk 'BEGIN {  print "Month Crates"
              print "----- ------" }
            { print $1, $2 }' inventory-shipped
```

When run, the program prints the following:

```
Month Crates
----- ------
Jan 13
Feb 15
Mar 15
...
```

The only problem, however, is that the headings and the table data don't line up! We can fix this by printing some spaces between the two fields:

```
awk 'BEGIN { print "Month Crates"
             print "----- ------" }
           { print $1, "     ", $2 }' inventory-shipped
```

Lining up columns this way can get pretty complicated when there are many columns to fix. Counting spaces for two or three columns is simple, but any more than this can take up a lot of time. This is why the printf statement was created (see the section "Using printf Statements for Fancier Printing" later in this chapter); one of its specialties is lining up columns of data.

 You can continue either a print or printf statement simply by putting a newline after any comma (see the section "awk Statements Versus Lines" in Chapter 1, *Getting Started with awk*).

Output Separators

As mentioned previously, a print statement contains a list of items separated by commas. In the output, the items are normally separated by single spaces. However, this doesn't need to be the case; a single space is only the default. Any string of characters may be used as the *output field separator* by setting the built-in variable OFS. The initial value of this variable is the string " "—that is, a single space.

The output from an entire `print` statement is called an *output record*. Each `print` statement outputs one output record, and then outputs a string called the *output record separator* (or ORS). The initial value of ORS is the string "\n"; i.e., a newline character. Thus, each `print` statement normally makes a separate line.

In order to change how output fields and records are separated, assign new values to the variables OFS and ORS. The usual place to do this is in the BEGIN rule (see the section "The BEGIN and END Special Patterns" in Chapter 6), so that it happens before any input is processed. It can also be done with assignments on the command line, before the names of the input files, or using the *−v* command-line option (see the section "Command-Line Options" in Chapter 11, *Running awk and gawk*). The following example prints the first and second fields of each input record, separated by a semicolon, with a blank line added after each newline:

```
$ awk 'BEGIN { OFS = ";"; ORS = "\n\n" }
>             { print $1, $2 }' BBS-list
aardvark;555-5553

alpo-net;555-3412

barfly;555-7685
...
```

If the value of ORS does not contain a newline, the program's output is run together on a single line.

Controlling Numeric Output with print

When the `print` statement is used to print numeric values, *awk* internally converts the number to a string of characters and prints that string. *awk* uses the `sprintf` function to do this conversion (see the section "String-Manipulation Functions" in Chapter 8, *Functions*). For now, it suffices to say that the `sprintf` function accepts a *format specification* that tells it how to format numbers (or strings), and that there are a number of different ways in which numbers can be formatted. The different format specifications are discussed more fully in the section "Format-Control Letters" later in this chapter.

The built-in variable OFMT contains the default format specification that `print` uses with `sprintf` when it wants to convert a number to a string for printing. The default value of OFMT is "%.6g". The way `print` prints numbers can be changed by supplying different format specifications as the value of OFMT, as shown in the following example:

```
$ awk 'BEGIN {
>    OFMT = "%.0f"  # print numbers as integers (rounds)
>    print 17.23, 17.54 }'
17 18
```

According to the POSIX standard, *awk*'s behavior is undefined if OFMT contains anything but a floating-point conversion specification. (d.c.)

Using printf Statements for Fancier Printing

For more precise control over the output format than what is normally provided by print, use printf. printf can be used to specify the width to use for each item, as well as various formatting choices for numbers (such as what output base to use, whether to print an exponent, whether to print a sign, and how many digits to print after the decimal point). This is done by supplying a string, called the *format string*, that controls how and where to print the other arguments.

Introduction to the printf Statement

A simple printf statement looks like this:

```
printf format, item1, item2, ...
```

The entire list of arguments may optionally be enclosed in parentheses. The parentheses are necessary if any of the item expressions use the > relational operator; otherwise, it can be confused with a redirection (see the section "Redirecting Output of print and printf" later in this chapter).

The difference between printf and print is the *format* argument. This is an expression whose value is taken as a string; it specifies how to output each of the other arguments. It is called the *format string*.

The format string is very similar to that in the ISO C library function printf. Most of *format* is text to output verbatim. Scattered among this text are *format specifiers*—one per item. Each format specifier says to output the next item in the argument list at that place in the format.

The printf statement does not automatically append a newline to its output. It outputs only what the format string specifies. So if a newline is needed, you must include one in the format string. The output separator variables OFS and ORS have no effect on printf statements. For example:

```
$ awk 'BEGIN {
>     ORS = "\nOUCH!\n"; OFS = "+"
>     msg = "Dont Panic!"
>     printf "%s\n", msg
> }'
Dont Panic!
```

Here, neither the + nor the OUCH! appear when the message is printed.

Format-Control Letters

A format specifier starts with the character % and ends with a *format-control letter*—it tells the printf statement how to output one item. The format-control letter specifies what *kind* of value to print. The rest of the format specifier is made up of optional *modifiers* that control *how* to print the value, such as the field width. Here is a list of the format-control letters:

%c   This prints a number as an ASCII character; thus, printf "%c", 65 outputs the letter A. (The output for a string value is the first character of the string.)

%d, %i

These are equivalent; they both print a decimal integer. (The %i specification is for compatibility with ISO C.)

%e, %E

These print a number in scientific (exponential) notation; for example:

```
printf "%4.3e\n", 1950
```

prints 1.950e+03, with a total of four significant figures, three of which follow the decimal point. (The 4.3 represents two modifiers, discussed in the next section.) %E uses E instead of e in the output.

%f   This prints a number in floating-point notation. For example:

```
printf "%4.3f", 1950
```

prints 1950.000, with a total of four significant figures, three of which follow the decimal point. (The 4.3 represents two modifiers, discussed in the next section.)

%g, %G

These print a number in either scientific notation or in floating-point notation, whichever uses fewer characters; if the result is printed in scientific notation, %G uses E instead of e.

%o   This prints an unsigned octal integer.

%s   This prints a string.

%u   This prints an unsigned decimal integer. (This format is of marginal use, because all numbers in *awk* are floating-point; it is provided primarily for compatibility with C.)

%x, %X

These print an unsigned hexadecimal integer; %X uses the letters A through F instead of a through f.

%% This isn't a format-control letter, but it does have meaning—the sequence `%%` outputs one `%`; it does not consume an argument and it ignores any modifiers.

 When using the integer format-control letters for values that are outside the range of a C `long` integer, *gawk* switches to the `%g` format specifier. Other versions of *awk* may print invalid values or do something else entirely. (d.c.)

Modifiers for printf Formats

A format specification can also include *modifiers* that can control how much of the item's value is printed, as well as how much space it gets. The modifiers come between the `%` and the format-control letter. We will use the small box "□" in the following examples to represent spaces in the output. Here are the possible modifiers, in the order in which they may appear:

N$ An integer constant followed by a `$` is a *positional specifier*. Normally, format specifications are applied to arguments in the order given in the format string. With a positional specifier, the format specification is applied to a specific argument, instead of what would be the next argument in the list. Positional specifiers begin counting with one. Thus:

```
printf "%s %s\n", "don't", "panic"
printf "%2$s %1$s\n", "panic", "don't"
```

prints the famous friendly message twice.

At first glance, this feature doesn't seem to be of much use. It is in fact a *gawk* extension, intended for use in translating messages at runtime. See the section "Rearranging printf Arguments" in Chapter 9, *Internationalization with gawk*, which describes how and why to use positional specifiers. For now, we will not use them.

- The minus sign, used before the *width* modifier (see later in this list), says to left-justify the argument within its specified width. Normally, the argument is printed right-justified in the specified width. Thus:

```
printf "%-4s", "foo"
```

prints foo□.

space
    For numeric conversions, prefix positive values with a space and negative values with a minus sign.

+ The plus sign, used before the *width* modifier (see later in this list), says to always supply a sign for numeric conversions, even if the data to format is positive. The + overrides the space modifier.

Use an "alternate form" for certain control letters. For %o, supply a leading zero. For %x and %X, supply a leading 0x or 0X for a nonzero result. For %e, %E, and %f, the result always contains a decimal point. For %g and %G, trailing zeros are not removed from the result.

0 A leading 0 (zero) acts as a flag that indicates that output should be padded with zeros instead of spaces. This applies even to non-numeric output formats. (d.c.) This flag only has an effect when the field width is wider than the value to print.

width

> *width* is a number specifying the desired minimum width of a field. Inserting any number between the % sign and the format-control character forces the field to expand to this width. The default way to do this is to pad with spaces on the left. For example:

```
printf "%4s", "foo"
```

> prints □foo.

> The value of *width* is a minimum width, not a maximum. If the item value requires more than *width* characters, it can be as wide as necessary. Thus, the following:

```
printf "%4s", "foobar"
```

> prints foobar.

> Preceding the *width* with a minus sign causes the output to be padded with spaces on the right, instead of on the left.

.prec

> A period followed by an integer constant specifies the precision to use when printing. The meaning of the precision varies by control letter:

%e, %E, %f

> Number of digits to the right of the decimal point.

%g, %G

> Maximum number of significant digits.

`%d, %i, %o, %u, %x, %X`
> Minimum number of digits to print.

`%s`   Maximum number of characters from the string that should print.

Thus, the following:

```
printf "%.4s", "foobar"
```

prints `foob`.

The C library `printf`'s dynamic *width* and *prec* capability (for example, `"%*.*s"`) is supported. Instead of supplying explicit *width* and/or *prec* values in the format string, they are passed in the argument list. For example:

```
w = 5
p = 3
s = "abcdefg"
printf "%*.*s\n", w, p, s
```

is exactly equivalent to:

```
s = "abcdefg"
printf "%5.3s\n", s
```

Both programs output ⊔⊔abc. Earlier versions of *awk* did not support this capability. If you must use such a version, you may simulate this feature by using concatenation to build up the format string, like so:

```
w = 5
p = 3
s = "abcdefg"
printf "%" w "." p "s\n", s
```

This is not particularly easy to read but it does work.

C programmers may be used to supplying additional `l`, `L`, and `h` modifiers in `printf` format strings. These are not valid in *awk*. Most *awk* implementations silently ignore these modifiers. If *--lint* is provided on the command line (see the section "Command-Line Options" in Chapter 11), *gawk* warns about their use. If *--posix* is supplied, their use is a fatal error.

Examples Using printf

The following is a simple example of how to use `printf` to make an aligned table:

```
awk '{ printf "%-10s %s\n", $1, $2 }' BBS-list
```

This command prints the names of the bulletin boards (`$1`) in the file *BBS-list* as a string of 10 characters that are left-justified. It also prints the phone numbers (`$2`) next on the line. This produces an aligned two-column table of names and phone numbers, as shown here:

```
$ awk '{ printf "%-10s %s\n", $1, $2 }' BBS-list
aardvark   555-5553
alpo-net   555-3412
barfly     555-7685
bites      555-1675
camelot    555-0542
core       555-2912
fooey      555-1234
foot       555-6699
macfoo     555-6480
sdace      555-3430
sabafoo    555-2127
```

In this case, the phone numbers had to be printed as strings because the numbers are separated by a dash. Printing the phone numbers as numbers would have produced just the first three digits: 555. This would have been pretty confusing.

It wasn't necessary to specify a width for the phone numbers because they are last on their lines. They don't need to have spaces after them.

The table could be made to look even nicer by adding headings to the tops of the columns. This is done using the BEGIN pattern (see the section "The BEGIN and END Special Patterns" in Chapter 6) so that the headers are only printed once, at the beginning of the *awk* program:

```
awk 'BEGIN { print "Name      Number"
             print "----      ------" }
     { printf "%-10s %s\n", $1, $2 }' BBS-list
```

The above example mixed print and printf statements in the same program. Using just printf statements can produce the same results:

```
awk 'BEGIN { printf "%-10s %s\n", "Name", "Number"
             printf "%-10s %s\n", "----", "------" }
     { printf "%-10s %s\n", $1, $2 }' BBS-list
```

Printing each column heading with the same format specification used for the column elements ensures that the headings are aligned just like the columns.

The fact that the same format specification is used three times can be emphasized by storing it in a variable, like this:

```
awk 'BEGIN { format = "%-10s %s\n"
             printf format, "Name", "Number"
             printf format, "----", "------" }
     { printf format, $1, $2 }' BBS-list
```

At this point, it would be a worthwhile exercise to use the printf statement to line up the headings and table data for the *inventory-shipped* example that was covered earlier in the section on the print statement (see the section "The print Statement" earlier in this chapter).

Redirecting Output of print and printf

So far, the output from print and printf has gone to the standard output, usually
the terminal. Both print and printf can also send their output to other places.
This is called *redirection*.

A redirection appears after the print or printf statement. Redirections in *awk* are
written just like redirections in shell commands, except that they are written inside
the *awk* program.

There are four forms of output redirection: output to a file, output appended to a
file, output through a pipe to another command, and output to a coprocess. They
are all shown for the print statement, but they work identically for printf:

print *items* > *output-file*

> This type of redirection prints the items into the output file named *output-file*.
> The filename *output-file* can be any expression. Its value is changed to a string
> and then used as a filename (see Chapter 5, *Expressions*).
>
> When this type of redirection is used, the *output-file* is erased before the first
> output is written to it. Subsequent writes to the same *output-file* do not erase
> *output-file*, but append to it. (This is different from how you use redirections
> in shell scripts.) If *output-file* does not exist, it is created. For example, here is
> how an *awk* program can write a list of BBS names to one file named *name-
> list*, and a list of phone numbers to another file named *phone-list*:
>
> ```
> $ awk '{ print $2 > "phone-list"
> >         print $1 > "name-list" }' BBS-list
> $ cat phone-list
> 555-5553
> 555-3412
> ...
> $ cat name-list
> aardvark
> alpo-net
> ...
> ```

Each output file contains one name or number per line.

print *items* >> *output-file*

> This type of redirection prints the items into the pre-existing output file named
> *output-file*. The difference between this and the single-> redirection is that the
> old contents (if any) of *output-file* are not erased. Instead, the *awk* output is
> appended to the file. If *output-file* does not exist, then it is created.

print *items* | *command*

> It is also possible to send output to a program through a pipe instead of into a
> file. This type of redirection opens a pipe to *command* and writes the values
> of *items* through this pipe to a process created to execute *command*.

The redirection argument *command* is actually an *awk* expression. Its value is converted to a string whose contents give the shell command to be run. For example, the following produces two files, one unsorted list of BBS names, and one list sorted in reverse alphabetical order:

```
awk '{ print $1 > "names.unsorted"
       command = "sort -r > names.sorted"
       print $1 | command }' BBS-list
```

The unsorted list is written with an ordinary redirection, while the sorted list is written by piping through the *sort* utility.

The next example uses redirection to mail a message to the mailing list bug-system. This might be useful when trouble is encountered in an *awk* script run periodically for system maintenance:

```
report = "mail bug-system"
print "Awk script failed:", $0 | report
m = ("at record number " FNR " of " FILENAME)
print m | report
close(report)
```

The message is built using string concatenation and saved in the variable m. It's then sent down the pipeline to the *mail* program. (The parentheses group the items to concatenate—see the section "String Concatenation" in Chapter 5.)

The close function is called here because it's a good idea to close the pipe as soon as all the intended output has been sent to it. See the section "Closing Input and Output Redirections" later in this chapter for more information.

This example also illustrates the use of a variable to represent a *file* or *command*—it is not necessary to always use a string constant. Using a variable is generally a good idea, because *awk* requires that the string value be spelled identically every time.

print *items* |& *command*

This type of redirection prints the items to the input of *command*. The difference between this and the single-| redirection is that the output from *command* can be read with getline. Thus *command* is a coprocess, which works together with, but subsidiary to, the *awk* program.

This feature is a *gawk* extension, and is not available in POSIX *awk*. See the section "Two-Way Communications with Another Process" in Chapter 10, *Advanced Features of gawk*, for a more complete discussion.

Redirecting output using >, >>, |, or |& asks the system to open a file, pipe, or coprocess only if the particular *file* or *command* you specify has not already been written to by your program or if it has been closed since it was last written to.

It is a common error to use > redirection for the first print to a file, and then to use >> for subsequent output:

```
# clear the file
print "Don't panic" > "guide.txt"
...
# append
print "Avoid improbability generators" >> "guide.txt"
```

This is indeed how redirections must be used from the shell. But in *awk*, it isn't necessary. In this kind of case, a program should use > for all the print statements, since the output file is only opened once.

As mentioned earlier (see the section "Points to Remember About getline" in Chapter 3, *Reading Input Files*), many *awk* implementations limit the number of pipelines that an *awk* program may have open to just one! In *gawk*, there is no such limit. *gawk* allows a program to open as many pipelines as the underlying operating system permits.

Piping into sh

A particularly powerful way to use redirection is to build command lines and pipe them into the shell, *sh*. For example, suppose you have a list of files brought over from a system where all the filenames are stored in uppercase, and you wish to rename them to have names in all lowercase. The following program is both simple and efficient:

```
{ printf("mv %s %s\n", $0, tolower($0)) | "sh" }

END { close("sh") }
```

The tolower function returns its argument string with all uppercase characters converted to lowercase (see the section "String-Manipulation Functions" in Chapter 8). The program builds up a list of command lines, using the *mv* utility to rename the files. It then sends the list to the shell for execution.

Special Filenames in gawk

gawk provides a number of special filenames that it interprets internally. These filenames provide access to standard file descriptors, process-related information, and TCP/IP networking.

Special Files for Standard Descriptors

Running programs conventionally have three input and output streams already available to them for reading and writing. These are known as the *standard input*, *standard output*, and *standard error output*. These streams are, by default, connected to your terminal, but they are often redirected with the shell, via the <, <<, >, >>, >&, and | operators. Standard error is typically used for writing error messages; the reason there are two separate streams, standard output and standard error, is so that they can be redirected separately.

In other implementations of *awk*, the only way to write an error message to standard error in an *awk* program is as follows:

```
print "Serious error detected!" | "cat 1>&2"
```

This works by opening a pipeline to a shell command that can access the standard error stream that it inherits from the *awk* process. This is far from elegant, and it is also inefficient, because it requires a separate process. So people writing *awk* programs often don't do this. Instead, they send the error messages to the terminal, like this:

```
print "Serious error detected!" > "/dev/tty"
```

This usually has the same effect but not always: although the standard error stream is usually the terminal, it can be redirected; when that happens, writing to the terminal is not correct. In fact, if *awk* is run from a background job, it may not have a terminal at all. Then opening */dev/tty* fails.

gawk provides special filenames for accessing the three standard streams, as well as any other inherited open files. If the filename matches one of these special names when *gawk* redirects input or output, then it directly uses the stream that the filename stands for. These special filenames work for all operating systems that *gawk* has been ported to, not just those that are POSIX-compliant:

/dev/stdin
> The standard input (file descriptor 0).

/dev/stdout
> The standard output (file descriptor 1).

/dev/stderr
> The standard error output (file descriptor 2).

/dev/fd/N
> The file associated with file descriptor *N*. Such a file must be opened by the program initiating the *awk* execution (typically the shell). Unless special pains are taken in the shell from which *gawk* is invoked, only descriptors 0, 1, and 2 are available.

The filenames */dev/stdin*, */dev/stdout*, and */dev/stderr* are aliases for */dev/fd/0*, */dev/fd/1*, and */dev/fd/2*, respectively. However, they are more self-explanatory. The proper way to write an error message in a *gawk* program is to use */dev/stderr*, like this:

```
print "Serious error detected!" > "/dev/stderr"
```

Note the use of quotes around the filename. Like any other redirection, the value must be a string. It is a common error to omit the quotes, which leads to confusing results.

Special Files for Process-Related Information

gawk also provides special filenames that give access to information about the running *gawk* process. Each of these "files" provides a single record of information. To read them more than once, they must first be closed with the `close` function (see the section "Closing Input and Output Redirections" later in this chapter). The filenames are:

/dev/pid
> Reading this file returns the process ID of the current process, in decimal form, terminated with a newline.

/dev/ppid
> Reading this file returns the parent process ID of the current process, in decimal form, terminated with a newline.

/dev/pgrpid
> Reading this file returns the process group ID of the current process, in decimal form, terminated with a newline.

/dev/user
> Reading this file returns a single record terminated with a newline. The fields are separated with spaces. The fields represent the following information:
>
> $1   The return value of the `getuid` system call (the real user ID number).
>
> $2   The return value of the `geteuid` system call (the effective user ID number).
>
> $3   The return value of the `getgid` system call (the real group ID number).
>
> $4   The return value of the `getegid` system call (the effective group ID number).
>
> If there are any additional fields, they are the group IDs returned by the `getgroups` system call. (Multiple groups may not be supported on all systems.)

These special filenames may be used on the command line as datafiles, as well as for I/O redirections within an *awk* program. They may not be used as source files with the *–f* option.

 The special files that provide process-related information are now considered obsolete and will disappear entirely in the next release of *gawk*. *gawk* prints a warning message every time you use one of these files. To obtain process-related information, use the PROCINFO array. See section "Built-in Variables That Convey Information" in Chapter 6.

Special Files for Network Communications

Starting with Version 3.1 of *gawk*, *awk* programs can open a two-way TCP/IP connection, acting as either a client or a server. This is done using a special filename of the form:

```
/inet/protocol/local-port/remote-host/remote-port
```

The *protocol* is one of tcp, udp, or raw, and the other fields represent the other essential pieces of information for making a networking connection. These filenames are used with the |& operator for communicating with a coprocess (see the section "Two-Way Communications with Another Process" in Chapter 10). This is an advanced feature, mentioned here only for completeness. See Chapter 14, *Internetworking with gawk*, for an in-depth discussion with many examples.

Special Filename Caveats

Here is a list of things to bear in mind when using the special filenames that *gawk* provides:

- Recognition of these special filenames is disabled if *gawk* is in compatibility mode (see the section "Command-Line Options" in Chapter 11).

- As mentioned earlier, the special files that provide process-related information are now considered obsolete and will disappear entirely in the next release of *gawk*. *gawk* prints a warning message every time you use one of these files. To obtain process-related information, use the PROCINFO array. See the section "Built-in Variables" in Chapter 6.

- Starting with Version 3.1, *gawk always* interprets these special filenames.* For example, using /dev/fd/4 for output actually writes on file descriptor 4, and not on a new file descriptor that is dup'ed from file descriptor 4. Most of the time this does not matter; however, it is important to *not* close any of the files related to file descriptors 0, 1, and 2. Doing so results in unpredictable behavior.

Closing Input and Output Redirections

If the same filename or the same shell command is used with getline more than once during the execution of an *awk* program (see the section "Explicit Input with getline" in Chapter 3), the file is opened (or the command is executed) the first time only. At that time, the first record of input is read from that file or command. The next time the same file or command is used with getline, another record is read from it, and so on.

Similarly, when a file or pipe is opened for output, the filename or command associated with it is remembered by *awk*, and subsequent writes to the same file or command are appended to the previous writes. The file or pipe stays open until *awk* exits.

This implies that special steps are necessary in order to read the same file again from the beginning, or to rerun a shell command (rather than reading more output from the same command). The close function makes these things possible:

    close(*filename*)

or:

    close(*command*)

The argument *filename* or *command* can be any expression. Its value must *exactly* match the string that was used to open the file or start the command (spaces and other "irrelevant" characters included). For example, if you open a pipe with this:

    "sort -r names" | getline foo

then you must close it with this:

    close("sort -r names")

---

* Older versions of *gawk* would interpret these names internally only if the system did not actually have a a */dev/fd* directory or any of the other special files listed earlier. Usually this didn't make a difference, but sometimes it did; thus, it was decided to make *gawk*'s behavior consistent on all systems and to have it always interpret the special filenames itself.

Once this function call is executed, the next `getline` from that file or command, or the next `print` or `printf` to that file or command, reopens the file or reruns the command. Because the expression that you use to close a file or pipeline must exactly match the expression used to open the file or run the command, it is good practice to use a variable to store the filename or command. The previous example becomes the following:

```
sortcom = "sort -r names"
sortcom | getline foo
...
close(sortcom)
```

This helps avoid hard-to-find typographical errors in your *awk* programs. Here are some of the reasons for closing an output file:

- To write a file and read it back later on in the same *awk* program. Close the file after writing it, then begin reading it with `getline`.

- To write numerous files, successively, in the same *awk* program. If the files aren't closed, eventually *awk* may exceed a system limit on the number of open files in one process. It is best to close each one when the program has finished writing it.

- To make a command finish. When output is redirected through a pipe, the command reading the pipe normally continues to try to read input as long as the pipe is open. Often this means the command cannot really do its work until the pipe is closed. For example, if output is redirected to the *mail* program, the message is not actually sent until the pipe is closed.

- To run the same program a second time, with the same arguments. This is not the same thing as giving more input to the first run! For example, suppose a program pipes output to the *mail* program. If it outputs several lines redirected to this pipe without closing it, they make a single message of several lines. By contrast, if the program closes the pipe after each line of output, then each line makes a separate message.

If you use more files than the system allows you to have open, *gawk* attempts to multiplex the available open files among your datafiles. *gawk*'s ability to do this depends upon the facilities of your operating system, so it may not always work. It is therefore both good practice and good portability advice to always use `close` on your files when you are done with them. In fact, if you are using a lot of pipes, it is essential that you close commands when done. For example, consider something like this:

```
{
    ...
    command = ("grep " $1 " /some/file | my_prog -q " $3)
    while ((command | getline) > 0) {
        process output of command
    }
    # need close(command) here
}
```

Using close's Return Value

In many versions of Unix *awk*, the close function is actually a statement. It is a syntax error to try and use the return value from close: (d.c.)

```
command = "..."
command | getline info
retval = close(command)    # syntax error in most Unix awks
```

gawk treats close as a function. The return value is −1 if the argument names something that was never opened with a redirection, or if there is a system problem closing the file or process. In these cases, *gawk* sets the built-in variable ERRNO to a string describing the problem.

In *gawk*, when closing a pipe or coprocess, the return value is the exit status of the command. Otherwise, it is the return value from the system's close or fclose C functions when closing input or output files, respectively. This value is zero if the close succeeds, or −1 if it fails.

The return value for closing a pipeline is particularly useful. It allows you to get the output from a command as well as its exit status.

For POSIX-compliant systems, if the exit status is a number above 128, then the program was terminated by a signal. Subtract 128 to get the signal number:

```
exit_val = close(command)
if (exit_val > 128)
    print command, "died with signal", exit_val - 128
else
    print command, "exited with code", exit_val
```

Currently, in *gawk*, this only works for commands piping into getline. For commands piped into from print or printf, the return value from close is that of the library's pclose function.

This example creates a new pipeline based on data in *each* record. Without the call to close indicated in the comment, *awk* creates child processes to run the commands, until it eventually runs out of file descriptors for more pipelines.

Even though each command has finished (as indicated by the end-of-file return status from `getline`), the child process is not terminated;* more importantly, the file descriptor for the pipe is not closed and released until `close` is called or *awk* exits.

`close` will silently do nothing if given an argument that does not represent a file, pipe or coprocess that was opened with a redirection.

When using the `|&` operator to communicate with a coprocess, it is occasionally useful to be able to close one end of the two-way pipe without closing the other. This is done by supplying a second argument to `close`. As in any other call to `close`, the first argument is the name of the command or special file used to start the coprocess. The second argument should be a string, with either of the values `"to"` or `"from"`. Case does not matter. As this is an advanced feature, a more complete discussion is delayed until the section "Two-Way Communications with Another Process" in Chapter 10, which discusses it in more detail and gives an example.

---

* The technical terminology is rather morbid. The finished child is called a "zombie," and cleaning up after it is referred to as "reaping."

5

Expressions

Expressions are the basic building blocks of *awk* patterns and actions. An expression evaluates to a value that you can print, test, or pass to a function. Additionally, an expression can assign a new value to a variable or a field by using an assignment operator.

An expression can serve as a pattern or action statement on its own. Most other kinds of statements contain one or more expressions that specify the data on which to operate. As in other languages, expressions in *awk* include variables, array references, constants, and function calls, as well as combinations of these with various operators.

Constant Expressions

The simplest type of expression is the *constant*, which always has the same value. There are three types of constants: numeric, string, and regular expression.

Each is used in the appropriate context when you need a data value that isn't going to change. Numeric constants can have different forms, but are stored identically internally.

Numeric and String Constants

A *numeric constant* stands for a number. This number can be an integer, a decimal fraction, or a number in scientific (exponential) notation.* Here are some examples of numeric constants that all have the same value:

```
105
1.05e+2
1050e-1
```

A string constant consists of a sequence of characters enclosed in double-quotation marks. For example:

```
"parrot"
```

represents the string whose contents are `parrot`. Strings in *gawk* can be of any length, and they can contain any of the possible eight-bit ASCII characters including ASCII NUL (character code zero). Other *awk* implementations may have difficulty with some character codes.

Octal and Hexadecimal Numbers

In *awk*, all numbers are in decimal; i.e., base 10. Many other programming languages allow you to specify numbers in other bases, often octal (base 8) and hexadecimal (base 16). In octal, the numbers go 0, 1, 2, 3, 4, 5, 6, 7, 10, 11, 12, etc. Just as 11, in decimal, is 1 times 10 plus 1, so 11, in octal, is 1 times 8 plus 1. This equals 9 in decimal. In hexadecimal, there are 16 digits. Since the everyday decimal number system only has 10 digits (0–9), the letters a through f are used to represent the rest. (Case in the letters is usually irrelevant; hexadecimal a and A have the same value.) Thus, 11, in hexadecimal, is 1 times 16 plus 1, which equals 17 in decimal.

Just by looking at plain 11, you can't tell what base it's in. So, in C, C++, and other languages derived from C, there is a special notation to help signify the base.

---

* The internal representation of all numbers, including integers, uses double-precision floating-point numbers. On most modern systems, these are in IEEE 754 standard format.

Octal numbers start with a leading 0, and hexadecimal numbers start with a leading 0x or 0X:

11   Decimal value 11.
011   Octal 11, decimal value 9.
0x11 Hexadecimal 11, decimal value 17.

This example shows the difference:

```
$ gawk 'BEGIN { printf "%d, %d, %d\n", 011, 11, 0x11 }'
9, 11, 17
```

Being able to use octal and hexadecimal constants in your programs is most useful when working with data that cannot be represented conveniently as characters or as regular numbers, such as binary data of various sorts.

gawk allows the use of octal and hexadecimal constants in your program text. However, such numbers in the input data are not treated differently; doing so by default would break old programs. (If you really need to do this, use the —*non-decimal-data* command-line option; see the section "Allowing Nondecimal Input Data" in Chapter 10, *Advanced Features of gawk*.) If you have octal or hexadecimal data, you can use the strtonum function (see the section "String-Manipulation Functions" in Chapter 8, *Functions*) to convert the data into a number. Most of the time, you will want to use octal or hexadecimal constants when working with the built-in bit manipulation functions; see the section "Bit-Manipulation Functions of gawk" in Chapter 8 for more information.

Unlike some early C implementations, 8 and 9 are not valid in octal constants; e.g., *gawk* treats 018 as decimal 18:

```
$ gawk 'BEGIN { print "021 is", 021 ; print 018 }'
021 is 17
18
```

Octal and hexadecimal source code constants are a *gawk* extension. If *gawk* is in compatibility mode (see the section "Command-Line Options" in Chapter 11, *Running awk and gawk*), they are not available.

Regular Expression Constants

A regexp constant is a regular expression description enclosed in slashes, such as /^beginning and end$/. Most regexps used in *awk* programs are constant, but the ~ and !~ matching operators can also match computed or "dynamic" regexps (which are just ordinary strings or variables that contain a regexp).

A Constant's Base Does Not Affect Its Value

Once a numeric constant has been converted internally into a number, *gawk* no longer remembers what the original form of the constant was; the internal value is always used. This has particular consequences for conversion of numbers to strings:

```
$ gawk 'BEGIN { printf "0x11 is <%s>\n", 0x11 }'
0x11 is <17>
```

Using Regular Expression Constants

When used on the righthand side of the ~ or !~ operators, a regexp constant merely stands for the regexp that is to be matched. However, regexp constants (such as /foo/) may be used like simple expressions. When a regexp constant appears by itself, it has the same meaning as if it appeared in a pattern, i.e., ($0 ~ /foo/). (d.c.) See the section "Expressions as Patterns" in Chapter 6, *Patterns, Actions, and Variables*. This means that the following two code segments:

```
if ($0 ~ /barfly/ || $0 ~ /camelot/)
    print "found"
```

and:

```
if (/barfly/ || /camelot/)
    print "found"
```

are exactly equivalent. One rather bizarre consequence of this rule is that the following Boolean expression is valid, but does not do what the user probably intended:

```
# note that /foo/ is on the left of the ~
if (/foo/ ~ $1) print "found foo"
```

This code is "obviously" testing $1 for a match against the regexp /foo/. But in fact, the expression /foo/ ~ $1 actually means ($0 ~ /foo/) ~ $1. In other words, first match the input record against the regexp /foo/. The result is either zero or one, depending upon the success or failure of the match. That result is then matched against the first field in the record. Because it is unlikely that you would ever really want to make this kind of test, *gawk* issues a warning when it sees this construct in a program. Another consequence of this rule is that the assignment statement:

```
matches = /foo/
```

assigns either zero or one to the variable matches, depending upon the contents of the current input record. This feature of the language has never been well documented until the POSIX specification.

Constant regular expressions are also used as the first argument for the gensub, sub, and gsub functions, and as the second argument of the match function (see the section "String-Manipulation Functions" in Chapter 8). Modern implementations of *awk*, including *gawk*, allow the third argument of split to be a regexp constant, but some older implementations do not. (d.c.) This can lead to confusion when attempting to use regexp constants as arguments to user-defined functions (see the section "User-Defined Functions" in Chapter 8). For example:

```
function mysub(pat, repl, str, global)
{
    if (global)
        gsub(pat, repl, str)
    else
        sub(pat, repl, str)
    return str
}

{
    ...
    text = "hi! hi yourself!"
    mysub(/hi/, "howdy", text, 1)
    ...
}
```

In this example, the programmer wants to pass a regexp constant to the user-defined function mysub, which in turn passes it on to either sub or gsub. However, what really happens is that the pat parameter is either one or zero, depending upon whether or not $0 matches /hi/. *gawk* issues a warning when it sees a regexp constant used as a parameter to a user-defined function, since passing a truth value in this way is probably not what was intended.

Variables

Variables are ways of storing values at one point in your program for use later in another part of your program. They can be manipulated entirely within the program text, and they can also be assigned values on the *awk* command line.

Using Variables in a Program

Variables let you give names to values and refer to them later. Variables have already been used in many of the examples. The name of a variable must be a sequence of letters, digits, or underscores, and it may not begin with a digit. Case is significant in variable names; a and A are distinct variables.

A variable name is a valid expression by itself; it represents the variable's current value. Variables are given new values with *assignment operators, increment operators,* and *decrement operators.* See the section "Assignment Expressions" later in this chapter.

A few variables have special built-in meanings, such as FS (the field separator), and NF (the number of fields in the current input record). See the section "Built-in Variables" in Chapter 6 for a list of the built-in variables. These built-in variables can be used and assigned just like all other variables, but their values are also used or changed automatically by *awk.* All built-in variables' names are entirely uppercase.

Variables in *awk* can be assigned either numeric or string values. The kind of value a variable holds can change over the life of a program. By default, variables are initialized to the empty string, which is zero if converted to a number. There is no need to "initialize" each variable explicitly in *awk,* which is what you would do in C and in most other traditional languages.

Assigning Variables on the Command Line

Any *awk* variable can be set by including a *variable assignment* among the arguments on the command line when *awk* is invoked (see the section "Other Command-Line Arguments" in Chapter 11). Such an assignment has the following form:

```
variable=text
```

With it, a variable is set either at the beginning of the *awk* run or in between input files. When the assignment is preceded with the *−v* option, as in the following:

```
-v variable=text
```

the variable is set at the very beginning, even before the BEGIN rules are run. The *−v* option and its assignment must precede all the filename arguments, as well as the program text. (See the section "Command-Line Options" in Chapter 11 for more information about the *−v* option.) Otherwise, the variable assignment is performed at a time determined by its position among the input file arguments—after the processing of the preceding input file argument. For example:

```
awk '{ print $n }' n=4 inventory-shipped n=2 BBS-list
```

prints the value of field number n for all input records. Before the first file is read, the command line sets the variable n equal to four. This causes the fourth field to be printed in lines from the file *inventory-shipped.* After the first file has finished, but before the second file is started, n is set to two, so that the second field is printed in lines from *BBS-list*:

```
$ awk '{ print $n }' n=4 inventory-shipped n=2 BBS-list
15
24
...
555-5553
555-3412
...
```

Command-line arguments are made available for explicit examination by the *awk* program in the ARGV array (see the section "Using ARGC and ARGV" in Chapter 6). *awk* processes the values of command-line assignments for escape sequences (see the section "Escape Sequences" in Chapter 2, *Regular Expressions*). (d.c.)

Conversion of Strings and Numbers

Strings are converted to numbers and numbers are converted to strings, if the context of the *awk* program demands it. For example, if the value of either foo or bar in the expression foo + bar happens to be a string, it is converted to a number before the addition is performed. If numeric values appear in string concatenation, they are converted to strings. Consider the following:

```
two = 2; three = 3
print (two three) + 4
```

This prints the (numeric) value 27. The numeric values of the variables two and three are converted to strings and concatenated together. The resulting string is converted back to the number 23, to which 4 is then added.

If, for some reason, you need to force a number to be converted to a string, concatenate the empty string, "", with that number. To force a string to be converted to a number, add zero to that string. A string is converted to a number by interpreting any numeric prefix of the string as numerals: "2.5" converts to 2.5, "1e3" converts to 1000, and "25fix" has a numeric value of 25. Strings that can't be interpreted as valid numbers convert to zero.

The exact manner in which numbers are converted into strings is controlled by the *awk* built-in variable CONVFMT (see the section "Built-in Variables" in Chapter 6). Numbers are converted using the sprintf function with CONVFMT as the format specifier (see the section "String-Manipulation Functions" in Chapter 8).

CONVFMT's default value is "%.6g", which prints a value with at least six significant digits. For some applications, you might want to change it to specify more precision. On most modern machines, 17 digits is enough to capture a floating-point number's value exactly, most of the time.*

---

* Pathological cases can require up to 752 digits (!), but we doubt that you need to worry about this.

Strange results can occur if you set CONVFMT to a string that doesn't tell sprintf how to format floating-point numbers in a useful way. For example, if you forget the % in the format, *awk* converts all numbers to the same constant string. As a special case, if a number is an integer, then the result of converting it to a string is *always* an integer, no matter what the value of CONVFMT may be. Given the following code fragment:

```
CONVFMT = "%2.2f"
a = 12
b = a ""
```

b has the value "12", not "12.00". (d.c.)

Prior to the POSIX standard, *awk* used the value of OFMT for converting numbers to strings. OFMT specifies the output format to use when printing numbers with print. CONVFMT was introduced in order to separate the semantics of conversion from the semantics of printing. Both CONVFMT and OFMT have the same default value: "%.6g". In the vast majority of cases, old *awk* programs do not change their behavior. However, these semantics for OFMT are something to keep in mind if you must port your new style program to older implementations of *awk*. We recommend that instead of changing your programs, just port *gawk* itself. See the section "The print Statement" in Chapter 4, *Printing Output*, for more information on the print statement.

Arithmetic Operators

The *awk* language uses the common arithmetic operators when evaluating expressions. All of these arithmetic operators follow normal precedence rules and work as you would expect them to.

The following example uses a file named *grades*, which contains a list of student names as well as three test scores per student (it's a small class):

```
Pat    100 97 58
Sandy  84 72 93
Chris  72 92 89
```

This programs takes the file *grades* and prints the average of the scores:

```
$ awk '{ sum = $2 + $3 + $4 ; avg = sum / 3
>         print $1, avg }' grades
Pat 85
Sandy 83
Chris 84.3333
```

The following list provides the arithmetic operators in *awk*, in order from the highest precedence to the lowest:

– *x* Negation.

+ *x* Unary plus; the expression is converted to a number.

x ˆ *y*
x ** *y*

> Exponentiation; *x* raised to the *y* power. 2 ˆ 3 has the value eight; the character sequence ** is equivalent to ˆ.

x * *y*

> Multiplication.

x / *y*

> Division; because all numbers in *awk* are floating-point numbers, the result is *not* rounded to an integer—3 / 4 has the value 0.75. (It is a common mistake, especially for C programmers, to forget that *all* numbers in *awk* are floating-point, and that division of integer-looking constants produces a real number, not an integer.)

x % *y*

> Remainder; further discussion is provided in the text, just after this list.

x + *y*

> Addition.

x – *y*

> Subtraction.

Unary plus and minus have the same precedence, the multiplication operators all have the same precedence, and addition and subtraction have the same precedence.

When computing the remainder of *x* % *y*, the quotient is rounded toward zero to an integer and multiplied by *y*. This result is subtracted from *x*; this operation is sometimes known as "trunc-mod." The following relation always holds:

```
b * int(a / b) + (a % b) == a
```

One possibly undesirable effect of this definition of remainder is that *x* % *y* is negative if *x* is negative. Thus:

```
-17 % 8 = -1
```

In other *awk* implementations, the signedness of the remainder may be machine-dependent.

The POSIX standard only specifies the use of ^ for exponentiation. For maximum portability, do not use the ** operator.

String Concatenation

There is only one string operation: concatenation. It does not have a specific operator to represent it. Instead, concatenation is performed by writing expressions next to one another, with no operator. For example:

```
$ awk '{ print "Field number one: " $1 }' BBS-list
Field number one: aardvark
Field number one: alpo-net
...
```

Without the space in the string constant after the :, the line runs together. For example:

```
$ awk '{ print "Field number one:" $1 }' BBS-list
Field number one:aardvark
Field number one:alpo-net
...
```

Because string concatenation does not have an explicit operator, it is often necessary to insure that it happens at the right time by using parentheses to enclose the items to concatenate. For example, the following code fragment does not concatenate file and name as you might expect:

```
file = "file"
name = "name"
print "something meaningful" > file name
```

It is necessary to use the following:

```
print "something meaningful" > (file name)
```

Parentheses should be used around concatenation in all but the most common contexts, such as on the righthand side of =. Be careful about the kinds of expressions used in string concatenation. In particular, the order of evaluation of expressions used for concatenation is undefined in the *awk* language. Consider this example:

```
BEGIN {
    a = "don't"
    print (a " " (a = "panic"))
}
```

It is not defined whether the assignment to a happens before or after the value of a is retrieved for producing the concatenated value. The result could be either don't panic, or panic panic. The precedence of concatenation, when mixed with other operators, is often counter-intuitive. Consider this example:

```
$ awk 'BEGIN { print -12 " " -24 }'
-12-24
```

This "obviously" is concatenating −12, a space, and −24. But where did the space disappear to? The answer lies in the combination of operator precedences and *awk*'s automatic conversion rules. To get the desired result, write the program in the following manner:

```
$ awk 'BEGIN { print -12 " " (-24) }'
-12 -24
```

This forces *awk* to treat the − on the −24 as unary. Otherwise, it's parsed as follows:

```
    -12 (" " - 24)
→ -12 (0 - 24)
→ -12 (-24)
→ -12-24
```

As mentioned earlier, when doing concatenation, *parenthesize*. Otherwise, you're never quite sure what you'll get.

Assignment Expressions

An *assignment* is an expression that stores a (usually different) value into a variable. For example, let's assign the value one to the variable z:

```
    z = 1
```

After this expression is executed, the variable z has the value one. Whatever old value z had before the assignment is forgotten.

Assignments can also store string values. For example, the following stores the value "this food is good" in the variable message:

```
thing = "food"
predicate = "good"
message = "this " thing " is " predicate
```

This also illustrates string concatenation. The = sign is called an *assignment operator*. It is the simplest assignment operator because the value of the righthand operand is stored unchanged. Most operators (addition, concatenation, and so on) have no effect except to compute a value. If the value isn't used, there's no reason to use the operator. An assignment operator is different; it does produce a value, but even if you ignore it, the assignment still makes itself felt through the alteration of the variable. We call this a *side effect*.

The lefthand operand of an assignment need not be a variable (see the section "Variables" earlier in this chapter); it can also be a field (see the section "Changing the Contents of a Field in Chapter 3, *Reading Input Files*) or an array element (see Chapter 7, *Arrays in awk*). These are all called *lvalues*, which means they can appear on the lefthand side of an assignment operator. The righthand operand may be any expression; it produces the new value that the assignment stores in the specified variable, field, or array element. (Such values are called *rvalues*.)

It is important to note that variables do *not* have permanent types. A variable's type is simply the type of whatever value it happens to hold at the moment. In the following program fragment, the variable foo has a numeric value at first, and a string value later on:

```
foo = 1
print foo
foo = "bar"
print foo
```

When the second assignment gives foo a string value, the fact that it previously had a numeric value is forgotten.

String values that do not begin with a digit have a numeric value of zero. After executing the following code, the value of foo is five:

```
foo = "a string"
foo = foo + 5
```

 Using a variable as a number and then later as a string can be confusing and is poor programming style. The previous two examples illustrate how *awk* works, *not* how you should write *your* programs!

An assignment is an expression, so it has a value—the same value that is assigned. Thus, z = 1 is an expression with the value one. One consequence of this is that you can write multiple assignments together, such as:

```
x = y = z = 5
```

This example stores the value five in all three variables (x, y, and z). It does so because the value of z = 5, which is five, is stored into y and then the value of y = z = 5, which is five, is stored into x.

Assignments may be used anywhere an expression is called for. For example, it is valid to write x != (y = 1) to set y to one, and then test whether x equals one. But this style tends to make programs hard to read; such nesting of assignments should be avoided, except perhaps in a one-shot program.

Aside from =, there are several other assignment operators that do arithmetic with the old value of the variable. For example, the operator += computes a new value by adding the righthand value to the old value of the variable. Thus, the following assignment adds five to the value of foo:

```
foo += 5
```

This is equivalent to the following:

```
foo = foo + 5
```

Use whichever makes the meaning of your program clearer.

There are situations where using += (or any assignment operator) is *not* the same as simply repeating the lefthand operand in the righthand expression. For example:

```
# Thanks to Pat Rankin for this example
BEGIN {
    foo[rand()] += 5
    for (x in foo)
        print x, foo[x]

    bar[rand()] = bar[rand()] + 5
    for (x in bar)
        print x, bar[x]
}
```

The indices of bar are practically guaranteed to be different, because rand returns different values each time it is called. (Arrays and the rand function haven't been covered yet. See Chapter 7 and the section "Numeric Functions" in Chapter 8 for more information.) This example illustrates an important fact about assignment operators: the lefthand expression is only evaluated *once*. It is up to the implementation as to which expression is evaluated first, the lefthand or the righthand. Consider this example:

```
i = 1
a[i += 2] = i + 1
```

The value of a[3] could be either two or four.

Table 5-1 lists the arithmetic assignment operators. In each case, the righthand operand is an expression whose value is converted to a number.

Table 5-1. Arithmetic Assignment Operators

Operator	Effect
`lvalue += increment`	Adds *increment* to the value of *lvalue*.
`lvalue -= decrement`	Subtracts *decrement* from the value of *lvalue*.
`lvalue *= coefficient`	Multiplies the value of *lvalue* by *coefficient*.
`lvalue /= divisor`	Divides the value of *lvalue* by *divisor*.
`lvalue %= modulus`	Sets *lvalue* to its remainder by *modulus*.
`lvalue ^= power`	Raises *lvalue* to the power *power*.
`lvalue **= power`	Raises *lvalue* to the power *power*.

 Only the `^=` operator is specified by POSIX. For maximum portability, do not use the `**=` operator.

Syntactic Ambiguities Between /= and Regular Expressions

There is a syntactic ambiguity between the `/=` assignment operator and regexp constants whose first character is an `=`. (d.c.) This is most notable in commercial *awk* versions. For example:

```
$ awk /==/ /dev/null
awk: syntax error at source line 1
 context is
        >>> /= <<<
awk: bailing out at source line 1
```

A workaround is:

```
awk '/[=]=/' /dev/null
```

gawk does not have this problem, nor do the other freely available versions described in the section "Other Freely Available awk Implementations" in Appendix B, *Installing gawk*.

Increment and Decrement Operators

Increment and *decrement operators* increase or decrease the value of a variable by one. An assignment operator can do the same thing, so the increment operators add no power to the *awk* language; however, they are convenient abbreviations for very common operations.

The operator used for adding one is written ++. It can be used to increment a variable either before or after taking its value. To pre-increment a variable v, write ++v. This adds one to the value of v—that new value is also the value of the expression. (The assignment expression v += 1 is completely equivalent.) Writing the ++ after the variable specifies post-increment. This increments the variable value just the same; the difference is that the value of the increment expression itself is the variable's *old* value. Thus, if foo has the value four, then the expression foo++ has the value four, but it changes the value of foo to five. In other words, the operator returns the old value of the variable, but with the side effect of incrementing it.

The post-increment foo++ is nearly the same as writing (foo += 1) - 1. It is not perfectly equivalent because all numbers in *awk* are floating-point—in floating-point, foo + 1 - 1 does not necessarily equal foo. But the difference is minute as long as you stick to numbers that are fairly small (less than 10^{12}).

Fields and array elements are incremented just like variables. (Use $(i++) when you want to do a field reference and a variable increment at the same time. The parentheses are necessary because of the precedence of the field reference operator $.)

The decrement operator -- works just like ++, except that it subtracts one instead of adding it. As with ++, it can be used before the lvalue to pre-decrement or after it to post-decrement. Following is a summary of increment and decrement expressions:

++*lvalue*
> This expression increments *lvalue*, and the new value becomes the value of the expression.

lvalue++
> This expression increments *lvalue*, but the value of the expression is the *old* value of *lvalue*.

--*lvalue*
> This expression is like ++*lvalue*, but instead of adding, it subtracts. It decrements *lvalue* and delivers the value that is the result.

lvalue--

This expression is like *lvalue++*, but instead of adding, it subtracts. It decrements *lvalue*. The value of the expression is the *old* value of *lvalue*.

Operator Evaluation Order

What happens for something like the following?

```
b = 6
print b += b++
```

Or something even stranger?

```
b = 6
b += ++b + b++
print b
```

In other words, when do the various side effects prescribed by the postfix operators (b++) take effect? When side effects happen is *implementation defined.* In other words, it is up to the particular version of *awk*. The result for the first example may be 12 or 13, and for the second, it may be 22 or 23.

In short, doing things like this is not recommended and definitely not anything that you can rely upon for portability. You should avoid such things in your own programs.

True and False in awk

Many programming languages have a special representation for the concepts of "true" and "false." Such languages usually use the special constants true and false, or perhaps their uppercase equivalents. However, *awk* is different. It borrows a very simple concept of true and false from C. In *awk*, any nonzero numeric value *or* any nonempty string value is true. Any other value (zero or the null string "") is false. The following program prints "A strange truth value" three times:

```
BEGIN {
    if (3.1415927)
        print "A strange truth value"
    if ("Four Score And Seven Years Ago")
        print "A strange truth value"
    if (j = 57)
        print "A strange truth value"
}
```

There is a surprising consequence of the "nonzero or non-null" rule: the string constant "0" is actually true, because it is non-null. (d.c.)

Variable Typing and Comparison Expressions

Unlike other programming languages, *awk* variables do not have a fixed type. Instead, they can be either a number or a string, depending upon the value that is assigned to them.

The 1992 POSIX standard introduced the concept of a *numeric string*, which is simply a string that looks like a number—for example, " +2". This concept is used for determining the type of a variable. The type of the variable is important because the types of two variables determine how they are compared. In *gawk*, variable typing follows these rules:

- A numeric constant or the result of a numeric operation has the *numeric* attribute.

- A string constant or the result of a string operation has the *string* attribute.

- Fields, `getline` input, `FILENAME`, `ARGV` elements, `ENVIRON` elements, and the elements of an array created by `split` that are numeric strings have the *strnum* attribute. Otherwise, they have the *string* attribute. Uninitialized variables also have the *strnum* attribute.

- Attributes propagate across assignments but are not changed by any use.

The last rule is particularly important. In the following program, `a` has numeric type, even though it is later used in a string operation:

```
BEGIN {
    a = 12.345
    b = a " is a cute number"
    print b
}
```

When two operands are compared, either string comparison or numeric comparison may be used. This depends upon the attributes of the operands, according to the following symmetric matrix:

	STRING	NUMERIC	STRNUM
STRING	string	string	string
NUMERIC	string	numeric	numeric
STRNUM	string	numeric	numeric

The basic idea is that user input that looks numeric—and *only* user input—should be treated as numeric, even though it is actually made of characters and is therefore also a string. Thus, for example, the string constant " +3.14" is a string, even though it looks numeric, and is *never* treated as number for comparison purposes.

In short, when one operand is a "pure" string, such as a string constant, then a string comparison is performed. Otherwise, a numeric comparison is performed.*

Comparison expressions compare strings or numbers for relationships such as equality. They are written using *relational operators*, which are a superset of those in C. Table 5-2 describes them.

Table 5-2. Relational Operators

Expression	Result
x < *y*	True if *x* is less than *y*.
x <= *y*	True if *x* is less than or equal to *y*.
x > *y*	True if *x* is greater than *y*.
x >= *y*	True if *x* is greater than or equal to *y*.
x == *y*	True if *x* is equal to *y*.
x != *y*	True if *x* is not equal to *y*.
x ~ *y*	True if the string *x* matches the regexp denoted by *y*.
x !~ *y*	True if the string *x* does not match the regexp denoted by *y*.
subscript in array	True if the array *array* has an element with the subscript *subscript*.

Comparison expressions have the value one if true and zero if false. When comparing operands of mixed types, numeric operands are converted to strings using the value of CONVFMT (see the section "Conversion of Strings and Numbers" earlier in this chapter).

Strings are compared by comparing the first character of each, then the second character of each, and so on. Thus, "10" is less than "9". If there are two strings where one is a prefix of the other, the shorter string is less than the longer one. Thus, "abc" is less than "abcd".

It is very easy to accidentally mistype the == operator and leave off one of the = characters. The result is still valid *awk* code, but the program does not do what is intended:

```
if (a = b)    # oops! should be a == b
    ...
else
    ...
```

Unless b happens to be zero or the null string, the if part of the test always succeeds. Because the operators are so similar, this kind of error is very difficult to spot when scanning the source code.

---

* The POSIX standard is under revision. The revised standard's rules for typing and comparison are the same as just described for *gawk*.

The following list illustrates the kind of comparison *gawk* performs, as well as what the result of the comparison is:

1.5 <= 2.0
> Numeric comparison (true)

"abc" >= "xyz"
> String comparison (false)

1.5 != " +2"
> String comparison (true)

"1e2" < "3"
> String comparison (true)

a = 2; b = "2"
a == b
> String comparison (true)

a = 2; b = " +2"
a == b
> String comparison (false)

In the next example:

```
$ echo 1e2 3 | awk '{ print ($1 < $2) ? "true" : "false" }'
false
```

the result is `false` because both $1 and $2 are user input. They are numeric strings—therefore both have the *strnum* attribute, dictating a numeric comparison. The purpose of the comparison rules and the use of numeric strings is to attempt to produce the behavior that is "least surprising," while still "doing the right thing." String comparisons and regular expression comparisons are very different. For example:

```
x == "foo"
```

has the value one, or is true if the variable x is precisely foo. By contrast:

```
x ~ /foo/
```

has the value one if x contains foo, such as "Oh, what a fool am I!".

The righthand operand of the ~ and !~ operators may be either a regexp constant (/.../) or an ordinary expression. In the latter case, the value of the expression as a string is used as a dynamic regexp (see the section "How to Use Regular Expressions" and the section "Using Dynamic Regexps" in Chapter 2).

In modern implementations of *awk*, a constant regular expression in slashes by itself is also an expression. The regexp /`regexp`/ is an abbreviation for the following comparison expression:

```
$0 ~ /regexp/
```

One special place where /foo/ is *not* an abbreviation for $0 ~ /foo/ is when it is the righthand operand of ~ or !~. See the section "Using Regular Expression Constants" earlier in this chapter, where this is discussed in more detail.

Boolean Expressions

A *Boolean expression* is a combination of comparison expressions or matching expressions, using the Boolean operators "or" (||), "and" (&&), and "not" (!), along with parentheses to control nesting. The truth value of the Boolean expression is computed by combining the truth values of the component expressions. Boolean expressions are also referred to as *logical expressions*. The terms are equivalent.

Boolean expressions can be used wherever comparison and matching expressions can be used. They can be used in if, while, do, and for statements (see the section "Control Statements in Actions" in Chapter 6). They have numeric values (one if true, zero if false) that come into play if the result of the Boolean expression is stored in a variable or used in arithmetic.

In addition, every Boolean expression is also a valid pattern, so you can use one as a pattern to control the execution of rules. The Boolean operators are:

boolean1 && *boolean2*
> True if both *boolean1* and *boolean2* are true. For example, the following statement prints the current input record if it contains both 2400 and foo:
>
> ```
> if ($0 ~ /2400/ && $0 ~ /foo/) print
> ```
>
> The subexpression *boolean2* is evaluated only if *boolean1* is true. This can make a difference when *boolean2* contains expressions that have side effects. In the case of $0 ~ /foo/ && ($2 == bar++), the variable bar is not incremented if there is no substring foo in the record.

boolean1 || *boolean2*
> True if at least one of *boolean1* or *boolean2* is true. For example, the following statement prints all records in the input that contain *either* 2400 or foo or both:
>
> ```
> if ($0 ~ /2400/ || $0 ~ /foo/) print
> ```
>
> The subexpression *boolean2* is evaluated only if *boolean1* is false. This can make a difference when *boolean2* contains expressions that have side effects.

! *boolean*

True if *boolean* is false. For example, the following program prints no home! in the unusual event that the HOME environment variable is not defined:

```
BEGIN { if (! ("HOME" in ENVIRON))
              print "no home!" }
```

(The in operator is described in the section "Referring to an Array Element" in Chapter 7.)

The && and || operators are called *short-circuit* operators because of the way they work. Evaluation of the full expression is "short-circuited" if the result can be determined part way through its evaluation.

Statements that use && or || can be continued simply by putting a newline after them. But you cannot put a newline in front of either of these operators without using backslash continuation (see the section "awk Statements Versus Lines" in Chapter 1, *Getting Started with awk*).

The actual value of an expression using the ! operator is either one or zero, depending upon the truth value of the expression it is applied to. The ! operator is often useful for changing the sense of a flag variable from false to true and back again. For example, the following program is one way to print lines in between special bracketing lines:

```
$1 == "START"   { interested = ! interested; next }
interested == 1 { print }
$1 == "END"     { interested = ! interested; next }
```

The variable interested, as with all *awk* variables, starts out initialized to zero, which is also false. When a line is seen whose first field is START, the value of interested is toggled to true, using !. The next rule prints lines as long as interested is true. When a line is seen whose first field is END, interested is toggled back to false.

 The next statement is discussed in the section "The next Statement" in Chapter 6. next tells *awk* to skip the rest of the rules, get the next record, and start processing the rules over again at the top. The reason it's there is to avoid printing the bracketing START and END lines.

Conditional Expressions

A *conditional expression* is a special kind of expression that has three operands. It allows you to use one expression's value to select one of two other expressions. The conditional expression is the same as in the C language, as shown here:

```
selector ? if-true-exp : if-false-exp
```

There are three subexpressions. The first, *selector*, is always computed first. If it is "true" (not zero or not null), then *if-true-exp* is computed next and its value becomes the value of the whole expression. Otherwise, *if-false-exp* is computed next and its value becomes the value of the whole expression. For example, the following expression produces the absolute value of **x**:

```
x >= 0 ? x : -x
```

Each time the conditional expression is computed, only one of *if-true-exp* and *if-false-exp* is used; the other is ignored. This is important when the expressions have side effects. For example, this conditional expression examines element i of either array **a** or array **b**, and increments i:

```
x == y ? a[i++] : b[i++]
```

This is guaranteed to increment i exactly once, because each time only one of the two increment expressions is executed and the other is not. See Chapter 7 for more information about arrays.

As a minor *gawk* extension, a statement that uses ?: can be continued simply by putting a newline after either character. However, putting a newline in front of either character does not work without using backslash continuation (see the section "awk Statements Versus Lines" in Chapter 1). If *--posix* is specified (see the section "Command-Line Options" in Chapter 11), then this extension is disabled.

Function Calls

A *function* is a name for a particular calculation. This enables you to ask for it by name at any point in the program. For example, the function sqrt computes the square root of a number.

A fixed set of functions are *built-in*, which means they are available in every *awk* program. The sqrt function is one of these. See the section "Built-in Functions" in Chapter 8 for a list of built-in functions and their descriptions. In addition, you can define functions for use in your program. See the section "User-Defined Functions" in Chapter 8 for instructions on how to do this.

The way to use a function is with a *function call* expression, which consists of the function name followed immediately by a list of *arguments* in parentheses. The arguments are expressions that provide the raw materials for the function's calculations. When there is more than one argument, they are separated by commas. If there are no arguments, just write () after the function name. The following examples show function calls with and without arguments:

```
sqrt(x^2 + y^2)        # one argument
atan2(y, x)            # two arguments
rand()                 # no arguments
```

 Do not put any space between the function name and the open parenthesis! A user-defined function name looks just like the name of a variable—a space would make the expression look like concatenation of a variable with an expression inside parentheses.

With built-in functions, space before the parenthesis is harmless, but it is best not to get into the habit of using space to avoid mistakes with user-defined functions. Each function expects a particular number of arguments. For example, the sqrt function must be called with a single argument, the number of which to take the square root:

```
sqrt(argument)
```

Some of the built-in functions have one or more optional arguments. If those arguments are not supplied, the functions use a reasonable default value. See the section "Built-in Functions" in Chapter 8 for full details. If arguments are omitted in calls to user-defined functions, then those arguments are treated as local variables and initialized to the empty string (see the section "User-Defined Functions" in Chapter 8).

Like every other expression, the function call has a value, which is computed by the function based on the arguments you give it. In this example, the value of sqrt(*argument*) is the square root of *argument*. A function can also have side effects, such as assigning values to certain variables or doing I/O. The following program reads numbers, one number per line, and prints the square root of each one:

```
$ awk '{ print "The square root of", $1, "is", sqrt($1) }'
1
The square root of 1 is 1
3
The square root of 3 is 1.73205
5
The square root of 5 is 2.23607
Ctrl-d
```

Operator Precedence (How Operators Nest)

Operator precedence determines how operators are grouped when different operators appear close by in one expression. For example, * has higher precedence than +; thus, a + b * c means to multiply b and c, and then add a to the product (i.e., a + (b * c)).

The normal precedence of the operators can be overruled by using parentheses. Think of the precedence rules as saying where the parentheses are assumed to be. In fact, it is wise to always use parentheses whenever there is an unusual combination of operators, because other people who read the program may not remember what the precedence is in this case. Even experienced programmers occasionally forget the exact rules, which leads to mistakes. Explicit parentheses help prevent any such mistakes.

When operators of equal precedence are used together, the leftmost operator groups first, except for the assignment, conditional, and exponentiation operators, which group in the opposite order. Thus, a - b + c groups as (a - b) + c and a = b = c groups as a = (b = c).

The precedence of prefix unary operators does not matter as long as only unary operators are involved, because there is only one way to interpret them: innermost first. Thus, $++i means $(++i) and ++$x means ++($x). However, when another operator follows the operand, then the precedence of the unary operators can matter. $x^2 means ($x)^2, but -x^2 means -(x^2), because - has lower precedence than ^, whereas $ has higher precedence. This list presents *awk*'s operators, in order of highest to lowest precedence:

(...)
    Grouping.

$ Field.

++ --
    Increment, decrement.

^ **
    Exponentiation. These operators group right to left.

+ - !
    Unary plus, minus, logical "not."

* / %
    Multiplication, division, modulus.

`+ -`

Addition, subtraction.

String Concatenation

No special symbol is used to indicate concatenation. The operands are simply written side by side (see the earlier section "String Concatenation").

`< <= == !=`
`> >= >> | |&`

Relational and redirection. The relational operators and the redirections have the same precedence level. Characters such as > serve both as relationals and as redirections; the context distinguishes between the two meanings.

Note that the I/O redirection operators in `print` and `printf` statements belong to the statement level, not to expressions. The redirection does not produce an expression that could be the operand of another operator. As a result, it does not make sense to use a redirection operator near another operator of lower precedence without parentheses. Such combinations (for example, `print foo > a ? b : c`), result in syntax errors. The correct way to write this statement is `print foo > (a ? b : c)`.

`~ !~`

Matching, nonmatching.

`in` Array membership.

`&&` Logical "and."

`||` Logical "or."

`?:` Conditional. This operator groups right to left.

`= += -= *=`
`/= %= ^= **=`

Assignment. These operators group right to left.

 The `|&`, `**`, and `**=` operators are not specified by POSIX. For maximum portability, do not use them.

6
Patterns, Actions, and Variables

As you have already seen, each *awk* statement consists of a pattern with an associated action. This chapter describes how you build patterns and actions, what kinds of things you can do within actions, and *awk*'s built-in variables.

The pattern-action rules and the statements available for use within actions form the core of *awk* programming. In a sense, everything covered in this text up to here has been the foundation that programs are built on top of. Now it's time to start building something useful.

Pattern Elements

Patterns in *awk* control the execution of rules—a rule is executed when its pattern matches the current input record. The following is a summary of the types of *awk* pattern types:

`/regular expression/`

> A regular expression. It matches when the text of the input record fits the regular expression. (See Chapter 2, *Regular Expressions.*)

`expression`

> A single expression. It matches when its value is nonzero (if a number) or non-null (if a string). (See the section "Expressions as Patterns" later in this chapter.)

`pat1, pat2`

> A pair of patterns separated by a comma, specifying a range of records. The range includes both the initial record that matches *pat1* and the final record that matches *pat2*. (See the section "Specifying Record Ranges with Patterns" later in this chapter.)

```
BEGIN
END
```

Special patterns for you to supply startup or cleanup actions for your *awk* program. (See the section "The BEGIN and END Special Patterns" later in this chapter.)

empty

The empty pattern matches every input record. (See the section "The Empty Pattern" later in this chapter.)

Regular Expressions as Patterns

Regular expressions are one of the first kinds of patterns presented in this book. This kind of pattern is simply a regexp constant in the pattern part of a rule. Its meaning is $0 ~ /pattern/. The pattern matches when the input record matches the regexp. For example:

```
/foo|bar|baz/   { buzzwords++ }
END             { print buzzwords, "buzzwords seen" }
```

Expressions as Patterns

Any *awk* expression is valid as an *awk* pattern. The pattern matches if the expression's value is nonzero (if a number) or non-null (if a string). The expression is reevaluated each time the rule is tested against a new input record. If the expression uses fields such as $1, the value depends directly on the new input record's text; otherwise, it depends on only what has happened so far in the execution of the *awk* program.

Comparison expressions, using the comparison operators described in the section "Variable Typing and Comparison Expressions" in Chapter 5, *Expressions*, are a very common kind of pattern. Regexp matching and nonmatching are also very common expressions. The left operand of the ~ and !~ operators is a string. The right operand is either a constant regular expression enclosed in slashes (/*regexp*/), or any expression whose string value is used as a dynamic regular expression (see the section "Using Dynamic Regexps" in Chapter 2). The following example prints the second field of each input record whose first field is precisely foo:

```
$ awk '$1 == "foo" { print $2 }' BBS-list
```

(There is no output, because there is no BBS site with the exact name foo.) Contrast this with the following regular expression match, which accepts any record with a first field that contains foo:

```
$ awk '$1 ~ /foo/ { print $2 }' BBS-list
555-1234
555-6699
555-6480
555-2127
```

A regexp constant as a pattern is also a special case of an expression pattern. The expression /foo/ has the value one if foo appears in the current input record. Thus, as a pattern, /foo/ matches any record containing foo.

Boolean expressions are also commonly used as patterns. Whether the pattern matches an input record depends on whether its subexpressions match. For example, the following command prints all the records in *BBS-list* that contain both 2400 and foo:

```
$ awk '/2400/ && /foo/' BBS-list
fooey        555-1234     2400/1200/300     B
```

The following command prints all records in *BBS-list* that contain *either* 2400 or foo (or both, of course):

```
$ awk '/2400/ || /foo/' BBS-list
alpo-net     555-3412     2400/1200/300     A
bites        555-1675     2400/1200/300     A
fooey        555-1234     2400/1200/300     B
foot         555-6699     1200/300          B
macfoo       555-6480     1200/300          A
sdace        555-3430     2400/1200/300     A
sabafoo      555-2127     1200/300          C
```

The following command prints all records in *BBS-list* that do *not* contain the string foo:

```
$ awk '! /foo/' BBS-list
aardvark     555-5553     1200/300          B
alpo-net     555-3412     2400/1200/300     A
barfly       555-7685     1200/300          A
bites        555-1675     2400/1200/300     A
camelot      555-0542     300               C
core         555-2912     1200/300          C
sdace        555-3430     2400/1200/300     A
```

The subexpressions of a Boolean operator in a pattern can be constant regular expressions, comparisons, or any other *awk* expressions. Range patterns are not expressions, so they cannot appear inside Boolean patterns. Likewise, the special patterns BEGIN and END, which never match any input record, are not expressions and cannot appear inside Boolean patterns.

Specifying Record Ranges with Patterns

A *range pattern* is made of two patterns separated by a comma, in the form *beg-pat, endpat*. It is used to match ranges of consecutive input records. The first pattern, *begpat*, controls where the range begins, while *endpat* controls where the pattern ends. For example, the following:

```
awk '$1 == "on", $1 == "off"' myfile
```

prints every record in *myfile* between on/off pairs, inclusive.

A range pattern starts out by matching *begpat* against every input record. When a record matches *begpat*, the range pattern is *turned on* and the range pattern matches this record as well. As long as the range pattern stays turned on, it automatically matches every input record read. The range pattern also matches *endpat* against every input record; when this succeeds, the range pattern is turned off again for the following record. Then the range pattern goes back to checking *begpat* against each record.

The record that turns on the range pattern and the one that turns it off both match the range pattern. If you don't want to operate on these records, you can write `if` statements in the rule's action to distinguish them from the records you are interested in.

It is possible for a pattern to be turned on and off by the same record. If the record satisfies both conditions, then the action is executed for just that record. For example, suppose there is text between two identical markers (e.g., the % symbol), each on its own line, that should be ignored. A first attempt would be to combine a range pattern that describes the delimited text with the `next` statement (not discussed yet, see the section "The next Statement" later in this chapter). This causes *awk* to skip any further processing of the current record and start over again with the next input record. Such a program looks like this:

```
/^%$/,/^%$/    { next }
               { print }
```

This program fails because the range pattern is both turned on and turned off by the first line, which just has a % on it. To accomplish this task, write the program in the following manner, using a flag:

```
/^%$/    { skip = ! skip; next }
skip == 1 { next } # skip lines with 'skip' set
```

In a range pattern, the comma (,) has the lowest precedence of all the operators (i.e., it is evaluated last). Thus, the following program attempts to combine a range pattern with another, simpler test:

```
echo Yes | awk '/1/,/2/ || /Yes/'
```

The intent of this program is (/1/,/2/) || /Yes/. However, *awk* interprets this as /1/, (/2/ || /Yes/). This cannot be changed or worked around; range patterns do not combine with other patterns:

```
$ echo yes | gawk '(/1/,/2/) || /Yes/'
gawk: cmd. line:1: (/1/,/2/) || /Yes/
gawk: cmd. line:1:           ^ parse error
gawk: cmd. line:2: (/1/,/2/) || /Yes/
gawk: cmd. line:2:                    ^ unexpected newline
```

The BEGIN and END Special Patterns

All the patterns described so far are for matching input records. The BEGIN and END special patterns are different. They supply startup and cleanup actions for *awk* programs. BEGIN and END rules must have actions; there is no default action for these rules because there is no current record when they run. BEGIN and END rules are often referred to as "BEGIN and END blocks" by long-time *awk* programmers.

Startup and cleanup actions

A BEGIN rule is executed once only, before the first input record is read. Likewise, an END rule is executed once only, after all the input is read. For example:

```
$ awk '
> BEGIN { print "Analysis of \"foo\"" }
> /foo/ { ++n }
> END   { print "\"foo\" appears", n, "times." }' BBS-list
Analysis of "foo"
"foo" appears 4 times.
```

This program finds the number of records in the input file *BBS-list* that contain the string foo. The BEGIN rule prints a title for the report. There is no need to use the BEGIN rule to initialize the counter n to zero, since *awk* does this automatically (see the section "Variables" in Chapter 5). The second rule increments the variable n every time a record containing the pattern foo is read. The END rule prints the value of n at the end of the run.

The special patterns BEGIN and END cannot be used in ranges or with Boolean operators (indeed, they cannot be used with any operators). An *awk* program may have multiple BEGIN and/or END rules. They are executed in the order in which they appear: all the BEGIN rules at startup and all the END rules at termination. BEGIN and END rules may be intermixed with other rules. This feature was added in the 1987 version of *awk* and is included in the POSIX standard. The original (1978) version of *awk* required that the BEGIN rule was at the beginning of the program, and that the END rule was at the end, and only allowed one of each. This is no longer required, but it is a good idea to follow this template in terms of program organization and readability.

Multiple BEGIN and END rules are useful for writing library functions, because each library file can have its own BEGIN and/or END rule to do its own initialization and/or cleanup. The order in which library functions are named on the command-line controls the order in which their BEGIN and END rules are executed. Therefore, you have to be careful when writing such rules in library files so that the order in which they are executed doesn't matter. See the section "Command-Line Options" in Chapter 11, *Running awk and gawk*, for more information on using library functions. See Chapter 12, *A Library of awk Functions*, for a number of useful library functions.

If an *awk* program has only a BEGIN rule and no other rules, then the program exits after the BEGIN rule is run.* However, if an END rule exists, then the input is read, even if there are no other rules in the program. This is necessary in case the END rule checks the FNR and NR variables.

Input/Output from BEGIN and END rules

There are several (sometimes subtle) points to remember when doing I/O from a BEGIN or END rule. The first has to do with the value of $0 in a BEGIN rule. Because BEGIN rules are executed before any input is read, there simply is no input record, and therefore no fields, when executing BEGIN rules. References to $0 and the fields yield a null string or zero, depending upon the context. One way to give $0 a real value is to execute a getline command without a variable (see the section "Explicit Input with getline" in Chapter 3, *Reading Input Files*). Another way is simply to assign a value to $0.

The second point is similar to the first but from the other direction. Traditionally, due largely to implementation issues, $0 and NF were *undefined* inside an END rule. The POSIX standard specifies that NF is available in an END rule. It contains the number of fields from the last input record. Most probably due to an oversight, the standard does not say that $0 is also preserved, although logically one would think that it should be. In fact, *gawk* does preserve the value of $0 for use in END rules. Be aware, however, that Unix *awk*, and possibly other implementations, do not.

The third point follows from the first two. The meaning of print inside a BEGIN or END rule is the same as always: print $0. If $0 is the null string, then this prints an empty line. Many long time *awk* programmers use an unadorned print in BEGIN and END rules, to mean print "", relying on $0 being null. Although one might generally get away with this in BEGIN rules, it is a very bad idea in END rules, at least in *gawk*. It is also poor style, since if an empty line is needed in the output, the program should print one explicitly.

---

* The original version of *awk* used to keep reading and ignoring input until the end of the file was seen.

Finally, the next and nextfile statements are not allowed in a BEGIN rule, because the implicit read-a-record-and-match-against-the-rules loop has not started yet. Similarly, those statements are not valid in an END rule, since all the input has been read. (See the section "The next Statement" and section "Using gawk's nextfile Statement" later in this chapter.)

The Empty Pattern

An empty (i.e., nonexistent) pattern is considered to match *every* input record. For example, the program:

```
awk '{ print $1 }' BBS-list
```

prints the first field of every record.

Using Shell Variables in Programs

awk programs are often used as components in larger programs written in shell. For example, it is very common to use a shell variable to hold a pattern that the *awk* program searches for. There are two ways to get the value of the shell variable into the body of the *awk* program.

The most common method is to use shell quoting to substitute the variable's value into the program inside the script. For example, in the following program:

```
echo -n "Enter search pattern: "
read pattern
awk "/$pattern/ "'{ nmatches++ }
     END { print nmatches, "found" }' /path/to/data
```

the *awk* program consists of two pieces of quoted text that are concatenated together to form the program. The first part is double-quoted, which allows substitution of the pattern variable inside the quotes. The second part is single-quoted.

Variable substitution via quoting works, but can be potentially messy. It requires a good understanding of the shell's quoting rules (see the section "Shell-Quoting Issues" in Chapter 1, *Getting Started with awk*), and it's often difficult to correctly match up the quotes when reading the program.

A better method is to use *awk*'s variable assignment feature (see the section "Assigning Variables on the Command Line" in Chapter 5) to assign the shell variable's value to an *awk* variable's value. Then use dynamic regexps to match the pattern (see the section "Using Dynamic Regexps" in Chapter 2). The following shows how to redo the previous example using this technique:

```
echo -n "Enter search pattern: "
read pattern
awk -v pat="$pattern" '$0 ~ pat { nmatches++ }
                END { print nmatches, "found" }' /path/to/data
```

Now, the *awk* program is just one single-quoted string. The assignment –v pat="$pattern" still requires double quotes, in case there is whitespace in the value of $pattern. The *awk* variable pat could be named pattern too, but that would be more confusing. Using a variable also provides more flexibility, since the variable can be used anywhere inside the program—for printing, as an array subscript, or for any other use—without requiring the quoting tricks at every point in the program.

Actions

An *awk* program or script consists of a series of rules and function definitions interspersed. (Functions are described later. See the section "User-Defined Functions" in Chapter 8, *Functions*.) A rule contains a pattern and an action, either of which (but not both) may be omitted. The purpose of the *action* is to tell *awk* what to do once a match for the pattern is found. Thus, in outline, an *awk* program generally looks like this:

```
[pattern] [{ action }]
[pattern] [{ action }]
...
function name(args) { ... }
...
```

An action consists of one or more *awk statements*, enclosed in curly braces ({ }). Each statement specifies one thing to do. The statements are separated by newlines or semicolons. The curly braces around an action must be used even if the action contains only one statement, or if it contains no statements at all. However, if you omit the action entirely, omit the curly braces as well. An omitted action is equivalent to { print $0 }:

```
/foo/ { }    # match foo, do nothing -- empty action
/foo/        # match foo, print the record -- omitted action
```

The following types of statements are supported in *awk*:

Expressions

Call functions or assign values to variables (see Chapter 5). Executing this kind of statement simply computes the value of the expression. This is useful when the expression has side effects (see the section "Assignment Expressions" in Chapter 5).

Control statements

Specify the control flow of *awk* programs. The *awk* language gives you C-like constructs (if, for, while, and do) as well as a few special ones (see the section "Control Statements in Actions" later in this chapter).

Compound statements

Consist of one or more statements enclosed in curly braces. A compound statement is used in order to put several statements together in the body of an if, while, do, or for statement.

Input statements

Use the getline command (see the section "Explicit Input with getline" in Chapter 3). Also supplied in *awk* are the next statement (see the section "The next Statement" later in this chapter) and the nextfile statement (see the section "Using gawk's nextfile Statement" later in this chapter).

Output statements

Such as print and printf. See Chapter 4, *Printing Output.*

Deletion statements

For deleting array elements. See the section "The delete Statement" in Chapter 7, *Arrays in awk.*

Control Statements in Actions

Control statements, such as if, while, and so on, control the flow of execution in *awk* programs. Most of the control statements in *awk* are patterned on similar statements in C.

All the control statements start with special keywords, such as if and while, to distinguish them from simple expressions. Many control statements contain other statements. For example, the if statement contains another statement that may or may not be executed. The contained statement is called the *body.* To include more than one statement in the body, group them into a single *compound statement* with curly braces, separating them with newlines or semicolons.

The if-else Statement

The if-else statement is *awk*'s decision-making statement. It looks like this:

```
if (condition) then-body [else else-body]
```

The *condition* is an expression that controls what the rest of the statement does. If the *condition* is true, *then-body* is executed; otherwise, *else-body* is executed. The else part of the statement is optional. The condition is considered false if its value is zero or the null string; otherwise, the condition is true. Refer to the following:

```
if (x % 2 == 0)
    print "x is even"
else
    print "x is odd"
```

In this example, if the expression x % 2 == 0 is true (that is, if the value of x is evenly divisible by two), then the first print statement is executed; otherwise, the second print statement is executed. If the else keyword appears on the same line as *then-body* and *then-body* is not a compound statement (i.e., not surrounded by curly braces), then a semicolon must separate *then-body* from the else. To illustrate this, the previous example can be rewritten as:

```
if (x % 2 == 0) print "x is even"; else
    print "x is odd"
```

If the ; is left out, *awk* can't interpret the statement and it produces a syntax error. Don't actually write programs this way, because a human reader might fail to see the else if it is not the first thing on its line.

The while Statement

In programming, a *loop* is a part of a program that can be executed two or more times in succession. The while statement is the simplest looping statement in *awk*. It repeatedly executes a statement as long as a condition is true. For example:

```
while (condition)
    body
```

body is a statement called the *body* of the loop, and *condition* is an expression that controls how long the loop keeps running. The first thing the while statement does is test the *condition*. If the *condition* is true, it executes the statement *body*. After *body* has been executed, *condition* is tested again, and if it is still true, *body* is executed again. This process repeats until the *condition* is no longer true. If the *condition* is initially false, the body of the loop is never executed and *awk* continues with the statement following the loop. This example prints the first three fields of each record, one per line:

```
awk '{ i = 1
    while (i <= 3) {
        print $i
        i++
    }
}' inventory-shipped
```

The body of this loop is a compound statement enclosed in braces, containing two statements. The loop works in the following manner: first, the value of i is set to one. Then, the while statement tests whether i is less than or equal to three. This is true when i equals one, so the i-th field is printed. Then the i++ increments the value of i and the loop repeats. The loop terminates when i reaches four.

A newline is not required between the condition and the body; however using one makes the program clearer unless the body is a compound statement or else is very simple. The newline after the open-brace that begins the compound statement is not required either, but the program is harder to read without it.

The do-while Statement

The do loop is a variation of the while looping statement. The do loop executes the *body* once and then repeats the *body* as long as the *condition* is true. It looks like this:

```
do
    body
while (condition)
```

Even if the *condition* is false at the start, the *body* is executed at least once (and only once, unless executing *body* makes *condition* true). Contrast this with the corresponding while statement:

```
while (condition)
    body
```

This statement does not execute *body* even once if the *condition* is false to begin with. The following is an example of a do statement:

```
{    i = 1
    do {
        print $0
        i++
    } while (i <= 10)
}
```

This program prints each input record 10 times. However, it isn't a very realistic example, since in this case an ordinary while would do just as well. This situation reflects actual experience; only occasionally is there a real use for a do statement.

The for Statement

The for statement makes it more convenient to count iterations of a loop. The general form of the for statement looks like this:

```
for (initialization; condition; increment)
    body
```

The *initialization, condition,* and *increment* parts are arbitrary *awk* expressions, and *body* stands for any *awk* statement.

The `for` statement starts by executing *initialization*. Then, as long as the *condition* is true, it repeatedly executes *body* and then *increment*. Typically, *initialization* sets a variable to either zero or one, *increment* adds one to it, and *condition* compares it against the desired number of iterations. For example:

```
awk '{ for (i = 1; i <= 3; i++)
          print $i
}' inventory-shipped
```

This prints the first three fields of each input record, with one field per line.

It isn't possible to set more than one variable in the *initialization* part without using a multiple assignment statement such as x = y = 0. This makes sense only if all the initial values are equal. (But it is possible to initialize additional variables by writing their assignments as separate statements preceding the `for` loop.)

The same is true of the *increment* part. Incrementing additional variables requires separate statements at the end of the loop. The C compound expression, using C's comma operator, is useful in this context but it is not supported in *awk*.

Most often, *increment* is an increment expression, as in the previous example. But this is not required; it can be any expression whatsoever. For example, the following statement prints all the powers of two between 1 and 100:

```
for (i = 1; i <= 100; i *= 2)
    print i
```

If there is nothing to be done, any of the three expressions in the parentheses following the `for` keyword may be omitted. Thus, `for (; x > 0;)` is equivalent to `while (x > 0)`. If the *condition* is omitted, it is treated as true, effectively yielding an *infinite loop* (i.e., a loop that never terminates).

In most cases, a `for` loop is an abbreviation for a `while` loop, as shown here:

```
initialization
while (condition) {
    body
    increment
}
```

The only exception is when the `continue` statement (see the section "The continue Statement" later in this chapter) is used inside the loop. Changing a `for` statement to a `while` statement in this way can change the effect of the `continue` statement inside the loop.

The *awk* language has a `for` statement in addition to a `while` statement because a `for` loop is often both less work to type and more natural to think of. Counting the number of iterations is very common in loops. It can be easier to think of this counting as part of looping rather than as something to do inside the loop.

The break Statement

The `break` statement jumps out of the innermost `for`, `while`, or `do` loop that encloses it. The following example finds the smallest divisor of any integer, and also identifies prime numbers:

```
# find smallest divisor of num
{
    num = $1
    for (div = 2; div*div <= num; div++)
        if (num % div == 0)
            break
    if (num % div == 0)
        printf "Smallest divisor of %d is %d\n", num, div
    else
        printf "%d is prime\n", num
}
```

When the remainder is zero in the first `if` statement, *awk* immediately *breaks out* of the containing `for` loop. This means that *awk* proceeds immediately to the statement following the loop and continues processing. (This is very different from the `exit` statement, which stops the entire *awk* program. See the section "The exit Statement" later in this chapter.)

Th following program illustrates how the *condition* of a `for` or `while` statement could be replaced with a `break` inside an `if`:

```
# find smallest divisor of num
{
    num = $1
    for (div = 2; ; div++) {
        if (num % div == 0) {
            printf "Smallest divisor of %d is %d\n", num, div
            break
        }
        if (div*div > num) {
            printf "%d is prime\n", num
            break
        }
    }
}
```

The `break` statement has no meaning when used outside the body of a loop. However, although it was never documented, historical implementations of *awk* treated the `break` statement outside of a loop as if it were a `next` statement (see the section "The next Statement" later in this chapter). Recent versions of Unix *awk* no longer allow this usage. *gawk* supports this use of `break` only if *−−traditional* has been specified on the command line (see the section "Command-Line Options" in Chapter 11). Otherwise, it is treated as an error, since the POSIX standard specifies that `break` should only be used inside the body of a loop. (d.c.)

The continue Statement

As with break, the continue statement is used only inside for, while, and do loops. It skips over the rest of the loop body, causing the next cycle around the loop to begin immediately. Contrast this with break, which jumps out of the loop altogether.

The continue statement in a for loop directs *awk* to skip the rest of the body of the loop and resume execution with the increment-expression of the for statement. The following program illustrates this fact:

```
BEGIN {
    for (x = 0; x <= 20; x++) {
        if (x == 5)
            continue
        printf "%d ", x
    }
    print ""
}
```

This program prints all the numbers from 0 to 20—except for 5, for which the printf is skipped. Because the increment x++ is not skipped, x does not remain stuck at 5. Contrast the for loop from the previous example with the following while loop:

```
BEGIN {
    x = 0
    while (x <= 20) {
        if (x == 5)
            continue
        printf "%d ", x
        x++
    }
    print ""
}
```

This program loops forever once x reaches 5.

The continue statement has no meaning when used outside the body of a loop. Historical versions of *awk* treated a continue statement outside a loop the same way they treated a break statement outside a loop: as if it were a next statement. Recent versions of Unix *awk* no longer work this way, and *gawk* allows it only if *––traditional* is specified on the command line (see the section "Command-Line Options" in Chapter 11). Just like the break statement, the POSIX standard specifies that continue should only be used inside the body of a loop. (d.c.)

The next Statement

The next statement forces *awk* to immediately stop processing the current record and go on to the next record. This means that no further rules are executed for the current record, and the rest of the current rule's action isn't executed.

Contrast this with the effect of the getline function (see the section "Explicit Input with getline" in Chapter 3). That also causes *awk* to read the next record immediately, but it does not alter the flow of control in any way (i.e., the rest of the current action executes with a new input record).

At the highest level, *awk* program execution is a loop that reads an input record and then tests each rule's pattern against it. If you think of this loop as a for statement whose body contains the rules, then the next statement is analogous to a continue statement. It skips to the end of the body of this implicit loop and executes the increment (which reads another record).

For example, suppose an *awk* program works only on records with four fields, and it shouldn't fail when given bad input. To avoid complicating the rest of the program, write a "weed out" rule near the beginning, in the following manner:

```
NF != 4 {
    err = sprintf("%s:%d: skipped: NF != 4\n", FILENAME, FNR)
    print err > "/dev/stderr"
    next
}
```

Because of the next statement, the program's subsequent rules won't see the bad record. The error message is redirected to the standard error output stream, as error messages should be. For more detail see the section "Special Filenames in gawk" in Chapter 4.

According to the POSIX standard, the behavior is undefined if the next statement is used in a BEGIN or END rule. *gawk* treats it as a syntax error. Although POSIX permits it, some other *awk* implementations don't allow the next statement inside function bodies (see the section "User-Defined Functions" in Chapter 8). Just as with any other next statement, a next statement inside a function body reads the next record and starts processing it with the first rule in the program. If the next statement causes the end of the input to be reached, then the code in any END rules is executed. See the section "The BEGIN and END Special Patterns" earlier in this chapter.

Using gawk's nextfile Statement

gawk provides the nextfile statement, which is similar to the next statement. However, instead of abandoning processing of the current record, the nextfile statement instructs *gawk* to stop processing the current datafile.

The `nextfile` statement is a *gawk* extension. In most other *awk* implementations, or if *gawk* is in compatibility mode (see the section "Command-Line Options" in Chapter 11), `nextfile` is not special.

Upon execution of the `nextfile` statement, FILENAME is updated to the name of the next datafile listed on the command line, FNR is reset to one, ARGIND is incremented, and processing starts over with the first rule in the program. (ARGIND hasn't been introduced yet. See the section "Built-in Variables" later in this chapter.) If the `nextfile` statement causes the end of the input to be reached, then the code in any END rules is executed. See the section "The BEGIN and END Special Patterns" earlier in this chapter.

The `nextfile` statement is useful when there are many datafiles to process but it isn't necessary to process every record in every file. Normally, in order to move on to the next datafile, a program has to continue scanning the unwanted records. The `nextfile` statement accomplishes this much more efficiently.

While one might think that `close(FILENAME)` would accomplish the same as `nextfile`, this isn't true. `close` is reserved for closing files, pipes, and coprocesses that are opened with redirections. It is not related to the main processing that *awk* does with the files listed in ARGV.

If it's necessary to use an *awk* version that doesn't support `nextfile`, see the section "Implementing nextfile as a Function" in Chapter 12 for a user-defined function that simulates the `nextfile` statement.

The current version of the Bell Laboratories *awk* (see the section "Other Freely Available awk Implementations" in Appendix B, *Installing gawk*) also supports `nextfile`. However, it doesn't allow the `nextfile` statement inside function bodies (see the section "User-Defined Functions" in Chapter 8). *gawk* does; a `nextfile` inside a function body reads the next record and starts processing it with the first rule in the program, just as any other `nextfile` statement.

 Versions of *gawk* prior to 3.0 used two words (`next file`) for the `nextfile` statement. In Version 3.0, this was changed to one word, because the treatment of `file` was inconsistent. When it appeared after `next`, `file` was a keyword; otherwise, it was a regular identifier. The old usage is no longer accepted; `next file` generates a syntax error.

The exit Statement

The exit statement causes *awk* to immediately stop executing the current rule and to stop processing input; any remaining input is ignored. The exit statement is written as follows:

    exit [*return code*]

When an exit statement is executed from a BEGIN rule, the program stops processing everything immediately. No input records are read. However, if an END rule is present, as part of executing the exit statement, the END rule is executed (see the section "The BEGIN and END Special Patterns" earlier in this chapter). If exit is used as part of an END rule, it causes the program to stop immediately.

An exit statement that is not part of a BEGIN or END rule stops the execution of any further automatic rules for the current record, skips reading any remaining input records, and executes the END rule if there is one.

In such a case, if you don't want the END rule to do its job, set a variable to nonzero before the exit statement and check that variable in the END rule. See the section "Assertions" in Chapter 12 for an example that does this.

If an argument is supplied to exit, its value is used as the exit status code for the *awk* process. If no argument is supplied, exit returns status zero (success). In the case where an argument is supplied to a first exit statement, and then exit is called a second time from an END rule with no argument, *awk* uses the previously supplied exit value. (d.c.)

For example, suppose an error condition occurs that is difficult or impossible to handle. Conventionally, programs report this by exiting with a nonzero status. An *awk* program can do this using an exit statement with a nonzero argument, as shown in the following example:

```
BEGIN {
    if (("date" | getline date_now) <= 0) {
        print "Can't get system date" > "/dev/stderr"
        exit 1
    }
    print "current date is", date_now
    close("date")
}
```

Built-in Variables

Most *awk* variables are available to use for your own purposes; they never change unless your program assigns values to them, and they never affect anything unless your program examines them. However, a few variables in *awk* have special built-in meanings. *awk* examines some of these automatically, so that they enable you to tell *awk* how to do certain things. Others are set automatically by *awk*, so that they carry information from the internal workings of *awk* to your program.

This section documents all the built-in variables of *gawk*, most of which are also documented in the chapters describing their areas of activity.

Built-in Variables That Control awk

The following is an alphabetical list of variables that you can change to control how *awk* does certain things. The variables that are specific to *gawk* are marked with a pound sign (#):

BINMODE #

> On non-POSIX systems, this variable specifies use of binary mode for all I/O. Numeric values of one, two, or three specify that input files, output files, or all files, respectively, should use binary I/O. Alternatively, string values of "r" or "w" specify that input files and output files, respectively, should use binary I/O. A string value of "rw" or "wr" indicates that all files should use binary I/O. Any other string value is equivalent to "rw", but *gawk* generates a warning message. BINMODE is described in more detail in the section "Using gawk on PC Operating Systems" in Appendix B.

> This variable is a *gawk* extension. In other *awk* implementations (except *mawk*, see the section "Other Freely Available awk Implementations" in Appendix B), or if *gawk* is in compatibility mode (see the section "Command-Line Options" in Chapter 11), it is not special.

CONVFMT

> This string controls conversion of numbers to strings (see the section "Conversion of Strings and Numbers" in Chapter 5). It works by being passed, in effect, as the first argument to the sprintf function (see the section "String-Manipulation Functions" in Chapter 8). Its default value is "%.6g". CONVFMT was introduced by the POSIX standard.

FIELDWIDTHS #

> This is a space-separated list of columns that tells *gawk* how to split input with fixed columnar boundaries. Assigning a value to FIELDWIDTHS overrides the use of FS for field splitting. See the section "Reading Fixed-Width Data" in Chapter 3 for more information.

If *gawk* is in compatibility mode (see the section "Command-Line Options" in Chapter 11), then FIELDWIDTHS has no special meaning, and field-splitting operations occur based exclusively on the value of FS.

FS

This is the input field separator (see the section "Specifying How Fields Are Separated" in Chapter 3). The value is a single-character string or a multi-character regular expression that matches the separations between fields in an input record. If the value is the null string (""), then each character in the record becomes a separate field. (This behavior is a *gawk* extension. POSIX *awk* does not specify the behavior when FS is the null string.)

The default value is " ", a string consisting of a single space. As a special exception, this value means that any sequence of spaces, tabs, and/or new-lines is a single separator.* It also causes spaces, tabs, and newlines at the beginning and end of a record to be ignored.

You can set the value of FS on the command line using the *–F* option:

```
awk -F, 'program' input-files
```

If *gawk* is using FIELDWIDTHS for field splitting, assigning a value to FS causes *gawk* to return to the normal, FS-based field splitting. An easy way to do this is to simply say FS = FS, perhaps with an explanatory comment.

IGNORECASE #

If IGNORECASE is nonzero or non-null, then all string comparisons and all regular expression matching are case independent. Thus, regexp matching with ~ and !~, as well as the gensub, gsub, index, match, split, and sub functions, record termination with RS, and field splitting with FS, all ignore case when doing their particular regexp operations. However, the value of IGNORECASE does *not* affect array subscripting. See the section "Case Sensitivity in Matching" in Chapter 2.

If *gawk* is in compatibility mode (see the section "Command-Line Options" in Chapter 11), then IGNORECASE has no special meaning. Thus, string and regexp operations are always case-sensitive.

LINT #

When this variable is true (nonzero or non-null), *gawk* behaves as if the *––lint* command-line option is in effect. (see the section "Command-Line Options" in Chapter 11). With a value of "fatal", lint warnings become fatal errors. Any other true value prints nonfatal warnings. Assigning a false value to LINT turns off the lint warnings.

---

* In POSIX *awk*, newline does not count as whitespace.

This variable is a *gawk* extension. It is not special in other *awk* implementations. Unlike the other special variables, changing LINT does affect the production of lint warnings, even if *gawk* is in compatibility mode. Much as the *--lint* and *--traditional* options independently control different aspects of *gawk*'s behavior, the control of lint warnings during program execution is independent of the flavor of *awk* being executed.

OFMT

This string controls conversion of numbers to strings (see the section "Conversion of Strings and Numbers" in Chapter 5) for printing with the print statement. It works by being passed as the first argument to the sprintf function (see the section "String-Manipulation Functions" in Chapter 8). Its default value is "%.6g". Earlier versions of *awk* also used OFMT to specify the format for converting numbers to strings in general expressions; this is now done by CONVFMT.

OFS

This is the output field separator (see the section "Output Separators" in Chapter 4). It is output between the fields printed by a print statement. Its default value is " ", a string consisting of a single space.

ORS

This is the output record separator. It is output at the end of every print statement. Its default value is "\n", the newline character. (See the section "Output Separators" in Chapter 4.)

RS

This is *awk*'s input record separator. Its default value is a string containing a single newline character, which means that an input record consists of a single line of text. It can also be the null string, in which case records are separated by runs of blank lines. If it is a regexp, records are separated by matches of the regexp in the input text. (See the section "How Input Is Split into Records" in Chapter 3.)

The ability for RS to be a regular expression is a *gawk* extension. In most other *awk* implementations, or if *gawk* is in compatibility mode (see the section "Command-Line Options" in Chapter 11), just the first character of RS's value is used.

SUBSEP

This is the subscript separator. It has the default value of "\034" and is used to separate the parts of the indices of a multidimensional array. Thus, the expression foo["A", "B"] really accesses foo["A\034B"] (see the section "Multidimensional Arrays" in Chapter 7).

TEXTDOMAIN #

This variable is used for internationalization of programs at the *awk* level. It sets the default text domain for specially marked string constants in the source text, as well as for the dcgettext and bindtextdomain functions (see Chapter 9, *Internationalization with gawk*). The default value of TEXTDOMAIN is "messages".

This variable is a *gawk* extension. In other *awk* implementations, or if *gawk* is in compatibility mode (see the section "Command-Line Options" in Chapter 11), it is not special.

Built-in Variables That Convey Information

The following is an alphabetical list of variables that *awk* sets automatically on certain occasions in order to provide information to your program. The variables that are specific to *gawk* are marked with a pound sign (#):

ARGC, ARGV

The command-line arguments available to *awk* programs are stored in an array called ARGV. ARGC is the number of command-line arguments present. See the section "Other Command-Line Arguments" in Chapter 11. Unlike most *awk* arrays, ARGV is indexed from 0 to ARGC − 1. In the following example:

```
$ awk 'BEGIN {
>           for (i = 0; i < ARGC; i++)
>               print ARGV[i]
>     }' inventory-shipped BBS-list
awk
inventory-shipped
BBS-list
```

ARGV[0] contains "awk", ARGV[1] contains "inventory-shipped", and ARGV[2] contains "BBS-list". The value of ARGC is three, one more than the index of the last element in ARGV, because the elements are numbered from zero.

The names ARGC and ARGV, as well as the convention of indexing the array from 0 to ARGC − 1, are derived from the C language's method of accessing command-line arguments.

The value of ARGV[0] can vary from system to system. Also, you should note that the program text is *not* included in ARGV, nor are any of *awk*'s command-line options. See the section "Using ARGC and ARGV" later in this chapter for information about how *awk* uses these variables.

ARGIND #

The index in ARGV of the current file being processed. Every time *gawk* opens a new datafile for processing, it sets ARGIND to the index in ARGV of the filename. When *gawk* is processing the input files, FILENAME == ARGV[ARGIND] is always true.

This variable is useful in file processing; it allows you to tell how far along you are in the list of datafiles as well as to distinguish between successive instances of the same filename on the command line.

While you can change the value of ARGIND within your *awk* program, *gawk* automatically sets it to a new value when the next file is opened.

This variable is a *gawk* extension. In other *awk* implementations, or if *gawk* is in compatibility mode (see the section "Command-Line Options" in Chapter 11), it is not special.

ENVIRON

An associative array that contains the values of the environment. The array indices are the environment variable names; the elements are the values of the particular environment variables. For example, ENVIRON["HOME"] might be */home/arnold*. Changing this array does not affect the environment passed on to any programs that *awk* may spawn via redirection or the system function.

Some operating systems may not have environment variables. On such systems, the ENVIRON array is empty (except for ENVIRON["AWKPATH"]; see the section "The AWKPATH Environment Variable" in Chapter 11).

ERRNO #

If a system error occurs during a redirection for getline, during a read for getline, or during a close operation, then ERRNO contains a string describing the error.

This variable is a *gawk* extension. In other *awk* implementations, or if *gawk* is in compatibility mode (see the section "Command-Line Options" in Chapter 11), it is not special.

FILENAME

The name of the file that *awk* is currently reading. When no datafiles are listed on the command line, *awk* reads from the standard input and FILENAME is set to "-". FILENAME is changed each time a new file is read (see Chapter 3). Inside a BEGIN rule, the value of FILENAME is "", since there are no input files being processed yet.* (d.c.) Note, though, that using getline (see the section "Explicit Input with getline" in Chapter 3) inside a BEGIN rule can give FILE-NAME a value.

FNR

The current record number in the current file. FNR is incremented each time a new record is read (see the section "Explicit Input with getline" in Chapter 3). It is reinitialized to zero each time a new input file is started.

---

* Some early implementations of Unix *awk* initialized FILENAME to "-", even if there were datafiles to be processed. This behavior was incorrect and should not be relied upon in your programs.

NF

The number of fields in the current input record. NF is set each time a new record is read, when a new field is created or when $0 changes (see the section "Examining Fields" in Chapter 3).

NR

The number of input records *awk* has processed since the beginning of the program's execution (see the section "How Input Is Split into Records" in Chapter 3). NR is incremented each time a new record is read.

PROCINFO #

The elements of this array provide access to information about the running *awk* program. The following elements (listed alphabetically) are guaranteed to be available:

PROCINFO["egid"]

The value of the getegid system call.

PROCINFO["euid"]

The value of the geteuid system call.

PROCINFO["FS"]

This is "FS" if field splitting with FS is in effect, or it is "FIELDWIDTHS" if field splitting with FIELDWIDTHS is in effect.

PROCINFO["gid"]

The value of the getgid system call.

PROCINFO["pgrpid"]

The process group ID of the current process.

PROCINFO["pid"]

The process ID of the current process.

PROCINFO["ppid"]

The parent process ID of the current process.

PROCINFO["uid"]

The value of the getuid system call.

On some systems, there may be elements in the array, "group1" through "group*N*" for some *N*. *N* is the number of supplementary groups that the process has. Use the in operator to test for these elements (see the section "Referring to an Array Element" in Chapter 7).

This array is a *gawk* extension. In other *awk* implementations, or if *gawk* is in compatibility mode (see the section "Command-Line Options" in Chapter 11), it is not special.

RLENGTH

The length of the substring matched by the `match` function (see the section "String-Manipulation Functions" in Chapter 8). RLENGTH is set by invoking the `match` function. Its value is the length of the matched string, or −1 if no match is found.

RSTART

The start index in characters of the substring that is matched by the `match` function (see the section "String-Manipulation Functions" in Chapter 8). RSTART is set by invoking the `match` function. Its value is the position of the string where the matched substring starts, or zero if no match was found.

RT #

This is set each time a record is read. It contains the input text that matched the text denoted by RS, the record separator.

This variable is a *gawk* extension. In other *awk* implementations, or if *gawk* is in compatibility mode (see the section "Command-Line Options" in Chapter 11), it is not special.

Changing NR and FNR

awk increments NR and FNR each time it reads a record, instead of setting them to the absolute value of the number of records read. This means that a program can change these variables and their new values are incremented for each record. (d.c.) This is demonstrated in the following example:

```
$ echo '1
> 2
> 3
> 4' | awk 'NR == 2 { NR = 17 }
> { print NR }'
1
17
18
19
```

Before FNR was added to the *awk* language (see the section "Major Changes Between V7 and SVR3.1" in Appendix A, *The Evolution of the awk Language*), many *awk* programs used this feature to track the number of records in a file by resetting NR to zero when FILENAME changed.

Using ARGC and ARGV

The previous section "Built-in Variables That Convey Information" presented the
following program describing the information contained in ARGC and ARGV:

```
$ awk 'BEGIN {
>         for (i = 0; i < ARGC; i++)
>             print ARGV[i]
>      }' inventory-shipped BBS-list
awk
inventory-shipped
BBS-list
```

In this example, ARGV[0] contains awk, ARGV[1] contains inventory-shipped, and
ARGV[2] contains BBS-list. Notice that the *awk* program is not entered in ARGV.
The other special command-line options, with their arguments, are also not
entered. This includes variable assignments done with the –*v* option (see the section "Command-Line Options" in Chapter 11). Normal variable assignments on the
command line *are* treated as arguments and do show up in the ARGV array:

```
$ cat showargs.awk
BEGIN {
    printf "A=%d, B=%d\n", A, B
    for (i = 0; i < ARGC; i++)
        printf "\tARGV[%d] = %s\n", i, ARGV[i]
}
END   { printf "A=%d, B=%d\n", A, B }
$ awk -v A=1 -f showargs.awk B=2 /dev/null
A=1, B=0
        ARGV[0] = awk
        ARGV[1] = B=2
        ARGV[2] = /dev/null
A=1, B=2
```

A program can alter ARGC and the elements of ARGV. Each time *awk* reaches the
end of an input file, it uses the next element of ARGV as the name of the next input
file. By storing a different string there, a program can change which files are read.
Use - to represent the standard input. Storing additional elements and incrementing ARGC causes additional files to be read.

If the value of ARGC is decreased, that eliminates input files from the end of the list.
By recording the old value of ARGC elsewhere, a program can treat the eliminated
arguments as something other than filenames.

To eliminate a file from the middle of the list, store the null string ("") into ARGV in
place of the file's name. As a special feature, *awk* ignores filenames that have been
replaced with the null string. Another option is to use the delete statement to
remove elements from ARGV (see the section "The delete Statement" in Chapter 7).

All of these actions are typically done in the BEGIN rule, before actual processing of the input begins. See the section "Splitting a Large File into Pieces" and the section "Duplicating Output into Multiple Files" in Chapter 13, *Practical awk Programs*, for examples of each way of removing elements from ARGV. The following fragment processes ARGV in order to examine, and then remove, command-line options:

```
BEGIN {
    for (i = 1; i < ARGC; i++) {
        if (ARGV[i] == "-v")
            verbose = 1
        else if (ARGV[i] == "-d")
            debug = 1
        else if (ARGV[i] ~ /^-?/) {
            e = sprintf("%s: unrecognized option -- %c",
                    ARGV[0], substr(ARGV[i], 1, ,1))
            print e > "/dev/stderr"
        } else
            break
        delete ARGV[i]
    }
}
```

To actually get the options into the *awk* program, end the *awk* options with −− and then supply the *awk* program's options, in the following manner:

```
awk -f myprog -- -v -d file1 file2 ...
```

This is not necessary in *gawk*. Unless −−*posix* has been specified, *gawk* silently puts any unrecognized options into ARGV for the *awk* program to deal with. As soon as it sees an unknown option, *gawk* stops looking for other options that it might otherwise recognize. The previous example with *gawk* would be:

```
gawk -f myprog -d -v file1 file2 ...
```

Because *−d* is not a valid *gawk* option, it and the following *−v* are passed on to the *awk* program.

7

Arrays in awk

An *array* is a table of values called *elements*. The elements of an array arc distinguished by their indices. *Indices* may be either numbers or strings.

This chapter describes how arrays work in *awk*, how to use array elements, how to scan through every element in an array, and how to remove array elements. It also describes how *awk* simulates multidimensional arrays, as well as some of the less obvious points about array usage. The chapter finishes with a discussion of *gawk*'s facility for sorting an array based on its indices.

awk maintains a single set of names that may be used for naming variables, arrays, and functions (see the section "User-Defined Functions" in Chapter 8, *Functions*). Thus, you cannot have a variable and an array with the same name in the same *awk* program.

Introduction to Arrays

The *awk* language provides one-dimensional arrays for storing groups of related strings or numbers. Every *awk* array must have a name. Array names have the same syntax as variable names; any valid variable name would also be a valid array name. But one name cannot be used in both ways (as an array and as a variable) in the same *awk* program.

Arrays in *awk* superficially resemble arrays in other programming languages, but there are fundamental differences. In *awk*, it isn't necessary to specify the size of an array before starting to use it. Additionally, any number or string in *awk*, not just consecutive integers, may be used as an array index.

In most other languages, arrays must be *declared* before use, including a specification of how many elements or components they contain. In such languages, the declaration causes a contiguous block of memory to be allocated for that many elements. Usually, an index in the array must be a positive integer. For example, the index zero specifies the first element in the array, which is actually stored at the beginning of the block of memory. Index one specifies the second element, which is stored in memory right after the first element, and so on. It is impossible to add more elements to the array, because it has room only for as many elements as given in the declaration. (Some languages allow arbitrary starting and ending indices—e.g., 15 .. 27—but the size of the array is still fixed when the array is declared.)

A contiguous array of four elements might look like Figure 7-1 conceptually, if the element values are 8, "foo", "", and 30.

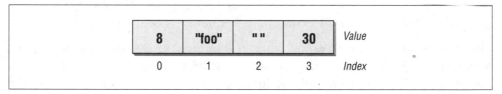

Figure 7-1. Array indexing

Only the values are stored; the indices are implicit from the order of the values. Here, 8 is the value at index zero, because 8 appears in the position with zero elements before it.

Arrays in *awk* are different—they are *associative*. This means that each array is a collection of pairs: an index and its corresponding array element value:

Index	Value
3	30
2	`"foo"`
0	8
2	`" "`

The pairs are shown in jumbled order because their order is irrelevant.

One advantage of associative arrays is that new pairs can be added at any time. For example, suppose a tenth element is added to the array whose value is `"number ten"`. The result is:

Index	Value
10	`"number ten"`
3	30
1	`"foo"`
0	8
2	`" "`

Now the array is *sparse*, which just means some indices are missing. It has elements 0–3 and 10, but doesn't have elements 4, 5, 6, 7, 8, or 9.

Another consequence of associative arrays is that the indices don't have to be positive integers. Any number, or even a string, can be an index. For example, the following is an array that translates words from English to French:

Index	Value
`"dog"`	`"chien"`
`"cat"`	`"chat"`
`"one"`	`"un"`
1	`"un"`

Here we decided to translate the number one in both spelled-out and numeric form—thus illustrating that a single array can have both numbers and strings as indices. In fact, array subscripts are always strings; this is discussed in more detail in the section "Using Numbers to Subscript Arrays" later in this chapter. Here, the number 1 isn't double-quoted, since *awk* automatically converts it to a string.

The value of IGNORECASE has no effect upon array subscripting. The identical string value used to store an array element must be used to retrieve it. When *awk* creates an array (e.g., with the split built-in function), that array's indices are consecutive integers starting at one. (See the section "String-Manipulation Functions" in Chapter 8.)

awk's arrays are efficient—the time to access an element is independent of the number of elements in the array.

Referring to an Array Element

The principal way to use an array is to refer to one of its elements. An array reference is an expression as follows:

```
array[index]
```

Here, *array* is the name of an array. The expression *index* is the index of the desired element of the array.

The value of the array reference is the current value of that array element. For example, foo[4.3] is an expression for the element of array foo at index 4.3.

A reference to an array element that has no recorded value yields a value of "", the null string. This includes elements that have not been assigned any value as well as elements that have been deleted (see the section "The delete Statement" later in this chapter). Such a reference automatically creates that array element, with the null string as its value. (In some cases, this is unfortunate, because it might waste memory inside *awk*.)

To determine whether an element exists in an array at a certain index, use the following expression:

```
index in array
```

This expression tests whether the particular index exists, without the side effect of creating that element if it is not present. The expression has the value one (true) if *array[index]* exists and zero (false) if it does not exist. For example, this statement tests whether the array frequencies contains the index 2:

```
if (2 in frequencies)
    print "Subscript 2 is present."
```

Note that this is *not* a test of whether the array frequencies contains an element whose *value* is two. There is no way to do that except to scan all the elements. Also, this *does not* create frequencies[2], while the following (incorrect) alternative does:

```
if (frequencies[2] != "")
    print "Subscript 2 is present."
```

Assigning Array Elements

Array elements can be assigned values just like *awk* variables:

```
array[subscript] = value
```

array is the name of an array. The expression *subscript* is the index of the element of the array that is assigned a value. The expression *value* is the value to assign to that element of the array.

Basic Array Example

The following program takes a list of lines, each beginning with a line number, and prints them out in order of line number. The line numbers are not in order when they are first read—instead they are scrambled. This program sorts the lines by making an array using the line numbers as subscripts. The program then prints out the lines in sorted order of their numbers. It is a very simple program and gets confused upon encountering repeated numbers, gaps, or lines that don't begin with a number:

```
{
    if ($1 > max)
        max = $1
    arr[$1] = $0
}

END {
    for (x = 1; x <= max; x++)
        print arr[x]
}
```

The first rule keeps track of the largest line number seen so far; it also stores each line into the array arr, at an index that is the line's number. The second rule runs after all the input has been read, to print out all the lines. When this program is run with the following input:

```
5  I am the Five man
2  Who are you?  The new number two!
4  . . . And four on the floor
1  Who is number one?
3  I three you.
```

Its output is:

```
1  Who is number one?
2  Who are you?  The new number two!
3  I three you.
4  . . . And four on the floor
5  I am the Five man
```

If a line number is repeated, the last line with a given number overrides the others. Gaps in the line numbers can be handled with an easy improvement to the program's END rule, as follows:

```
END {
    for (x = 1; x <= max; x++)
        if (x in arr)
            print arr[x]
}
```

Scanning All Elements of an Array

In programs that use arrays, it is often necessary to use a loop that executes once for each element of an array. In other languages, where arrays are contiguous and indices are limited to positive integers, this is easy: all the valid indices can be found by counting from the lowest index up to the highest. This technique won't do the job in *awk*, because any number or string can be an array index. So *awk* has a special kind of for statement for scanning an array:

```
for (var in array)
    body
```

This loop executes *body* once for each index in *array* that the program has previously used, with the variable *var* set to that index.

The following program uses this form of the for statement. The first rule scans the input records and notes which words appear (at least once) in the input, by storing a one into the array used with the word as index. The second rule scans the elements of used to find all the distinct words that appear in the input. It prints each word that is more than 10 characters long and also prints the number of such words. See the section "String-Manipulation Functions" in Chapter 8 for more information on the built-in function length:

```
# Record a 1 for each word that is used at least once
{
    for (i = 1; i <= NF; i++)
        used[$i] = 1
}

# Find number of distinct words more than 10 characters long
END {
    for (x in used)
        if (length(x) > 10) {
            ++num_long_words
            print x
        }
    print num_long_words, "words longer than 10 characters"
}
```

See the section "Generating Word-Usage Counts" in Chapter 13, *Practical awk Programs*, for a more detailed example of this type.

The order in which elements of the array are accessed by this statement is determined by the internal arrangement of the array elements within *awk* and cannot be controlled or changed. This can lead to problems if new elements are added to *array* by statements in the loop body; it is not predictable whether the for loop will reach them. Similarly, changing *var* inside the loop may produce strange results. It is best to avoid such things.

The delete Statement

To remove an individual element of an array, use the delete statement:

```
delete array[index]
```

Once an array element has been deleted, any value the element once had is no longer available. It is as if the element had never been referred to or had been given a value. The following is an example of deleting elements in an array:

```
for (i in frequencies)
    delete frequencies[i]
```

This example removes all the elements from the array frequencies. Once an element is deleted, a subsequent for statement to scan the array does not report that element and the in operator to check for the presence of that element returns zero (i.e., false):

```
delete foo[4]
if (4 in foo)
    print "This will never be printed"
```

It is important to note that deleting an element is *not* the same as assigning it a null value (the empty string, ""). For example:

```
foo[4] = ""
if (4 in foo)
    print "This is printed, even though foo[4] is empty"
```

It is not an error to delete an element that does not exist. If *--lint* is provided on the command line (see the section "Command-Line Options" in Chapter 11, *Running awk and gawk*), *gawk* issues a warning message when an element that is not in the array is deleted.

All the elements of an array may be deleted with a single statement by leaving off the subscript in the `delete` statement, as follows:

```
delete array
```

This ability is a *gawk* extension; it is not available in compatibility mode (see the section "Command-Line Options" in Chapter 11).

Using this version of the `delete` statement is about three times more efficient than the equivalent loop that deletes each element one at a time.

The following statement provides a portable but nonobvious way to clear out an array:*

```
split("", array)
```

The `split` function (see the section "String-Manipulation Functions" in Chapter 8) clears out the target array first. This call asks it to split apart the null string. Because there is no data to split out, the function simply clears the array and then returns.

Deleting an array does not change its type; you cannot delete an array and then use the array's name as a scalar (i.e., a regular variable). For example, the following does not work:

```
a[1] = 3; delete a; a = 3
```

Using Numbers to Subscript Arrays

An important aspect about arrays to remember is that *array subscripts are always strings*. When a numeric value is used as a subscript, it is converted to a string value before being used for subscripting (see the section "Conversion of Strings and Numbers" in Chapter 5, *Expressions*). This means that the value of the built-in variable CONVFMT can affect how your program accesses elements of an array. For example:

```
xyz = 12.153
data[xyz] = 1
CONVFMT = "%2.2f"
if (xyz in data)
    printf "%s is in data\n", xyz
else
    printf "%s is not in data\n", xyz
```

---

* Thanks to Michael Brennan for pointing this out.

This prints 12.15 is not in data. The first statement gives xyz a numeric value. Assigning to data[xyz] subscripts data with the string value "12.153" (using the default conversion value of CONVFMT, "%.6g"). Thus, the array element data["12.153"] is assigned the value one. The program then changes the value of CONVFMT. The test (xyz in data) generates a new string value from xyz—this time "12.15"—because the value of CONVFMT only allows two significant digits. This test fails, since "12.15" is a different string from "12.153".

According to the rules for conversions (see the section "Conversion of Strings and Numbers" in Chapter 5), integer values are always converted to strings as integers, no matter what the value of CONVFMT may happen to be. So the usual case of the following works:

```
for (i = 1; i <= maxsub; i++)
    do something with array[i]
```

The "integer values always convert to strings as integers" rule has an additional consequence for array indexing. Octal and hexadecimal constants (see the section "Octal and Hexadecimal Numbers" in Chapter 5) are converted internally into numbers, and their original form is forgotten. This means, for example, that array[17], array[021], and array[0x11] all refer to the same element!

As with many things in *awk*, the majority of the time things work as one would expect them to. But it is useful to have a precise knowledge of the actual rules which sometimes can have a subtle effect on your programs.

Using Uninitialized Variables as Subscripts

Suppose it's necessary to write a program to print the input data in reverse order. A reasonable attempt to do so (with some test data) might look like this:

```
$ echo 'line 1
> line 2
> line 3' | awk '{ l[lines] = $0; ++lines }
> END {
>     for (i = lines-1; i >= 0; --i)
>         print l[i]
> }'
line 3
line 2
```

Unfortunately, the very first line of input data did not come out in the output!

At first glance, this program should have worked. The variable lines is uninitialized, and uninitialized variables have the numeric value zero. So, *awk* should have printed the value of l[0].

The issue here is that subscripts for *awk* arrays are *always* strings. Uninitialized variables, when used as strings, have the value "", not zero. Thus, line 1 ends up stored in l[""]. The following version of the program works correctly:

```
{ l[lines++] = $0 }
END {
    for (i = lines - 1; i >= 0; --i)
        print l[i]
}
```

Here, the ++ forces lines to be numeric, thus making the "old value" numeric zero. This is then converted to "0" as the array subscript.

Even though it is somewhat unusual, the null string ("") is a valid array subscript. (d.c.) *gawk* warns about the use of the null string as a subscript if *—lint* is provided on the command line (see the section "Command-Line Options" in Chapter 11).

Multidimensional Arrays

A multidimensional array is an array in which an element is identified by a sequence of indices instead of a single index. For example, a two-dimensional array requires two indices. The usual way (in most languages, including *awk*) to refer to an element of a two-dimensional array named grid is with grid[x,y].

Multidimensional arrays are supported in *awk* through concatenation of indices into one string. *awk* converts the indices into strings (see the section "Conversion of Strings and Numbers" in Chapter 5) and concatenates them together, with a separator between them. This creates a single string that describes the values of the separate indices. The combined string is used as a single index into an ordinary, one-dimensional array. The separator used is the value of the built-in variable SUB-SEP.

For example, suppose we evaluate the expression foo[5,12] = "value" when the value of SUBSEP is "@". The numbers 5 and 12 are converted to strings and concatenated with an @ between them, yielding "5@12"; thus, the array element foo["5@12"] is set to "value".

Once the element's value is stored, *awk* has no record of whether it was stored with a single index or a sequence of indices. The two expressions foo[5,12] and foo[5 SUBSEP 12] are always equivalent.

The default value of SUBSEP is the string "\034", which contains a nonprinting character that is unlikely to appear in an *awk* program or in most input data. The usefulness of choosing an unlikely character comes from the fact that index values that contain a string matching SUBSEP can lead to combined strings that are ambiguous. Suppose that SUBSEP is "@"; then foo["a@b", "c"] and foo["a", "b@c"] are indistinguishable because both are actually stored as foo["a@b@c"].

To test whether a particular index sequence exists in a multidimensional array, use the same operator (in) that is used for single dimensional arrays. Write the whole sequence of indices in parentheses, separated by commas, as the left operand:

```
(subscript1, subscript2, ...) in array
```

The following example treats its input as a two-dimensional array of fields; it rotates this array 90 degrees clockwise and prints the result. It assumes that all lines have the same number of elements:

```
{
    if (max_nf < NF)
        max_nf = NF
    max_nr = NR
    for (x = 1; x <= NF; x++)
        vector[x, NR] = $x
}

END {
    for (x = 1; x <= max_nf; x++) {
        for (y = max_nr; y >= 1; --y)
            printf("%s ", vector[x, y])
        printf("\n")
    }
}
```

When given the input:

```
1 2 3 4 5 6
2 3 4 5 6 1
3 4 5 6 1 2
4 5 6 1 2 3
```

the program produces the following output:

```
4 3 2 1
5 4 3 2
6 5 4 3
1 6 5 4
2 1 6 5
3 2 1 6
```

Scanning Multidimensional Arrays

There is no special for statement for scanning a "multidimensional" array. There cannot be one because, in truth, there are no multidimensional arrays or elements—there is only a multidimensional *way of accessing* an array.

However, if your program has an array that is always accessed as multidimensional, you can get the effect of scanning it by combining the scanning for statement (see the section "Scanning All Elements of an Array" earlier in this chapter) with the built-in `split` function (see the section "String-Manipulation Functions" in Chapter 8). It works in the following manner:

```
for (combined in array) {
    split(combined, separate, SUBSEP)
    ...
}
```

This sets the variable `combined` to each concatenated combined index in the array, and splits it into the individual indices by breaking it apart where the value of SUB-SEP appears. The individual indices then become the elements of the array `separate`.

Thus, if a value is previously stored in `array[1, "foo"]`; then an element with index `"1\034foo"` exists in `array`. (Recall that the default value of SUBSEP is the character with code 034.) Sooner or later, the `for` statement finds that index and does an iteration with the variable `combined` set to `"1\034foo"`. Then the `split` function is called as follows:

```
split("1\034foo", separate, "\034")
```

The result is to set `separate[1]` to `"1"` and `separate[2]` to `"foo"`. Presto! The original sequence of separate indices is recovered.

Sorting Array Values and Indices with gawk

The order in which an array is scanned with a `for (i in array)` loop is essentially arbitrary. In most *awk* implementations, sorting an array requires writing a sort function. While this can be educational for exploring different sorting algorithms, usually that's not the point of the program. *gawk* provides the built-in `asort` function (see the section "String-Manipulation Functions" in Chapter 8) that sorts an array. For example:

```
populate the array data
n = asort(data)
for (i = 1; i <= n; i++)
    do something with data[i]
```

After the call to `asort`, the array `data` is indexed from 1 to some number n, the total number of elements in `data`. (This count is `asort`'s return value.) `data[1]` $\leq$ `data[2]` $\leq$ `data[3]`, and so on. The comparison of array elements is done using *gawk*'s usual comparison rules (see the section "Variable Typing and Comparison Expressions" in Chapter 5).

An important side effect of calling `asort` is that *the array's original indices are irrevocably lost.* As this isn't always desirable, `asort` accepts a second argument:

```
populate the array source
n = asort(source, dest)
for (i = 1; i <= n; i++)
    do something with dest[i]
```

In this case, *gawk* copies the `source` array into the `dest` array and then sorts `dest`, destroying its indices. However, the `source` array is not affected.

Often, what's needed is to sort on the values of the *indices* instead of the values of the elements. To do this, use a helper array to hold the sorted index values, and then access the original array's elements. It works in the following way:

```
populate the array data
# copy indices
j = 1
for (i in data) {
    ind[j] = i     # index value becomes element value
    j++
}
n = asort(ind)     # index values are now sorted
for (i = 1; i <= n; i++)
    do something with data[ind[i]]
```

Sorting the array by replacing the indices provides maximal flexibility. To traverse the elements in decreasing order, use a loop that goes from *n* down to 1, either over the elements or over the indices.

Copying array indices and elements isn't expensive in terms of memory. Internally, *gawk* maintains *reference counts* to data. For example, when `asort` copies the first array to the second one, there is only one copy of the original array elements' data, even though both arrays use the values. Similarly, when copying the indices from `data` to `ind`, there is only one copy of the actual index strings.

As with array subscripts, the value of `IGNORECASE` does not affect array sorting.

8

Functions

This chapter describes *awk*'s built-in functions, which fall into three categories: numeric, string, and I/O. *gawk* provides additional groups of functions to work with values that represent time, do bit manipulation, and internationalize and localize programs.

Besides the built-in functions, *awk* has provisions for writing new functions that the rest of a program can use. The second half of this chapter describes these *user-defined functions*.

Built-in Functions

Built-in functions are always available for your *awk* program to call. This section defines all the built-in functions in *awk*; some of these are mentioned in other sections but are summarized here for your convenience.

Calling Built-in Functions

To call one of *awk*'s built-in functions, write the name of the function followed by arguments in parentheses. For example, `atan2(y + z, 1)` is a call to the function `atan2` and has two arguments.

Whitespace is ignored between the built-in function name and the open parenthesis, and it is good practice to avoid using whitespace there. User-defined functions do not permit whitespace in this way, and it is easier to avoid mistakes by following a simple convention that always works—no whitespace after a function name.

Each built-in function accepts a certain number of arguments. In some cases, arguments can be omitted. The defaults for omitted arguments vary from function to function and are described under the individual functions. In some *awk* implementations, extra arguments given to built-in functions are ignored. However, in *gawk*, it is a fatal error to give extra arguments to a built-in function.

When a function is called, expressions that create the function's actual parameters are evaluated completely before the call is performed. For example, in the following code fragment:

```
i = 4
j = sqrt(i++)
```

the variable i is incremented to the value 5 before sqrt is called with a value of 4 for its actual parameter. The order of evaluation of the expressions used for the function's parameters is undefined. Thus, avoid writing programs that assume that parameters are evaluated from left to right or from right to left. For example:

```
i = 5
j = atan2(i++, i *= 2)
```

If the order of evaluation is left to right, then i first becomes 6, and then 12, and atan2 is called with the two arguments 6 and 12. But if the order of evaluation is right to left, i first becomes 10, then 11, and atan2 is called with the two arguments 11 and 10.

Numeric Functions

The following list describes all of the built-in functions that work with numbers. Optional parameters are enclosed in square brackets ([ ]):

int(*x*)

> This returns the nearest integer to *x*, located between *x* and zero and truncated toward zero.
>
> For example, int(3) is 3, int(3.9) is 3, int(-3.9) is −3, and int(-3) is −3 as well.

sqrt(*x*)

> This returns the positive square root of *x*. *gawk* reports an error if *x* is negative. Thus, sqrt(4) is 2.

exp(*x*)

> This returns the exponential of *x* (e^x) or reports an error if *x* is out of range. The range of values *x* can have depends on your machine's floating-point representation.

`log(x)`

This returns the natural logarithm of *x*, if *x* is positive; otherwise, it reports an error.

`sin(x)`

This returns the sine of *x*, with *x* in radians.

`cos(x)`

This returns the cosine of *x*, with *x* in radians.

`atan2(y, x)`

This returns the arctangent of *y* / *x* in radians.

`rand()`

This returns a random number. The values of `rand` are uniformly distributed between zero and one. The value is never zero and never one.*

Often random integers are needed instead. Following is a user-defined function that can be used to obtain a random non-negative integer less than *n*:

```
function randint(n) {
    return int(n * rand())
}
```

The multiplication produces a random number greater than zero and less than n. Using `int`, this result is made into an integer between zero and n − 1, inclusive.

The following example uses a similar function to produce random integers between one and *n*. This program prints a new random number for each input record:

```
# Function to roll a simulated die.
function roll(n) { return 1 + int(rand() * n) }

# Roll 3 six-sided dice and
# print total number of points.
{
    printf("%d points\n",
            roll(6)+roll(6)+roll(6))
}
```

---

* The C version of `rand` is known to produce fairly poor sequences of random numbers. However, nothing requires that an *awk* implementation use the C `rand` to implement the *awk* version of `rand`. In fact, *gawk* uses the BSD `random` function, which is considerably better than `rand`, to produce random numbers.

In most *awk* implementations, including *gawk*, rand starts generating numbers from the same starting number, or *seed*, each time you run *awk*. Thus, a program generates the same results each time you run it. The numbers are random within one *awk* run but predictable from run to run. This is convenient for debugging, but if you want a program to do different things each time it is used, you must change the seed to a value that is different in each run. To do this, use srand.

srand([*x*])

The function srand sets the starting point, or seed, for generating random numbers to the value *x*.

Each seed value leads to a particular sequence of random numbers.* Thus, if the seed is set to the same value a second time, the same sequence of random numbers is produced again.

Different *awk* implementations use different random-number generators internally. Don't expect the same *awk* program to produce the same series of random numbers when executed by different versions of *awk*.

If the argument *x* is omitted, as in srand(), then the current date and time of day are used for a seed. This is the way to get random numbers that are truly unpredictable.

The return value of srand is the previous seed. This makes it easy to keep track of the seeds in case you need to consistently reproduce sequences of random numbers.

String-Manipulation Functions

The functions in this section look at or change the text of one or more strings. Optional parameters are enclosed in square brackets ([ ]). Those functions that are specific to *gawk* are marked with a pound sign (#):

asort(*source* [, *dest*]) #

asort is a *gawk*-specific extension, returning the number of elements in the array *source*. The contents of *source* are sorted using *gawk*'s normal rules for comparing values, and the indices of the sorted values of *source* are replaced with sequential integers starting with one. If the optional array *dest* is speci-

---

* Computer-generated random numbers really are not truly random. They are technically known as "pseudorandom." This means that while the numbers in a sequence appear to be random, you can in fact generate the same sequence of random numbers over and over again.

fied, then *source* is duplicated into *dest*. *dest* is then sorted, leaving the indices of *source* unchanged. For example, if the contents of a are as follows:

```
a["last"] = "de"
a["first"] = "sac"
a["middle"] = "cul"
```

A call to asort:

```
asort(a)
```

results in the following contents of a:

```
a[1] = "cul"
a[2] = "de"
a[3] = "sac"
```

The asort function is described in more detail in the section "Sorting Array Values and Indices with gawk" in Chapter 7, *Arrays in awk*. asort is a *gawk* extension; it is not available in compatibility mode (see the section "Command-Line Options" in Chapter 11, *Running awk and gawk*).

index(*in, find*)

This searches the string *in* for the first occurrence of the string *find*, and returns the position in characters at which that occurrence begins in the string *in*. Consider the following example:

```
$ awk 'BEGIN { print index("peanut", "an") }'
3
```

If *find* is not found, index returns zero. (Remember that string indices in *awk* start at one.)

length([*string*])

This returns the number of characters in *string*. If *string* is a number, the length of the digit string representing that number is returned. For example, length("abcde") is 5. By contrast, length(15 * 35) works ·out to 3. In this example, 15 * 35 = 525, and 525 is then converted to the string "525", which has three characters.

If no argument is supplied, length returns the length of $0.

 In older versions of *awk*, the length function could be called without any parentheses. Doing so is marked as "deprecated" in the POSIX standard. This means that while a program can do this, it is a feature that can eventually be removed from a future version of the standard. Therefore, for programs to be maximally portable, always supply the parentheses.

match(*string, regexp* [, *array*])

The match function searches *string* for the longest, leftmost substring matched by the regular expression, *regexp*. It returns the character position, or *index*, at which that substring begins (one, if it starts at the beginning of *string*). If no match is found, it returns zero.

The order of the first two arguments is backwards from most other string functions that work with regular expressions, such as sub and gsub. It might help to remember that for match, the order is the same as for the ~ operator: *string* ~ *regexp*.

The match function sets the built-in variable RSTART to the index. It also sets the built-in variable RLENGTH to the length in characters of the matched substring. If no match is found, RSTART is set to zero, and RLENGTH to −1.

For example:

```
{
    if ($1 == "FIND")
        regex = $2
    else {
        where = match($0, regex)
        if (where != 0)
            print "Match of", regex, "found at",
                            where, "in", $0
    }
}
```

This program looks for lines that match the regular expression stored in the variable regex. This regular expression can be changed. If the first word on a line is FIND, regex is changed to be the second word on that line. Therefore, if given:

```
FIND ru+n
My program runs
but not very quickly
FIND Melvin
JF+KM
This line is property of Reality Engineering Co.
Melvin was here.
```

awk prints:

```
Match of ru+n found at 12 in My program runs
Match of Melvin found at 1 in Melvin was here.
```

If *array* is present, it is cleared, and then the 0th element of *array* is set to the entire portion of *string* matched by *regexp*. If *regexp* contains parentheses, the integer-indexed elements of *array* are set to contain the portion of *string* matching the corresponding parenthesized subexpression. For example:

```
$ echo foooobazbarrrrr |
> gawk '{ match($0, /(fo+).+(ba*r)/, arr)
>           print arr[1], arr[2] }'
foooo barrrrr
```

The *array* argument to match is a *gawk* extension. In compatibility mode (see
the section "Command-Line Options" in Chapter 11), using a third argument is
a fatal error.

split(*string, array* [, *fieldsep*])

> This function divides *string* into pieces separated by *fieldsep* and stores the
> pieces in *array*. The first piece is stored in array[1], the second piece in
> array[2], and so forth. The string value of the third argument, *fieldsep*, is a
> regexp describing where to split *string* (much as FS can be a regexp describ-
> ing where to split input records). If *fieldsep* is omitted, the value of FS is used.
> split returns the number of elements created. If *string* does not match *field-
> sep*, *array* is empty and split returns zero.

> The split function splits strings into pieces in a manner similar to the way
> input lines are split into fields. For example:

```
split("cul-de-sac", a, "-")
```

> splits the string cul-de-sac into three fields using – as the separator. It sets the
> contents of the array a as follows:

```
a[1] = "cul"
a[2] = "de"
a[3] = "sac"
```

> The value returned by this call to split is three.

> As with input field-splitting, when the value of *fieldsep* is " ", leading and
> trailing whitespace is ignored, and the elements are separated by runs of
> whitespace. Also as with input field-splitting, if *fieldsep* is the null string, each
> individual character in the string is split into its own array element. (This is a
> *gawk*-specific extension.)

> Modern implementations of *awk*, including *gawk*, allow the third argument to
> be a regexp constant (/abc/) as well as a string. (d.c.) The POSIX standard
> allows this as well.

> Before splitting the string, split deletes any previously existing elements in
> the array *array*. If *string* does not match *fieldsep* at all, *array* has one element
> only. The value of that element is the original *string*.

sprintf(*format, expression1, ...*)

This returns (without printing) the string that `printf` would have printed out with the same arguments (see the section "Using printf Statements for Fancier Printing" in Chapter 4, *Printing Output*). For example:

```
pival = sprintf("pi = %.2f (approx.)", 22/7)
```

assigns the string `"pi = 3.14 (approx.)"` to the variable `pival`.

strtonum(*str*) #

Examines *str* and returns its numeric value. If *str* begins with a leading 0, `strtonum` assumes that *str* is an octal number. If *str* begins with a leading 0x or 0X, `strtonum` assumes that *str* is a hexadecimal number. For example:

```
$ echo 0x11 | gawk '{ printf "%d\n", strtonum($1) }'
17
```

Using the `strtonum` function is *not* the same as adding zero to a string value; the automatic coercion of strings to numbers works only for decimal data, not for octal or hexadecimal.*

`strtonum` is a *gawk* extension; it is not available in compatibility mode (see the section "Command-Line Options" in Chapter 11).

sub(*regexp, replacement* [, *target*])

The `sub` function alters the value of *target*. It searches this value, which is treated as a string, for the leftmost, longest substring matched by the regular expression *regexp*. Then the entire string is changed by replacing the matched text with *replacement*. The modified string becomes the new value of *target*.

This function is peculiar because *target* is not simply used to compute a value, and not just any expression will do—it must be a variable, field, or array element so that `sub` can store a modified value there. If this argument is omitted, then the default is to use and alter $0. For example:

```
str = "water, water, everywhere"
sub(/at/, "ith", str)
```

sets str to `"wither, water, everywhere"`, by replacing the leftmost longest occurrence of at with ith.

The `sub` function returns the number of substitutions made (either one or zero).

---

* Unless you use the *--non-decimal-data* option, which isn't recommended. See the section "Allowing Nondecimal Input Data" in Chapter 10, *Advanced Features of gawk*, for more information.

If the special character & appears in *replacement*, it stands for the precise sub-string that was matched by *regexp*. (If the regexp can match more than one string, then this precise substring may vary.) For example:

```
{ sub(/candidate/, "& and his wife"); print }
```

changes the first occurrence of candidate to candidate and his wife on each input line. Here is another example:

```
$ awk 'BEGIN {
>       str = "daabaaa"
>       sub(/a+/, "C&C", str)
>       print str
> }'
dCaaCbaaa
```

This shows how & can represent a nonconstant string and also illustrates the "leftmost, longest" rule in regexp matching (see the section "How Much Text Matches?" in Chapter 2, *Regular Expressions*).

The effect of this special character (&) can be turned off by putting a backslash before it in the string. As usual, to insert one backslash in the string, you must write two backslashes. Therefore, write \\& in a string constant to include a literal & in the replacement. For example, the following shows how to replace the first | on each line with an &:

```
{ sub(/\|/, "\\&"); print }
```

As mentioned, the third argument to sub must be a variable, field or array reference. Some versions of *awk* allow the third argument to be an expression that is not an *lvalue*. In such a case, sub still searches for the pattern and returns zero or one, but the result of the substitution (if any) is thrown away because there is no place to put it. Such versions of *awk* accept expressions such as the following:

```
sub(/USA/, "United States", "the USA and Canada")
```

For historical compatibility, *gawk* accepts erroneous code, such as in the previous example. However, using any other nonchangeable object as the third parameter causes a fatal error and your program will not run.

Finally, if the *regexp* is not a regexp constant, it is converted into a string, and then the value of that string is treated as the regexp to match.

gsub(*regexp, replacement* [, *target*])

This is similar to the sub function, except gsub replaces *all* of the longest, left-most, *nonoverlapping* matching substrings it can find. The g in gsub stands for "global," which means replace everywhere. For example:

```
{ gsub(/Britain/, "United Kingdom"); print }
```

replaces all occurrences of the string Britain with United Kingdom for all input records.

The gsub function returns the number of substitutions made. If the variable to search and alter (*target*) is omitted, then the entire input record ($0) is used. As in sub, the characters & and \ are special, and the third argument must be assignable.

gensub(*regexp, replacement, how* [, *target*]) #

gensub is a general substitution function. Like sub and gsub, it searches the target string *target* for matches of the regular expression *regexp*. Unlike sub and gsub, the modified string is returned as the result of the function and the original target string is *not* changed. If *how* is a string beginning with g or G, then it replaces all matches of *regexp* with *replacement*. Otherwise, *how* is treated as a number that indicates which match of *regexp* to replace. If no *target* is supplied, $0 is used.

gensub provides an additional feature that is not available in sub or gsub: the ability to specify components of a regexp in the replacement text. This is done by using parentheses in the regexp to mark the components and then specifying \\N in the replacement text, where *N* is a digit from 1 to 9. For example:

```
$ gawk '
> BEGIN {
>        a = "abc def"
>        b = gensub(/(.+) (.+)/, "\\2 \\1", "g", a)
>        print b
> }'
def abc
```

As with sub, you must type two backslashes in order to get one into the string. In the replacement text, the sequence \0 represents the entire matched text, as does the character &.

The following example shows how you can use the third argument to control which match of the regexp should be changed:

```
$ echo a b c a b c |
> gawk '{ print gensub(/a/, "AA", 2) }'
a b c AA b c
```

In this case, $0 is used as the default target string. gensub returns the new string as its result, which is passed directly to print for printing.

If the *how* argument is a string that does not begin with g or G, or if it is a number that is less than or equal to zero, only one substitution is performed. If *how* is zero, *gawk* issues a warning message.

If *regexp* does not match *target*, gensub's return value is the original unchanged value of *target*.

gensub is a *gawk* extension; it is not available in compatibility mode (see the section "Command-Line Options" in Chapter 11).

substr(*string*, *start* [, *length*])

This returns a *length*-character-long substring of *string*, starting at character number *start*. The first character of a string is character number one.* For example, substr("washington", 5, 3) returns "ing".

If *length* is not present, this function returns the whole suffix of *string* that begins at character number *start*. For example, substr("washington", 5) returns "ington". The whole suffix is also returned if *length* is greater than the number of characters remaining in the string, counting from character *start*.

The string returned by substr *cannot* be assigned. Thus, it is a mistake to attempt to change a portion of a string, as shown in the following example:

```
string = "abcdef"
# try to get "abCDEf", won't work
substr(string, 3, 3) = "CDE"
```

It is also a mistake to use substr as the third argument of sub or gsub:

```
gsub(/xyz/, "pdq", substr($0, 5, 20))  # WRONG
```

(Some commercial versions of *awk* do in fact let you use substr this way, but doing so is not portable.)

If you need to replace bits and pieces of a string, combine substr with string concatenation, in the following manner:

```
string = "abcdef"
...
string = substr(string, 1, 2) "CDE" substr(string, 6)
```

tolower(*string*)

This returns a copy of *string*, with each uppercase character in the string replaced with its corresponding lowercase character. Nonalphabetic characters are left unchanged. For example, tolower("MiXeD cAsE 123") returns "mixed case 123".

toupper(*string*)

This returns a copy of *string*, with each lowercase character in the string replaced with its corresponding uppercase character. Nonalphabetic characters are left unchanged. For example, toupper("MiXeD cAsE 123") returns "MIXED CASE 123".

---

* This is different from C and C++, in which the first character is number zero.

More about \ and & with sub, gsub, and gensub

When using sub, gsub, or gensub, and trying to get literal backslashes and amper-
sands into the replacement text, you need to remember that there are several levels of *escape processing* going on.

First, there is the *lexical* level, which is when *awk* reads your program and builds
an internal copy of it that can be executed. Then there is the runtime *level*, which
is when *awk* actually scans the replacement string to determine what to generate.

At both levels, *awk* looks for a defined set of characters that can come after a
backslash. At the lexical level, it looks for the escape sequences listed in the section "Escape Sequences" in Chapter 2. Thus, for every \ that *awk* processes at the
runtime level, type two backslashes at the lexical level. When a character that is
not valid for an escape sequence follows the \, Unix *awk* and *gawk* both simply
remove the initial \ and put the next character into the string. Thus, for example,
"a\qb" is treated as "aqb".

At the runtime level, the various functions handle sequences of \ and & differently.
The situation is (sadly) somewhat complex. Historically, the sub and gsub functions
treated the two character sequence \& specially; this sequence was replaced in the
generated text with a single &. Any other \ within the *replacement* string that did
not precede an & was passed through unchanged. This is illustrated in Table 8-1.

Table 8-1. Historical Escape Sequence Processing for sub and gsub

You type	sub sees	sub generates
\&	&	The matched text
\\&	\&	A literal &
\\\&	\&	A literal &
\\\\&	\\&	A literal \&
\\\\\&	\\&	A literal \&
\\\\\\&	\\\&	A literal \\&
\\q	\q	A literal \q

Table 8-1 shows both the lexical-level processing, where an odd number of backslashes becomes an even number at the runtime level, as well as the runtime processing done by sub. (For the sake of simplicity, the rest of the following tables
only show the case of even numbers of backslashes entered at the lexical level.)

The problem with the historical approach is that there is no way to get a literal \
followed by the matched text.

The 1992 POSIX standard attempted to fix this problem. The standard says that sub
and gsub look for either a \ or an & after the \. If either one follows a \, that

character is output literally. The interpretation of \ and & then becomes as shown in Table 8-2.

Table 8-2. 1992 POSIX Rules for sub and gsub Escape Sequence Processing

You type	sub sees	sub generates
&	&	The matched text
\\&	\&	A literal &
\\\\&	\\&	A literal \, then the matched text
\\\\\\&	\\\&	A literal \&

This appears to solve the problem. Unfortunately, the phrasing of the standard is unusual. It says, in effect, that \ turns off the special meaning of any following character, but for anything other than \ and &, such special meaning is undefined. This wording leads to two problems:

- Backslashes must now be doubled in the *replacement* string, breaking historical *awk* programs.

- To make sure that an *awk* program is portable, *every* character in the *replacement* string must be preceded with a backslash.*

The POSIX standard is under revision. Because of the problems just listed, proposed text for the revised standard reverts to rules that correspond more closely to the original existing practice. The proposed rules have special cases that make it possible to produce a \ preceding the matched text:

In a nutshell, at the runtime level, there are now three special sequences of characters (\\\&, \\&, and \&) whereas historically there was only one. However, as in the historical case, any \ that is not part of one of these three sequences is not special and appears in the output literally.

gawk 3.0 and 3.1 follow these proposed POSIX rules for sub and gsub. Whether these proposed rules will actually become codified into the standard is unknown at this point. Subsequent *gawk* releases will track the standard and implement whatever the final version specifies; this book will be updated as well.†

The rules for gensub are considerably simpler. At the runtime level, whenever *gawk* sees a \, if the following character is a digit, then the text that matched the corresponding parenthesized subexpression is placed in the generated output. Otherwise, no matter what character follows the \, it appears in the generated text and the \ does not, as shown in Table 8-3.

---

* This consequence was certainly unintended.

† As this book went to press, we learned that the POSIX standard will not use these rules. However, it was too late to change *gawk* for the 3.1 release. *gawk* behaves as described here.

Table 8-3. Escape Sequence Processing for gensub

You type	gensub sees	gensub generates
&	&	The matched text
\\&	\&	A literal &
\\\\	\\	A literal \
\\\\&	\\&	A literal \, then the matched text
\\\\\\&	\\\&	A literal \&
\\q	\q	A literal q

Because of the complexity of the lexical and runtime level processing and the special cases for sub and gsub, we recommend the use of *gawk* and gensub when you have to do substitutions.

Matching the Null String

In *awk*, the * operator can match the null string. This is particularly important for the sub, gsub, and gensub functions. For example:

```
$ echo abc | awk '{ gsub(/m*/, "X"); print }'
XaXbXcX
```

Although this makes a certain amount of sense, it can be surprising.

Input/Output Functions

The following functions relate to input/output (I/O). Optional parameters are enclosed in square brackets ([ ]):

close(*filename* [, *how*])

Close the file *filename* for input or output. Alternatively, the argument may be a shell command that was used for creating a coprocess, or for redirecting to or from a pipe; then the coprocess or pipe is closed. See the section "Closing Input and Output Redirections" in Chapter 4 for more information.

When closing a coprocess, it is occasionally useful to first close one end of the two-way pipe and then to close the other. This is done by providing a second argument to close. This second argument should be one of the two string values "to" or "from", indicating which end of the pipe to close. Case in the string does not matter. See the section "Two-Way Communications with Another Process" in Chapter 10, which discusses this feature in more detail and gives an example.

`fflush([`*`filename`*`])`

> Flush any buffered output associated with *filename*, which is either a file opened for writing or a shell command for redirecting output to a pipe or coprocess.
>
> Many utility programs *buffer* their output; i.e., they save information to write to a disk file or terminal in memory until there is enough for it to be worthwhile to send the data to the output device. This is often more efficient than writing every little bit of information as soon as it is ready. However, sometimes it is necessary to force a program to *flush* its buffers; that is, write the information to its destination, even if a buffer is not full. This is the purpose of the `fflush` function—*gawk* also buffers its output and the `fflush` function forces *gawk* to flush its buffers.
>
> `fflush` was added to the Bell Laboratories research version of *awk* in 1994; it is not part of the POSIX standard and is not available if *--posix* has been specified on the command line (see the section "Command-Line Options" in Chapter 11).
>
> *gawk* extends the `fflush` function in two ways. The first is to allow no argument at all. In this case, the buffer for the standard output is flushed. The second is to allow the null string (`""`) as the argument. In this case, the buffers for *all* open output files and pipes are flushed.
>
> `fflush` returns zero if the buffer is successfully flushed; otherwise, it returns −1. In the case where all buffers are flushed, the return value is zero only if all buffers were flushed successfully. Otherwise, it is −1, and *gawk* warns about the problem *filename*.
>
> *gawk* also issues a warning message if you attempt to flush a file or pipe that was opened for reading (such as with `getline`), or if *filename* is not an open file, pipe, or coprocess. In such a case, `fflush` returns −1, as well.

`system(`*`command`*`)`

> Executes operating-system commands and then return to the *awk* program. The `system` function executes the command given by the string *command*. It returns the status returned by the command that was executed as its value.
>
> For example, if the following fragment of code is put in your *awk* program:
>
> ```
> END {
>     system("date | mail -s 'awk run done' root")
> }
> ```
>
> the system administrator is sent mail when the *awk* program finishes processing input and begins its end-of-input processing.

Note that redirecting `print` or `printf` into a pipe is often enough to accomplish your task. If you need to run many commands, it is more efficient to simply print them down a pipeline to the shell:

```
while (more stuff to do)
    print command | "/bin/sh"
close("/bin/sh")
```

However, if your *awk* program is interactive, `system` is useful for cranking up large self-contained programs, such as a shell or an editor. Some operating systems cannot implement the `system` function. `system` causes a fatal error if it is not supported.

Interactive Versus Noninteractive Buffering

As a side point, buffering issues can be even more confusing, depending upon whether your program is *interactive*, i.e., communicating with a user sitting at a keyboard.[*]

Interactive programs generally *line buffer* their output; i.e., they write out every line. Noninteractive programs wait until they have a full buffer, which may be many lines of output. Here is an example of the difference:

```
$ awk '{ print $1 + $2 }'
1 1
2
2 3
5
Ctrl-d
```

Each line of output is printed immediately. Compare that behavior with this example:

```
$ awk '{ print $1 + $2 }' | cat
1 1
2 3
Ctrl-d
2
5
```

Here, no output is printed until after the Ctrl-d is typed, because it is all buffered and sent down the pipe to *cat* in one shot.

---

[*] A program is interactive if the standard output is connected to a terminal device.

Controlling Output Buffering with system

The `fflush` function provides explicit control over output buffering for individual files and pipes. However, its use is not portable to many other *awk* implementations. An alternative method to flush output buffers is to call `system` with a null string as its argument:

```
system("")   # flush output
```

gawk treats this use of the `system` function as a special case and is smart enough not to run a shell (or other command interpreter) with the empty command. Therefore, with *gawk*, this idiom is not only useful, it is also efficient. While this method should work with other *awk* implementations, it does not necessarily avoid starting an unnecessary shell. (Other implementations may only flush the buffer associated with the standard output and not necessarily all buffered output.)

If you think about what a programmer expects, it makes sense that `system` should flush any pending output. The following program:

```
BEGIN {
    print "first print"
    system("echo system echo")
    print "second print"
}
```

must print:

```
first print
system echo
second print
```

and not:

```
system echo
first print
second print
```

If *awk* did not flush its buffers before calling `system`, you would see the latter (undesirable) output.

Using gawk's Timestamp Functions

awk programs are commonly used to process log files containing timestamp information, indicating when a particular log record was written. Many programs log their timestamp in the form returned by the `time` system call, which is the number of seconds since a particular epoch. On POSIX-compliant systems, it is the number of seconds since 1970-01-01 00:00:00 UTC, not counting leap seconds.[*] All known POSIX-compliant systems support timestamps from 0 through $2^{31} - 1$, which is

---

[*] See the Glossary, especially the entries "Epoch" and "UTC."

sufficient to represent times through 2038-01-19 03:14:07 UTC. Many systems support a wider range of timestamps, including negative timestamps that represent times before the epoch.

In order to make it easier to process such log files and to produce useful reports, *gawk* provides the following functions for working with timestamps. They are *gawk* extensions; they are not specified in the POSIX standard, nor are they in any other known version of *awk*.* Optional parameters are enclosed in square brackets ([ ]):

systime()

> This function returns the current time as the number of seconds since the system epoch. On POSIX systems, this is the number of seconds since 1970-01-01 00:00:00 UTC, not counting leap seconds. It may be a different number on other systems.

mktime(*datespec*)

> This function turns *datespec* into a timestamp in the same form as is returned by systime. It is similar to the function of the same name in ISO C. The argument, *datespec*, is a string of the form "YYYY MM DD HH MM SS [DST]". The string consists of six or seven numbers representing, respectively, the full year including century, the month from 1 to 12, the day of the month from 1 to 31, the hour of the day from 0 to 23, the minute from 0 to 59, the second from 0 to 60,† and an optional daylight-savings flag.

> The values of these numbers need not be within the ranges specified; for example, an hour of −1 means 1 hour before midnight. The origin-zero Gregorian calendar is assumed, with year 0 preceding year 1 and year −1 preceding year 0. The time is assumed to be in the local timezone. If the daylight-savings flag is positive, the time is assumed to be daylight savings time; if zero, the time is assumed to be standard time; and if negative (the default), mktime attempts to determine whether daylight savings time is in effect for the specified time.

> If *datespec* does not contain enough elements or if the resulting time is out of range, mktime returns −1.

strftime([*format* [, *timestamp*]])

> This function returns a string. It is similar to the function of the same name in ISO C. The time specified by *timestamp* is used to produce a string, based on the contents of the *format* string. The *timestamp* is in the same format as the

---

* The GNU *date* utility can also do many of the things described here. Its use may be preferable for simple time-related operations in shell scripts.

† Occasionally there are minutes in a year with a leap second, which is why the seconds can go up to 60.

value returned by the systime function. If no *timestamp* argument is supplied, *gawk* uses the current time of day as the timestamp. If no *format* argument is supplied, strftime uses "%a %b %d %H:%M:%S %Z %Y". This format string produces output that is (almost) equivalent to that of the *date* utility. (Versions of *gawk* prior to 3.0 require the *format* argument.)

The systime function allows you to compare a timestamp from a log file with the current time of day. In particular, it is easy to determine how long ago a particular record was logged. It also allows you to produce log records using the "seconds since the epoch" format.

The mktime function allows you to convert a textual representation of a date and time into a timestamp. This makes it easy to do before/after comparisons of dates and times, particularly when dealing with date and time data coming from an external source, such as a log file.

The strftime function allows you to easily turn a timestamp into human-readable information. It is similar in nature to the sprintf function (see the section "String-Manipulation Functions" earlier in this chapter), in that it copies nonformat specification characters verbatim to the returned string, while substituting date and time values for format specifications in the *format* string.

strftime is guaranteed by the 1999 ISO C standard* to support the following date format specifications:

%a   The locale's abbreviated weekday name.

%A   The locale's full weekday name.

%b   The locale's abbreviated month name.

%B   The locale's full month name.

%c   The locale's "appropriate" date and time representation. (This is %A %B %d %T %Y in the "C" locale.)

%C   The century. This is the year divided by 100 and truncated to the next lower integer.

%d   The day of the month as a decimal number (01–31).

%D   Equivalent to specifying %m/%d/%y.

%e   The day of the month, padded with a space if it is only one digit.

---

* As this is a recent standard, not every system's strftime necessarily supports all of the conversions listed here.

%F Equivalent to specifying %Y-%m-%d. This is the ISO 8601 date format.

%g The year modulo 100 of the ISO week number, as a decimal number (00–99). For example, January 1, 1993 is in week 53 of 1992. Thus, the year of its ISO week number is 1992, even though its year is 1993. Similarly, December 31, 1973 is in week 1 of 1974. Thus, the year of its ISO week number is 1974, even though its year is 1973.

%G The full year of the ISO week number, as a decimal number.

%h Equivalent to %b.

%H The hour (24-hour clock) as a decimal number (00–23).

%I The hour (12-hour clock) as a decimal number (01–12).

%j The day of the year as a decimal number (001–366).

%m The month as a decimal number (01–12).

%M The minute as a decimal number (00–59).

%n A newline character (ASCII LF).

%p The locale's equivalent of the AM/PM designations associated with a 12-hour clock.

%r The locale's 12-hour clock time. (This is %I:%M:%S %p in the "C" locale.)

%R Equivalent to specifying %H:%M.

%S The second as a decimal number (00–60).

%t A tab character.

%T Equivalent to specifying %H:%M:%S.

%u The weekday as a decimal number (1–7). Monday is day one.

%U The week number of the year (the first Sunday as the first day of week one) as a decimal number (00–53).

%V The week number of the year (the first Monday as the first day of week one) as a decimal number (01–53). The method for determining the week number is as specified by ISO 8601. (To wit: if the week containing January 1 has four or more days in the new year, then it is week one; otherwise, it is week 53 of the previous year and the next week is week one.)

%w The weekday as a decimal number (0–6). Sunday is day zero.

%W The week number of the year (the first Monday as the first day of week one) as a decimal number (00–53).

%x The locale's "appropriate" date representation. (This is %A %B %d %Y in the "C" locale.)

%X The locale's "appropriate" time representation. (This is %T in the "C" locale.)

%y The year modulo 100 as a decimal number (00–99).

%Y The full year as a decimal number (e.g., 1995).

%z The time zone offset in a +HHMM format (e.g., the format necessary to produce RFC 822/RFC 1036 date headers).

%Z The time zone name or abbreviation; no characters if no time zone is determinable.

%Ec %EC %Ex %EX %Ey %EY %Od %Oe %OH
%OI %Om %OM %OS %Ou %OU %OV %Ow %OW %Oy

"Alternate representations" for the specifications that use only the second letter (%c, %C, and so on).* (These facilitate compliance with the POSIX *date* utility.)

%% A literal %.

If a conversion specifier is not one of the above, the behavior is undefined.†

Informally, a *locale* is the geographic place in which a program is meant to run. For example, a common way to abbreviate the date September 4, 1991 in the United States is "9/4/91." In many countries in Europe, however, it is abbreviated "4.9.91." Thus, the %x specification in a "US" locale might produce 9/4/91, while in a "EUROPE" locale, it might produce 4.9.91. The ISO C standard defines a default "C" locale, which is an environment that is typical of what most C programmers are used to.

A public-domain C version of strftime is supplied with *gawk* for systems that are not yet fully standards-compliant. It supports all of the just listed format specifications. If that version is used to compile *gawk* (see Appendix B, *Installing gawk*), then the following additional format specifications are available:

%k The hour (24-hour clock) as a decimal number (0–23). Single-digit numbers are padded with a space.

%l The hour (12-hour clock) as a decimal number (1–12). Single-digit numbers are padded with a space.

---

* If you don't understand any of this, don't worry about it; these facilities are meant to make it easier to "internationalize" programs. Other internationalization features are described in Chapter 9, *Internationalization with gawk*.

† This is because ISO C leaves the behavior of the C version of strftime undefined and *gawk* uses the system's version of strftime if it's there. Typically, the conversion specifier either does not appear in the returned string or appears literally.

%N The "Emperor/Era" name. Equivalent to %C.

%o The "Emperor/Era" year. Equivalent to %y.

%s The time as a decimal timestamp in seconds since the epoch.

%v The date in VMS format (e.g., 20-JUN-1991).

Additionally, the alternate representations are recognized but their normal representations are used.

This example is an _awk_ implementation of the POSIX _date_ utility. Normally, the _date_ utility prints the current date and time of day in a well-known format. However, if you provide an argument to it that begins with a +, _date_ copies nonformat specifier characters to the standard output and interprets the current time according to the format specifiers in the string. For example:

```
$ date '+Today is %A, %B %d, %Y.'
Today is Thursday, September 14, 2000.
```

Here is the _gawk_ version of the _date_ utility. It has a shell "wrapper" to handle the _-u_ option, which requires that _date_ run as if the time zone is set to UTC:

```
#! /bin/sh
#
# date --- approximate the P1003.2 'date' command

case $1 in
-u) TZ=UTC0      # use UTC
    export TZ
    shift ;;
esac

gawk 'BEGIN {
    format = "%a %b %d %H:%M:%S %Z %Y"
    exitval = 0

    if (ARGC > 2)
        exitval = 1
    else if (ARGC == 2) {
        format = ARGV[1]
        if (format ~ /^\+/)
            format = substr(format, 2)    # remove leading +
    }
    print strftime(format)
    exit exitval
}' "$@"
```

Bit-Manipulation Functions of gawk

Many languages provide the ability to perform *bitwise* operations on two integer numbers. In other words, the operation is performed on each successive pair of bits in the operands. Three common operations are bitwise AND, OR, and XOR. The operations are described in Table 8-4.

Table 8-4. Bitwise Operations

| | Bit Operator | | | | | |
	AND		OR		XOR	
Operands	0	1	0	1	0	1
0	0	0	0	1	0	1
1	0	1	1	1	1	0

As you can see, the result of an AND operation is 1 only when *both* bits are 1. The result of an OR operation is 1 if *either* bit is 1. The result of an XOR operation is 1 if either bit is 1, but not both. The next operation is the *complement*; the complement of 1 is 0 and the complement of 0 is 1. Thus, this operation "flips" all the bits of a given value.

Finally, two other common operations are to shift the bits left or right. For example, if you have a bit string 10111001 and you shift it right by three bits, you end up with 00010111.* If you start over again with 10111001 and shift it left by three bits, you end up with 11001000. *gawk* provides built-in functions that implement the bitwise operations just described. They are:

and(*v1, v2*)
> Returns the bitwise AND of the values provided by *v1* and *v2*.

or(*v1, v2*)
> Returns the bitwise OR of the values provided by *v1* and *v2*.

xor(*v1, v2*)
> Returns the bitwise XOR of the values provided by *v1* and *v2*.

compl(*val*)
> Returns the bitwise complement of *val*.

---

* This example shows that 0's come in on the left side. For *gawk*, this is always true, but in some languages, it's possible to have the left side fill with 1's. Caveat emptor.

lshift(*val, count*)

   Returns the value of *val*, shifted left by *count* bits.

rshift(*val, count*)

   Returns the value of *val*, shifted right by *count* bits.

For all of these functions, first the double-precision floating-point value is converted to a C unsigned long, then the bitwise operation is performed and then the result is converted back into a C double. (If you don't understand this paragraph, don't worry about it.)

Here is a user-defined function (see the section "User-Defined Functions" later in this chapter) that illustrates the use of these functions:

```
# bits2str --- turn a byte into readable 1's and 0's

function bits2str(bits,          data, mask)
{
    if (bits == 0)
        return "0"

    mask = 1
    for (; bits != 0; bits = rshift(bits, 1))
        data = (and(bits, mask) ? "1" : "0") data

    while ((length(data) % 8) != 0)
        data = "0" data

    return data
}

BEGIN {
    printf "123 = %s\n", bits2str(123)
    printf "0123 = %s\n", bits2str(0123)
    printf "0x99 = %s\n", bits2str(0x99)
    comp = compl(0x99)
    printf "compl(0x99) = %#x = %s\n", comp, bits2str(comp)
    shift = lshift(0x99, 2)
    printf "lshift(0x99, 2) = %#x = %s\n", shift, bits2str(shift)
    shift = rshift(0x99, 2)
    printf "rshift(0x99, 2) = %#x = %s\n", shift, bits2str(shift)
}
```

This program produces the following output when run:

```
$ gawk -f testbits.awk
123 = 01111011
0123 = 01010011
0x99 = 10011001
compl(0x99) = 0xffffff66 = 11111111111111111111111101100110
lshift(0x99, 2) = 0x264 = 0000001001100100
rshift(0x99, 2) = 0x26 = 00100110
```

The `bits2str` function turns a binary number into a string. The number 1 represents a binary value where the rightmost bit is set to 1. Using this mask, the function repeatedly checks the rightmost bit. ANDing the mask with the value indicates whether the rightmost bit is 1 or not. If so, a `"1"` is concatenated onto the front of the string. Otherwise, a `"0"` is added. The value is then shifted right by one bit and the loop continues until there are no more 1 bits.

If the initial value is zero it returns a simple `"0"`. Otherwise, at the end, it pads the value with zeros to represent multiples of 8-bit quantities. This is typical in modern computers.

The main code in the BEGIN rule shows the difference between the decimal and octal values for the same numbers (see the section "Octal and Hexadecimal Numbers" in Chapter 5, *Expressions*), and then demonstrates the results of the `compl`, `lshift`, and `rshift` functions.

Using gawk's String-Translation Functions

gawk provides facilities for internationalizing *awk* programs. These include the functions described in the following list. The descriptions here are purposely brief. See Chapter 9 for the full story. Optional parameters are enclosed in square brackets ([ ]):

`dcgettext(string [, domain [, category]])`
> This function returns the translation of *string* in text domain *domain* for locale category *category*. The default value for *domain* is the current value of TEXTDOMAIN. The default value for *category* is `"LC_MESSAGES"`.

`bindtextdomain(directory [, domain])`
> This function allows you to specify the directory in which *gawk* will look for message translation files, in case they will not or cannot be placed in the "standard" locations (e.g., during testing). It returns the directory in which *domain* is "bound."
>
> The default *domain* is the value of TEXTDOMAIN. If *directory* is the null string (`""`), then `bindtextdomain` returns the current binding for the given *domain*.

User-Defined Functions

Complicated *awk* programs can often be simplified by defining your own functions. User-defined functions can be called just like built-in ones (see the section "Function Calls" in Chapter 5), but it is up to you to define them, i.e., to tell *awk* what they should do.

Function Definition Syntax

Definitions of functions can appear anywhere between the rules of an *awk* program. Thus, the general form of an *awk* program is extended to include sequences of rules *and* user-defined function definitions. There is no need to put the definition of a function before all uses of the function. This is because *awk* reads the entire program before starting to execute any of it.

The definition of a function named *name* looks like this:

```
function name(parameter-list)
{
    body-of-function
}
```

name is the name of the function to define. A valid function name is like a valid variable name: a sequence of letters, digits, and underscores that doesn't start with a digit. Within a single *awk* program, any particular name can only be used as a variable, array, or function.

parameter-list is a list of the function's arguments and local variable names, separated by commas. When the function is called, the argument names are used to hold the argument values given in the call. The local variables are initialized to the empty string. A function cannot have two parameters with the same name, nor may it have a parameter with the same name as the function itself.

The *body-of-function* consists of *awk* statements. It is the most important part of the definition, because it says what the function should actually *do*. The argument names exist to give the body a way to talk about the arguments; local variables exist to give the body places to keep temporary values.

Argument names are not distinguished syntactically from local variable names. Instead, the number of arguments supplied when the function is called determines how many argument variables there are. Thus, if three argument values are given, the first three names in *parameter-list* are arguments and the rest are local variables.

It follows that if the number of arguments is not the same in all calls to the function, some of the names in *parameter-list* may be arguments on some occasions and local variables on others. Another way to think of this is that omitted arguments default to the null string.

Usually when you write a function, you know how many names you intend to use for arguments and how many you intend to use as local variables. It is conventional to place some extra space between the arguments and the local variables, in order to document how your function is supposed to be used.

During execution of the function body, the arguments and local variable values hide, or *shadow*, any variables of the same names used in the rest of the program. The shadowed variables are not accessible in the function definition, because there is no way to name them while their names have been taken away for the local variables. All other variables used in the *awk* program can be referenced or set normally in the function's body.

The arguments and local variables last only as long as the function body is executing. Once the body finishes, you can once again access the variables that were shadowed while the function was running.

The function body can contain expressions that call functions. They can even call this function, either directly or by way of another function. When this happens, we say the function is *recursive*. The act of a function calling itself is called *recursion*.

In many *awk* implementations, including *gawk*, the keyword function may be abbreviated func. However, POSIX only specifies the use of the keyword function. This actually has some practical implications. If *gawk* is in POSIX-compatibility mode (see the section "Command-Line Options" in Chapter 11), then the following statement does *not* define a function:

```
func foo() { a = sqrt($1) ; print a }
```

Instead it defines a rule that, for each record, concatenates the value of the variable func with the return value of the function foo. If the resulting string is non-null, the action is executed. This is probably not what is desired. (*awk* accepts this input as syntactically valid, because functions may be used before they are defined in *awk* programs.)

To ensure that your *awk* programs are portable, always use the keyword function when defining a function.

Function Definition Examples

Here is an example of a user-defined function, called myprint, that takes a number and prints it in a specific format:

```
function myprint(num)
{
     printf "%6.3g\n", num
}
```

To illustrate, here is an *awk* rule that uses our myprint function:

```
$3 > 0     { myprint($3) }
```

This program prints, in our special format, all the third fields that contain a positive number in our input. Therefore, when given the following:

```
 1.2   3.4    5.6   7.8
 9.10 11.12 -13.14 15.16
17.18 19.20  21.22 23.24
```

this program, using our function to format the results, prints:

```
 5.6
21.2
```

This function deletes all the elements in an array:

```
function delarray(a,    i)
{
    for (i in a)
        delete a[i]
}
```

When working with arrays, it is often necessary to delete all the elements in an array and start over with a new list of elements (see the section "The delete Statement" in Chapter 7). Instead of having to repeat this loop everywhere that you need to clear out an array, your program can just call `delarray`. (This guarantees portability. The use of `delete` *array* to delete the contents of an entire array is a nonstandard extension.)

The following is an example of a recursive function. It takes a string as an input parameter and returns the string in backwards order. Recursive functions must always have a test that stops the recursion. In this case, the recursion terminates when the starting position is zero, i.e., when there are no more characters left in the string:

```
function rev(str, start)
{
    if (start == 0)
        return ""

    return (substr(str, start, 1) rev(str, start - 1))
}
```

If this function is in a file named *rev.awk*, it can be tested this way:

```
$ echo "Don't Panic!" |
> gawk --source '{ print rev($0, length($0)) }' -f rev.awk
!cinaP t'noD
```

The C `ctime` function takes a timestamp and returns it in a string, formatted in a well-known fashion. The following example uses the built-in `strftime` function (see the section "Using gawk's Timestamp Functions" earlier in this chapter) to create an *awk* version of `ctime`:

```
# ctime.awk
#
# awk version of C ctime(3) function

function ctime(ts,      format)
{
    format = "%a %b %d %H:%M:%S %Z %Y"
    if (ts == 0)
        ts = systime()        # use current time as default
    return strftime(format, ts)
}
```

Calling User-Defined Functions

Calling a function means causing the function to run and do its job. A function call is an expression and its value is the value returned by the function.

A function call consists of the function name followed by the arguments in parentheses. *awk* expressions are what you write in the call for the arguments. Each time the call is executed, these expressions are evaluated, and the values are the actual arguments. For example, here is a call to foo with three arguments (the first being a string concatenation):

```
foo(x y, "lose", 4 * z)
```

 Whitespace characters (spaces and tabs) are not allowed between the function name and the open-parenthesis of the argument list. If you write whitespace by mistake, *awk* might think that you mean to concatenate a variable with an expression in parentheses. However, it notices that you used a function name and not a variable name, and reports an error.

When a function is called, it is given a *copy* of the values of its arguments. This is known as *call by value*. The caller may use a variable as the expression for the argument, but the called function does not know this—it only knows what value the argument had. For example, if you write the following code:

```
foo = "bar"
z = myfunc(foo)
```

then you should not think of the argument to myfunc as being "the variable foo." Instead, think of the argument as the string value "bar". If the function myfunc alters the values of its local variables, this has no effect on any other variables. Thus, if myfunc does this:

```
function myfunc(str)
{
    print str
    str = "zzz"
    print str
}
```

to change its first argument variable `str`, it does *not* change the value of `foo` in the caller. The role of `foo` in calling `myfunc` ended when its value (`"bar"`) was computed. If `str` also exists outside of `myfunc`, the function body cannot alter this outer value, because it is shadowed during the execution of `myfunc` and cannot be seen or changed from there.

However, when arrays are the parameters to functions, they are *not* copied. Instead, the array itself is made available for direct manipulation by the function. This is usually called *call by reference*. Changes made to an array parameter inside the body of a function *are* visible outside that function.

Changing an array parameter inside a function can be very dangerous if you do not watch what you are doing. For example:

```
function changeit(array, ind, nvalue)
{
    array[ind] = nvalue
}

BEGIN {
    a[1] = 1; a[2] = 2; a[3] = 3
    changeit(a, 2, "two")
    printf "a[1] = %s, a[2] = %s, a[3] = %s\n",
            a[1], a[2], a[3]
}
```

prints `a[1] = 1, a[2] = two, a[3] = 3`, because `changeit` stores `"two"` in the second element of `a`.

Some *awk* implementations allow you to call a function that has not been defined. They only report a problem at runtime when the program actually tries to call the function. For example:

```
BEGIN {
    if (0)
        foo()
    else
        bar()
}
function bar() { ... }
# note that 'foo' is not defined
```

Because the `if` statement will never be true, it is not really a problem that `foo` has not been defined. Usually, though, it is a problem if a program calls an undefined function.

If *--lint* is specified (see the section "Command-Line Options" in Chapter 11), *gawk* reports calls to undefined functions.

Some *awk* implementations generate a runtime error if you use the `next` statement (see the section "The next Statement" in Chapter 6, *Patterns, Actions, and Variables*) inside a user-defined function. *gawk* does not have this limitation.

The return Statement

The body of a user-defined function can contain a `return` statement. This statement returns control to the calling part of the *awk* program. It can also be used to return a value for use in the rest of the *awk* program. It looks like this:

```
return [expression]
```

The *expression* part is optional. If it is omitted, then the returned value is undefined, and therefore, unpredictable.

A `return` statement with no value expression is assumed at the end of every function definition. So if control reaches the end of the function body, then the function returns an unpredictable value. *awk* does *not* warn you if you use the return value of such a function.

Sometimes, you want to write a function for what it does, not for what it returns. Such a function corresponds to a `void` function in C or to a `procedure` in Pascal. Thus, it may be appropriate to not return any value; simply bear in mind that if you use the return value of such a function, you do so at your own risk.

The following is an example of a user-defined function that returns a value for the largest number among the elements of an array:

```
function maxelt(vec,    i, ret)
{
    for (i in vec) {
        if (ret == "" || vec[i] > ret)
            ret = vec[i]
    }
    return ret
}
```

You call `maxelt` with one argument, which is an array name. The local variables `i` and `ret` are not intended to be arguments; while there is nothing to stop you from passing several arguments to `maxelt`, the results would be strange. The extra space before `i` in the function parameter list indicates that `i` and `ret` are not supposd to be arguments. You should follow this convention when defining functions.

The following program uses the `maxelt` function. It loads an array, calls `maxelt`, and then reports the maximum number in that array:

```
function maxelt(vec,    i, ret)
{
    for (i in vec) {
        if (ret == "" || vec[i] > ret)
            ret = vec[i]
    }
    return ret
}

# Load all fields of each record into nums.
{
    for(i = 1; i <= NF; i++)
        nums[NR, i] = $i
}

END {
    print maxelt(nums)
}
```

Given the following input:

```
 1 5 23 8 16
44 3 5 2 8 26
256 291 1396 2962 100
-6 467 998 1101
99385 11 0 225
```

the program reports (predictably) that `99385` is the largest number in the array.

Functions and Their Effects on Variable Typing

awk is a very fluid language. It is possible that *awk* can't tell if an identifier represents a regular variable or an array until runtime. Here is an annotated sample program:

```
function foo(a)
{
    a[1] = 1    # parameter is an array
}

BEGIN {
    b = 1
    foo(b)   # invalid: fatal type mismatch

    foo(x)   # x uninitialized, becomes an array dynamically
    x = 1    # now not allowed, runtime error
}
```

Usually, such things aren't a big issue, but it's worth being aware of them.

9

Internationalization with gawk

Once upon a time, computer makers wrote software that worked only in English. Eventually, hardware and software vendors noticed that if their systems worked in the native languages of non-English-speaking countries, they were able to sell more systems. As a result, internationalization and localization of programs and software systems became a common practice.

Until recently, the ability to provide internationalization was largely restricted to programs written in C and C++. This chapter describes the underlying library *gawk* uses for internationalization, as well as how *gawk* makes internationalization features available at the *awk* program level. Having internationalization available at the *awk* level gives software developers additional flexibility—they are no longer required to write in C when internationalization is a requirement.

Internationalization and Localization

Internationalization means writing (or modifying) a program once, in such a way that it can use multiple languages without requiring further source-code changes. *Localization* means providing the data necessary for an internationalized program to work in a particular language. Most typically, these terms refer to features such as the language used for printing error messages, the language used to read responses, and information related to how numerical and monetary values are printed and read.

GNU gettext

The facilities in GNU `gettext` focus on messages; strings printed by a program, either directly or via formatting with `printf` or `sprintf`.*

When using GNU `gettext`, each application has its own *text domain*. This is a unique name, such as `kpilot` or `gawk`, that identifies the application. A complete application may have multiple components—programs written in C or C++, as well as scripts written in *sh* or *awk*. All of the components use the same text domain.

To make the discussion concrete, assume we're writing an application named *guide*. Internationalization consists of the following steps, in this order:

1. The programmer goes through the source for all of *guide*'s components and marks each string that is a candidate for translation. For example, `"`-F':
    option required"` is a good candidate for translation. A table with strings of option names is not (e.g., *gawk*'s *--profile* option should remain the same, no matter what the local language).

2. The programmer indicates the application's text domain (`"guide"`) to the get-text library, by calling the `textdomain` function.

3. Messages from the application are extracted from the source code and collected into a portable object file (*guide.po*), which lists the strings and their translations. The translations are initially empty. The original (usually English) messages serve as the key for lookup of the translations.

4. For each language with a translator, *guide.po* is copied and translations are created and shipped with the application.

5. Each language's *.po* file is converted into a binary message object (*.mo*) file. A message object file contains the original messages and their translations in a binary format that allows fast lookup of translations at runtime.

6. When *guide* is built and installed, the binary translation files are installed in a standard place.

7. For testing and development, it is possible to tell `gettext` to use *.mo* files in a different directory than the standard one by using the `bindtextdomain` function.

8. At runtime, *guide* looks up each string via a call to `gettext`. The returned string is the translated string if available, or the original string if not.

---

* For some operating systems, the *gawk* port doesn't support GNU `gettext`. This applies most notably to the PC operating systems. As such, these features are not available if you are using one of those operating systems. Sorry.

9. If necessary, it is possible to access messages from a different text domain
    than the one belonging to the application, without having to switch the appli-
    cation's default text domain back and forth.

In C (or C++), the string marking and dynamic translation lookup are accomplished by wrapping each string in a call to gettext:

```
printf(gettext("Don't Panic!\n"));
```

The tools that extract messages from source code pull out all strings enclosed in
calls to gettext.

The GNU gettext developers, recognizing that typing gettext over and over again
is both painful and ugly to look at, use the macro _ (an underscore) to make
things easier:

```
/* In the standard header file: */
#define _(str) gettext(str)

/* In the program text: */
printf(_("Don't Panic!\n"));
```

This reduces the typing overhead to just three extra characters per string and is
considerably easier to read as well. There are locale *categories* for different types
of locale-related information. The defined locale categories that gettext knows
about are:

LC_MESSAGES

Text messages. This is the default category for gettext operations, but it is
possible to supply a different one explicitly, if necessary. (It is almost never
necessary to supply a different category.)

LC_COLLATE

Text-collation information; i.e., how different characters and/or groups of
characters sort in a given language.

LC_CTYPE

Character-type information (alphabetic, digit, upper- or lowercase, and so on).
This information is accessed via the POSIX character classes in regular expressions, such as /[[:alnum:]]/ (see the section "Regular Expression Operators"
in Chapter 2, *Regular Expressions*).

LC_MONETARY

Monetary information, such as the currency symbol, and whether the symbol
goes before or after a number.

LC_NUMERIC

Numeric information, such as which characters to use for the decimal point and the thousands separator.*

LC_RESPONSE

Response information, such as how "yes" and "no" appear in the local language, and possibly other information as well.

LC_TIME

Time- and date-related information, such as 12- or 24-hour clock, month printed before or after day in a date, local month abbreviations, and so on.

LC_ALL

All of the above. (Not too useful in the context of gettext.)

Internationalizing awk Programs

gawk provides the following variables and functions for internationalization:

TEXTDOMAIN

This variable indicates the application's text domain. For compatibility with GNU gettext, the default value is "messages".

_"your message here"

String constants marked with a leading underscore are candidates for translation at runtime. String constants without a leading underscore are not translated.

dcgettext(*string* [, *domain* [, *category*]])

This built-in function returns the translation of *string* in text domain *domain* for locale category *category*. The default value for *domain* is the current value of TEXTDOMAIN. The default value for *category* is "LC_MESSAGES".

If you supply a value for *category*, it must be a string equal to one of the known locale categories described in the previous section. You must also supply a text domain. Use TEXTDOMAIN if you want to use the current domain.

 The order of arguments to the *awk* version of the dcgettext function is purposely different from the order for the C version. The *awk* version's order was chosen to be simple and to allow for reasonable *awk*-style default arguments.

---

* Americans use a comma every three decimal places and a period for the decimal point, while many Europeans do exactly the opposite: 1,234.56 versus 1.234,56.

`bindtextdomain(`*directory* [, *domain*]`)`

> This built-in function allows you to specify the directory in which `gettext`
> looks for *.mo* files, in case they will not or cannot be placed in the standard
> locations (e.g., during testing). It returns the directory in which *domain* is
> "bound."
>
> The default *domain* is the value of TEXTDOMAIN. If *directory* is the null string
> ("`"`"`"`"), then `bindtextdomain` returns the current binding for the given *domain*.

To use these facilities in your *awk* program, follow the steps outlined in the previous section, like so:

1. Set the variable TEXTDOMAIN to the text domain of your program. This is best
    done in a BEGIN rule (see the section "The BEGIN and END Special Patterns"
    in Chapter 6, *Patterns, Actions, and Variables*), or it can also be done via the
    −*v* command-line option (see the section "Command-Line Options" in Chapter
    11, *Running awk and gawk*):

    ```
    BEGIN {
        TEXTDOMAIN = "guide"
        ...
    }
    ```

2. Mark all translatable strings with a leading underscore (_) character. It *must*
    be adjacent to the opening quote of the string. For example:

    ```
    print _"hello, world"
    x = _"you goofed"
    printf(_"Number of users is %d\n", nusers)
    ```

3. If you are creating strings dynamically, you can still translate them, using the
    `dcgettext` built-in function:

    ```
    message = nusers " users logged in"
    message = dcgettext(message, "adminprog")
    print message
    ```

    Here, the call to `dcgettext` supplies a different text domain ("`adminprog`") in
    which to find the message, but it uses the default "`LC_MESSAGES`" category.

4. During development, you might want to put the *.mo* file in a private directory
    for testing. This is done with the `bindtextdomain` built-in function:

    ```
    BEGIN {
        TEXTDOMAIN = "guide"     # our text domain
        if (Testing) {
            # where to find our files
            bindtextdomain("testdir")
            # joe is in charge of adminprog
            bindtextdomain("../joe/testdir", "adminprog")
        }
        ...
    }
    ```

See the section "A Simple Internationalization Example" later in this chapter for an example program showing the steps to create and use translations from *awk*.

Translating awk Programs

Once a program's translatable strings have been marked, they must be extracted to create the initial *.po* file. As part of translation, it is often helpful to rearrange the order in which arguments to printf are output.

gawk's *—gen–po* command-line option extracts the messages and is discussed next. After that, printf's ability to rearrange the order for printf arguments at run-time is covered.

Extracting Marked Strings

Once your *awk* program is working, and all the strings have been marked and you've set (and perhaps bound) the text domain, it is time to produce translations. First, use the *—gen–po* command-line option to create the initial *.po* file:

```
$ gawk --gen-po -f guide.awk > guide.po
```

When run with *—gen–po*, *gawk* does not execute your program. Instead, it parses it as usual and prints all marked strings to standard output in the format of a GNU gettext Portable Object file. Also included in the output are any constant strings that appear as the first argument to dcgettext.* See the section "A Simple Internationalization Example" later in this chapter for the full list of steps to go through to create and test translations for *guide*.

Rearranging printf Arguments

Format strings for printf and sprintf (see the section "Using printf Statements for Fancier Printing" in Chapter 4, *Printing Output*) present a special problem for translation. Consider the following:†

```
printf(_"String `%s' has %d characters\n", string, length(string)))
```

A possible German translation for this might be:

```
"%d Zeichen lang ist die Zeichenkette `%s'\n"
```

The problem should be obvious: the order of the format specifications is different from the original! Even though gettext can return the translated string at runtime, it cannot change the argument order in the call to printf.

---

* Eventually, the *xgettext* utility that comes with GNU gettext will be taught to automatically run gawk *--gen-po* for *.awk* files, freeing the translator from having to do it manually.

† This example is borrowed from the GNU gettext manual.

To solve this problem, `printf` format specificiers may have an additional optional element, which we call a *positional specifier*. For example:

```
"%2$d Zeichen lang ist die Zeichenkette '%1$s'\n"
```

Here, the positional specifier consists of an integer count, which indicates which argument to use, and a $. Counts are one-based, and the format string itself is *not* included. Thus, in the following example, `string` is the first argument and `length(string)` is the second:

```
$ gawk 'BEGIN {
>       string = "Dont Panic"
>       printf _"%2$d characters live in \"%1$s\"\n",
>                         string, length(string)
> }'
10 characters live in "Dont Panic"
```

If present, positional specifiers come first in the format specification, before the flags, the field width, and/or the precision.

Positional specifiers can be used with the dynamic field width and precision capability:

```
$ gawk 'BEGIN {
>       printf("%*.*s\n", 10, 20, "hello")
>       printf("%3$*2$.*1$s\n", 20, 10, "hello")
> }'
hello
hello
```

When using * with a positional specifier, the * comes first, then the integer position, and then the $. This is somewhat counterintuitive.

gawk does not allow you to mix regular format specifiers and those with positional specifiers in the same string:

```
$ gawk 'BEGIN { printf _"%d %3$s\n", 1, 2, "hi" }'
gawk: cmd. line:1: fatal: must use 'count$' on all formats or none
```

There are some pathological cases that *gawk* may fail to diagnose. In such cases, the output may not be what you expect. It's still a bad idea to try mixing them, even if *gawk* doesn't detect it.

Although positional specifiers can be used directly in *awk* programs, their primary purpose is to help in producing correct translations of format strings into languages different from the one in which the program is first written.

awk Portability Issues

gawk's internationalization features were purposely chosen to have as little impact as possible on the portability of *awk* programs that use them to other versions of *awk*. Consider this program:

```
BEGIN {
    TEXTDOMAIN = "guide"
    if (Test_Guide)   # set with -v
        bindtextdomain("/test/guide/messages")
    print _"don't panic!"
}
```

As written, it won't work on other versions of *awk*. However, it is actually almost portable, requiring very little change:

- Assignments to TEXTDOMAIN won't have any effect, since TEXTDOMAIN is not special in other *awk* implementations.

- Non-GNU versions of *awk* treat marked strings as the concatenation of a variable named _ with the string following it.* Typically, the variable _ has the null string ("") as its value, leaving the original string constant as the result.

- By defining "dummy" functions to replace dcgettext and bindtextdomain, the *awk* program can be made to run, but all the messages are output in the original language. For example:

    ```
    function bindtextdomain(dir, domain)
    {
        return dir
    }

    function dcgettext(string, domain, category)
    {
        return string
    }
    ```

- The use of positional specifications in printf or sprintf is *not* portable. To support gettext at the C level, many systems' C versions of sprintf do support positional specifiers. But it works only if enough arguments are supplied in the function call. Many versions of *awk* pass printf formats and arguments unchanged to the underlying C library version of sprintf, but only one format and argument at a time. What happens if a positional specification is used is

---

* This is good fodder for an "Obfuscated *awk*" contest.

anybody's guess. However, since the positional specifications are primarily for use in *translated* format strings, and since non-GNU *awks* never retrieve the translated string, this should not be a problem in practice.

A Simple Internationalization Example

Now let's look at a step-by-step example of how to internationalize and localize a simple *awk* program, using *guide.awk* as our original source:

```
BEGIN {
    TEXTDOMAIN = "guide"
    bindtextdomain(".")  # for testing
    print _"Don't Panic"
    print _"The Answer Is", 42
    print "Pardon me, Zaphod who?"
}
```

Run gawk --gen-po to create the *.po* file:

```
$ gawk --gen-po -f guide.awk > guide.po
```

This produces:

```
#: guide.awk:4
msgid "Don't Panic"
msgstr ""

#: guide.awk:5
msgid "The Answer Is"
msgstr ""
```

This original portable object file is saved and reused for each language into which the application is translated. The msgid is the original string and the msgstr is the translation.

 Strings not marked with a leading underscore do not appear in the *guide.po* file.

Next, the messages must be translated. Here is a translation to a hypothetical dialect of English, called "Mellow":*

```
$ cp guide.po guide-mellow.po
Add translations to guide-mellow.po ...
```

---

* Perhaps it would be better if it were called "Hippy." Ah, well.

Following are the translations:

```
#: guide.awk:4
msgid "Don't Panic"
msgstr "Hey man, relax!"

#: guide.awk:5
msgid "The Answer Is"
msgstr "Like, the scoop is"
```

The next step is to make the directory to hold the binary message object file and then to create the *guide.mo* file. The directory layout shown here is standard for GNU gettext on GNU/Linux systems. Other versions of gettext may use a different layout:

```
$ mkdir en_US en_US/LC_MESSAGES
```

The *msgfmt* utility does the conversion from human-readable *.po* file to machine-readable *.mo* file. By default, *msgfmt* creates a file named *messages*. This file must be renamed and placed in the proper directory so that *gawk* can find it:

```
$ msgfmt guide-mellow.po
$ mv messages en_US/LC_MESSAGES/guide.mo
```

Finally, we run the program to test it:

```
$ gawk -f guide.awk
Hey man, relax!
Like, the scoop is 42
Pardon me, Zaphod who?
```

If the two replacement functions for dcgettext and bindtextdomain (see the section "awk Portability Issues" earlier in this chapter) are in a file named *libintl.awk*, then we can run *guide.awk* unchanged as follows:

```
$ gawk --posix -f guide.awk -f libintl.awk
Don't Panic
The Answer Is 42
Pardon me, Zaphod who?
```

gawk Can Speak Your Language

As of Version 3.1, *gawk* itself has been internationalized using the GNU gettext package. (GNU gettext is described in complete detail in *GNU gettext tools*.) As of this writing, the latest version of GNU gettext is Version 0.10.37 (*ftp://gnudist.gnu.org/gnu/gettext/gettext-0.10.37.tar.gz*).

If a translation of *gawk*'s messages exists, then *gawk* produces usage messages, warnings, and fatal errors in the local language.

On systems that do not use Version 2 (or later) of the GNU C library, you should configure *gawk* with the *--with-included-gettext* option before compiling and installing it. See the section "Additional Configuration Options" in Appendix B, *Installing gawk,* for more information.

Advanced Features of gawk

This chapter discusses advanced features in *gawk*. It's a bit of a "grab bag" of items that are otherwise unrelated to each other. First, a command-line option allows *gawk* to recognize nondecimal numbers in input data, not just in *awk* programs. Next, two-way I/O, discussed briefly in earlier parts of this book, is described in full detail, along with the basics of TCP/IP networking and BSD portal files. Finally, *gawk* can *profile* an *awk* program, making it possible to tune it for performance.

The section "Adding New Built-in Functions to gawk" in Appendix C, *Implementation Notes*, discusses the ability to dynamically add new built-in functions to *gawk*. As this feature is still immature and likely to change, its description is relegated to an appendix.

Allowing Nondecimal Input Data

If you run *gawk* with the *--non–decimal–data* option, you can have nondecimal constants in your input data:

```
$ echo 0123 123 0x123 |
> gawk --non-decimal-data '{ printf "%d, %d, %d\n", $1, $2, $3 }'
83, 123, 291
```

For this feature to work, write your program so that *gawk* treats your data as numeric:

```
$ echo 0123 123 0x123 | gawk '{ print $1, $2, $3 }'
0123 123 0x123
```

The print statement treats its expressions as strings. Although the fields can act as numbers when necessary, they are still strings, so print does not try to treat them numerically. You may need to add zero to a field to force it to be treated as a number. For example:

```
$ echo 0123 123 0x123 | gawk --non-decimal-data '
> { print $1, $2, $3
>     print $1 + 0, $2 + 0, $3 + 0 }'
0123 123 0x123
83 123 291
```

Because it is common to have decimal data with leading zeros, and because using it could lead to surprising results, the default is to leave this facility disabled. If you want it, you must explicitly request it.

 Use of this option is not recommended. It can break old programs very badly. Instead, use the strtonum function to convert your data (see the section "Octal and Hexadecimal Numbers" in Chapter 5, *Expressions*). This makes your programs easier to write and easier to read, and leads to less surprising results.

Two-Way Communications with Another Process

It is often useful to be able to send data to a separate program for processing and then read the result. This can always be done with temporary files:

```
# write the data for processing
tempfile = ("/tmp/mydata." PROCINFO["pid"])
while (not done with data)
    print data | ("subprogram > " tempfile)
close("subprogram > " tempfile)

# read the results, remove tempfile when done
while ((getline newdata < tempfile) > 0)
    process newdata appropriately
close(tempfile)
system("rm " tempfile)
```

This works, but not elegantly.

Starting with Version 3.1 of *gawk*, it is possible to open a *two-way* pipe to another process. The second process is termed a *coprocess*, since it runs in parallel with *gawk*. The two-way connection is created using the new |& operator (borrowed from the Korn shell, *ksh*):*

```
do {
    print data |& "subprogram"
    "subprogram" |& getline results
} while (data left to process)
close("subprogram")
```

The first time an I/O operation is executed using the |& operator, *gawk* creates a two-way pipeline to a child process that runs the other program. Output created with `print` or `printf` is written to the program's standard input, and output from the program's standard output can be read by the *gawk* program using `getline`. As is the case with processes started by |, the subprogram can be any program, or pipeline of programs, that can be started by the shell.

There are some cautionary items to be aware of:

- As the code inside *gawk* currently stands, the coprocess's standard error goes to the same place that the parent *gawk*'s standard error goes. It is not possible to read the child's standard error separately.

- I/O buffering may be a problem. *gawk* automatically flushes all output down the pipe to the child process. However, if the coprocess does not flush its output, *gawk* may hang when doing a `getline` in order to read the coprocess's results. This could lead to a situation known as *deadlock*, where each process is waiting for the other one to do something.

It is possible to close just one end of the two-way pipe to a coprocess, by supplying a second argument to the `close` function of either `"to"` or `"from"` (see the section "Closing Input and Output Redirections" in Chapter 4, *Printing Output*). These strings tell *gawk* to close the end of the pipe that sends data to the process or the end that reads from it, respectively.

This is particularly necessary in order to use the system *sort* utility as part of a coprocess; *sort* must read *all* of its input data before it can produce any output. The *sort* program does not receive an end-of-file indication until *gawk* closes the write end of the pipe.

---

* This is very different from the same operator in the C shell, *csh*.

When you have finished writing data to the *sort* utility, you can close the "to" end of the pipe, and then start reading sorted data via getline. For example:

```
BEGIN {
    command = "LC_ALL=C sort"
    n = split("abcdefghijklmnopqrstuvwxyz", a, "")

    for (i = n; i > 0; i--)
        print a[i] |& command
    close(command, "to")

    while ((command |& getline line) > 0)
        print "got", line
    close(command)
}
```

This program writes the letters of the alphabet in reverse order, one per line, down the two-way pipe to *sort*. It then closes the write end of the pipe, so that *sort* receives an end-of-file indication. This causes *sort* to sort the data and write the sorted data back to the *gawk* program. Once all of the data has been read, *gawk* terminates the coprocess and exits.

As a side note, the assignment LC_ALL=C in the *sort* command ensures traditional Unix (ASCII) sorting from *sort*.

Using gawk for Network Programming

In addition to being able to open a two-way pipeline to a coprocess on the same system (see the section "Two-Way Communications with Another Process" earlier in this chapter), it is possible to make a two-way connection to another process on another system across an IP networking connection.

You can think of this as just a *very long* two-way pipeline to a coprocess. The way *gawk* decides that you want to use TCP/IP networking is by recognizing special filenames that begin with /inet/.

The full syntax of the special filename is */inet/protocol/local-port/remote-host/ remote-port*. The components are:

protocol

> The protocol to use over IP. This must be either tcp, udp, or raw, for a TCP, UDP, or raw IP connection, respectively. The use of TCP is recommended for most applications.

The use of raw sockets is not currently supported in Version 3.1 of *gawk.*

local-port

The local TCP or UDP port number to use. Use a port number of 0 when you want the system to pick a port. This is what you should do when writing a TCP or UDP client. You may also use a well-known service name, such as smtp or http, in which case *gawk* attempts to determine the predefined port number using the C getservbyname function.

remote-host

The IP address or fully-qualified domain name of the Internet host to which you want to connect.

remote-port

The TCP or UDP port number to use on the given *remote-host*. Again, use 0 if you don't care, or else a well-known service name.

Consider the following very simple example:

```
BEGIN {
    Service = "/inet/tcp/0/localhost/daytime"
    Service |& getline
    print $0
    close(Service)
}
```

This program reads the current date and time from the local system's TCP daytime server. It then prints the results and closes the connection.

Because this topic is extensive, the use of *gawk* for TCP/IP programming is documented separately. See Chapter 14, *Internetworking with gawk*, for a much more complete introduction and discussion, as well as extensive examples.

Using gawk with BSD Portals

Similar to the */inet* special files, if *gawk* is configured with the *--enable-portals* option (see the section "Compiling gawk for Unix" in Appendix B, *Installing gawk*), *gawk* treats files whose pathnames begin with /p as 4.4 BSD-style portals.

When used with the |& operator, *gawk* opens the file for two-way communications. The operating system's portal mechanism then manages creating the process associated with the portal and the corresponding communications with the portal's process.

Profiling Your awk Programs

Beginning with Version 3.1 of *gawk*, you may produce execution traces of your *awk* programs. This is done with a specially compiled version of *gawk*, called *pgawk* ("profiling *gawk*").

pgawk is identical in every way to *gawk*, except that when it has finished running, it creates a profile of your program in a file named *awkprof.out*. Because it is profiling, it also executes up to 45% slower than *gawk* normally does.

As shown in the following example, the *—profile* option can be used to change the name of the file where *pgawk* will write the profile:

```
$ pgawk --profile=myprog.prof -f myprog.awk data1 data2
```

In the above example, *pgawk* places the profile in *myprog.prof* instead of in *awkprof.out*.

Regular *gawk* also accepts this option. When called with just *—profile*, *gawk* "pretty prints" the program into *awkprof.out*, without any execution counts. You may supply an option to *—profile* to change the filename. Here is a sample session showing a simple *awk* program, its input data, and the results from running *pgawk*. First, the *awk* program:

```
BEGIN { print "First BEGIN rule" }

END { print "First END rule" }

/foo/ {
    print "matched /foo/, gosh"
    for (i = 1; i <= 3; i++)
        sing()
}

{
    if (/foo/)
        print "if is true"
    else
        print "else is true"
}

BEGIN { print "Second BEGIN rule" }

END { print "Second END rule" }

function sing(    dummy)
{
    print "I gotta be me!"
}
```

Following is the input data:

```
foo
bar
baz
foo
junk
```

Here is the *awkprof.out* that results from running *pgawk* on this program and data (this example also illustrates that *awk* programmers sometimes have to work late):

```
        # gawk profile, created Sun Aug 13 00:00:15 2000

        # BEGIN block(s)

        BEGIN {
    1           print "First BEGIN rule"
    1           print "Second BEGIN rule"
        }

        # Rule(s)

    5   /foo/   { # 2
    2           print "matched /foo/, gosh"
    6           for (i = 1; i <= 3; i++) {
    6                   sing()
                }
        }

    5   {
    5           if (/foo/) { # 2
    2                   print "if is true"
    3           } else {
    3                   print "else is true"
                }
        }

        # END block(s)

        END {
    1           print "First END rule"
    1           print "Second END rule"
        }

        # Functions, listed alphabetically

    6   function sing(dummy)
        {
    6           print "I gotta be me!"
        }
```

This example illustrates many of the basic rules for profiling output. The rules are as follows:

- The program is printed in the order BEGIN rule, pattern/action rules, END rule and functions, listed alphabetically. Multiple BEGIN and END rules are merged together.

- Pattern-action rules have two counts. The first count, to the left of the rule, shows how many times the rule's pattern was *tested*. The second count, to the right of the rule's opening left brace in a comment, shows how many times the rule's action was *executed*. The difference between the two indicates how many times the rule's pattern evaluated to false.

- Similarly, the count for an if-else statement shows how many times the condition was tested. To the right of the opening left brace for the if's body is a count showing how many times the condition was true. The count for the else indicates how many times the test failed.

- The count for a loop header (such as for or while) shows how many times the loop test was executed. (Because of this, you can't just look at the count on the first statement in a rule to determine how many times the rule was executed. If the first statement is a loop, the count is misleading.)

- For user-defined functions, the count next to the function keyword indicates how many times the function was called. The counts next to the statements in the body show how many times those statements were executed.

- The layout uses "K&R" style with tabs. Braces are used everywhere, even when the body of an if, else, or loop is only a single statement.

- Parentheses are used only where needed, as indicated by the structure of the program and the precedence rules. For example, (3 + 5) * 4 means add three plus five, then multiply the total by four. However, 3 + 5 * 4 has no parentheses, and means 3 + (5 * 4).

- All string concatenations are parenthesized too. (This could be made a bit smarter.)

- Parentheses are used around the arguments to print and printf only when the print or printf statement is followed by a redirection. Similarly, if the target of a redirection isn't a scalar, it gets parenthesized.

- *pgawk* supplies leading comments in front of the BEGIN and END rules, the pattern/action rules, and the functions.

The profiled version of your program may not look exactly like what you typed when you wrote it. This is because *pgawk* creates the profiled version by "pretty printing" its internal representation of the program. The advantage to this is that *pgawk* can produce a standard representation. The disadvantage is that all source-code comments are lost, as are the distinctions among multiple BEGIN and END rules. Also, things such as:

```
/foo/
```

come out as:

```
/foo/   {
    print $0
}
```

which is correct, but possibly surprising.

Besides creating profiles when a program has completed, *pgawk* can produce a profile while it is running. This is useful if your *awk* program goes into an infinite loop and you want to see what has been executed. To use this feature, run *pgawk* in the background:

```
$ pgawk -f myprog &
[1] 13992
```

The shell prints a job number and process ID number; in this case, 13992. Use the *kill* command to send the USR1 signal to *pgawk*:

```
$ kill -USR1 13992
```

As usual, the profiled version of the program is written to *awkprof.out*, or to a different file if you use the *--profile* option.

Along with the regular profile, as shown earlier, the profile includes a trace of any active functions:

```
# Function Call Stack:

#   3. baz
#   2. bar
#   1. foo
# -- main --
```

You may send *pgawk* the USR1 signal as many times as you like. Each time, the profile and function call trace are appended to the output profile file.

If you use the HUP signal instead of the USR1 signal, *pgawk* produces the profile and the function call trace and then exits.

11

Running awk and gawk

This chapter covers how to run *awk*, both POSIX-standard and *gawk*-specific command-line options, and what *awk* and *gawk* do with non-option arguments. It then proceeds to cover how *gawk* searches for source files, obsolete options and/or features, and known bugs in *gawk*. This chapter rounds out the discussion of *awk* as a program and as a language.

While a number of the options and features described here were discussed in passing earlier in the book, this chapter provides the full details.

Invoking awk

There are two ways to run *awk*—with an explicit program or with one or more program files. Here are templates for both of them; items enclosed in [...] in these templates are optional:

```
awk [options] -f progfile [--] file ...
awk [options] [--] 'program' file ...
```

Besides traditional one-letter POSIX-style options, *gawk* also supports GNU long options.

It is possible to invoke *awk* with an empty program:

```
awk '' datafile1 datafile2
```

Doing so makes little sense, though; *awk* exits silently when given an empty program. If *—lint* has been specified on the command line, *gawk* issues a warning that the program is empty.

Command-Line Options

Options begin with a dash and consist of a single character. GNU-style long options consist of two dashes and a keyword. The keyword can be abbreviated, as long as the abbreviation allows the option to be uniquely identified. If the option takes an argument, then the keyword is either immediately followed by an equals sign (=) and the argument's value, or the keyword and the argument's value are separated by whitespace. If a particular option with a value is given more than once, it is the last value that counts.

Each long option for *gawk* has a corresponding POSIX-style option. The long and short options are interchangeable in all contexts. The options and their meanings are as follows:

-F *fs*

--field-separator *fs*

> Sets the FS variable to *fs* (see the section "Specifying How Fields Are Separated" in Chapter 3, *Reading Input Files*).

-f *source-file*

--file *source-file*

> Indicates that the *awk* program is to be found in *source-file* instead of in the first non-option argument.

-v *var=val*

--assign *var=val*

> Sets the variable *var* to the value *val before* execution of the program begins. Such variable values are available inside the BEGIN rule (see the section "Other Command-Line Arguments" later in this chapter).

> The *–v* option can only set one variable, but it can be used more than once, setting another variable each time, like this: awk -v foo=1 -v bar=2 ....

> Using *–v* to set the values of the built-in variables may lead to surprising results. *awk* will reset the values of those variables as it needs to, possibly ignoring any predefined value you may have given.

–mf *N*

–mr *N*

> Sets various memory limits to the value *N*. The f flag sets the maximum number of fields and the r flag sets the maximum record size. These two flags and the *–m* option are from the Bell Laboratories research version of Unix *awk*. They are provided for compatibility but otherwise ignored by *gawk*, since

gawk has no predefined limits. (The Bell Laboratories *awk* no longer needs these options; it continues to accept them to avoid breaking old programs.)

-W *gawk-opt*

Following the POSIX standard, implementation-specific options are supplied as arguments to the −*W* option. These options also have corresponding GNU-style long options. Note that the long options may be abbreviated, as long as the abbreviations remain unique. The full list of *gawk*-specific options is provided next.

-- Signals the end of the command-line options. The following arguments are not treated as options even if they begin with -. This interpretation of −− follows the POSIX argument parsing conventions.

This is useful if you have filenames that start with -, or in shell scripts, if you have filenames that will be specified by the user that could start with -.

The previous list described options mandated by the POSIX standard, as well as options available in the Bell Laboratories version of *awk*. The following list describes *gawk*-specific options:

-W compat, -W traditional, --compat, --traditional

Specifies *compatibility mode*, in which the GNU extensions to the *awk* language are disabled, so that *gawk* behaves just like the Bell Laboratories research version of Unix *awk*. −−*traditional* is the preferred form of this option. See the section "Extensions in gawk Not in POSIX awk" in Appendix A, *The Evolution of the awk Language*, which summarizes the extensions. Also see the section "Downward Compatibility and Debugging" in Appendix C, *Implementation Notes*.

-W copyright
--copyright

Print the short version of the General Public License and then exit.

-W copyleft
--copyleft

Just like −−*copyright*.

-W dump-variables[=*file*]
--dump-variables[=*file*]

Prints a sorted list of global variables, their types, and final values to *file*. If no *file* is provided, *gawk* prints this list to the file named *awkvars.out* in the current directory.

Having a list of all global variables is a good way to look for typographical
errors in your programs. You would also use this option if you have a large
program with a lot of functions, and you want to be sure that your functions
don't inadvertently use global variables that you meant to be local. (This is a
particularly easy mistake to make with simple variable names like i, j, etc.)

`-W gen-po`

`--gen-po`

Analyzes the source program and generates a GNU `gettext` Portable Object
file on standard output for all string constants that have been marked for translation. See Chapter 9, *Internationalization with gawk*, for information about
this option.

`-W help, -W usage, --help, --usage`

Prints a "usage" message summarizing the short and long style options that
gawk accepts and then exits.

`-W lint[=fatal]`

`--lint[=fatal]`

Warn about constructs that are dubious or nonportable to other *awk* implementations. Some warnings are issued when *gawk* first reads your program.
Others are issued at runtime, as your program executes. With an optional
argument of `fatal`, lint warnings become fatal errors. This may be drastic, but
its use will certainly encourage the development of cleaner *awk* programs.

`-W lint-old`

`--lint-old`

Warns about constructs that are not available in the original version of *awk*
from Version 7 Unix (see the section "Major Changes Between V7 and
SVR3.1" in Appendix A).

`-W non-decimal-data`

`--non-decimal-data`

Enable automatic interpretation of octal and hexadecimal values in input data
(see the section "Allowing Nondecimal Input Data" in Chapter 10, *Advanced
Features of gawk*).

This option can severely break old programs. Use with care.

```
-W posix
--posix
```
> Operates in strict POSIX mode. This disables all *gawk* extensions (just like
> *—traditional*) and adds the following additional restrictions:
>
> - \x escape sequences are not recognized (see the section "Escape
>   Sequences" in Chapter 2, *Regular Expressions*).
>
> - Newlines do not act as whitespace to separate fields when FS is equal to a
>   single space (see the section "Examining Fields" in Chapter 3).
>
> - Newlines are not allowed after ? or : (see the section "Conditional Expres-
>   sions" in Chapter 5, *Expressions*).
>
> - The synonym func for the keyword function is not recognized (see the
>   section "Function Definition Syntax" in Chapter 8, *Functions*).
>
> - The ** and **= operators cannot be used in place of ^ and ^= (see the
>   section "Arithmetic Operators" in Chapter 5, and also see the section
>   "Assignment Expressions" in Chapter 5).
>
> - Specifying -Ft on the command line does not set the value of FS to be a
>   single tab character (see the section "Specifying How Fields Are Sepa-
>   rated" in Chapter 3).
>
> - The fflush built-in function is not supported (see the section "Input/Out-
>   put Functions" in Chapter 8).
>
> If you supply both *—traditional* and *—posix* on the command line, *—posix*
> takes precedence. *gawk* also issues a warning if both options are supplied.

```
-W profile[=file]
--profile[=file]
```
> Enable profiling of *awk* programs (see the section "Profiling Your awk Pro-
> grams" in Chapter 10). By default, profiles are created in a file named
> *awkprof.out*. The optional *file* argument allows you to specify a different file-
> name for the profile file.
>
> When run with *gawk*, the profile is just a "pretty printed" version of the pro-
> gram. When run with *pgawk*, the profile contains execution counts for each
> statement in the program in the left margin, and function call counts for each
> function.

```
-W re-interval
--re-interval
```
> Allow interval expressions (see the section "Regular Expression Operators" in
> Chapter 2) in regexps. Because interval expressions were traditionally not
> available in *awk*, *gawk* does not provide them by default. This prevents old
> *awk* programs from breaking.

-W source *program-text*

--source *program-text*

>   Allows you to mix source code in files with source code that you enter on the command line. Program source code is taken from the *program-text*. This is particularly useful when you have library functions that you want to use from your command-line programs (see the section "The AWKPATH Environment Variable" later in this chapter).

-W version

--version

>   Prints version information for this particular copy of *gawk*. This allows you to determine if your copy of *gawk* is up to date with respect to whatever the Free Software Foundation is currently distributing. It is also useful for bug reports (see the section "Reporting Problems and Bugs" in Appendix B, *Installing gawk*).

As long as program text has been supplied, any other options are flagged as invalid with a warning message but are otherwise ignored.

In compatibility mode, as a special case, if the value of *fs* supplied to the *–F* option is t, then FS is set to the tab character ("\t"). This is true only for *––traditional* and not for *––posix* (see the section "Specifying How Fields Are Separated" in Chapter 3).

The *–f* option may be used more than once on the command line. If it is, *awk* reads its program source from all of the named files, as if they had been concatenated together into one big file. This is useful for creating libraries of *awk* functions. These functions can be written once and then retrieved from a standard place, instead of having to be included into each individual program. (As mentioned in the section "Function Definition Syntax" in Chapter 8, function names must be unique.)

Library functions can still be used, even if the program is entered at the terminal, by specifying -f /dev/tty. After typing your program, type Ctrl-d (the end-of-file character) to terminate it. (You may also use -f - to read program source from the standard input but then you will not be able to also use the standard input as a source of data.)

Because it is clumsy using the standard *awk* mechanisms to mix source file and command-line *awk* programs, *gawk* provides the *––source* option. This does not require you to pre-empt the standard input for your source code; it allows you to easily mix command-line and library source code (see the section "The AWKPATH Environment Variable" later in this chapter).

If no *–f* or *––source* option is specified, then *gawk* uses the first nonoption command-line argument as the text of the program source code.

If the environment variable POSIXLY_CORRECT exists, then *gawk* behaves in strict POSIX mode, exactly as if you had supplied the *—posix* command-line option. Many GNU programs look for this environment variable to turn on strict POSIX mode. If *—lint* is supplied on the command line and *gawk* turns on POSIX mode because of POSIXLY_CORRECT, then it issues a warning message indicating that POSIX mode is in effect. You would typically set this variable in your shell's startup file. For a Bourne-compatible shell (such as bash), you would add these lines to the *.profile* file in your home directory:

```
POSIXLY_CORRECT=true
export POSIXLY_CORRECT
```

For a *csh*-compatible shell, you would add this line to the *.login* file in your home directory:

```
setenv POSIXLY_CORRECT true
```

Having POSIXLY_CORRECT set is not recommended for daily use, but it is good for testing the portability of your programs to other environments.

Other Command-Line Arguments

Any additional arguments on the command line are normally treated as input files to be processed in the order specified. However, an argument that has the form *var=value*, assigns the value *value* to the variable *var*—it does not specify a file at all. (This was discussed earlier in the section "Assigning Variables on the Command Line" in Chapter 5.)

All these arguments are made available to your *awk* program in the ARGV array (see the section "Built-in Variables" in Chapter 6, *Patterns, Actions, and Variables*). Command-line options and the program text (if present) are omitted from ARGV. All other arguments, including variable assignments, are included. As each element of ARGV is processed, *gawk* sets the variable ARGIND to the index in ARGV of the current element.

The distinction between filename arguments and variable-assignment arguments is made when *awk* is about to open the next input file. At that point in execution, it checks the filename to see whether it is really a variable assignment; if so, *awk* sets the variable instead of reading a file.

Therefore, the variables actually receive the given values after all previously specified files have been read. In particular, the values of variables assigned in this fashion are *not* available inside a BEGIN rule (see the section "The BEGIN and END Special Patterns" in Chapter 6), because such rules are run before *awk* begins scanning the argument list.

The variable values given on the command line are processed for escape sequences (see the section "Escape Sequences" in Chapter 2).

In some earlier implementations of *awk*, when a variable assignment occurred before any filenames, the assignment would happen *before* the BEGIN rule was executed. *awk*'s behavior was thus inconsistent; some command-line assignments were available inside the BEGIN rule, while others were not. Unfortunately, some applications came to depend upon this "feature." When *awk* was changed to be more consistent, the *–v* option was added to accommodate applications that depended upon the old behavior.

The variable assignment feature is most useful for assigning to variables such as RS, OFS, and ORS, which control input and output formats before scanning the datafiles. It is also useful for controlling state if multiple passes are needed over a datafile. For example:

```
awk 'pass == 1 { pass 1 stuff }
     pass == 2 { pass 2 stuff }' pass=1 mydata pass=2 mydata
```

Given the variable assignment feature, the *–F* option for setting the value of FS is not strictly necessary. It remains for historical compatibility.

The AWKPATH Environment Variable

In most *awk* implementations, you must supply a precise path name for each program file, unless the file is in the current directory. But in *gawk*, if the filename supplied to the *–f* option does not contain a /, then *gawk* searches a list of directories (called the *search path*), one by one, looking for a file with the specified name.

The search path is a string consisting of directory names separated by colons. *gawk* gets its search path from the AWKPATH environment variable. If that variable does not exist, *gawk* uses a default path, .:/usr/local/share/awk.* (Programs written for use by system administrators should use an AWKPATH variable that does not include the current directory, ".".)

The scarch path feature is particularly useful for building libraries of useful *awk* functions. The library files can be placed in a standard directory in the default path and then specified on the command line with a short filename. Otherwise, the full filename would have to be typed for each file.

---

* Your version of *gawk* may use a different directory; it will depend upon how *gawk* was built and installed. The actual directory is the value of $(datadir) generated when *gawk* was configured. You probably don't need to worry about this, though.

By using both the *––source* and *–f* options, your command-line *awk* programs can use facilities in *awk* library files (see Chapter 12, *A Library of awk Functions*). Path searching is not done if *gawk* is in compatibility mode. This is true for both *––traditional* and *––posix*. See the section "Command-Line Options" earlier in this chapter.

> If you want files in the current directory to be found, you must include the current directory in the path, either by including . explicitly in the path or by writing a null entry in the path. (A null entry is indicated by starting or ending the path with a colon or by placing two colons next to each other (::).) If the current directory is not included in the path, then files cannot be found in the current directory. This path search mechanism is identical to the shell's.

Starting with Version 3.0, if AWKPATH is not defined in the environment, *gawk* places its default search path into ENVIRON["AWKPATH"]. This makes it easy to determine the actual search path that *gawk* will use from within an *awk* program.

While you can change ENVIRON["AWKPATH"] within your *awk* program, this has no effect on the running program's behavior. This makes sense: the AWKPATH environment variable is used to find the program source files. Once your program is running, all the files have been found, and *gawk* no longer needs to use AWKPATH.

Obsolete Options and/or Features

For Version 3.1 of *gawk*, there are no deprecated command-line options from the previous version of *gawk*. The use of next file (two words) for nextfile was deprecated in *gawk* 3.0 but still worked. Starting with Version 3.1, the two-word usage is no longer accepted.

The process-related special files described in the section "Special Files for Process-Related Information" in Chapter 4, *Printing Output*, work as described, but are now considered deprecated. *gawk* prints a warning message every time they are used. (Use PROCINFO instead; see the section "Built-in Variables That Convey Information" in Chapter 6.) They will be removed from the next release of *gawk*.

Known Bugs in gawk

- The *−F* option for changing the value of FS (see the section "Command-Line Options" earlier in this chapter) is not necessary given the command-line variable assignment feature; it remains only for backward compatibility.

- Syntactically invalid single-character programs tend to overflow the parse stack, generating a rather unhelpful message. Such programs are surprisingly difficult to diagnose in the completely general case, and the effort to do so really is not worth it.

II

Using awk and gawk

Part II shows how to use *awk* and *gawk* for problem solving. There is lots of code here for you to read and learn from. This part contains the following chapters:

- Chapter 12, *A Library of awk Functions*
- Chapter 13, *Practical awk Programs*
- Chapter 14, *Internetworking with gawk*

12

A Library of awk Functions

The section "User-Defined Functions" in Chapter 8, *Functions*, describes how to write your own *awk* functions. Writing functions is important, because it allows you to encapsulate algorithms and program tasks in a single place. It simplifies programming, making program development more manageable, and making programs more readable.

One valuable way to learn a new programming language is to *read* programs in that language. To that end, this chapter and Chapter 13, *Practical awk Programs*, provide a good-sized body of code for you to read, and hopefully, to learn from.

This chapter presents a library of useful *awk* functions. Many of the sample programs presented later in this book use these functions. The functions are presented here in a progression from simple to complex.

The section "Extracting Programs from Texinfo Source Files" in Chapter 13 presents a program that you can use to extract the source code for these example library functions and programs from the Texinfo source for this book. (This has already been done as part of the *gawk* distribution.)

If you have written one or more useful, general-purpose *awk* functions and would like to contribute them to the author's collection of *awk* programs, see the section "How to Contribute" in the Preface for more information.

The programs in this chapter and in Chapter 13 freely use features that are *gawk*-specific. Rewriting these programs for different implementations of *awk* is pretty straightforward.

Diagnostic error messages are sent to */dev/stderr*. Use | "cat 1>&2", instead of > "/dev/stderr" if your system does not have a */dev/stderr*, or if you cannot use *gawk.*

A number of programs use `nextfile` (see the section "Using gawk's nextfile Statement" in Chapter 6, *Patterns, Actions, and Variables*) to skip any remaining input in the input file. The section "Implementing nextfile as a Function" later in this chapter shows you how to write a function that does the same thing.

Finally, some of the programs choose to ignore upper- and lowercase distinctions in their input. They do so by assigning one to IGNORECASE. You can achieve almost the same effect* by adding the following rule to the beginning of the program:

```
# ignore case
{ $0 = tolower($0) }
```

Also, verify that all regexp and string constants used in comparisons use only lowercase letters.

Naming Library Function Global Variables

Due to the way the *awk* language evolved, variables are either *global* (usable by the entire program) or *local* (usable just by a specific function). There is no intermediate state analogous to `static` variables in C.

Library functions often need to have global variables that they can use to preserve state information between calls to the function—for example, `getopt`'s variable `_opti` (see the section "Processing Command-Line Options" later in this chapter). Such variables are called *private*, since the only functions that need to use them are the ones in the library.

When writing a library function, you should try to choose names for your private variables that will not conflict with any variables used by either another library function or a user's main program. For example, a name like `i` or `j` is not a good choice, because user programs often use variable names like these for their own purposes.

The example programs shown in this chapter all start the names of their private variables with an underscore (_). Users generally don't use leading underscores in their variable names, so this convention immediately decreases the chances that the variable name will be accidentally shared with the user's program.

---

* The effects are not identical. Output of the transformed record will be in all lowercase, while IGNORECASE preserves the original contents of the input record.

In addition, several of the library functions use a prefix that helps indicate what function or set of functions use the variables—for example, _pw_byname in the user database routines (see the section "Reading the User Database" later in this chapter). This convention is recommended, since it even further decreases the chance of inadvertent conflict among variable names. Note that this convention is used equally well for variable names and for private function names as well.*

As a final note on variable naming, if a function makes global variables available for use by a main program, it is a good convention to start that variable's name with a capital letter—for example, getopt's Opterr and Optind variables (see the section "Processing Command-Line Options" later in this chapter). The leading capital letter indicates that it is global, while the fact that the variable name is not all capital letters indicates that the variable is not one of *awk*'s built-in variables, such as FS.

It is also important that *all* variables in library functions that do not need to save state are, in fact, declared local.† If this is not done, the variable could accidentally be used in the user's program, leading to bugs that are very difficult to track down:

```
function lib_func(x, y,    l1, l2)
{
    ...
    use variable some_var    # some_var should be local
    ...                      # but is not by oversight
}
```

A different convention, common in the Tcl community, is to use a single associative array to hold the values needed by the library function(s), or "package." This significantly decreases the number of actual global names in use. For example, the functions described in the section "Reading the User Database" later in this chapter might have used array elements PW_data["inited"], PW_data["total"], PW_data ["count"], and PW_data["awklib"], instead of _pw_inited, _pw_awklib, _pw_total, and _pw_count.

The conventions presented in this section are exactly that: conventions. You are not required to write your programs this way—we merely recommend that you do so.

---

* While all the library routines could have been rewritten to use this convention, this was not done, in order to show how my own *awk* programming style has evolved and to provide some basis for this discussion.

† *gawk*'s *—dump-variables* command-line option is useful for verifying this.

General Programming

This section presents a number of functions that are of general programming use.

Implementing nextfile as a Function

The nextfile statement, presented in the section "Using gawk's nextfile Statement" in Chapter 6, is a *gawk*-specific extension—it is not available in most other implementations of *awk*. This section shows two versions of a nextfile function that you can use to simulate *gawk*'s nextfile statement if you cannot use *gawk*.

A first attempt at writing a nextfile function is as follows:

```
# nextfile --- skip remaining records in current file
# this should be read in before the "main" awk program

function nextfile()    { _abandon_ = FILENAME; next }
_abandon_ == FILENAME  { next }
```

Because it supplies a rule that must be executed first, this file should be included before the main program. This rule compares the current datafile's name (which is always in the FILENAME variable) to a private variable named _abandon_. If the filename matches, then the action part of the rule executes a next statement to go on to the next record. (The use of _ in the variable name is a convention. It is discussed more fully in the section "Naming Library Function Global Variables" earlier in this chapter.)

The use of the next statement effectively creates a loop that reads all the records from the current datafile. The end of the file is eventually reached and a new datafile is opened, changing the value of FILENAME. Once this happens, the comparison of _abandon_ to FILENAME fails, and execution continues with the first rule of the "real" program.

The nextfile function itself simply sets the value of _abandon_ and then executes a next statement to start the loop.

This initial version has a subtle problem. If the same datafile is listed *twice* on the command line, one right after the other or even with just a variable assignment between them, this code skips right through the file a second time, even though it should stop when it gets to the end of the first occurrence. A second version of nextfile that remedies this problem is shown here:

```
# nextfile --- skip remaining records in current file
# correctly handle successive occurrences of the same file
# this should be read in before the "main" awk program

function nextfile()    { _abandon_ = FILENAME; next }
```

```
_abandon_ == FILENAME {
    if (FNR == 1)
        _abandon_ = ""
    else
        next
}
```

The `nextfile` function has not changed. It makes `_abandon_` equal to the current filename and then executes a `next` statement. The `next` statement reads the next record and increments `FNR` so that `FNR` is guaranteed to have a value of at least two. However, if `nextfile` is called for the last record in the file, then *awk* closes the current datafile and moves on to the next one. Upon doing so, `FILENAME` is set to the name of the new file and `FNR` is reset to one. If this next file is the same as the previous one, `_abandon_` is still equal to `FILENAME`. However, `FNR` is equal to one, telling us that this is a new occurrence of the file and not the one we were reading when the `nextfile` function was executed. In that case, `_abandon_` is reset to the empty string, so that further executions of this rule fail (until the next time that `nextfile` is called).

If `FNR` is not one, then we are still in the original datafile and the program executes a `next` statement to skip through it.

An important question to ask at this point is: given that the functionality of `nextfile` can be provided with a library file, why is it built into *gawk*? Adding features for little reason leads to larger, slower programs that are harder to maintain. The answer is that building `nextfile` into *gawk* provides significant gains in efficiency. If the `nextfile` function is executed at the beginning of a large datafile, *awk* still has to scan the entire file, splitting it up into records, just to skip over it. The built-in `nextfile` can simply close the file immediately and proceed to the next one, which saves a lot of time. This is particularly important in *awk*, because *awk* programs are generally I/O-bound (i.e., they spend most of their time doing input and output, instead of performing computations).

Assertions

When writing large programs, it is often useful to know that a condition or set of conditions is true. Before proceeding with a particular computation, you make a statement about what you believe to be the case. Such a statement is known as an *assertion*. The C language provides an `<assert.h>` header file and corresponding `assert` macro that the programmer can use to make assertions. If an assertion fails, the `assert` macro arranges to print a diagnostic message describing the condition that should have been true but was not, and then it kills the program. In C, using `assert` looks this:

```
#include <assert.h>

int myfunc(int a, double b)
{
    assert(a <= 5 && b >= 17.1);
    ...
}
```

If the assertion fails, the program prints a message similar to this:

```
prog.c:5: assertion failed: a <= 5 && b >= 17.1
```

The C language makes it possible to turn the condition into a string for use in printing the diagnostic message. This is not possible in *awk*, so this `assert` function also requires a string version of the condition that is being tested. Following is the function:

```
# assert --- assert that a condition is true. Otherwise exit.

function assert(condition, string)
{
    if (! condition) {
        printf("%s:%d: assertion failed: %s\n",
            FILENAME, FNR, string) > "/dev/stderr"
        _assert_exit = 1
        exit 1
    }
}

END {
    if (_assert_exit)
        exit 1
}
```

The `assert` function tests the `condition` parameter. If it is false, it prints a message to standard error, using the `string` parameter to describe the failed condition. It then sets the variable `_assert_exit` to one and executes the `exit` statement. The `exit` statement jumps to the `END` rule. If the `END` rules finds `_assert_exit` to be true, it exits immediately.

The purpose of the test in the `END` rule is to keep any other `END` rules from running. When an assertion fails, the program should exit immediately. If no assertions fail, then `_assert_exit` is still false when the `END` rule is run normally, and the rest of the program's `END` rules execute. For all of this to work correctly, *assert.awk* must be the first source file read by *awk*. The function can be used in a program in the following way:

```
function myfunc(a, b)
{
    assert(a <= 5 && b >= 17.1, "a <= 5 && b >= 17.1")
    ...
}
```

If the assertion fails, you see a message similar to the following:

```
mydata:1357: assertion failed: a <= 5 && b >= 17.1
```

There is a small problem with this version of `assert`. An `END` rule is automatically added to the program calling `assert`. Normally, if a program consists of just a `BEGIN` rule, the input files and/or standard input are not read. However, now that the program has an `END` rule, *awk* attempts to read the input datafiles or standard input (see the section "Startup and cleanup actions" in Chapter 6), most likely causing the program to hang as it waits for input.

There is a simple workaround to this: make sure the `BEGIN` rule always ends with an `exit` statement.

Rounding Numbers

The way `printf` and `sprintf` (see the section "Using printf Statements for Fancier Printing" in Chapter 4, *Printing Output*) perform rounding often depends upon the system's C `sprintf` subroutine. On many machines, `sprintf` rounding is "unbiased," which means it doesn't always round a trailing .5 up, contrary to naive expectations. In unbiased rounding, .5 rounds to even, rather than always up, so 1.5 rounds to 2 but 4.5 rounds to 4. This means that if you are using a format that does rounding (e.g., `"%.0f"`), you should check what your system does. The following function does traditional rounding; it might be useful if your *awk*'s `printf` does unbiased rounding:

```
# round.awk --- do normal rounding

function round(x,    ival, aval, fraction)
{
    ival = int(x)      # integer part, int() truncates

    # see if fractional part
    if (ival == x)   # no fraction
        return x
```

```
    if (x < 0) {
        aval = -x        # absolute value
        ival = int(aval)
        fraction = aval - ival
        if (fraction >= .5)
            return int(x) - 1    # -2.5 --> -3
        else
            return int(x)        # -2.3 --> -2
    } else {
        fraction = x - ival
        if (fraction >= .5)
            return ival + 1
        else
            return ival
    }
}

# test harness
{ print $0, round($0) }
```

The Cliff Random Number Generator

The Cliff random number generator[*] is a very simple random number generator that "passes the noise sphere test for randomness by showing no structure." It is easily programmed in less than 10 lines of *awk* code:

```
# cliff_rand.awk --- generate Cliff random numbers

BEGIN { _cliff_seed = 0.1 }

function cliff_rand()
{
    _cliff_seed = (100 * log(_cliff_seed)) % 1
    if (_cliff_seed < 0)
        _cliff_seed = - _cliff_seed
    return _cliff_seed
}
```

This algorithm requires an initial "seed" of 0.1. Each new value uses the current seed as input for the calculation. If the built-in rand function (see the section "Numeric Functions" in Chapter 8) isn't random enough, you might try using this function instead.

Translating Between Characters and Numbers

One commercial implementation of *awk* supplies a built-in function, ord, which takes a character and returns the numeric value for that character in the machine's character set. If the string passed to ord has more than one character, only the first one is used.

---

[*] *http://mathworld.wolfram.com/CliffRandomNumberGenerator.hmtl.*

The inverse of this function is chr (from the function of the same name in Pascal), which takes a number and returns the corresponding character. Both functions are written very nicely in *awk*; there is no real reason to build them into the *awk* interpreter:

```
# ord.awk --- do ord and chr

# Global identifiers:
#    _ord_:        numerical values indexed by characters
#    _ord_init:    function to initialize _ord_

BEGIN    { _ord_init() }

function _ord_init(    low, high, i, t)
{
    low = sprintf("%c", 7) # BEL is ascii 7
    if (low == "\a") {      # regular ascii
        low = 0
        high = 127
    } else if (sprintf("%c", 128 + 7) == "\a") {
        # ascii, mark parity
        low = 128
        high = 255
    } else {            # ebcdic(!)
        low = 0
        high = 255
    }

    for (i = low; i <= high; i++) {
        t = sprintf("%c", i)
        _ord_[t] = i
    }
}
```

Some explanation of the numbers used by chr is worthwhile. The most prominent character set in use today is ASCII. Although an 8-bit byte can hold 256 distinct values (from 0 to 255), ASCII only defines characters that use the values from 0 to 127.* In the now distant past, at least one minicomputer manufacturer used ASCII, but with mark parity, meaning that the leftmost bit in the byte is always 1. This means that on those systems, characters have numeric values from 128 to 255. Finally, large mainframe systems use the EBCDIC character set, which uses all 256 values. While there are other character sets in use on some older systems, they are not really worth worrying about:

---

* ASCII has been extended in many countries to use the values from 128 to 255 for country-specific characters. If your system uses these extensions, you can simplify _ord_init to simply loop from 0 to 255.

```
function ord(str,      c)
{
    # only first character is of interest
    c = substr(str, 1, 1)
    return _ord_[c]
}

function chr(c)
{
    # force c to be numeric by adding 0
    return sprintf("%c", c + 0)
}

#### test code ####
# BEGIN      \
# {
#     for (;;) {
#         printf("enter a character: ")
#         if (getline var <= 0)
#             break
#         printf("ord(%s) = %d\n", var, ord(var))
#     }
# }
```

An obvious improvement to these functions is to move the code for the _ord_init function into the body of the BEGIN rule. It was written this way initially for ease of development. There is a "test program" in a BEGIN rule, to test the function. It is commented out for production use.

Merging an Array into a String

When doing string processing, it is often useful to be able to join all the strings in an array into one long string. The following function, join, accomplishes this task. It is used later in several of the application programs (see Chapter 13).

Good function design is important; this function needs to be general but it should also have a reasonable default behavior. It is called with an array as well as the beginning and ending indices of the elements in the array to be merged. This assumes that the array indices are numeric—a reasonable assumption since the array was likely created with split (see the section "String-Manipulation Functions" in Chapter 8):

```
# join.awk --- join an array into a string

function join(array, start, end, sep,     result, i)
{
    if (sep == "")
        sep = " "
    else if (sep == SUBSEP) # magic value
        sep = ""
```

```
    result = array[start]
    for (i = start + 1; i <= end; i++)
        result = result sep array[i]
    return result
}
```

An optional additional argument is the separator to use when joining the strings back together. If the caller supplies a nonempty value, join uses it; if it is not supplied, it has a null value. In this case, join uses a single blank as a default separator for the strings. If the value is equal to SUBSEP, then join joins the strings with no separator between them. SUBSEP serves as a "magic" value to indicate that there should be no separation between the component strings.*

Managing the Time of Day

The systime and strftime functions described in the section "Using gawk's Time-stamp Functions" in Chapter 8 provide the minimum functionality necessary for dealing with the time of day in human readable form. While strftime is extensive, the control formats are not necessarily easy to remember or intuitively obvious when reading a program.

The following function, gettimeofday, populates a user-supplied array with preformatted time information. It returns a string with the current time formatted in the same way as the *date* utility:

```
# gettimeofday.awk --- get the time of day in a usable format

# Returns a string in the format of output of date(1)
# Populates the array argument time with individual values:
#    time["second"]       -- seconds (0 - 59)
#    time["minute"]       -- minutes (0 - 59)
#    time["hour"]         -- hours (0 - 23)
#    time["althour"]      -- hours (0 - 12)
#    time["monthday"]     -- day of month (1 - 31)
#    time["month"]        -- month of year (1 - 12)
#    time["monthname"]    -- name of the month
#    time["shortmonth"]   -- short name of the month
#    time["year"]         -- year modulo 100 (0 - 99)
#    time["fullyear"]     -- full year
#    time["weekday"]      -- day of week (Sunday = 0)
#    time["altweekday"]   -- day of week (Monday = 0)
#    time["dayname"]      -- name of weekday
#    time["shortdayname"] -- short name of weekday
#    time["yearday"]      -- day of year (0 - 365)
#    time["timezone"]     -- abbreviation of timezone name
#    time["ampm"]         -- AM or PM designation
#    time["weeknum"]      -- week number, Sunday first day
#    time["altweeknum"]   -- week number, Monday first day
```

---

* It would be nice if *awk* had an assignment operator for concatenation. The lack of an explicit operator for concatenation makes string operations more difficult than they really need to be.

```
function gettimeofday(time,     ret, now, i)
{
    # get time once, avoids unnecessary system calls
    now = systime()

    # return date(1)-style output
    ret = strftime("%a %b %d %H:%M:%S %Z %Y", now)

    # clear out target array
    delete time

    # fill in values, force numeric values to be
    # numeric by adding 0
    time["second"]      = strftime("%S", now) + 0
    time["minute"]      = strftime("%M", now) + 0
    time["hour"]        = strftime("%H", now) + 0
    time["althour"]     = strftime("%I", now) + 0
    time["monthday"]    = strftime("%d", now) + 0
    time["month"]       = strftime("%m", now) + 0
    time["monthname"]   = strftime("%B", now)
    time["shortmonth"]  = strftime("%b", now)
    time["year"]        = strftime("%y", now) + 0
    time["fullyear"]    = strftime("%Y", now) + 0
    time["weekday"]     = strftime("%w", now) + 0
    time["altweekday"]  = strftime("%u", now) + 0
    time["dayname"]     = strftime("%A", now)
    time["shortdayname"] = strftime("%a", now)
    time["yearday"]     = strftime("%j", now) + 0
    time["timezone"]    = strftime("%Z", now)
    time["ampm"]        = strftime("%p", now)
    time["weeknum"]     = strftime("%U", now) + 0
    time["altweeknum"]  = strftime("%W", now) + 0

    return ret
}
```

The string indices are easier to use and read than the various formats required by
strftime. The alarm program presented in the section "An Alarm Clock Program"
in Chapter 13 uses this function. A more general design for the gettimeofday function would have allowed the user to supply an optional timestamp value to use
instead of the current time.

Datafile Management

This section presents functions that are useful for managing command-line
datafiles.

Noting Datafile Boundaries

The BEGIN and END rules are each executed exactly once at the beginning and end of your *awk* program, respectively (see the section "The BEGIN and END Special Patterns" in Chapter 6). We (the *gawk* authors) once had a user who mistakenly thought that the BEGIN rule is executed at the beginning of each datafile and the END rule is executed at the end of each datafile. When informed that this was not the case, the user requested that we add new special patterns to *gawk*, named BEGIN_FILE and END_FILE, that would have the desired behavior. He even supplied us the code to do so.

Adding these special patterns to *gawk* wasn't necessary; the job can be done cleanly in *awk* itself, as illustrated by the following library program. It arranges to call two user-supplied functions, beginfile and endfile, at the beginning and end of each datafile. Besides solving the problem in only nine (!) lines of code, it does so *portably*; this works with any implementation of *awk*:

```
# transfile.awk
#
# Give the user a hook for filename transitions
#
# The user must supply functions beginfile() and endfile()
# that each take the name of the file being started or
# finished, respectively.

FILENAME != _oldfilename \
{
    if (_oldfilename != "")
        endfile(_oldfilename)
    _oldfilename = FILENAME
    beginfile(FILENAME)
}

END   { endfile(FILENAME) }
```

This file must be loaded before the user's "main" program, so that the rule it supplies is executed first.

This rule relies on *awk*'s FILENAME variable that automatically changes for each new datafile. The current filename is saved in a private variable, _oldfilename. If FILENAME does not equal _oldfilename, then a new datafile is being processed and it is necessary to call endfile for the old file. Because endfile should only be called if a file has been processed, the program first checks to make sure that _oldfilename is not the null string. The program then assigns the current filename to _oldfilename and calls beginfile for the file. Because, like all *awk* variables, _oldfilename is initialized to the null string, this rule executes correctly even for the first datafile.

The program also supplies an END rule to do the final processing for the last file. Because this END rule comes before any END rules supplied in the "main" program, endfile is called first. Once again the value of multiple BEGIN and END rules should be clear.

This version has same problem as the first version of nextfile (see the section "Implementing nextfile as a Function" earlier in this chapter). If the same datafile occurs twice in a row on the command line, then beginfile and endfile are not executed at the end of the first pass and at the beginning of the second pass. The following version solves the problem:

```
# ftrans.awk --- handle data file transitions
#
# user supplies beginfile() and endfile() functions

FNR == 1 {
    if (_filename_ != "")
        endfile(_filename_)
    _filename_ = FILENAME
    beginfile(FILENAME)
}


END   { endfile(_filename_) }
```

The section "Counting Things" in Chapter 13 shows how this library function can be used and how it simplifies writing the main program.

Rereading the Current File

Another request for a new built-in function was for a rewind function that would make it possible to reread the current file. The requesting user didn't want to have to use getline (see the section "Explicit Input with getline" in Chapter 3, *Reading Input Files*) inside a loop.

However, as long as you are not in the END rule, it is quite easy to arrange to immediately close the current input file and then start over with it from the top. For lack of a better name, we'll call it rewind:

```
# rewind.awk --- rewind the current file and start over

function rewind(     i)
{
    # shift remaining arguments up
    for (i = ARGC; i > ARGIND; i--)
        ARGV[i] = ARGV[i-1]

    # make sure gawk knows to keep going
    ARGC++
```

```
          # make current file next to get done
          ARGV[ARGIND+1] = FILENAME

          # do it
          nextfile
   }
```

This code relies on the ARGIND variable (see the section "Built-in Variables That Convey Information" in Chapter 6), which is specific to *gawk*. If you are not using *gawk*, you can use ideas presented in the section "Noting Datafile Boundaries" earlier in this chapter to either update ARGIND on your own or modify this code as appropriate.

The rewind function also relies on the nextfile keyword (see the section "Using gawk's nextfile Statement" in Chapter 6). See the section "Implementing nextfile as a Function" earlier in this chapter for a function version of nextfile.

Checking for Readable Datafiles

Normally, if you give *awk* a datafile that isn't readable, it stops with a fatal error. There are times when you might want to just ignore such files and keep going. You can do this by prepending the following program to your *awk* program:

```
# readable.awk --- library file to skip over unreadable files

BEGIN {
    for (i = 1; i < ARGC; i++) {
        if (ARGV[i] ~ /^[A-Za-z_][A-Za-z0-9_]*=.*/ \
            || ARGV[i] == "-")
            continue    # assignment or standard input
        else if ((getline junk < ARGV[i]) < 0) # unreadable
            delete ARGV[i]
        else
            close(ARGV[i])
    }
}
```

In *gawk*, the getline won't be fatal (unless *--posix* is in force). Removing the element from ARGV with delete skips the file (since it's no longer in the list).

Treating Assignments as Filenames

Occasionally, you might not want *awk* to process command-line variable assignments (see the section "Assigning Variables on the Command Line" in Chapter 5, *Expressions*). In particular, if you have filenames that contain an = character, *awk* treats the filename as an assignment, and does not process it.

Some users have suggested an additional command-line option for *gawk* to disable command-line assignments. However, some simple programming with a library file does the trick:

```
# noassign.awk --- library file to avoid the need for a
# special option that disables command-line assignments

function disable_assigns(argc, argv,    i)
{
    for (i = 1; i < argc; i++)
        if (argv[i] ~ /^[A-Za-z_][A-Za-z_0-9]*=.*/)
            argv[i] = ("./" argv[i])
}

BEGIN {
    if (No_command_assign)
        disable_assigns(ARGC, ARGV)
}
```

You then run your program this way:

```
awk -v No_command_assign=1 -f noassign.awk -f yourprog.awk *
```

The function works by looping through the arguments. It prepends ./ to any argument that matches the form of a variable assignment, turning that argument into a filename.

The use of No_command_assign allows you to disable command-line assignments at invocation time, by giving the variable a true value. When not set, it is initially zero (i.e., false), so the command-line arguments are left alone.

Processing Command-Line Options

Most utilities on POSIX compatible systems take options, or "switches," on the command line that can be used to change the way a program behaves. *awk* is an example of such a program (see the section "Command-Line Options" in Chapter 11, *Running awk and gawk*). Often, options take *arguments*; i.e., data that the program needs to correctly obey the command-line option. For example, *awk*'s *–F* option requires a string to use as the field separator. The first occurrence on the command line of either –– or a string that does not begin with – ends the options.

Modern Unix systems provide a C function named getopt for processing command-line arguments. The programmer provides a string describing the one-letter options. If an option requires an argument, it is followed in the string with a colon. getopt is also passed the count and values of the command-line arguments and is called in a loop. getopt processes the command-line arguments for option letters. Each time around the loop, it returns a single character representing the next option letter that it finds, or ? if it finds an invalid option. When it returns −1, there are no options left on the command line.

When using getopt, options that do not take arguments can be grouped together. Furthermore, options that take arguments require that the argument is present. The argument can immediately follow the option letter, or it can be a separate command-line argument.

Given a hypothetical program that takes three command-line options, −*a*, −*b*, and −*c*, where −*b* requires an argument, all of the following are valid ways of invoking the program:

```
prog -a -b foo -c data1 data2 data3
prog -ac -bfoo -- data1 data2 data3
prog -acbfoo data1 data2 data3
```

Notice that when the argument is grouped with its option, the rest of the argument is considered to be the option's argument. In this example, −*acbfoo* indicates that all of the −*a*, −*b*, and −*c* options were supplied, and that foo is the argument to the −*b* option.

getopt provides four external variables that the programmer can use:

optind
> The index in the argument value array (argv) in which the first nonoption command-line argument can be found.

optarg
> The string value of the argument to an option.

opterr
> Usually getopt prints an error message when it finds an invalid option. Setting opterr to zero disables this feature. (An application might want to print its own error message.)

optopt
> The letter representing the command-line option.

The following C fragment shows how getopt might process command-line arguments for *awk*:

```
int
main(int argc, char *argv[])
{
    ...
    /* print our own message */
    opterr = 0;
    while ((c = getopt(argc, argv, "v:f:F:W:")) != -1) {
        switch (c) {
```

```
      case 'f':    /* file */
         ...
         break;
      case 'F':    /* field separator */
         ...
         break;
      case 'v':    /* variable assignment */
         ...
         break;
      case 'W':    /* extension */
         ...
         break;
      case '?':
      default:
         usage();
         break;
      }
   }
   ...
}
```

As a side point, *gawk* actually uses the GNU `getopt_long` function to process both normal and GNU-style long options (see the section "Command-Line Options" in Chapter 11).

The abstraction provided by `getopt` is very useful and is quite handy in *awk* programs as well. Following is an *awk* version of `getopt`. This function highlights one of the greatest weaknesses in *awk*, which is that it is very poor at manipulating single characters. Repeated calls to `substr` are necessary for accessing individual characters (see the section "String-Manipulation Functions" in Chapter 8).*

The discussion that follows walks through the code a bit at a time:

```
# getopt.awk --- do C library getopt(3) function in awk

# External variables:
#    Optind -- index in ARGV of first nonoption argument
#    Optarg -- string value of argument to current option
#    Opterr -- if nonzero, print our own diagnostic
#    Optopt -- current option letter

# Returns:
#    -1     at end of options
#    ?      for unrecognized option
#    <c>    a character representing the current option

# Private Data:
#    _opti  -- index in multi-flag option, e.g., -abc
```

---

* This function was written before *gawk* acquired the ability to split strings into single characters using `""` as the separator. We have left it alone, since using `substr` is more portable.

The function starts out with a list of the global variables it uses, what the return values are, what they mean, and any global variables that are "private" to this library function. Such documentation is essential for any program, and particularly for library functions.

The getopt function first checks that it was indeed called with a string of options (the options parameter). If options has a zero length, getopt immediately returns −1:

```
function getopt(argc, argv, options,    thisopt, i)
{
    if (length(options) == 0)    # no options given
        return -1

    if (argv[Optind] == "--") {  # all done
        Optind++
        _opti = 0
        return -1
    } else if (argv[Optind] !~ /^-[^: \t\n\f\r\v\b]/) {
        _opti = 0
        return -1
    }
```

The next thing to check for is the end of the options. A −− ends the command-line options, as does any command-line argument that does not begin with a -. Optind is used to step through the array of command-line arguments; it retains its value across calls to getopt, because it is a global variable.

The regular expression that is used, /^-[^: \t\n\f\r\v\b]/, is perhaps a bit of overkill; it checks for a - followed by anything that is not whitespace and not a colon. If the current command-line argument does not match this pattern, it is not an option, and it ends option processing:

```
    if (_opti == 0)
        _opti = 2
    thisopt = substr(argv[Optind], _opti, 1)
    Optopt = thisopt
    i = index(options, thisopt)
    if (i == 0) {
        if (Opterr)
            printf("%c -- invalid option\n",
                thisopt) > "/dev/stderr"
        if (_opti >= length(argv[Optind])) {
            Optind++
            _opti = 0
        } else
            _opti++
        return "?"
    }
```

The _opti variable tracks the position in the current command-line argument
(argv[Optind]). If multiple options are grouped together with one - (e.g., *-abx*), it
is necessary to return them to the user one at a time.

If _opti is equal to zero, it is set to two, which is the index in the string of the
next character to look at (we skip the -, which is at position one). The variable
thisopt holds the character, obtained with substr. It is saved in Optopt for the
main program to use.

If thisopt is not in the options string, then it is an invalid option. If Opterr is
nonzero, getopt prints an error message on the standard error that is similar to the
message from the C version of getopt.

Because the option is invalid, it is necessary to skip it and move on to the next
option character. If _opti is greater than or equal to the length of the current command-line argument, it is necessary to move on to the next argument, so Optind is
incremented and _opti is reset to zero. Otherwise, Optind is left alone and _opti is
merely incremented.

In any case, because the option is invalid, getopt returns ?. The main program can
examine Optopt if it needs to know what the invalid option letter actually is. Continuing on:

```
if (substr(options, i + 1, 1) == ":") {
    # get option argument
    if (length(substr(argv[Optind], _opti + 1)) > 0)
        Optarg = substr(argv[Optind], _opti + 1)
    else
        Optarg = argv[++Optind]
    _opti = 0
} else
    Optarg = ""
```

If the option requires an argument, the option letter is followed by a colon in the
options string. If there are remaining characters in the current command-line argument (argv[Optind]), then the rest of that string is assigned to Optarg. Otherwise,
the next command-line argument is used (-xFOO versus -x FOO). In either case,
_opti is reset to zero, because there are no more characters left to examine in the
current command-line argument. Continuing:

```
if (_opti == 0 || _opti >= length(argv[Optind])) {
    Optind++
    _opti = 0
} else
    _opti++
return thisopt
}
```

Finally, if _opti is either zero or greater than the length of the current command-line argument, it means this element in argv is through being processed, so Optind is incremented to point to the next element in argv. If neither condition is true, then only _opti is incremented, so that the next option letter can be processed on the next call to getopt.

The BEGIN rule initializes both Opterr and Optind to one. Opterr is set to one, since the default behavior is for getopt to print a diagnostic message upon seeing an invalid option. Optind is set to one, since there's no reason to look at the program name, which is in ARGV[0]:

```
BEGIN {
    Opterr = 1    # default is to diagnose
    Optind = 1    # skip ARGV[0]

    # test program
    if (_getopt_test) {
        while ((_go_c = getopt(ARGC, ARGV, "ab:cd")) != -1)
            printf("c = <%c>, optarg = <%s>\n",
                _go_c, Optarg)
        printf("non-option arguments:\n")
        for (; Optind < ARGC; Optind++)
            printf("\tARGV[%d] = <%s>\n",
                Optind, ARGV[Optind])
    }
}
```

The rest of the BEGIN rule is a simple test program. Here is the result of two sample runs of the test program:

```
$ awk -f getopt.awk -v _getopt_test=1 -- -a -cbARG bax -x
c = <a>, optarg = <>
c = <c>, optarg = <>
c = <b>, optarg = <ARG>
non-option arguments:
        ARGV[3] = <bax>
        ARGV[4] = <-x>

$ awk -f getopt.awk -v _getopt_test=1 -- -a -x -- xyz abc
c = <a>, optarg = <>
x -- invalid option
c = <?>, optarg = <>
non-option arguments:
        ARGV[4] = <xyz>
        ARGV[5] = <abc>
```

In both runs, the first -- terminates the arguments to *awk*, so that it does not try to interpret the −*a*, etc., as its own options. Several of the sample programs presented in Chapter 13 use getopt to process their arguments.

Reading the User Database

The PROCINFO array (see the section "Built-in Variables" in Chapter 6) provides access to the current user's real and effective user and group ID numbers, and if available, the user's supplementary group set. However, because these are numbers, they do not provide very useful information to the average user. There needs to be some way to find the user information associated with the user and group ID numbers. This section presents a suite of functions for retrieving information from the user database. See the section "Reading the Group Database" later in this chapter for a similar suite that retrieves information from the group database.

The POSIX standard does not define the file where user information is kept. Instead, it provides the <pwd.h> header file and several C language subroutines for obtaining user information. The primary function is getpwent, for "get password entry." The "password" comes from the original user database file, */etc/passwd*, which stores user information, along with the encrypted passwords (hence the name).

While an *awk* program could simply read */etc/passwd* directly, this file may not contain complete information about the system's set of users.* To be sure you are able to produce a readable and complete version of the user database, it is necessary to write a small C program that calls getpwent. getpwent is defined as returning a pointer to a struct passwd. Each time it is called, it returns the next entry in the database. When there are no more entries, it returns NULL, the null pointer. When this happens, the C program should call endpwent to close the database. Following is *pwcat*, a C program that "cats" the password database:

```
/*
 * pwcat.c
 *
 * Generate a printable version of the password database
 */

#include <stdio.h>
#include <pwd.h>

int
main(argc, argv)
int argc;
char **argv;
{
    struct passwd *p;
```

---

* It is often the case that password information is stored in a network database.

```
            while ((p = getpwent()) != NULL)
                printf("%s:%s:%d:%d:%s:%s:%s\n",
                        p->pw_name, p->pw_passwd, p->pw_uid,
                        p->pw_gid, p->pw_gecos, p->pw_dir, p->pw_shell);

            endpwent();
            exit(0);
        }
```

If you don't understand C, don't worry about it. The output from *pwcat* is the user database, in the traditional */etc/passwd* format of colon-separated fields. The fields are:

Login name
> The user's login name.

Encrypted password
> The user's encrypted password. This may not be available on some systems.

User-ID
> The user's numeric user ID number.

Group-ID
> The user's numeric group ID number.

Full name
> The user's full name, and perhaps other information associated with the user.

Home directory
> The user's login (or "home") directory (familiar to shell programmers as $HOME).

Login shell
> The program that is run when the user logs in. This is usually a shell, such as bash.

A few lines representative of *pwcat*'s output are as follows:

```
$ pwcat
root:3Ov02d5VaUPB6:0:1:Operator:/:/bin/sh
nobody:*:65534:65534::/:
daemon:*:1:1::/:
sys:*:2:2::/:/bin/csh
bin:*:3:3::/bin:
arnold:xyzzy:2076:10:Arnold Robbins:/home/arnold:/bin/sh
miriam:yxaay:112:10:Miriam Robbins:/home/miriam:/bin/sh
andy:abcca2:113:10:Andy Jacobs:/home/andy:/bin/sh
    ...
```

With that introduction, following is a group of functions for getting user information. There are several functions here, corresponding to the C functions of the same names:

```
# passwd.awk --- access password file information

BEGIN {
    # tailor this to suit your system
    _pw_awklib = "/usr/local/libexec/awk/"
}

function _pw_init(    oldfs, oldrs, olddol0, pwcat, using_fw)
{
    if (_pw_inited)
        return

    oldfs = FS
    oldrs = RS
    olddol0 = $0
    using_fw = (PROCINFO["FS"] == "FIELDWIDTHS")
    FS = ":"
    RS = "\n"

    pwcat = _pw_awklib "pwcat"
    while ((pwcat | getline) > 0) {
        _pw_byname[$1] = $0
        _pw_byuid[$3] = $0
        _pw_bycount[++_pw_total] = $0
    }
    close(pwcat)
    _pw_count = 0
    _pw_inited = 1
    FS = oldfs
    if (using_fw)
        FIELDWIDTHS = FIELDWIDTHS
    RS = oldrs
    $0 = olddol0
}
```

The BEGIN rule sets a private variable to the directory where *pwcat* is stored. Because it is used to help out an *awk* library routine, we have chosen to put it in */usr/local/libexec/awk*; however, you might want it to be in a different directory on your system.

The function _pw_init keeps three copies of the user information in three associative arrays. The arrays are indexed by username (_pw_byname), by user-id number (_pw_byuid), and by order of occurrence (_pw_bycount). The variable _pw_inited is used for efficiency; _pw_init needs only to be called once.

Because this function uses getline to read information from *pwcat*, it first saves the values of FS, RS, and $0. It notes in the variable using_fw whether field splitting with FIELDWIDTHS is in effect or not. Doing so is necessary, since these functions could be called from anywhere within a user's program, and the user may have his own way of splitting records and fields.

The using_fw variable checks PROCINFO["FS"], which is "FIELDWIDTHS" if field splitting is being done with FIELDWIDTHS. This makes it possible to restore the correct field-splitting mechanism later. The test can only be true for *gawk*. It is false if using FS or on some other *awk* implementation.

The main part of the function uses a loop to read database lines, split the line into fields, and then store the line into each array as necessary. When the loop is done, _pw_init cleans up by closing the pipeline, setting _pw_inited to one, and restoring FS (and FIELDWIDTHS if necessary), RS, and $0. The use of _pw_count is explained shortly.

The getpwnam function takes a username as a string argument. If that user is in the database, it returns the appropriate line. Otherwise, it returns the null string:

```
function getpwnam(name)
{
    _pw_init()
    if (name in _pw_byname)
        return _pw_byname[name]
    return ""
}
```

Similarly, the getpwuid function takes a user-id number argument. If that user number is in the database, it returns the appropriate line. Otherwise, it returns the null string:

```
function getpwuid(uid)
{
    _pw_init()
    if (uid in _pw_byuid)
        return _pw_byuid[uid]
    return ""
}
```

The getpwent function simply steps through the database, one entry at a time. It uses _pw_count to track its current position in the _pw_bycount array:

```
function getpwent()
{
    _pw_init()
    if (_pw_count < _pw_total)
        return _pw_bycount[++_pw_count]
    return ""
}
```

The endpwent function resets _pw_count to zero, so that subsequent calls to getpwent start over again:

```
function endpwent()
{
    _pw_count = 0
}
```

A conscious design decision in this suite was made that requires each subroutine
to call _pw_init to initialize the database arrays. The overhead of running a separate process to generate the user database, and the I/O to scan it, are only
incurred if the user's main program actually calls one of these functions. If this
library file is loaded along with a user's program, but none of the routines are ever
called, then there is no extra runtime overhead. (The alternative is move the body
of _pw_init into a BEGIN rule, which always runs *pwcat*. This simplifies the code
but runs an extra process that may never be needed.)

In turn, calling _pw_init is not too expensive, because the _pw_inited variable
keeps the program from reading the data more than once. If you are worried
about squeezing every last cycle out of your *awk* program, the check of
_pw_inited could be moved out of _pw_init and duplicated in all the other functions. In practice, this is not necessary, since most *awk* programs are I/O-bound,
and it clutters up the code.

The *id* program in the section "Printing out User Information" in Chapter 13 uses
these functions.

Reading the Group Database

Much of the discussion presented in the previous section applies to the group
database as well. Although there has traditionally been a well-known file
(*/etc/group*) in a well-known format, the POSIX standard only provides a set of C
library routines (<grp.h> and getgrent) for accessing the information. Even though
this file may exist, it likely does not have complete information. Therefore, as with
the user database, it is necessary to have a small C program that generates the
group database as its output.

grcat, a C program that "cats" the group database, is as follows:

```
/*
 * grcat.c
 *
 * Generate a printable version of the group database
 */

#include <stdio.h>
#include <grp.h>
```

```
int
main(argc, argv)
int argc;
char **argv;
{
    struct group *g;
    int i;

    while ((g = getgrent()) != NULL) {
        printf("%s:%s:%d:", g->gr_name, g->gr_passwd,
                g->gr_gid);
        for (i = 0; g->gr_mem[i] != NULL; i++) {
            printf("%s", g->gr_mem[i]);
            if (g->gr_mem[i+1] != NULL)
                putchar(',');
        }
        putchar('\n');
    }
    endgrent();
    exit(0);
}
```

Each line in the group database represents one group. The fields are separated with colons and represent the following information:

Group name

> The group's name.

Group password

> The group's encrypted password. In practice, this field is never used; it is usually empty or set to *.

Group-ID

> The group's numeric group ID number; this number is unique within the file.

Group member list

> A comma-separated list of usernames. These users are members of the group. Modern Unix systems allow users to be members of several groups simultaneously. If your system does, then there are elements "group1" through "groupN" in PROCINFO for those group ID numbers. (Note that PROCINFO is a *gawk* extension; see the section "Built-in Variables" in Chapter 6.)

Here is what running *grcat* might produce:

```
$ grcat
wheel:*:0:arnold
nogroup:*:65534:
daemon:*:1:
kmem:*:2:
staff:*:10:arnold,miriam,andy
other:*:20:
...
```

Here are the functions for obtaining information from the group database. There are several, modeled after the C library functions of the same names:

```
# group.awk --- functions for dealing with the group file

BEGIN    \
{
    # Change to suit your system
    _gr_awklib = "/usr/local/libexec/awk/"
}

function _gr_init(    oldfs, oldrs, olddol0, grcat, using_fw, n, a, i)
{
    if (_gr_inited)
        return

    oldfs = FS
    oldrs = RS
    olddol0 = $0
    using_fw = (PROCINFO["FS"] == "FIELDWIDTHS")
    FS = ":"
    RS = "\n"

    grcat = _gr_awklib "grcat"
    while ((grcat | getline) > 0) {
        if ($1 in _gr_byname)
            _gr_byname[$1] = _gr_byname[$1] "," $4
        else
            _gr_byname[$1] = $0
        if ($3 in _gr_bygid)
            _gr_bygid[$3] = _gr_bygid[$3] "," $4
        else
            _gr_bygid[$3] = $0

        n = split($4, a, "[ \t]*,[ \t]*")
        for (i = 1; i <= n; i++)
            if (a[i] in _gr_groupsbyuser)
                _gr_groupsbyuser[a[i]] = \
                    _gr_groupsbyuser[a[i]] " " $1
            else
                _gr_groupsbyuser[a[i]] = $1

        _gr_bycount[++_gr_count] = $0
    }
    close(grcat)
    _gr_count = 0
    _gr_inited++
    FS = oldfs
    if (using_fw)
        FIELDWIDTHS = FIELDWIDTHS
    RS = oldrs
    $0 = olddol0
}
```

The BEGIN rule sets a private variable to the directory where *grcat* is stored. Because it is used to help out an *awk* library routine, we have chosen to put it in */usr/local/libexec/awk*. You might want it to be in a different directory on your system.

These routines follow the same general outline as the user database routines (see the section "Reading the User Database" earlier in this chapter). The _gr_inited variable is used to ensure that the database is scanned no more than once. The _gr_init function first saves FS, FIELDWIDTHS, RS, and $0, and then sets FS and RS to the correct values for scanning the group information.

The group information is stored is several associative arrays. The arrays are indexed by group name (_gr_byname), by group ID number (_gr_bygid), and by position in the database (_gr_bycount). There is an additional array indexed by username (_gr_groupsbyuser), which is a space-separated list of groups to which each user belongs.

Unlike the user database, it is possible to have multiple records in the database for the same group. This is common when a group has a large number of members. A pair of such entries might look like the following:

```
tvpeople:*:101:johnny,jay,arsenio
tvpeople:*:101:david,conan,tom,joan
```

For this reason, _gr_init looks to see if a group name or group ID number is already seen. If it is, then the usernames are simply concatenated onto the previous list of users. (There is actually a subtle problem with the code just presented. Suppose that the first time there were no names. This code adds the names with a leading comma. It also doesn't check that there is a $4.)

Finally, _gr_init closes the pipeline to *grcat*, restores FS (and FIELDWIDTHS if necessary), RS, and $0, initializes _gr_count to zero (it is used later), and makes _gr_inited nonzero.

The getgrnam function takes a group name as its argument, and if that group exists, it is returned. Otherwise, getgrnam returns the null string:

```
function getgrnam(group)
{
    _gr_init()
    if (group in _gr_byname)
        return _gr_byname[group]
    return ""
}
```

The getgrgid function is similar, it takes a numeric group ID and looks up the information associated with that group ID:

```
function getgrgid(gid)
{
    _gr_init()
    if (gid in _gr_bygid)
        return _gr_bygid[gid]
    return ""
}
```

The getgruser function does not have a C counterpart. It takes a username and returns the list of groups that have the user as a member:

```
function getgruser(user)
{
    _gr_init()
    if (user in _gr_groupsbyuser)
        return _gr_groupsbyuser[user]
    return ""
}
```

The getgrent function steps through the database one entry at a time. It uses _gr_count to track its position in the list:

```
function getgrent()
{
    _gr_init()
    if (++_gr_count in _gr_bycount)
        return _gr_bycount[_gr_count]
    return ""
}
```

The endgrent function resets _gr_count to zero so that getgrent can start over again:

```
function endgrent()
{
    _gr_count = 0
}
```

As with the user database routines, each function calls _gr_init to initialize the arrays. Doing so only incurs the extra overhead of running *grcat* if these functions are used (as opposed to moving the body of _gr_init into a BEGIN rule).

Most of the work is in scanning the database and building the various associative arrays. The functions that the user calls are themselves very simple, relying on *awk*'s associative arrays to do work.

The *id* program in the section "Printing out User Information" in Chapter 13 uses these functions.

13

Practical awk Programs

Chapter 12, *A Library of awk Functions*, presents the idea that reading programs in a language contributes to learning that language. This chapter continues that theme, presenting a potpourri of *awk* programs for your reading enjoyment. There are three sections. The first describes how to run the programs presented in this chapter.

The second presents *awk* versions of several common POSIX utilities. These are programs that you are hopefully already familiar with, and therefore, whose problems are understood. By reimplementing these programs in *awk*, you can focus on the *awk*-related aspects of solving the programming problem.

The third is a grab bag of interesting programs. These solve a number of different data-manipulation and management problems. Many of the programs are short, which emphasizes *awk*'s ability to do a lot in just a few lines of code.

Many of these programs use the library functions presented in Chapter 12.

Running the Example Programs

To run a given program, you would typically do something like this:

```
awk -f program -- options files
```

Here, *program* is the name of the *awk* program (such as *cut.awk*), *options* are any command-line options for the program that start with a -, and *files* are the actual datafiles.

If your system supports the #! executable interpreter mechanism (see the section "Executable awk Programs" in Chapter 1, *Getting Started with awk*), you can instead run your program directly:

```
cut.awk -c1-8 myfiles > results
```

If your *awk* is not *gawk*, you may instead need to use this:

```
cut.awk -- -c1-8 myfiles > results
```

Reinventing Wheels for Fun and Profit

This section presents a number of POSIX utilities that are implemented in *awk*. Reinventing these programs in *awk* is often enjoyable, because the algorithms can be very clearly expressed, and the code is usually very concise and simple. This is true because *awk* does so much for you.

It should be noted that these programs are not necessarily intended to replace the installed versions on your system. Instead, their purpose is to illustrate *awk* language programming for "real world" tasks.

Cutting out Fields and Columns

The *cut* utility selects, or "cuts," characters or fields from its standard input and sends them to its standard output. Fields are separated by tabs by default, but you may supply a command-line option to change the field *delimiter* (i.e., the field-separator character). *cut*'s definition of fields is less general than *awk*'s.

A common use of *cut* might be to pull out just the login name of logged-on users from the output of *who*. For example, the following pipeline generates a sorted, unique list of the logged-on users:

```
who | cut -c1-8 | sort | uniq
```

The options for *cut* are:

-c *list*

> Use *list* as the list of characters to cut out. Items within the list may be separated by commas, and ranges of characters can be separated with dashes. The list 1-8,15,22-35 specifies characters 1 through 8, 15, and 22 through 35.

-f *list*

> Use *list* as the list of fields to cut out.

-d *delim*

    Use *delim* as the field-separator character instead of the tab character.

-s Suppress printing of lines that do not contain the field delimiter.

The *awk* implementation of *cut* uses the getopt library function (see the section "Processing Command-Line Options" in Chapter 12) and the join library function (see the section "Merging an Array into a String" in Chapter 12).

The program begins with a comment describing the options, the library functions needed, and a usage function that prints out a usage message and exits. usage is called if invalid arguments are supplied:

```
# cut.awk --- implement cut in awk

# Options:
#     -f list      Cut fields
#     -d c         Field delimiter character
#     -c list      Cut characters
#
#     -s           Suppress lines without the delimiter
#
# Requires getopt and join library functions

function usage(    e1, e2)
{
    e1 = "usage: cut [-f list] [-d c] [-s] [files...]"
    e2 = "usage: cut [-c list] [files...]"
    print e1 > "/dev/stderr"
    print e2 > "/dev/stderr"
    exit 1
}
```

The variables e1 and e2 are used so that the function fits nicely on the page.

Next comes a BEGIN rule that parses the command-line options. It sets FS to a single-tab character, because that is *cut*'s default field separator. The output field separator is also set to be the same as the input field separator. Then getopt is used to step through the command-line options. One of the variables by_fields or by_chars is set to true, to indicate that processing should be done by fields or by characters, respectively. When cutting by characters, the output field separator is set to the null string:

```
BEGIN    \
{
    FS = "\t"     # default
    OFS = FS
    while ((c = getopt(ARGC, ARGV, "sf:c:d:")) != -1) {
        if (c == "f") {
            by_fields = 1
            fieldlist = Optarg
```

```
            } else if (c == "c") {
                by_chars = 1
                fieldlist = Optarg
                OFS = ""
            } else if (c == "d") {
                if (length(Optarg) > 1) {
                    printf("Using first character of %s" \
                        " for delimiter\n", Optarg) > "/dev/stderr"
                    Optarg = substr(Optarg, 1, 1)
                }
                FS = Optarg
                OFS = FS
                if (FS == " ")      # defeat awk semantics
                    FS = "[ ]"
            } else if (c == "s")
                suppress++
            else
                usage()
        }

    for (i = 1; i < Optind; i++)
        ARGV[i] = ""
```

Special care is taken when the field delimiter is a space. Using a single space (" ") for the value of FS is incorrect—*awk* would separate fields with runs of spaces, tabs, and/or newlines, and we want them to be separated with individual spaces. Also, note that after getopt is through, we have to clear out all the elements of ARGV from 1 to Optind, so that *awk* does not try to process the command-line options as filenames.

After dealing with the command-line options, the program verifies that the options make sense. Only one or the other of −c and −f should be used, and both require a field list. Then the program calls either set_fieldlist or set_charlist to pull apart the list of fields or characters:

```
    if (by_fields && by_chars)
        usage()

    if (by_fields == 0 && by_chars == 0)
        by_fields = 1      # default

    if (fieldlist == "") {
        print "cut: needs list for -c or -f" > "/dev/stderr"
        exit 1
    }

    if (by_fields)
        set_fieldlist()
    else
        set_charlist()
}
```

`set_fieldlist` is used to split the field list apart at the commas and into an array. Then, for each element of the array, it looks to see if it is actually a range, and if so, splits it apart. The range is verified to make sure the first number is smaller than the second. Each number in the list is added to the `flist` array, which simply lists the fields that will be printed. Normal field splitting is used. The program lets *awk* handle the job of doing the field splitting:

```
function set_fieldlist(          n, m, i, j, k, f, g)
{
    n = split(fieldlist, f, ",")
    j = 1    # index in flist
    for (i = 1; i <= n; i++) {
        if (index(f[i], "-") != 0) { # a range
            m = split(f[i], g, "-")
            if (m != 2 || g[1] >= g[2]) {
                printf("bad field list: %s\n",
                            f[i]) > "/dev/stderr"
                exit 1
            }
            for (k = g[1]; k <= g[2]; k++)
                flist[j++] = k
        } else
            flist[j++] = f[i]
    }
    nfields = j - 1
}
```

The `set_charlist` function is more complicated than `set_fieldlist`. The idea here is to use *gawk*'s FIELDWIDTHS variable (see the section "Reading Fixed-Width Data" in Chapter 3, *Reading Input Files*), which describes constant-width input. When using a character list, that is exactly what we have.

Setting up FIELDWIDTHS is more complicated than simply listing the fields that need to be printed. We have to keep track of the fields to print and also the intervening characters that have to be skipped. For example, suppose you wanted characters 1 through 8, 15, and 22 through 35. You would use –c 1-8,15,22-35. The necessary value for FIELDWIDTHS is "8 6 1 6 14". This yields five fields, and the fields to print are $1, $3, and $5. The intermediate fields are *filler*, which is stuff in between the desired data. `flist` lists the fields to print, and t tracks the complete field list, including filler fields:

```
function set_charlist(     field, i, j, f, g, t,
                            filler, last, len)
{
    field = 1   # count total fields
    n = split(fieldlist, f, ",")
    j = 1       # index in flist
    for (i = 1; i <= n; i++) {
        if (index(f[i], "-") != 0) { # range
            m = split(f[i], g, "-")
```

```
                    if (m != 2 || g[1] >= g[2]) {
                        printf("bad character list: %s\n",
                                    f[i]) > "/dev/stderr"
                        exit 1
                    }
                    len = g[2] - g[1] + 1
                    if (g[1] > 1)  # compute length of filler
                        filler = g[1] - last - 1
                    else
                        filler = 0
                    if (filler)
                        t[field++] = filler
                    t[field++] = len  # length of field
                    last = g[2]
                    flist[j++] = field - 1
                } else {
                    if (f[i] > 1)
                        filler = f[i] - last - 1
                    else
                        filler = 0
                    if (filler)
                        t[field++] = filler
                    t[field++] = 1
                    last = f[i]
                    flist[j++] = field - 1
                }
            }
        FIELDWIDTHS = join(t, 1, field - 1)
        nfields = j - 1
    }
```

Next is the rule that actually processes the data. If the *−s* option is given, then sup-press is true. The first if statement makes sure that the input record does have the field separator. If *cut* is processing fields, suppress is true, and the field separator character is not in the record, then the record is skipped.

If the record is valid, then *gawk* has split the data into fields, either using the char-acter in FS or using fixed-length fields and FIELDWIDTHS. The loop goes through the list of fields that should be printed. The corresponding field is printed if it contains data. If the next field also has data, then the separator character is written out between the fields:

```
    {
        if (by_fields && suppress && index($0, FS) != 0)
            next
```

```
        for (i = 1; i <= nfields; i++) {
            if ($flist[i] != "") {
                printf "%s", $flist[i]
                if (i < nfields && $flist[i+1] != "")
                    printf "%s", OFS
            }
        }
        print ""
    }
```

This version of *cut* relies on *gawk*'s FIELDWIDTHS variable to do the character-based cutting. While it is possible in other *awk* implementations to use substr (see the section "String-Manipulation Functions" in Chapter 8, *Functions*), it is also extremely painful. The FIELDWIDTHS variable supplies an elegant solution to the problem of picking the input line apart by characters.

Searching for Regular Expressions in Files

The *egrep* utility searches files for patterns. It uses regular expressions that are almost identical to those available in *awk* (see Chapter 2, *Regular Expressions*). It is used in the following manner:

```
egrep [ options ] 'pattern' files ...
```

The *pattern* is a regular expression. In typical usage, the regular expression is quoted to prevent the shell from expanding any of the special characters as file-name wildcards. Normally, *egrep* prints the lines that matched. If multiple file-names are provided on the command line, each output line is preceded by the name of the file and a colon.

The options to *egrep* are as follows:

-c   Print out a count of the lines that matched the pattern, instead of the lines themselves.

-s   Be silent. No output is produced and the exit value indicates whether the pattern was matched.

-v   Invert the sense of the test. *egrep* prints the lines that do *not* match the pattern and exits successfully if the pattern is not matched.

-i   Ignore case distinctions in both the pattern and the input data.

-l   Only print (list) the names of the files that matched, not the lines that matched.

-e *pattern*

Use *pattern* as the regexp to match. The purpose of the *−e* option is to allow patterns that start with a -.

This version uses the getopt library function (see the section "Processing Command-Line Options" in Chapter 12) and the file transition library program (see the section "Noting Datafile Boundaries" in Chapter 12).

The program begins with a descriptive comment and then a BEGIN rule that processes the command-line arguments with getopt. The *–i* (ignore case) option is particularly easy with *gawk*; we just use the IGNORECASE built-in variable (see the section "Built-in Variables" in Chapter 6, *Patterns, Actions, and Variables*):

```
# egrep.awk --- simulate egrep in awk

# Options:
#    -c     count of lines
#    -s     silent - use exit value
#    -v     invert test, success if no match
#    -i     ignore case
#    -l     print filenames only
#    -e     argument is pattern
#
# Requires getopt and file transition library functions

BEGIN {
    while ((c = getopt(ARGC, ARGV, "ce:svil")) != -1) {
        if (c == "c")
            count_only++
        else if (c == "s")
            no_print++
        else if (c == "v")
            invert++
        else if (c == "i")
            IGNORECASE = 1
        else if (c == "l")
            filenames_only++
        else if (c == "e")
            pattern = Optarg
        else
            usage()
    }
```

Next comes the code that handles the *egrep*-specific behavior. If no pattern is supplied with *–e*, the first nonoption on the command line is used. The *awk* command-line arguments up to ARGV[Optind] are cleared, so that *awk* won't try to process them as files. If no files are specified, the standard input is used, and if multiple files are specified, we make sure to note this so that the filenames can precede the matched lines in the output:

```
if (pattern == "")
    pattern = ARGV[Optind++]

for (i = 1; i < Optind; i++)
    ARGV[i] = ""
```

```
        if (Optind >= ARGC) {
            ARGV[1] = "-"
            ARGC = 2
        } else if (ARGC - Optind > 1)
            do_filenames++

#       if (IGNORECASE)
#           pattern = tolower(pattern)
}
```

The last two lines are commented out, since they are not needed in *gawk*. They should be uncommented if you have to use another version of *awk*.

The next set of lines should be uncommented if you are not using *gawk*. This rule translates all the characters in the input line into lowercase if the *−i* option is specified.* The rule is commented out since it is not necessary with *gawk*:

```
#{
#       if (IGNORECASE)
#           $0 = tolower($0)
#}
```

The `beginfile` function is called by the rule in *ftrans.awk* when each new file is processed. In this case, it is very simple; all it does is initialize a variable `fcount` to zero. `fcount` tracks how many lines in the current file matched the pattern (naming the parameter `junk` shows we know that `beginfile` is called with a parameter, but that we're not interested in its value):

```
function beginfile(junk)
{
    fcount = 0
}
```

The `endfile` function is called after each file has been processed. It affects the output only when the user wants a count of the number of lines that matched. `no_print` is true only if the exit status is desired. `count_only` is true if line counts are desired. *egrep* therefore only prints line counts if printing and counting are enabled. The output format must be adjusted depending upon the number of files to process. Finally, `fcount` is added to `total`, so that we know the total number of lines that matched the pattern:

```
function endfile(file)
{
    if (! no_print && count_only)
        if (do_filenames)
            print file ":" fcount
        else
            print fcount
```

---

* It also introduces a subtle bug; if a match happens, we output the translated line, not the original.

```
            total += fcount
   }
```

The following rule does most of the work of matching lines. The variable `matches` is true if the line matched the pattern. If the user wants lines that did not match, the sense of `matches` is inverted using the `!` operator. `fcount` is incremented with the value of `matches`, which is either one or zero, depending upon a successful or unsuccessful match. If the line does not match, the `next` statement just moves on to the next record.

A number of additional tests are made, but they are only done if we are not counting lines. First, if the user only wants exit status (`no_print` is true), then it is enough to know that *one* line in this file matched, and we can skip on to the next file with `nextfile`. Similarly, if we are only printing filenames, we can print the filename, and then skip to the next file with `nextfile`. Finally, each line is printed, with a leading filename and colon if necessary:

```
   {
       matches = ($0 ~ pattern)
       if (invert)
           matches = ! matches

       fcount += matches      # 1 or 0

       if (! matches)
           next

       if (! count_only) {
           if (no_print)
               nextfile

           if (filenames_only) {
               print FILENAME
               nextfile
           }

           if (do_filenames)
               print FILENAME ":" $0
           else
               print
       }
   }
```

The `END` rule takes care of producing the correct exit status. If there are no matches, the exit status is one; otherwise, it is zero:

```
   END    \
   {
       if (total == 0)
           exit 1
       exit 0
   }
```

The usage function prints a usage message in case of invalid options and then exits:

```
function usage(    e)
{
    e = "Usage: egrep [-csvil] -e pat [files ...]"
    e = e "\n\tegrep [-csvil] pat [files ...]"
    print e > "/dev/stderr"
    exit 1
}
```

The variable e is used so that the function fits nicely on the printed page.

Just a note on programming style: you may have noticed that the END rule uses backslash continuation, with the open brace on a line by itself. This is so that it more closely resembles the way functions are written. Many of the examples in this chapter use this style. You can decide for yourself if you like writing your BEGIN and END rules this way or not.

Printing out User Information

The *id* utility lists a user's real and effective user ID numbers, real and effective group ID numbers, and the user's group set, if any. *id* only prints the effective user ID and group ID only if they are different from the real ones. If possible, *id* also supplies the corresponding user and group names. The output might look like this:

```
$ id
uid=2076(arnold) gid=10(staff) groups=10(staff),4(tty)
```

This information is part of what is provided by *gawk*'s PROCINFO array (see the section "Built-in Variables" in Chapter 6). However, the *id* utility provides a more palatable output than just individual numbers.

Here is a simple version of *id* written in *awk*. It uses the user database library functions (see the section "Reading the User Database" in Chapter 12) and the group database library functions (see the section "Reading the Group Database" in Chapter 12).

The program is fairly straightforward. All the work is done in the BEGIN rule. The user and group ID numbers are obtained from PROCINFO. The code is repetitive. The entry in the user database for the real user ID number is split into parts at the :. The name is the first field. Similar code is used for the effective user ID number and the group numbers:

```
# id.awk --- implement id in awk
#
# Requires user and group library functions
# output is:
# uid=12(foo)  euid=34(bar)  gid=3(baz) \
#              egid=5(blat)  groups=9(nine),2(two),1(one)

BEGIN    \
{
    uid = PROCINFO["uid"]
    euid = PROCINFO["euid"]
    gid = PROCINFO["gid"]
    egid = PROCINFO["egid"]

    printf("uid=%d", uid)
    pw = getpwuid(uid)
    if (pw != "") {
        split(pw, a, ":")
        printf("(%s)", a[1])
    }

    if (euid != uid) {
        printf(" euid=%d", euid)
        pw = getpwuid(euid)
        if (pw != "") {
            split(pw, a, ":")
            printf("(%s)", a[1])
        }
    }

    printf(" gid=%d", gid)
    pw = getgrgid(gid)
    if (pw != "") {
        split(pw, a, ":")
        printf("(%s)", a[1])
    }

    if (egid != gid) {
        printf(" egid=%d", egid)
        pw = getgrgid(egid)
        if (pw != "") {
            split(pw, a, ":")
            printf("(%s)", a[1])
        }
    }
```

```
        for (i = 1; ("group" i) in PROCINFO; i++) {
            if (i == 1)
                printf(" groups=")
            group = PROCINFO["group" i]
            printf("%d", group)
            pw = getgrgid(group)
            if (pw != "") {
                split(pw, a, ":")
                printf("(%s)", a[1])
            }
            if (("group" (i+1)) in PROCINFO)
                printf(",")
        }

    print ""
}
```

The test in the `for` loop is worth noting. Any supplementary groups in the PROCINFO array have the indices `"group1"` through `"groupN"` for some *N*, i.e., the total number of supplementary groups. However, we don't know in advance how many of these groups there are.

This loop works by starting at one, concatenating the value with `"group"`, and then using `in` to see if that value is in the array. Eventually, `i` is incremented past the last group in the array and the loop exits.

The loop is also correct if there are *no* supplementary groups; then the condition is false the first time it's tested, and the loop body never executes.

Splitting a Large File into Pieces

The `split` program splits large text files into smaller pieces. Usage is as follows:

```
split [-count] file [ prefix ]
```

By default, the output files are named *xaa*, *xab*, and so on. Each file has 1000 lines in it, with the likely exception of the last file. To change the number of lines in each file, supply a number on the command line preceded with a minus; e.g., –500 for files with 500 lines in them instead of 1000. To change the name of the output files to something like *myfileaa*, *myfileab*, and so on, supply an additional argument that specifies the filename prefix.

Here is a version of `split` in *awk*. It uses the `ord` and `chr` functions presented in the section "Translating Between Characters and Numbers" in Chapter 12.

The program first sets its defaults, and then tests to make sure there are not too many arguments. It then looks at each argument in turn. The first argument could be a minus sign followed by a number. If it is, this happens to look like a negative number, so it is made positive, and that is the count of lines. The data filename is skipped over and the final argument is used as the prefix for the output filenames:

```
# split.awk --- do split in awk
#
# Requires ord and chr library functions
# usage: split [-num] [file] [outname]

BEGIN {
    outfile = "x"     # default
    count = 1000
    if (ARGC > 4)
        usage()

    i = 1
    if (ARGV[i] ~ /^-[0-9]+$/) {
        count = -ARGV[i]
        ARGV[i] = ""
        i++
    }
    # test argv in case reading from stdin instead of file
    if (i in ARGV)
        i++    # skip data file name
    if (i in ARGV) {
        outfile = ARGV[i]
        ARGV[i] = ""
    }

    s1 = s2 = "a"
    out = (outfile s1 s2)
}
```

The next rule does most of the work. tcount (temporary count) tracks how many
lines have been printed to the output file so far. If it is greater than count, it is time
to close the current file and start a new one. s1 and s2 track the current suffixes
for the filename. If they are both z, the file is just too big. Otherwise, s1 moves to
the next letter in the alphabet and s2 starts over again at a:

```
{
    if (++tcount > count) {
        close(out)
        if (s2 == "z") {
            if (s1 == "z") {
                printf("split: %s is too large to split\n",
                        FILENAME) > "/dev/stderr"
                exit 1
            }
            s1 = chr(ord(s1) + 1)
            s2 = "a"
        } else
            s2 = chr(ord(s2) + 1)
        out = (outfile s1 s2)
        tcount = 1
    }
    print > out
}
```

The usage function simply prints an error message and exits:

```
function usage(    e)
{
    e = "usage: split [-num] [file] [outname]"
    print e > "/dev/stderr"
    exit 1
}
```

The variable e is used so that the function fits nicely on the page.

This program is a bit sloppy; it relies on *awk* to automatically close the last file instead of doing it in an END rule. It also assumes that letters are contiguous in the character set, which isn't true for EBCDIC systems.

Duplicating Output into Multiple Files

The tee program is known as a "pipe fitting." tee copies its standard input to its standard output and also duplicates it to the files named on the command line. Its usage is as follows:

```
tee [-a] file ...
```

The *−a* option tells tee to append to the named files, instead of truncating them and starting over.

The BEGIN rule first makes a copy of all the command-line arguments into an array named copy. ARGV[0] is not copied, since it is not needed. tee cannot use ARGV directly, since *awk* attempts to process each filename in ARGV as input data.

If the first argument is *−a*, then the flag variable append is set to true, and both ARGV[1] and copy[1] are deleted. If ARGC is less than two, then no filenames were supplied and tee prints a usage message and exits. Finally, *awk* is forced to read the standard input by setting ARGV[1] to "-" and ARGC to two:

```
# tee.awk --- tee in awk

BEGIN    \
{
    for (i = 1; i < ARGC; i++)
        copy[i] = ARGV[i]

    if (ARGV[1] == "-a") {
        append = 1
        delete ARGV[1]
        delete copy[1]
        ARGC--
    }
```

```
        if (ARGC < 2) {
            print "usage: tee [-a] file ..." > "/dev/stderr"
            exit 1
        }
        ARGV[1] = "-"
        ARGC = 2
    }
```

The single rule does all the work. Since there is no pattern, it is executed for each line of input. The body of the rule simply prints the line into each file on the command line, and then to the standard output:

```
    {
        # moving the if outside the loop makes it run faster
        if (append)
            for (i in copy)
                print >> copy[i]
        else
            for (i in copy)
                print > copy[i]
        print
    }
```

It is also possible to write the loop this way:

```
    for (i in copy)
        if (append)
            print >> copy[i]
        else
            print > copy[i]
```

This is more concise but it is also less efficient. The `if` is tested for each record and for each output file. By duplicating the loop body, the `if` is only tested once for each input record. If there are *N* input records and *M* output files, the first method only executes *N* `if` statements, while the second executes $N \times M$ `if` statements.

Finally, the END rule cleans up by closing all the output files:

```
    END    \
    {
        for (i in copy)
            close(copy[i])
    }
```

Printing Nonduplicated Lines of Text

The *uniq* utility reads sorted lines of data on its standard input, and by default removes duplicate lines. In other words, it only prints unique lines—hence the name. *uniq* has a number of options. The usage is as follows:

```
uniq [-udc [-n]] [+n] [ input file [ output file ]]
```

The options for *uniq* are:

−d Print only repeated lines.

−u Print only nonrepeated lines.

−c Count lines. This option overrides −*d* and −*u*. Both repeated and nonrepeated lines are counted.

−*n* Skip *n* fields before comparing lines. The definition of fields is similar to *awk*'s default: nonwhitespace characters separated by runs of spaces and/or tabs.

+*n* Skip *n* characters before comparing lines. Any fields specified with −*n* are skipped first.

input file
    Data is read from the input file named on the command line, instead of from the standard input.

output file
    The generated output is sent to the named output file, instead of to the standard output.

Normally *uniq* behaves as if both the −*d* and −*u* options are provided.

uniq uses the getopt library function (see the section "Processing Command-Line Options" in Chapter 12) and the join library function (see the section "Merging an Array into a String" in Chapter 12).

The program begins with a usage function and then a brief outline of the options and their meanings in a comment. The BEGIN rule deals with the command-line arguments and options. It uses a trick to get getopt to handle options of the form −25, treating such an option as the option letter 2 with an argument of 5. If indeed two or more digits are supplied (Optarg looks like a number), Optarg is concatenated with the option digit and then the result is added to zero to make it into a number. If there is only one digit in the option, then Optarg is not needed. In this case, Optind must be decremented so that getopt processes it next time. This code is admittedly a bit tricky.

If no options are supplied, then the default is taken, to print both repeated and nonrepeated lines. The output file, if provided, is assigned to outputfile. Early on, outputfile is initialized to the standard output, */dev/stdout*:

```
# uniq.awk --- do uniq in awk
#
# Requires getopt and join library functions
```

```
function usage(    e)
{
    e = "Usage: uniq [-udc [-n]] [+n] [ in [ out ]]"
    print e > "/dev/stderr"
    exit 1
}

# -c    count lines. overrides -d and -u
# -d    only repeated lines
# -u    only non-repeated lines
# -n    skip n fields
# +n    skip n characters, skip fields first

BEGIN    \
{
    count = 1
    outputfile = "/dev/stdout"
    opts = "udc0:1:2:3:4:5:6:7:8:9:"
    while ((c = getopt(ARGC, ARGV, opts)) != -1) {
        if (c == "u")
            non_repeated_only++
        else if (c == "d")
            repeated_only++
        else if (c == "c")
            do_count++
        else if (index("0123456789", c) != 0) {
            # getopt requires args to options
            # this messes us up for things like -5
            if (Optarg ~ /^[0-9]+$/)
                fcount = (c Optarg) + 0
            else {
                fcount = c + 0
                Optind--
            }
        } else
            usage()
    }

    if (ARGV[Optind] ~ /^\+[0-9]+$/) {
        charcount = substr(ARGV[Optind], 2) + 0
        Optind++
    }

    for (i = 1; i < Optind; i++)
        ARGV[i] = ""

    if (repeated_only == 0 && non_repeated_only == 0)
        repeated_only = non_repeated_only = 1

    if (ARGC - Optind == 2) {
        outputfile = ARGV[ARGC - 1]
        ARGV[ARGC - 1] = ""
    }
}
```

The following function, `are_equal`, compares the current line, $0, to the previous line, `last`. It handles skipping fields and characters. If no field count and no character count are specified, `are_equal` simply returns one or zero depending upon the result of a simple string comparison of `last` and $0. Otherwise, things get more complicated. If fields have to be skipped, each line is broken into an array using `split` (see the section "String-Manipulation Functions" in Chapter 8); the desired fields are then joined back into a line using `join`. The joined lines are stored in `clast` and `cline`. If no fields are skipped, `clast` and `cline` are set to `last` and $0, respectively. Finally, if characters are skipped, `substr` is used to strip off the leading `charcount` characters in `clast` and `cline`. The two strings are then compared and `are_equal` returns the result:

```
function are_equal(    n, m, clast, cline, alast, aline)
{
    if (fcount == 0 && charcount == 0)
        return (last == $0)

    if (fcount > 0) {
        n = split(last, alast)
        m = split($0, aline)
        clast = join(alast, fcount+1, n)
        cline = join(aline, fcount+1, m)
    } else {
        clast = last
        cline = $0
    }
    if (charcount) {
        clast = substr(clast, charcount + 1)
        cline = substr(cline, charcount + 1)
    }

    return (clast == cline)
}
```

The following two rules are the body of the program. The first one is executed only for the very first line of data. It sets `last` equal to $0, so that subsequent lines of text have something to be compared to.

The second rule does the work. The variable `equal` is one or zero, depending upon the results of `are_equal`'s comparison. If *uniq* is counting repeated lines, and the lines are equal, then it increments the `count` variable. Otherwise, it prints the line and resets `count`, since the two lines are not equal.

If *uniq* is not counting, and if the lines are equal, `count` is incremented. Nothing is printed, since the point is to remove duplicates. Otherwise, if *uniq* is counting repeated lines and more than one line is seen, or if *uniq* is counting nonrepeated lines and only one line is seen, then the line is printed, and `count` is reset.

Finally, similar logic is used in the END rule to print the final line of input data:

```
NR == 1 {
    last = $0
    next
}

{
    equal = are_equal()

    if (do_count) {     # overrides -d and -u
        if (equal)
            count++
        else {
            printf("%4d %s\n", count, last) > outputfile
            last = $0
            count = 1    # reset
        }
        next
    }

    if (equal)
        count++
    else {
        if ((repeated_only && count > 1) ||
            (non_repeated_only && count == 1))
                print last > outputfile
        last = $0
        count = 1
    }
}

END {
    if (do_count)
        printf("%4d %s\n", count, last) > outputfile
    else if ((repeated_only && count > 1) ||
            (non_repeated_only && count == 1))
        print last > outputfile
}
```

Counting Things

The *wc* (word count) utility counts lines, words, and characters in one or more input files. Its usage is as follows:

```
wc [-lwc] [ files ... ]
```

If no files are specified on the command line, *wc* reads its standard input. If there are multiple files, it also prints total counts for all the files. The options and their meanings are shown in the following list:

-l Count only lines.

-w Count only words. A "word" is a contiguous sequence of nonwhitespace characters, separated by spaces and/or tabs. Luckily, this is the normal way *awk* separates fields in its input data.

-c Count only characters.

Implementing *wc* in *awk* is particularly elegant, since *awk* does a lot of the work for us; it splits lines into words (i.e., fields) and counts them, it counts lines (i.e., records), and it can easily tell us how long a line is.

This uses the getopt library function (see the section "Processing Command-Line Options" in Chapter 12) and the file-transition functions (see the section "Noting Datafile Boundaries" in Chapter 12).

This version has one notable difference from traditional versions of *wc*: it always prints the counts in the order lines, words, and characters. Traditional versions note the order of the *–l*, *–w*, and *–c* options on the command line, and print the counts in that order.

The BEGIN rule does the argument processing. The variable print_total is true if more than one file is named on the command line:

```
# wc.awk --- count lines, words, characters

# Options:
#     -l     only count lines
#     -w     only count words
#     -c     only count characters
#
# Default is to count lines, words, characters
#
# Requires getopt and file transition library functions

BEGIN {
    # let getopt print a message about
    # invalid options. we ignore them
    while ((c = getopt(ARGC, ARGV, "lwc")) != -1) {
        if (c == "l")
            do_lines = 1
        else if (c == "w")
            do_words = 1
        else if (c == "c")
            do_chars = 1
    }
    for (i = 1; i < Optind; i++)
        ARGV[i] = ""

    # if no options, do all
    if (! do_lines && ! do_words && ! do_chars)
        do_lines = do_words = do_chars = 1
```

```
        print_total = (ARGC - i > 2)
}
```

The `beginfile` function is simple; it just resets the counts of lines, words, and characters to zero, and saves the current filename in `fname`:

```
function beginfile(file)
{
    chars = lines = words = 0
    fname = FILENAME
}
```

The `endfile` function adds the current file's numbers to the running totals of lines, words, and characters.* It then prints out those numbers for the file that was just read. It relies on `beginfile` to reset the numbers for the following datafile:

```
function endfile(file)
{
    tchars += chars
    tlines += lines
    twords += words
    if (do_lines)
        printf "\t%d", lines
    if (do_words)
        printf "\t%d", words
    if (do_chars)
        printf "\t%d", chars
    printf "\t%s\n", fname
}
```

There is one rule that is executed for each line. It adds the length of the record, plus one, to `chars`. Adding one plus the record length is needed because the new-line character separating records (the value of RS) is not part of the record itself, and thus not included in its length. Next, `lines` is incremented for each line read, and `words` is incremented by the value of NF, which is the number of "words" on this line:

```
# do per line
{
    chars += length($0) + 1    # get newline
    lines++
    words += NF
}
```

---

* *wc* can't just use the value of FNR in `endfile`. If you examine the code in the section "Noting Datafile Boundaries" in Chapter 12, you will see that FNR has already been reset by the time `endfile` is called.

Finally, the END rule simply prints the totals for all the files:

```
END {
    if (print_total) {
        if (do_lines)
            printf "\t%d", tlines
        if (do_words)
            printf "\t%d", twords
        if (do_chars)
            printf "\t%d", tchars
        print "\ttotal"
    }
}
```

A Grab Bag of awk Programs

This section is a large "grab bag" of miscellaneous programs. We hope you find them both interesting and enjoyable.

Finding Duplicated Words in a Document

A common error when writing large amounts of prose is to accidentally duplicate words. Typically you will see this in text as something like "the program does the following..." When the text is online, often the duplicated words occur at the end of one line and the beginning of another, making them very difficult to spot.

This program, *dupword.awk*, scans through a file one line at a time and looks for adjacent occurrences of the same word. It also saves the last word on a line (in the variable prev) for comparison with the first word on the next line.

The first two statements make sure that the line is all lowercase, so that, for example, "The" and "the" compare equal to each other. The next statement replaces nonalphanumeric and nonwhitespace characters with spaces, so that punctuation does not affect the comparison either. The characters are replaced with spaces so that formatting controls don't create nonsense words (e.g., the Texinfo @code{NF} becomes codeNF if punctuation is simply deleted). The record is then resplit into fields, yielding just the actual words on the line, and ensuring that there are no empty fields.

If there are no fields left after removing all the punctuation, the current record is skipped. Otherwise, the program loops through each word, comparing it to the previous one:

```
# dupword.awk --- find duplicate words in text
```

```
{
    $0 = tolower($0)
    gsub(/[^[:alnum:][:blank:]]/, " ");
    $0 = $0              # re-split
    if (NF == 0)
        next
    if ($1 == prev)
        printf("%s:%d: duplicate %s\n",
            FILENAME, FNR, $1)
    for (i = 2; i <= NF; i++)
        if ($i == $(i-1))
            printf("%s:%d: duplicate %s\n",
                FILENAME, FNR, $i)
    prev = $NF
}
```

An Alarm Clock Program

The following program is a simple "alarm clock" program. You give it a time of day and an optional message. At the specified time, it prints the message on the standard output. In addition, you can give it the number of times to repeat the message as well as a delay between repetitions.

This program uses the gettimeofday function from the section "Managing the Time of Day" in Chapter 12.

All the work is done in the BEGIN rule. The first part is argument checking and setting of defaults: the delay, the count, and the message to print. If the user supplied a message without the ASCII BEL character (known as the "alert" character, "\a"), then it is added to the message. (On many systems, printing the ASCII BEL generates an audible alert. Thus when the alarm goes off, the system calls attention to itself in case the user is not looking at the computer or terminal.) Here is the program:

```
# alarm.awk --- set an alarm
#
# Requires gettimeofday library function

# usage: alarm time [ "message" [ count [ delay ] ] ]

BEGIN    \
{
    # Initial argument sanity checking
    usage1 = "usage: alarm time ['message' [count [delay]]]"
    usage2 = sprintf("\t(%s) time ::= hh:mm", ARGV[1])
```

```
if (ARGC < 2) {
    print usage1 > "/dev/stderr"
    print usage2 > "/dev/stderr"
    exit 1
} else if (ARGC == 5) {
    delay = ARGV[4] + 0
    count = ARGV[3] + 0
    message = ARGV[2]
} else if (ARGC == 4) {
    count = ARGV[3] + 0
    message = ARGV[2]
} else if (ARGC == 3) {
    message = ARGV[2]
} else if (ARGV[1] !~ /[0-9]?[0-9]:[0-9][0-9]/) {
    print usage1 > "/dev/stderr"
    print usage2 > "/dev/stderr"
    exit 1
}

# set defaults for once we reach the desired time
if (delay == 0)
    delay = 180     # 3 minutes
if (count == 0)
    count = 5
if (message == "")
    message = sprintf("\aIt is now %s!\a", ARGV[1])
else if (index(message, "\a") == 0)
    message = "\a" message "\a"
```

The next section of code turns the alarm time into hours and minutes, converts it (if necessary) to a 24-hour clock, and then turns that time into a count of the seconds since midnight. Next it turns the current time into a count of seconds since midnight. The difference between the two is how long to wait before setting off the alarm:

```
# split up alarm time
split(ARGV[1], atime, ":")
hour = atime[1] + 0     # force numeric
minute = atime[2] + 0   # force numeric

# get current broken down time
gettimeofday(now)

# if time given is 12-hour hours and it's after that
# hour, e.g., 'alarm 5:30' at 9 a.m. means 5:30 p.m.,
# then add 12 to real hour
if (hour < 12 && now["hour"] > hour)
    hour += 12

# set target time in seconds since midnight
target = (hour * 60 * 60) + (minute * 60)
```

```
# get current time in seconds since midnight
current = (now["hour"] * 60 * 60) + \
          (now["minute"] * 60) + now["second"]

# how long to sleep for
naptime = target - current
if (naptime <= 0) {
    print "time is in the past!" > "/dev/stderr"
    exit 1
}
```

Finally, the program uses the `system` function (see the section "Input/Output Functions" in Chapter 8) to call the *sleep* utility. The *sleep* utility simply pauses for the given number of seconds. If the exit status is not zero, the program assumes that *sleep* was interrupted and exits. If *sleep* exited with an OK status (zero), then the program prints the message in a loop, again using *sleep* to delay for however many seconds are necessary:

```
# zzzzzz..... go away if interrupted
if (system(sprintf("sleep %d", naptime)) != 0)
    exit 1

# time to notify!
command = sprintf("sleep %d", delay)
for (i = 1; i <= count; i++) {
    print message
    # if sleep command interrupted, go away
    if (system(command) != 0)
        break
}

    exit 0
}
```

Transliterating Characters

The system *tr* utility transliterates characters. For example, it is often used to map uppercase letters into lowercase for further processing:

```
generate data | tr 'A-Z' 'a-z' | process data ...
```

tr requires two lists of characters.* When processing the input, the first character in the first list is replaced with the first character in the second list, the second character in the first list is replaced with the second character in the second list, and so on. If there are more characters in the "from" list than in the "to" list, the last character of the "to" list is used for the remaining characters in the "from" list.

---

* On some older System V systems, including Solaris, *tr* may require that the lists be written as range expressions enclosed in square brackets (`[a-z]`) and quoted, to prevent the shell from attempting a filename expansion. This is not a feature.

Some time ago, a user proposed that a transliteration function should be added to *gawk*. The following program was written to prove that character transliteration could be done with a user-level function. This program is not as complete as the system *tr* utility but it does most of the job.

The *translate* program demonstrates one of the few weaknesses of standard *awk*: dealing with individual characters is very painful, requiring repeated use of the `substr`, `index`, and `gsub` built-in functions (see the section "String-Manipulation Functions" in Chapter 8).* There are two functions. The first, `stranslate`, takes three arguments:

`from`
>   A list of characters from which to translate.

`to`
>   A list of characters from which to translate.

`target`
>   The string on which to do the translation

Associative arrays make the translation part fairly easy. `t_ar` holds the "to" characters, indexed by the "from" characters. Then a simple loop goes through `from`, one character at a time. For each character in `from`, if the character appears in `target`, `gsub` is used to change it to the corresponding to character.

The `translate` function simply calls `stranslate` using $0 as the target. The main program sets two global variables, `FROM` and `TO`, from the command line, and then changes `ARGV` so that *awk* reads from the standard input.

Finally, the processing rule simply calls `translate` for each record:

```
# translate.awk --- do tr-like stuff

# Bugs: does not handle things like: tr A-Z a-z, it has
# to be spelled out. However, if 'to' is shorter than 'from',
# the last character in 'to' is used for the rest of 'from'.

function stranslate(from, to, target,      lf, lt, t_ar, i, c)
{
    lf = length(from)
    lt = length(to)
    for (i = 1; i <= lt; i++)
        t_ar[substr(from, i, 1)] = substr(to, i, 1)
    if (lt < lf)
        for (; i <= lf; i++)
            t_ar[substr(from, i, 1)] = substr(to, lt, 1)
```

---

* This program was written before *gawk* acquired the ability to split each character in a string into separate array elements.

```
    for (i = 1; i <= lf; i++) {
        c = substr(from, i, 1)
        if (index(target, c) > 0)
            gsub(c, t_ar[c], target)
    }
    return target
}

function translate(from, to)
{
    return $0 = stranslate(from, to, $0)
}

# main program
BEGIN {
    if (ARGC < 3) {
        print "usage: translate from to" > "/dev/stderr"
        exit
    }
    FROM = ARGV[1]
    TO = ARGV[2]
    ARGC = 2
    ARGV[1] = "-"
}

{
    translate(FROM, TO)
    print
}
```

While it is possible to do character transliteration in a user-level function, it is not necessarily efficient, and we (the *gawk* authors) started to consider adding a built-in function. However, shortly after writing this program, we learned that the System V Release 4 *awk* had added the `toupper` and `tolower` functions (see the section "String-Manipulation Functions" in Chapter 8). These functions handle the vast majority of the cases where character transliteration is necessary, and so we chose to simply add those functions to *gawk* as well and then leave well enough alone.

An obvious improvement to this program would be to set up the `t_ar` array only once, in a `BEGIN` rule. However, this assumes that the "from" and "to" lists will never change throughout the lifetime of the program.

Printing Mailing Labels

This next script reads lists of names and addresses and generates mailing labels. Each page of labels has 20 labels on it, 2 across and 10 down. The addresses are guaranteed to be no more than 5 lines of data. Each address is separated from the next by a blank line.

The basic idea is to read 20 labels worth of data. Each line of each label is stored in the `line` array. The single rule takes care of filling the `line` array and printing the page when 20 labels have been read.

The BEGIN rule simply sets RS to the empty string, so that *awk* splits records at blank lines (see the section "How Input Is Split into Records" in Chapter 3). It sets MAXLINES to 100, since 100 is the maximum number of lines on the page (20 * 5 = 100).

Most of the work is done in the `printpage` function. The label lines are stored sequentially in the `line` array. But they have to print horizontally; `line[1]` next to `line[6]`, `line[2]` next to `line[7]`, and so on. Two loops are used to accomplish this. The outer loop, controlled by `i`, steps through every 10 lines of data; this is each row of labels. The inner loop, controlled by `j`, goes through the lines within the row. As `j` goes from 0 to 4, `i+j` is the `j`-th line in the row, and `i+j+5` is the entry next to it. The output ends up looking something like this:

```
line 1          line 6
line 2          line 7
line 3          line 8
line 4          line 9
line 5          line 10
...
```

As a final note, an extra blank line is printed at lines 21 and 61, to keep the output lined up on the labels. This is dependent on the particular brand of labels in use when the program was written. You will also note that there are 2 blank lines at the top and 2 blank lines at the bottom.

The END rule arranges to flush the final page of labels; there may not have been an even multiple of 20 labels in the data:

```
# labels.awk --- print mailing labels

# Each label is 5 lines of data that may have blank lines.
# The label sheets have 2 blank lines at the top and 2 at
# the bottom.

BEGIN    { RS = "" ; MAXLINES = 100 }

function printpage(    i, j)
{
    if (Nlines <= 0)
        return

    printf "\n\n"        # header
```

```
        for (i = 1; i <= Nlines; i += 10) {
            if (i == 21 || i == 61)
                print ""
            for (j = 0; j < 5; j++) {
                if (i + j > MAXLINES)
                    break
                printf "  %-41s %s\n", line[i+j], line[i+j+5]
            }
            print ""
        }

        printf "\n\n"        # footer

        for (i in line)
            line[i] = ""
    }

    # main rule
    {
        if (Count >= 20) {
            printpage()
            Count = 0
            Nlines = 0
        }
        n = split($0, a, "\n")
        for (i = 1; i <= n; i++)
            line[++Nlines] = a[i]
        for (; i <= 5; i++)
            line[++Nlines] = ""
        Count++
    }

    END     \
    {
        printpage()
    }
```

Generating Word-Usage Counts

The following *awk* program prints the number of occurrences of each word in its input. It illustrates the associative nature of *awk* arrays by using strings as subscripts. It also demonstrates the for *index* in *array* mechanism. Finally, it shows how *awk* is used in conjunction with other utility programs to do a useful task of some complexity with a minimum of effort. Some explanations follow the program listing:

```
    # Print list of word frequencies
    {
        for (i = 1; i <= NF; i++)
            freq[$i]++
    }
```

```
END {
    for (word in freq)
        printf "%s\t%d\n", word, freq[word]
}
```

This program has two rules. The first rule, because it has an empty pattern, is executed for every input line. It uses *awk*'s field-accessing mechanism (see the section "Examining Fields" in Chapter 3) to pick out the individual words from the line, and the built-in variable NF (see the section "Built-in Variables" in Chapter 6) to know how many fields are available. For each input word, it increments an element of the array freq to reflect that the word has been seen an additional time.

The second rule, because it has the pattern END, is not executed until the input has been exhausted. It prints out the contents of the freq table that has been built up inside the first action. This program has several problems that would prevent it from being useful by itself on real text files:

- Words are detected using the *awk* convention that fields are separated just by whitespace. Other characters in the input (except newlines) don't have any special meaning to *awk*. This means that punctuation characters count as part of words.

- The *awk* language considers upper- and lowercase characters to be distinct. Therefore, "bartender" and "Bartender" are not treated as the same word. This is undesirable, since in normal text, words are capitalized if they begin sentences, and a frequency analyzer should not be sensitive to capitalization.

- The output does not come out in any useful order. You're more likely to be interested in which words occur most frequently or in having an alphabetized table of how frequently each word occurs.

The way to solve these problems is to use some of *awk*'s more advanced features. First, we use tolower to remove case distinctions. Next, we use gsub to remove punctuation characters. Finally, we use the system *sort* utility to process the output of the *awk* script. Here is the new version of the program:

```
# wordfreq.awk --- print list of word frequencies

{
    $0 = tolower($0)    # remove case distinctions
    gsub(/[^[:alnum:]_[:blank:]]/, "", $0)  # remove punctuation
    for (i = 1; i <= NF; i++)
        freq[$i]++
}

END {
    for (word in freq)
        printf "%s\t%d\n", word, freq[word]
}
```

Assuming we have saved this program in a file named *wordfreq.awk*, and that the data is in *file1*, the following pipeline:

```
awk -f wordfreq.awk file1 | sort +1 -nr
```

produces a table of the words appearing in *file1* in order of decreasing frequency. The *awk* program suitably massages the data and produces a word frequency table, which is not ordered.

The *awk* script's output is then sorted by the *sort* utility and printed on the terminal. The options given to *sort* specify a sort that uses the second field of each input line (skipping one field), that the sort keys should be treated as numeric quantities (otherwise 15 would come before 5), and that the sorting should be done in descending (reverse) order.

The *sort* could even be done from within the program, by changing the END action to:

```
END {
    sort = "sort +1 -nr"
    for (word in freq)
        printf "%s\t%d\n", word, freq[word] | sort
    close(sort)
}
```

This way of sorting must be used on systems that do not have true pipes at the command-line (or batch-file) level. See the general operating system documentation for more information on how to use the *sort* program.

Removing Duplicates from Unsorted Text

The *uniq* program (see the section "Printing Nonduplicated Lines of Text" earlier in this chapter) removes duplicate lines from *sorted* data.

Suppose, however, you need to remove duplicate lines from a datafile but that you want to preserve the order the lines are in. A good example of this might be a shell history file. The history file keeps a copy of all the commands you have entered, and it is not unusual to repeat a command several times in a row. Occasionally you might want to compact the history by removing duplicate entries. Yet it is desirable to maintain the order of the original commands.

This simple program does the job. It uses two arrays. The `data` array is indexed by the text of each line. For each line, `data[$0]` is incremented. If a particular line has not been seen before, then `data[$0]` is zero. In this case, the text of the line is stored in `lines[count]`. Each element of `lines` is a unique command, and the indices of `lines` indicate the order in which those lines are encountered. The END rule simply prints out the lines, in order:

```
# histsort.awk --- compact a shell history file
# Thanks to Byron Rakitzis for the general idea

{
    if (data[$0]++ == 0)
        lines[++count] = $0
}

END {
    for (i = 1; i <= count; i++)
        print lines[i]
}
```

This program also provides a foundation for generating other useful information. For example, using the following `print` statement in the `END` rule indicates how often a particular command is used:

```
print data[lines[i]], lines[i]
```

This works because `data[$0]` is incremented each time a line is seen.

Extracting Programs from Texinfo Source Files

Both this chapter and Chapter 12 present a large number of *awk* programs. If you want to experiment with these programs, it is tedious to have to type them in by hand. Here we present a program that can extract parts of a Texinfo input file into separate files.

This book is written in Texinfo, the GNU project's document formatting language.[*] A single Texinfo source file can be used to produce both printed and online documentation. Texinfo is fully documented in the book *Texinfo—The GNU Documentation Format*, available from the Free Software Foundation.

For our purposes, it is enough to know three things about Texinfo input files:

- The "at" symbol (@) is special in Texinfo, much as the backslash (\) is in C or *awk*. Literal @ symbols are represented in Texinfo source files as @@.

- Comments start with either @c or @comment. The file-extraction program works by using special comments that start at the beginning of a line.

- Lines containing @group and @end group commands bracket example text that should not be split across a page boundary. (Unfortunately, TEX isn't always smart enough to do things exactly right, and we have to give it some help.)

The following program, *extract.awk*, reads through a Texinfo source file and does two things, based on the special comments. Upon seeing @c system ..., it runs a command, by extracting the command text from the control line and passing it on

---

[*] The book was translated into DocBook XML for the O'Reilly & Associates edition.

to the `system` function (see the section "Input/Output Functions" in Chapter 8). Upon seeing @c file *filename*, each subsequent line is sent to the file *filename*, until @c endfile is encountered. The rules in *extract.awk* match either @c or @comment by letting the `omment` part be optional. Lines containing @group and @end group are simply removed. *extract.awk* uses the `join` library function (see the section "Merging an Array into a String" in Chapter 12).

The example programs in the online Texinfo source for *Effective awk Programming* (*gawk.texi*) have all been bracketed inside file and endfile lines. The *gawk* distribution uses a copy of *extract.awk* to extract the sample programs and install many of them in a standard directory where *gawk* can find them. The Texinfo file looks something like this:

```
...
This program has a @code{BEGIN} rule,
that prints a nice message:

@example
@c file examples/messages.awk
BEGIN @{ print "Don't panic!" @}
@c end file
@end example

It also prints some final advice:

@example
@c file examples/messages.awk
END @{ print "Always avoid bored archeologists!" @}
@c end file
@end example
...
```

extract.awk begins by setting IGNORECASE to one, so that mixed upper- and lower-case letters in the directives won't matter.

The first rule handles calling `system`, checking that a command is given (NF is at least three) and also checking that the command exits with a zero-exit status, signifying OK:

```
# extract.awk --- extract files and run programs
#                  from texinfo files

BEGIN     { IGNORECASE = 1 }

/^@c(omment)?[ \t]+system/      \
{
    if (NF < 3) {
        e = (FILENAME ":" FNR)
        e = (e  ": badly formed `system' line")
        print e > "/dev/stderr"
        next
    }
```

```
    $1 = ""
    $2 = ""
    stat = system($0)
    if (stat != 0) {
        e = (FILENAME ":" FNR)
        e = (e ": warning: system returned " stat)
        print e > "/dev/stderr"
    }
}
```

The variable e is used so that the function fits nicely on the page.

The second rule handles moving data into files. It verifies that a filename is given in the directive. If the file named is not the current file, then the current file is closed. Keeping the current file open until a new file is encountered allows the use of the > redirection for printing the contents, keeping open file management simple.

The for loop does the work. It reads lines using getline (see the section "Explicit Input with getline" in Chapter 3). For an unexpected end of file, it calls the unexpected_eof function. If the line is an "endfile" line, then it breaks out of the loop. If the line is an @group or @end group line, then it ignores it and goes on to the next line. Similarly, comments within examples are also ignored.

Most of the work is in the following few lines. If the line has no @ symbols, the program can print it directly. Otherwise, each leading @ must be stripped off. To remove the @ symbols, the line is split into separate elements of the array a, using the split function (see the section "String-Manipulation Functions" in Chapter 8). The @ symbol is used as the separator character. Each element of a that is empty indicates two successive @ symbols in the original line. For each two empty elements (@@ in the original file), we have to add a single @ symbol back in.

When the processing of the array is finished, join is called with the value of SUBSEP, to rejoin the pieces back into a single line. That line is then printed to the output file:

```
/^@c(omment)?[ \t]+file/        \
{
    if (NF != 3) {
        e = (FILENAME ":" FNR ": badly formed `file' line")
        print e > "/dev/stderr"
        next
    }
    if ($3 != curfile) {
        if (curfile != "")
            close(curfile)
        curfile = $3
    }
```

```
    for (;;) {
        if ((getline line) <= 0)
            unexpected_eof()
        if (line ~ /^@c(omment)?[ \t]+endfile/)
            break
        else if (line ~ /^@(end[ \t]+)?group/)
            continue
        else if (line ~ /^@c(omment+)?[ \t]+/)
            continue
        if (index(line, "@") == 0) {
            print line > curfile
            continue
        }
        n = split(line, a, "@")
        # if a[1] == "", means leading @,
        # don't add one back in.
        for (i = 2; i <= n; i++) {
            if (a[i] == "") { # was an @@
                a[i] = "@"
                if (a[i+1] == "")
                    i++
            }
        }
        print join(a, 1, n, SUBSEP) > curfile
    }
}
```

An important thing to note is the use of the > redirection. Output done with > only opens the file once; it stays open and subsequent output is appended to the file (see the section "Redirecting Output of print and printf" in Chapter 4, *Printing Output*). This makes it easy to mix program text and explanatory prose for the same sample source file (as has been done here!) without any hassle. The file is only closed when a new data filename is encountered or at the end of the input file.

Finally, the function unexpected_eof prints an appropriate error message and then exits. The END rule handles the final cleanup, closing the open file:

```
function unexpected_eof()
{
    printf("%s:%d: unexpected EOF or error\n",
            FILENAME, FNR) > "/dev/stderr"
    exit 1
}

END {
    if (curfile)
        close(curfile)
}
```

A Simple Stream Editor

The *sed* utility is a *stream editor,* a program that reads a stream of data, makes changes to it, and passes it on. It is often used to make global changes to a large file or to a stream of data generated by a pipeline of commands. While *sed* is a complicated program in its own right, its most common use is to perform global substitutions in the middle of a pipeline:

```
command1 < orig.data | sed 's/old/new/g' | command2 > result
```

Here, s/old/new/g tells *sed* to look for the regexp old on each input line and glob-ally replace it with the text new, i.e., all the occurrences on a line. This is similar to *awk*'s gsub function (see the section "String-Manipulation Functions" in Chapter 8).

The following program, *awksed.awk,* accepts at least two command-line arguments. the pattern to look for and the text to replace it with. Any additional arguments are treated as data filenames to process. If none are provided, the standard input is used:

```
# awksed.awk --- do s/foo/bar/g using just print
#     Thanks to Michael Brennan for the idea

function usage()
{
    print "usage: awksed pat repl [files...]" > "/dev/stderr"
    exit 1
}

BEGIN {
    # validate arguments
    if (ARGC < 3)
        usage()

    RS = ARGV[1]
    ORS = ARGV[2]

    # don't use arguments as files
    ARGV[1] = ARGV[2] = ""
}

# look ma, no hands!
{
    if (RT == "")
        printf "%s", $0
    else
        print
}
```

The program relies on *gawk*'s ability to have RS be a regexp, as well as on the set-ting of RT to the actual text that terminates the record (see the section "How Input Is Split into Records" in Chapter 3).

The idea is to have RS be the pattern to look for. *gawk* automatically sets $0 to the text between matches of the pattern. This is text that we want to keep, unmodified. Then, by setting ORS to the replacement text, a simple print statement outputs the text we want to keep, followed by the replacement text.

There is one wrinkle to this scheme, which is what to do if the last record doesn't end with text that matches RS. Using a print statement unconditionally prints the replacement text, which is not correct. However, if the file did not end in text that matches RS, RT is set to the null string. In this case, we can print $0 using printf (see the section "Using printf Statements for Fancier Printing" in Chapter 4).

The BEGIN rule handles the setup, checking for the right number of arguments and calling usage if there is a problem. Then it sets RS and ORS from the command-line arguments and sets ARGV[1] and ARGV[2] to the null string, so that they are not treated as filenames (see the section "Using ARGC and ARGV" in Chapter 6).

The usage function prints an error message and exits. Finally, the single rule handles the printing scheme outlined above, using print or printf as appropriate, depending upon the value of RT.

An Easy Way to Use Library Functions

Using library functions in *awk* can be very beneficial. It encourages code reuse and the writing of general functions. Programs are smaller and therefore clearer. However, using library functions is only easy when writing *awk* programs; it is painful when running them, requiring multiple –*f* options. If *gawk* is unavailable, then so too is the AWKPATH environment variable and the ability to put *awk* functions into a library directory (see the section "Command-Line Options" in Chapter 11, *Running awk and gawk*). It would be nice to be able to write programs in the following manner:

```
# library functions
@include getopt.awk
@include join.awk
...

# main program
BEGIN {
    while ((c = getopt(ARGC, ARGV, "a:b:cde")) != -1)
        ...
    ...
}
```

The following program, *igawk.sh*, provides this service. It simulates *gawk*'s searching of the AWKPATH variable and also allows *nested* includes; i.e., a file that is included with @include can contain further @include statements. *igawk* makes an effort to only include files once, so that nested includes don't accidentally include a library function twice.

igawk should behave just like *gawk* externally. This means it should accept all of *gawk*'s command-line arguments, including the ability to have multiple source files specified via *–f*, and the ability to mix command-line and library source files.

The program is written using the POSIX Shell (*sh*) command language. It works as follows:

1. Loop through the arguments, saving anything that doesn't represent *awk* source code for later, when the expanded program is run.

2. For any arguments that do represent *awk* text, put the arguments into a temporary file that will be expanded. There are two cases:

    a. Literal text, provided with *--source* or *--source=*. This text is just echoed directly. The *echo* program automatically supplies a trailing newline.

    b. Source filenames, provided with *–f.* We use a neat trick and echo @include filename into the temporary file. Since the file-inclusion program works the way *gawk* does, this gets the text of the file included into the program at the correct point.

3. Run an *awk* program (naturally) over the temporary file to expand @include statements. The expanded program is placed in a second temporary file.

4. Run the expanded program with *gawk* and any other original command-line arguments that the user supplied (such as the data filenames).

The initial part of the program turns on shell tracing if the first argument is debug. Otherwise, a shell trap statement arranges to clean up any temporary files on program exit or upon an interrupt.

The next part loops through all the command-line arguments. There are several cases of interest:

-- This ends the arguments to *igawk*. Anything else should be passed on to the user's *awk* program without being evaluated.

-W This indicates that the next option is specific to *gawk*. To make argument processing easier, the *–W* is appended to the front of the remaining arguments and the loop continues. (This is an *sh* programming trick. Don't worry about it if you are not familiar with *sh*.)

−v, −F

These are saved and passed on to *gawk.*

−f, −−file, −−file=, -Wfile=

The filename is saved to the temporary file */tmp/ig.s.$$* with an @include state-
ment. The *sed* utility is used to remove the leading option part of the argu-
ment (e.g., −−file=).

−−source, −−source=, -Wsource=

The source text is echoed into */tmp/ig.s.$$*.

−−version, -Wversion

igawk prints its version number, runs gawk −version to get the *gawk* version
information, and then exits.

If none of the −*f,* −−*file,* −*Wfile,* −−*source,* or −*Wsource* arguments are supplied,
then the first nonoption argument should be the *awk* program. If there are no
command-line arguments left, *igawk* prints an error message and exits. Otherwise,
the first argument is echoed into */tmp/ig.s.$$*. In any case, after the arguments
have been processed, */tmp/ig.s.$$* contains the complete text of the original *awk*
program.

The $$ in *sh* represents the current process ID number. It is often used in shell
programs to generate unique temporary filenames. This allows multiple users to
run *igawk* without worrying that the temporary filenames will clash. The program
is as follows:

```
#! /bin/sh
# igawk --- like gawk but do @include processing

if [ "$1" = debug ]
then
    set -x
    shift
else
    # cleanup on exit, hangup, interrupt, quit, termination
    trap 'rm -f /tmp/ig.[se].$$' 0 1 2 3 15
fi

while [ $# -ne 0 ] # loop over arguments
do
    case $1 in
    --)     shift; break;;

    -W)     shift
            set -- -W"$@"
            continue;;

    -[vF])  opts="$opts $1 '$2'"
            shift;;
```

```
        -[vF]*) opts="$opts '$1'" ;;

        -f)     echo @include "$2" >> /tmp/ig.s.$$
                shift;;

        -f*)    f=`echo "$1" | sed 's/-f//'`
                echo @include "$f" >> /tmp/ig.s.$$ ;;

        -?file=*)    # -Wfile or --file
                f=`echo "$1" | sed 's/-.file=//'`
                echo @include "$f" >> /tmp/ig.s.$$ ;;

        -?file)      # get arg, $2
                echo @include "$2" >> /tmp/ig.s.$$
                shift;;

        -?source=*)  # -Wsource or --source
                t=`echo "$1" | sed 's/-.source=//'`
                echo "$t" >> /tmp/ig.s.$$ ;;

        -?source)    # get arg, $2
                echo "$2" >> /tmp/ig.s.$$
                shift;;

        -?version)
                echo igawk: version 1.0 1>&2
                gawk --version
                exit 0 ;;

        -[W-]*) opts="$opts '$1'" ;;

        *)      break;;
        esac
        shift
done

if [ ! -s /tmp/ig.s.$$ ]
then
    if [ -z "$1" ]
    then
        echo igawk: no program! 1>&2
        exit 1
    else
        echo "$1" > /tmp/ig.s.$$
        shift
    fi
fi

# at this point, /tmp/ig.s.$$ has the program
```

The *awk* program to process @include directives reads through the program, one line at a time, using getline (see the section "Explicit Input with getline" in Chapter 3). The input filenames and @include statements are managed using a stack. As each @include is encountered, the current filename is "pushed" onto the stack and the file named in the `@include` directive becomes the current filename. As each file is finished, the stack is "popped," and the previous input file becomes the current input file again. The process is started by making the original file the first one on the stack.

The `pathto` function does the work of finding the full path to a file. It simulates *gawk*'s behavior when searching the AWKPATH environment variable (see the section "The AWKPATH Environment Variable" in Chapter 11). If a filename has a / in it, no path search is done. Otherwise, the filename is concatenated with the name of each directory in the path, and an attempt is made to open the generated filename. The only way to test if a file can be read in *awk* is to go ahead and try to read it with `getline`; this is what `pathto` does.* If the file can be read, it is closed and the filename is returned:

```
gawk -- '
# process @include directives

function pathto(file,    i, t, junk)
{
    if (index(file, "/") != 0)
        return file

    for (i = 1; i <= ndirs; i++) {
        t = (pathlist[i] "/" file)
        if ((getline junk < t) > 0) {
            # found it
            close(t)
            return t
        }
    }
    return ""
}
```

The main program is contained inside one `BEGIN` rule. The first thing it does is set up the `pathlist` array that `pathto` uses. After splitting the path on :, null elements are replaced with ".", which represents the current directory:

```
BEGIN {
    path = ENVIRON["AWKPATH"]
    ndirs = split(path, pathlist, ":")
    for (i = 1; i <= ndirs; i++) {
        if (pathlist[i] == "")
            pathlist[i] = "."
    }
```

---

* On some very old versions of *awk*, the test `getline junk < t` can loop forever if the file exists but is empty. Caveat emptor.

The stack is initialized with ARGV[1], which will be */tmp/ig.s.$$*. The main loop comes next. Input lines are read in succession. Lines that do not start with @include are printed verbatim. If the line does start with @include, the filename is in $2. pathto is called to generate the full path. If it cannot, then we print an error message and continue.

The next thing to check is if the file is included already. The processed array is indexed by the full filename of each included file and it tracks this information for us. If the file is seen again, a warning message is printed. Otherwise, the new filename is pushed onto the stack and processing continues.

Finally, when getline encounters the end of the input file, the file is closed and the stack is popped. When stackptr is less than zero, the program is done:

```
        stackptr = 0
        input[stackptr] = ARGV[1]  # ARGV[1] is first file

        for (; stackptr >= 0; stackptr--) {
            while ((getline < input[stackptr]) > 0) {
                if (tolower($1) != "@include") {
                    print
                    continue
                }
                fpath = pathto($2)
                if (fpath == "") {
                    printf("igawk:%s:%d: cannot find %s\n",
                        input[stackptr], FNR, $2) > "/dev/stderr"
                    continue
                }
                if (! (fpath in processed)) {
                    processed[fpath] = input[stackptr]
                    input[++stackptr] = fpath  # push onto stack
                } else
                    print $2, "included in", input[stackptr],
                        "already included in",
                        processed[fpath] > "/dev/stderr"
            }
            close(input[stackptr])
        }
    }' /tmp/ig.s.$$ > /tmp/ig.e.$$
```

The last step is to call *gawk* with the expanded program, along with the original options and command-line arguments that the user supplied. *gawk*'s exit status is passed back on to *igawk*'s calling program:

```
    eval gawk -f /tmp/ig.e.$$ $opts -- "$@"

    exit $?
```

This version of *igawk* represents my third attempt at this program. There are three key simplifications that make the program work better:

- Using @include even for the files named with *–f* makes building the initial collected *awk* program much simpler; all the @include processing can be done once.

- Not trying to save the line read with getline when testing for the file's accessibility for use with the main program complicates things considerably.

- Using a getline loop in the BEGIN rule does it all in one place. It is not necessary to call out to a separate loop for processing nested @include statements.

Also, this program illustrates that it is often worthwhile to combine *sh* and *awk* programming together. You can usually accomplish quite a lot, without having to resort to low-level programming in C or C++, and it is frequently easier to do certain kinds of string and argument manipulation using the shell than it is in *awk*.

Finally, *igawk* shows that it is not always necessary to add new features to a program; they can often be layered on top. With *igawk*, there is no real reason to build @include processing into *gawk* itself.

As an additional example of this, consider the idea of having two files in a directory in the search path:

default.awk
    This file contains a set of default library functions, such as getopt and assert.

site.awk
    This file contains library functions that are specific to a site or installation; i.e., locally developed functions. Having a separate file allows *default.awk* to change with new *gawk* releases, without requiring the system administrator to update it each time by adding the local functions.

One user suggested that *gawk* be modified to automatically read these files upon startup. Instead, it would be very simple to modify *igawk* to do this. Since *igawk* can process nested @include directives, *default.awk* could simply contain @include statements for the desired library functions.

14

Internetworking with gawk

This chapter describes *gawk*'s networking features in depth, including a number of interesting examples and the reusable core of a *gawk*-based web server. The chapter is adapted from *TCP/IP Internetworking with gawk*, by Jürgen Kahrs and Arnold Robbins, which is a separate document distributed with *gawk*.

Networking with gawk

The *awk* programming language was originally developed as a pattern-matching language for writing short programs to perform data manipulation tasks. *awk*'s strength is the manipulation of textual data that is stored in files. It was never meant to be used for networking purposes. To exploit its features in a networking context, it's necessary to use an access mode for network connections that resembles the access of files as closely as possible.

awk is also meant to be a prototyping language. It is used to demonstrate feasibility and to play with features and user interfaces. This can be done with file-like handling of network connections. *gawk* trades the lack of many of the advanced features of the TCP/IP family of protocols for the convenience of simple connection handling. The advanced features are available when programming in C or Perl. In fact, the network programming in this section is very similar to what is described in books such as *Internet Programming with Python*, *Advanced Perl Programming*, and *Web Client Programming with Perl* (O'Reilly).

However, you can do the programming here without first having to learn object-oriented ideology; underlying languages such as Tcl/Tk, Perl, Python; or all of the libraries necessary to extend these languages before they are ready for the Internet.

This section demonstrates how to use the TCP protocol. The other protocols are much less important for most users (UDP) or even untractable (RAW).

gawk's Networking Mechanisms

The |& operator introduced in *gawk* 3.1 for use in communicating with a *coprocess* is described in the section "Two-Way Communications with Another Process" in Chapter 10, *Advanced Features of gawk*. It shows how to do two-way I/O to a separate process, sending it data with print or printf and reading data with get-line. If you haven't read it already, you should go back and review that material now.

gawk transparently extends the two-way I/O mechanism to simple networking through the use of special filenames. When a "coprocess" that matches the special files we are about to describe is started, *gawk* creates the appropriate network connection, and then two-way I/O proceeds as usual.

At the C, C++, and Perl level, networking is accomplished via *sockets*, an Application Programming Interface (API) originally developed at the University of California at Berkeley that is now used almost universally for TCP/IP networking. Socket-level programming, while fairly straightforward, requires paying attention to a number of details, as well as using binary data. It is not well-suited for use from a high-level language like *awk*. The special files provided in *gawk* hide the details from the programmer, making things much simpler and easier to use.

The special filename for network access is made up of several fields, all of which are mandatory:

```
/inet/protocol/localport/hostname/remoteport
```

The */inet/* field is, of course, constant when accessing the network. The *localport* and *remoteport* fields do not have a meaning when used with */inet/raw* because "ports" only apply to TCP and UDP. So, when using */inet/raw*, the port fields always have to be 0.

The fields of the special filename

This section explains the meaning of all the other fields, as well as the range of values and the defaults. All of the fields are mandatory. To let the system pick a value, or if the field doesn't apply to the protocol, specify it as 0:

protocol

Determines which member of the TCP/IP family of protocols is selected to transport the data across the network. There are three possible values (always written in lowercase): tcp, udp, and raw. The exact meaning of each is explained later in this section.

localport

Determines which port on the local machine is used to communicate across the network. It has no meaning with */inet/raw* and must therefore be 0. Application-level clients usually use 0 to indicate they do not care which local port is used—instead they specify a remote port to connect to. It is vital for application-level servers to use a number different from 0 here because their service has to be available at a specific publicly known port number. It is possible to use a name from */etc/services* here.

hostname

Determines which remote host is to be at the other end of the connection. Application-level servers must fill this field with a 0 to indicate their being open for all other hosts to connect to them and enforce connection level server behavior this way. It is not possible for an application-level server to restrict its availability to one remote host by entering a hostname here. Application-level clients must enter a name different from 0. The name can be either symbolic (e.g., jpl-devvax.jpl.nasa.gov) or numeric (e.g., 128.149.1.143).

remoteport

Determines which port on the remote machine is used to communicate across the network. It has no meaning with */inet/raw* and must therefore be 0. For */inet/tcp* and */inet/udp*, application-level clients *must* use a number other than 0 to indicate to which port on the remote machine they want to connect. Application-level servers must not fill this field with a 0. Instead they specify a local port to which clients connect. It is possible to use a name from */etc/services* here.

Experts in network programming will notice that the usual client/server asymmetry found at the level of the socket API is not visible here. This is for the sake of simplicity of the high-level concept. If this asymmetry is necessary for your application, use another language. For *gawk*, it is more important to enable users to write a client program with a minimum of code. What happens when first accessing a network connection is seen in the following pseudocode:

```
if ((name of remote host given) && (other side accepts connection)) {
    rendez-vous successful; transmit with getline or print
} else {
    if ((other side did not accept) && (localport == 0))
        exit unsuccessful
```

```
    if (TCP) {
        set up a server accepting connections
        this means waiting for the client on the other side to connect
    } else
        ready
}
```

The exact behavior of this algorithm depends on the values of the fields of the special filename. When in doubt, Table 14-1 gives you the combinations of values and their meaning. If this table is too complicated, focus on the three lines printed in bold. All the examples in this section use only the patterns printed in **bold** letters.

Table 14-1. /inet Special File Components

Protocol	Local Port	Host Name	Remote Port	Resulting Connection-Level Behavior
tcp	**0**	**x**	**x**	**Dedicated client, fails if immediately connecting to a server on the other side fails**
udp	0	x	x	Dedicated client
raw	0	x	0	Dedicated client, works only as root
tcp, udp	**x**	**x**	**x**	**Client, switches to dedicated server if necessary**
tcp, udp	**x**	**0**	**0**	**Dedicated server**
raw	0	0	0	Dedicated server, works only as root
tcp, udp, raw	x	x	0	Invalid
tcp, udp, raw	0	0	x	Invalid
tcp, udp, raw	x	0	x	Invalid
tcp, udp	0	0	0	Invalid
tcp, udp	0	x	0	Invalid
raw	x	0	0	Invalid
raw	0	x	x	Invalid
raw	x	x	x	Invalid

In general, TCP is the preferred mechanism to use. It is the simplest protocol to understand and to use. Use the others only if circumstances demand low-overhead.

Comparing protocols

This section develops a pair of programs (sender and receiver) that do nothing but send a timestamp from one machine to another. The sender and the receiver are implemented with each of the three protocols available and demonstrate the differences between them.

/inet/tcp

Once again, always use TCP. (Use UDP when low overhead is a necessity, and use RAW for network experimentation.) The first example is the sender program:

```
# Server
BEGIN {
    print strftime() |& "/inet/tcp/8888/0/0"
    close("/inet/tcp/8888/0/0")
}
```

The receiver is very simple:

```
# Client
BEGIN {
    "/inet/tcp/0/localhost/8888" |& getline
    print $0
    close("/inet/tcp/0/localhost/8888")
}
```

TCP guarantees that the bytes arrive at the receiving end in exactly the same order that they were sent. No byte is lost (except for broken connections), doubled, or out of order. Some overhead is necessary to accomplish this, but this is the price to pay for a reliable service. It does matter which side starts first. The sender/server has to be started first, and it waits for the receiver to read a line.

/inet/udp

The server and client programs that use UDP are almost identical to their TCP counterparts; only the *protocol* has changed. As before, it does matter which side starts first. The receiving side blocks and waits for the sender. In this case, the receiver/client has to be started first:

```
# Server
BEGIN {
    print strftime() |& "/inet/udp/8888/0/0"
    close("/inet/udp/8888/0/0")
}
```

The receiver is almost identical to the TCP receiver:

```
# Client
BEGIN {
    "/inet/udp/0/localhost/8888" |& getline
    print $0
    close("/inet/udp/0/localhost/8888")
}
```

UDP cannot guarantee that the datagrams at the receiving end will arrive in exactly the same order they were sent. Some datagrams could be lost, some doubled, and some out of order. But no overhead is necessary to accomplish this. This unreliable behavior is good enough for tasks such as data acquisition, logging, and even stateless services like NFS.

/inet/raw

This is an IP-level protocol. Only root is allowed to access this special file. It is meant to be the basis for implementing and experimenting with transport-level protocols.* In the most general case, the sender has to supply the encapsulating header bytes in front of the packet and the receiver has to strip the additional bytes from the message.

RAW receivers cannot receive packets sent with TCP or UDP because the operating system does not deliver the packets to a RAW receiver. The operating system knows about some of the protocols on top of IP and decides on its own which packet to deliver to which process. Therefore, the UDP receiver must be used for receiving UDP datagrams sent with the RAW sender. This is a dark corner, not only of *gawk*, but also of TCP/IP.

For extended experimentation with protocols, look into the approach implemented in a tool called SPAK. This tool reflects the hierarchical layering of protocols (encapsulation) in the way data streams are piped out of one program into the next one. It shows which protocol is based on which other (lower-level) protocol by looking at the command-line ordering of the program calls. Cleverly thought out, SPAK is much better than *gawk*'s */inet* for learning the meaning of each and every bit in the protocol headers.

The next example uses the RAW protocol to emulate the behavior of UDP. The sender program is the same as above, but with some additional bytes that fill the places of the UDP fields:

```
BEGIN {
    Message = "Hello world\n"
    SourcePort = 0
    DestinationPort = 8888
    MessageLength = length(Message)+8
    RawService = "/inet/raw/0/localhost/0"
    printf("%c%c%c%c%c%c%c%c%s",
        SourcePort/256, SourcePort%256,
        DestinationPort/256, DestinationPort%256,
        MessageLength/256, MessageLength%256,
        0, 0, Message) |& RawService
    fflush(RawService)
    close(RawService)
}
```

---

* This special file is reserved, but not otherwise currently implemented.

Since this program tries to emulate the behavior of UDP, it checks if the RAW sender is understood by the UDP receiver but not if the RAW receiver can understand the UDP sender. In a real network, the RAW receiver is hardly of any use because it gets every IP packet that comes across the network. There are usually so many packets that *gawk* would be too slow for processing them. Only on a network with little traffic can the IP-level receiver program be tested. Programs for analyzing IP traffic on modem or ISDN channels should be possible.

Port numbers do not have a meaning when using */inet/raw*. Their fields have to be 0. Only TCP and UDP use ports. Receiving data from */inet/raw* is difficult, not only because of processing speed but also because data is usually binary and not restricted to ASCII. This implies that line separation with RS does not work as usual.

Establishing a TCP Connection

Let's observe a network connection at work. Type in the following program and watch the output. Within a second, it connects via TCP (*/inet/tcp*) to the machine it is running on (localhost) and asks the service daytime on the machine what time it is:

```
BEGIN {
    "/inet/tcp/0/localhost/daytime" |& getline
    print $0
    close("/inet/tcp/0/localhost/daytime")
}
```

Even experienced *awk* users will find the second line strange in two respects:

- A special file is used as a shell command that pipes its output into getline. One would rather expect to see the special file being read like any other file (getline < "/inet/tcp/0/localhost/daytime").

- The operator |& has not been part of any *awk* implementation (until now). It is actually the only extension of the *awk* language needed (apart from the special files) to introduce network access.

The |& operator was introduced in *gawk* 3.1 in order to overcome the crucial restriction that access to files and pipes in *awk* is always unidirectional. It was formerly impossible to use both access modes on the same file or pipe. Instead of changing the whole concept of file access, the |& operator behaves exactly like the usual pipe operator except for two additions:

- Normal shell commands connected to their *gawk* program with a |& pipe can be accessed bidirectionally. The |& turns out to be a quite general, useful, and natural extension of *awk*.

- Pipes that consist of a special filename for network connections are not executed as shell commands. Instead, they can be read and written to, just like a full-duplex network connection.

In the earlier example, the |& operator tells getline to read a line from the special file */inet/tcp/0/localhost/daytime*. We could also have printed a line into the special file. But instead we just read a line with the time, printed it, and closed the connection. (While we could just let *gawk* close the connection by finishing the program, in this book we are pedantic and always explicitly close the connections.)

Troubleshooting Connection Problems

It may well be that for some reason the program shown in the previous example does not run on your machine. When looking at possible reasons for this, you will learn much about typical problems that arise in network programming. First of all, your implementation of *gawk* may not support network access because it is a pre-3.1 version or you do not have a network interface in your machine. Perhaps your machine uses some other protocol, such as DECnet or Novell's IPX. For the rest of this section, we will assume you work on a Unix machine that supports TCP/IP. If the previous example program does not run on your machine, it may help to replace the name localhost with the name of your machine or its IP address. If it does, you could replace localhost with the name of another machine in your vicinity—this way, the program connects to another machine. Now you should see the date and time being printed by the program, otherwise your machine may not support the daytime service. Try changing the service to chargen or ftp. This way, the program connects to other services that should give you some response. If you are curious, you should have a look at your */etc/services* file. It could look like this:

```
# /etc/services:
#
# Network services, Internet style
#
# Name       Number/Protcol  Alternate name # Comments

echo         7/tcp
echo         7/udp
discard      9/tcp           sink null
discard      9/udp           sink null
daytime      13/tcp
daytime      13/udp
chargen      19/tcp          ttytst source
chargen      19/udp          ttytst source
ftp          21/tcp
telnet       23/tcp
smtp         25/tcp          mail
finger       79/tcp
```

```
www         80/tcp       http       # WorldWideWeb HTTP
www         80/udp       # HyperText Transfer Protocol
pop-2       109/tcp      postoffice    # POP version 2
pop-2       109/udp
pop-3       110/tcp      # POP version 3
pop-3       110/udp
nntp        119/tcp      readnews untp  # USENET News
irc         194/tcp      # Internet Relay Chat
irc         194/udp
...
```

Here, you find a list of services that traditional Unix machines usually support. If your GNU/Linux machine does not do so, it may be that these services are switched off in some startup script. Systems running some flavor of Microsoft Windows usually do *not* support these services. Nevertheless, it *is* possible to do networking with *gawk* on Microsoft Windows.* The first column of the file gives the name of the service, and the second column gives a unique number and the protocol that one can use to connect to this service. The rest of the line is treated as a comment. You see that some services (echo) support TCP as well as UDP.

Interacting with a Network Service

The next program makes use of the possibility to really interact with a network service by printing something into the special file. It asks the so-called *finger* service if a user of the machine is logged in. When testing this program, try to change localhost to some other machine name in your local network:

```
BEGIN {
    NetService = "/inet/tcp/0/localhost/finger"
    print "name" |& NetService
    while ((NetService |& getline) > 0)
        print $0
    close(NetService)
}
```

After telling the service on the machine which user to look for, the program repeatedly reads lines that come as a reply. When no more lines are coming (because the service has closed the connection), the program also closes the connection. Try replacing "name" with your login name (or the name of someone else logged in). For a list of all users currently logged in, replace *name* with an empty string ("").

The final close command could be safely deleted from the above script, because the operating system closes any open connection by default when a script reaches

---

* On Microsoft Windows, the equivalent of */etc/services* resides in the file *c:\windows\services.*

the end of execution. In order to avoid portability problems, it is best to always close connections explicitly. With the Linux kernel, for example, proper closing results in flushing of buffers. Letting the close happen by default may result in discarding buffers.

When looking at */etc/services* you may have noticed that the daytime service is also available with udp. In the earlier example, change tcp to udp, and change finger to daytime. After starting the modified program, you will see the expected day and time message. The program then hangs, because it waits for more lines coming from the service. However, they never come. This behavior is a consequence of the differences between TCP and UDP. When using UDP, neither party is automatically informed about the other closing the connection. Continuing to experiment this way reveals many other subtle differences between TCP and UDP. To avoid such trouble, one should always remember the advice Douglas E. Comer and David Stevens give in Volume III of their series *Internetworking with TCP* (page 14):

> When designing client-server applications, beginners are strongly advised to use TCP because it provides reliable, connection-oriented communication. Programs only use UDP if the application protocol handles reliability, the application requires hardware broadcast or multicast, or the application cannot tolerate virtual circuit overhead.

Setting up a Service

The preceding programs behaved as clients that connect to a server somewhere on the Internet and request a particular service. Now we will set up such a service to mimic the behavior of the daytime service. Such a server does not know in advance who is going to connect to it over the network. Therefore, we cannot insert a name for the host to connect to in our special filename.

Start the following program in one window. Notice that the service does not have the name daytime, but the number 8888. From looking at */etc/services*, you know that names like daytime are just mnemonics for predetermined 16-bit integers. Only the system administrator (root) could enter our new service into */etc/services* with an appropriate name. Also notice that the service name has to be entered into a different field of the special filename because we are setting up a server, not a client:

```
BEGIN {
    print strftime() |& "/inet/tcp/8888/0/0"
    close("/inet/tcp/8888/0/0")
}
```

Now open another window on the same machine. Copy the client program given as the first example (see the section "Establishing a TCP Connection" earlier in this chapter) to a new file and edit it, changing the name daytime to 8888. Then start the modified client. You should get a reply like this:

```
Sat Sep 27 19:08:16 CEST 1997
```

Both programs explicitly close the connection.

Now we will intentionally make a mistake to see what happens when the name 8888 (the so-called port) is already used by another service. Start the server program in both windows. The first one works, but the second one complains that it could not open the connection. Each port on a single machine can only be used by one server program at a time. Now terminate the server program and change the name 8888 to echo. After restarting it, the server program does not run any more, and you know why: there is already an echo service running on your machine. But even if this isn't true, you would not get your own echo server running on a Unix machine, because the ports with numbers smaller than 1024 (echo is at port 7) are reserved for root. On machines running some flavor of Microsoft Windows, there is no restriction that reserves ports 1 to 1024 for a privileged user; hence, you can start an echo server there.

Turning this short server program into something really useful is simple. Imagine a server that first reads a filename from the client through the network connection, then does something with the file and sends a result back to the client. The server-side processing could be:

```
BEGIN {
    NetService = "/inet/tcp/8888/0/0"
    NetService |& getline
    CatPipe    = ("cat " $1)    # sets $0 and the fields
    while ((CatPipe | getline) > 0)
        print $0 |& NetService
    close(NetService)
}
```

and we would have a remote copying facility. Such a server reads the name of a file from any client that connects to it and transmits the contents of the named file across the net. The server-side processing could also be the execution of a command that is transmitted across the network. From this example, you can see how simple it is to open up a security hole on your machine. If you allow clients to connect to your machine and execute arbitrary commands, anyone would be free to do rm -rf *.

Reading Email

The distribution of email is usually done by dedicated email servers that communicate with your machine using special protocols. To receive email, we will use the Post Office Protocol (POP). Sending can be done with the much older Simple Mail Transfer Protocol (SMTP).

When you type in the following program, replace the *emailhost* by the name of your local email server. Ask your administrator if the server has a POP service, and then use its name or number in the program below. Now the program is ready to connect to your email server, but it will not succeed in retrieving your mail because it does not yet know your login name or password. Replace them in the program, and it shows you the first email the server has in store:

```
BEGIN {
    POPService  = "/inet/tcp/0/emailhost/pop3"
    RS = ORS = "\r\n"
    print "user name"              |& POPService
    POPService                     |& getline
    print "pass password"          |& POPService
    POPService                     |& getline
    print "retr 1"                 |& POPService
    POPService                     |& getline
    if ($1 != "+OK") exit
    print "quit"                   |& POPService
    RS = "\r\n\\.\r\n"
    POPService |& getline
    print $0
    close(POPService)
}
```

The record separators RS and ORS are redefined because the protocol (POP) requires CR-LF to separate lines. After identifying yourself to the email service, the command `retr 1` instructs the service to send the first of all your email messages in line. If the service replies with something other than +OK, the program exits; maybe there is no email. Otherwise, the program first announces that it intends to finish reading email, and then redefines RS in order to read the entire email as multiline input in one record. From the POP RFC, we know that the body of the email always ends with a single line containing a single dot. The program looks for this using RS = "\r\n\\.\r\n". When it finds this sequence in the mail message, it quits. You can invoke this program as often as you like; it does not delete the message it reads, but instead leaves it on the server.

Reading a Web Page

Retrieving a web page from a web server is as simple as retrieving email from an email server. We only have to use a similar, but not identical, protocol and a different port. The name of the protocol is HyperText Transfer Protocol (HTTP) and the port number is usually 80. As in the preceding section, ask your administrator about the name of your local web server or proxy web server and its port number for HTTP requests.

The following program employs a rather crude approach toward retrieving a web page. It uses the prehistoric syntax of HTTP 0.9, which almost all web servers still support. The most noticeable thing about it is that the program directs the request to the local proxy server whose name you insert in the special filename (which in turn calls www.yahoo.com):

```
BEGIN {
    RS = ORS = "\r\n"
    HttpService = "/inet/tcp/0/proxy/80"
    print "GET http://www.yahoo.com"        |& HttpService
    while ((HttpService |& getline) > 0)
        print $0
    close(HttpService)
}
```

Again, lines are separated by a redefined RS and ORS. The GET request that we send to the server is the only kind of HTTP request that existed when the Web was created in the early 1990s. HTTP calls this GET request a "method," which tells the service to transmit a web page (here the home page of the Yahoo! search engine). Version 1.0 added the request methods HEAD and POST. The current version of HTTP is 1.1,* and knows the additional request methods OPTIONS, PUT, DELETE, and TRACE. You can fill in any valid web address, and the program prints the HTML code of that page to your screen.

Notice the similarity between the responses of the POP and HTTP services. First, you get a header that is terminated by an empty line, and then you get the body of the page in HTML. The lines of the headers also have the same form as in POP. There is the name of a parameter, then a colon, and finally the value of that parameter.

Images (*.png* or *.gif* files) can also be retrieved this way, but then you get binary data that should be redirected into a file. Another application is calling a CGI (Common Gateway Interface) script on some server. CGI scripts are used when the contents of a web page are not constant, but generated instantly at the moment you send a request for the page. For example, to get a detailed report

---

* Version 1.0 of HTTP was defined in RFC 1945. HTTP 1.1 was initially specified in RFC 2068. In June 1999, RFC 2068 was made obsolete by RFC 2616, an update without any substantial changes.

about the current quotes of Motorola stock shares, call a CGI script at Yahoo! with the following:

```
get = "GET http://quote.yahoo.com/q?s=MOT&d=t"
print get |& HttpService
```

You can also request weather reports this way.

A Primitive Web Service

Now we know enough about HTTP to set up a primitive web service that just says "Hello, world" when someone connects to it with a browser. Compared to the situation in the preceding section, our program changes the role. It tries to behave just like the server we have observed. Since we are setting up a server here, we have to insert the port number in the *localport* field of the special filename. The other two fields (*hostname* and *remoteport*) have to contain a 0 because we do not know in advance which host will connect to our service.

In the early 1990s, all a server had to do was send an HTML document and close the connection. Here, we adhere to the modern syntax of HTTP. The steps are as follows:

1. Send a status line telling the web browser that everything is okay.

2. Send a line to tell the browser how many bytes follow in the body of the message. This was not necessary earlier because both parties knew that the document ended when the connection closed. Nowadays it is possible to stay connected after the transmission of one web page. This is to avoid the network traffic necessary for repeatedly establishing TCP connections for requesting several images. Thus, there is the need to tell the receiving party how many bytes will be sent. The header is terminated as usual with an empty line.

3. Send the "Hello, world" body in HTML. The useless while loop swallows the request of the browser. We could actually omit the loop, and on most machines the program would still work. First, start the following program:

```
BEGIN {
    RS = ORS = "\r\n"
    HttpService = "/inet/tcp/8080/0/0"
    Hello = "<HTML><HEAD>" \
            "<TITLE>A Famous Greeting</TITLE></HEAD>" \
            "<BODY><H1>Hello, world</H1></BODY></HTML>"
    Len = length(Hello) + length(ORS)
    print "HTTP/1.0 200 OK"              |& HttpService
    print "Content-Length: " Len ORS     |& HttpService
    print Hello                          |& HttpService
    while ((HttpService |& getline) > 0)
        continue
    close(HttpService)
}
```

Now, on the same machine, start your favorite browser and let it point to *http://localhost:8080* (the browser needs to know on which port our server is listening for requests). If this does not work, the browser probably tries to connect to a proxy server that does not know your machine. If so, change the browser's configuration so that the browser does not try to use a proxy to connect to your machine.

A Web Service with Interaction

Setting up a web service that allows user interaction is more difficult and shows us the limits of network access in *gawk*. In this section, we develop a main program (a BEGIN pattern and its action) that will become the core of event-driven execution controlled by a graphical user interface (GUI). Each HTTP event that the user triggers by some action within the browser is received in this central procedure. Parameters and menu choices are extracted from this request, and an appropriate measure is taken according to the user's choice. For example:

```
BEGIN {
    if (MyHost == "") {
        "uname -n" | getline MyHost
        close("uname -n")
    }
    if (MyPort ==  0) MyPort = 8080
    HttpService = "/inet/tcp/" MyPort "/0/0"
    MyPrefix    = "http://" MyHost ":" MyPort
    SetUpServer()
    while ("awk" != "complex") {
        RS = ORS = "\r\n"        # header lines are terminated this way
        Status    = 200          # this means OK
        Reason    = "OK"
        Header    = TopHeader
        Document  = TopDoc
        Footer    = TopFooter
        if       (GETARG["Method"] == "GET") {
            HandleGET()
        } else if (GETARG["Method"] == "HEAD") {
            # not yet implemented
        } else if (GETARG["Method"] != "") {
            print "bad method", GETARG["Method"]
        }
        Prompt = Header Document Footer
        print "HTTP/1.0", Status, Reason    |& HttpService
        print "Connection: Close"           |& HttpService
        print "Pragma: no-cache"            |& HttpService
        len = length(Prompt) + length(ORS)
        print "Content-length:", len        |& HttpService
        print ORS Prompt                    |& HttpService
```

```
        # ignore all the header lines
        while ((HttpService |& getline) > 0)
            continue
        close(HttpService)               # stop talking to this client
        HttpService |& getline           # wait for new client request
        print systime(), strftime(), $0  # do some logging
        CGI_setup($1, $2, $3)            # read request parameters
    }
}
```

This web server presents menu choices in the form of HTML links. Therefore, it has to tell the browser the name of the host it is residing on. When starting the server, the user may supply the name of the host from the command line with gawk -v MyHost="Rumpelstilzchen". If the user does not do this, the server looks up the name of the host it is running on for later use as a web address in HTML documents. The same applies to the port number. These values are inserted later into the HTML content of the web pages to refer to the home system.

Each server that is built around this core has to initialize some application-dependent variables (such as the default home page) in a procedure SetUpServer, which is called immediately before entering the infinite loop of the server. For now, we will write an instance that initiates a trivial interaction. With this home page, the client user can click on two possible choices, and receive the current date either in human-readable format or in seconds since 1970:

```
function SetUpServer() {
  TopHeader = "<HTML><HEAD>"
  TopHeader = TopHeader "<title>My name is GAWK, GNU AWK</title></HEAD>"
  TopDoc    = "<BODY><h2>\
      Do you prefer your date <A HREF=" MyPrefix "/human>human</A> or\
      <A HREF=" MyPrefix "/POSIX>POSIXed</A>?</h2>" ORS ORS
  TopFooter = "</BODY></HTML>"
}
```

On the first run through the main loop, the default line terminators are set and the default home page is copied to the actual home page. Since this is the first run, GETARG["Method"] is not initialized yet, hence the case selection over the method does nothing. Now that the home page is initialized, the server can start communicating to a client browser.

It does so by printing the HTTP header into the network connection (print ... |& HttpService). This command blocks execution of the server script until a client connects. If this server script is compared with the primitive one we wrote before, you will notice two additional lines in the header. The first instructs the browser to close the connection after each request. The second tells the browser that it should never try to *remember* earlier requests that had identical web addresses (no caching). Otherwise, it could happen that the browser retrieves the time of day in the previous example just once, and later it takes the web page from the cache, always displaying the same time of day although time advances each second.

Having supplied the initial home page to the browser with a valid document stored in the parameter Prompt, it closes the connection and waits for the next request. When the request comes, a log line is printed that allows us to see which request the server receives. The final step in the loop is to call the function CGI_setup, which reads all the lines of the request (coming from the browser), processes them, and stores the transmitted parameters in the array PARAM. The complete text of these application-independent functions can be found in the section "A Simple CGI Library" later in this chapter. For now, we use a simplified version of CGI_setup:

```
function CGI_setup(    method, uri, version, i) {
    delete GETARG;          delete MENU;         delete PARAM
    GETARG["Method"] = $1; GETARG["URI"] = $2; GETARG["Version"] = $3
    i = index($2, "?")
    if (i > 0) {             # is there a "?" indicating a CGI request?
        split(substr($2, 1, i-1), MENU, "[/:]")
        split(substr($2, i+1), PARAM, "&")
        for (i in PARAM) {
            j = index(PARAM[i], "=")
            GETARG[substr(PARAM[i], 1, j-1)] = substr(PARAM[i], j+1)
        }
    } else {          # there is no "?", no need for splitting PARAMs
        split($2, MENU, "[/:]")
    }
}
```

At first, the function clears all variables used for global storage of request parameters. The rest of the function serves the purpose of filling the global parameters with the extracted new values. To accomplish this, the name of the requested resource is split into parts and stored for later evaluation. If the request contains a ?, then the request has CGI variables seamlessly appended to the web address. Everything in front of the ? is split up into menu items, and everything behind the ? is a list of *variable=value* pairs (separated by &) that also need splitting. This way, CGI variables are isolated and stored. This procedure lacks recognition of special characters that are transmitted in coded form.* Here, any optional request header and body parts are ignored. We do not need header parameters and the request body. However, when refining our approach or working with the POST and PUT methods, reading the header and body becomes inevitable. Header parameters should then be stored in a global array as well as the body.

---

* As defined in RFC 2068.

On each subsequent run through the main loop, one request from a browser is received, evaluated, and answered according to the user's choice. This can be done by letting the value of the HTTP method guide the main loop into execution of the procedure HandleGET, which evaluates the user's choice. In this case, we have only one hierarchical level of menus, but in the general case, menus are nested. The menu choices at each level are separated by /, just as in filenames. Notice how simple it is to construct menus of arbitrary depth:

```
function HandleGET() {
    if (      MENU[2] == "human") {
        Footer = strftime() TopFooter
    } else if (MENU[2] == "POSIX") {
        Footer = systime()  TopFooter
    }
}
```

The disadvantage of this approach is that our server is slow and can handle only one request at a time. Its main advantage, however, is that the server consists of just one *gawk* program. No need for installing an *httpd*, and no need for static separate HTML files, CGI scripts, or root privileges. This is rapid prototyping. This program can be started on the same host that runs your browser. Then let your browser point to *http://localhost:8080*.

It is also possible to include images into the HTML pages. Most browsers support the not very well-known *.xbm* format, which may contain only monochrome pictures but is an ASCII format. Binary images are possible but not so easy to handle. Another way of including images is to generate them with a tool such as GNUPlot, by calling the tool with the system function or through a pipe.

A Simple CGI Library

In the section "A Web Service with Interaction" earlier in this chapter, we saw the function CGI_setup as part of the web server "core logic" framework. The code presented there handles almost everything necessary for CGI requests. One thing it doesn't do is handle encoded characters in the requests. For example, an & is encoded as a percent sign followed by the hexadecimal value: %26. These encoded values should be decoded. Following is a simple library to perform these tasks. This code is used for all web server examples used throughout the rest of this book. If you want to use it for your own web server, store the source code into a file named *inetlib.awk*. Then you can include these functions into your code by placing the following statement into your program (on the first line of your script):

```
@include inetlib.awk
```

But beware, this mechanism is only possible if you invoke your web server script with *igawk* instead of the usual *awk* or *gawk*. Here is the code:

```
# CGI Library and core of a web server

# Global arrays
#   GETARG --- arguments to CGI GET command
#   MENU   --- menu items (path names)
#   PARAM  --- parameters of form x=y

# Optional variable MyHost contains host address
# Optional variable MyPort contains port number
# Needs TopHeader, TopDoc, TopFooter
# Sets MyPrefix, HttpService, Status, Reason

BEGIN {
    if (MyHost == "") {
        "uname -n" | getline MyHost
        close("uname -n")
    }
    if (MyPort ==  0) MyPort = 8080
    HttpService = "/inet/tcp/" MyPort "/0/0"
    MyPrefix    = "http://" MyHost ":" MyPort
    SetUpServer()
    while ("awk" != "complex") {
        RS = ORS    = "\r\n"      # header lines are terminated this way
        Status      = 200         # this means OK
        Reason      = "OK"
        Header      = TopHeader
        Document    = TopDoc
        Footer      = TopFooter
        if      (GETARG["Method"] == "GET") {
            HandleGET()
        } else if (GETARG["Method"] == "HEAD") {
            # not yet implemented
        } else if (GETARG["Method"] != "") {
            print "bad method", GETARG["Method"]
        }
        Prompt = Header Document Footer
        print "HTTP/1.0", Status, Reason    |& HttpService
        print "Connection: Close"           |& HttpService
        print "Pragma: no-cache"            |& HttpService
        len = length(Prompt) + length(ORS)
        print "Content-length:", len        |& HttpService
        print ORS Prompt                    |& HttpService
        # ignore all the header lines
        while ((HttpService |& getline) > 0)
            continue
        close(HttpService)                  # stop talking to this client
        HttpService |& getline              # wait for new client request
        print systime(), strftime(), $0     # do some logging
        CGI_setup($1, $2, $3)
    }
}
```

```
function CGI_setup(   method, uri, version, i)
{
    delete GETARG
    delete MENU
    delete PARAM
    GETARG["Method"] = method
    GETARG["URI"] = uri
    GETARG["Version"] = version

    i = index(uri, "?")
    if (i > 0) {   # is there a "?" indicating a CGI request?
        split(substr(uri, 1, i-1), MENU, "[/:]")
        split(substr(uri, i+1), PARAM, "&")
        for (i in PARAM) {
            PARAM[i] = _CGI_decode(PARAM[i])
            j = index(PARAM[i], "=")
            GETARG[substr(PARAM[i], 1, j-1)] = substr(PARAM[i], j+1)
        }
    } else {    # there is no "?", no need for splitting PARAMs
        split(uri, MENU, "[/:]")
    }
    for (i in MENU)      # decode characters in path
        if (i > 4)       # but not those in host name
            MENU[i] = _CGI_decode(MENU[i])
}
```

This isolates the details in a single function, CGI_setup. Decoding of encoded characters is pushed off to a helper function, _CGI_decode. The use of the leading underscore (_) in the function name is intended to indicate that it is an "internal" function, although there is nothing to enforce this:

```
function _CGI_decode(str,    hexdigs, i, pre, code1, code2, val, result)
{
    hexdigs = "123456789abcdef"

    i = index(str, "%")
    if (i == 0) # no work to do
        return str

    do {
        pre = substr(str, 1, i-1)    # part before %xx
        code1 = substr(str, i+1, 1) # first hex digit
        code2 = substr(str, i+2, 1) # second hex digit
        str = substr(str, i+3)       # rest of string

        code1 = tolower(code1)
        code2 = tolower(code2)
        val = index(hexdigs, code1) * 16 \
                + index(hexdigs, code2)

        result = result pre sprintf("%c", val)
        i = index(str, "%")
    } while (i != 0)
```

```
            if (length(str) > 0)
                result = result str
            return result
    }
```

This works by splitting the string apart around an encoded character. The two digits are converted to lowercase characters and looked up in a string of hex digits. Note that 0 is not in the string on purpose; index returns zero when it's not found, automatically giving the correct value! Once the hexadecimal value is converted from characters in a string into a numerical value, sprintf converts the value back into a real character. The following is a simple test harness for the above functions:

```
    BEGIN {
        CGI_setup("GET",
            "http://www.gnu.org/cgi-bin/foo?p1=stuff&p2=stuff%26junk" \
            "&percent=a %25 sign",
            "1.0")
        for (i in MENU)
            printf "MENU[\"%s\"] = %s\n", i, MENU[i]
        for (i in PARAM)
            printf "PARAM[\"%s\"] = %s\n", i, PARAM[i]
        for (i in GETARG)
            printf "GETARG[\"%s\"] = %s\n", i, GETARG[i]
    }
```

And this is the result when we run it:

```
    $ gawk -f testserv.awk
    MENU["4"] = www.gnu.org
    MENU["5"] = cgi-bin
    MENU["6"] = foo
    MENU["1"] = http
    MENU["2"] =
    MENU["3"] =
    PARAM["1"] = p1=stuff
    PARAM["2"] = p2=stuff&junk
    PARAM["3"] = percent=a % sign
    GETARG["p1"] = stuff
    GETARG["percent"] = a % sign
    GETARG["p2"] = stuff&junk
    GETARG["Method"] = GET
    GETARG["Version"] = 1.0
    GETARG["URI"] = http://www.gnu.org/cgi-bin/foo?p1=stuff&p2=stuff%26junk
                    &percent=a %25 sign
```

A Simple Web Server

In the preceding section, we built the core logic for event-driven GUIs. In this section, we finally extend the core to a real application. No one would actually write a commercial web server in *gawk*, but it is instructive to see that it is feasible in principle.

The application is ELIZA, the famous program by Joseph Weizenbaum that mimics the behavior of a professional psychotherapist when talking to you. Weizenbaum would certainly object to this description, but this is part of the legend around ELIZA. Take the site-independent core logic and append the following code:

```
function SetUpServer() {
  SetUpEliza()
  TopHeader = "<HTML><title>An HTTP-based System with GAWK</title>\
    <HEAD><META HTTP-EQUIV=\"Content-Type\"\
    CONTENT=\"text/html; charset=iso-8859-1\"></HEAD>\
    <BODY BGCOLOR=\"#ffffff\" TEXT=\"#000000\" LINK=\"#0000ff\"\
    VLINK=\"#0000ff\" ALINK=\"#0000ff\"> <A NAME=\"top\">"
  TopDoc    = "\
    <h2>Please choose one of the following actions:</h2>\
    <UL>\
    <LI><A HREF=" MyPrefix "/AboutServer>About this server</A></LI>\
    <LI><A HREF=" MyPrefix "/AboutELIZA>About Eliza</A></LI>\
    <LI><A HREF=" MyPrefix "/StartELIZA>Start talking to Eliza</A></LI>\
    </UL>"
  TopFooter = "</BODY></HTML>"
}
```

SetUpServer is similar to the previous example, except for calling another function, SetUpEliza. This approach can be used to implement other kinds of servers. The only changes needed to do so are hidden in the functions SetUpServer and HandleGET. Perhaps it might be necessary to implement other HTTP methods. The *igawk* program that comes with *gawk* may be useful for this process.

When extending this example to a complete application, the first thing to do is to implement the function SetUpServer to initialize the HTML pages and some variables. These initializations determine the way your HTML pages look (colors, titles, menu items, etc.).

The function HandleGET is a nested case selection that decides which page the user wants to see next. Each nesting level refers to a menu level of the GUI. Each case implements a certain action of the menu. On the deepest level of case selection, the handler essentially knows what the user wants and stores the answer into the variable that holds the HTML page contents:

```
function HandleGET() {
    # A real HTTP server would treat some parts of the URI as a file name.
    # We take parts of the URI as menu choices and go on accordingly.
    if (MENU[2] == "AboutServer") {
        Document    = "This is not a CGI script.\
            This is an httpd, an HTML file, and a CGI script all \
            in one GAWK script. It needs no separate www-server, \
            no installation, and no root privileges.\
            <p>To run it, do this:</p><ul>\
            <li> start this script with \"gawk -f httpserver.awk\",</li>\
            <li> and on the same host let your www browser open location\
```

```
             \"http://localhost:8080\"</li>\
             </ul>\<p>\ Details of HTTP come from:</p><ul>\
             <li>Hethmon:  Illustrated Guide to HTTP</p>\
             <li>RFC 2068</li></ul><p>JK 14.9.1997</p>"
    } else if (MENU[2] == "AboutELIZA") {
        Document    = "This is an implementation of the famous ELIZA\
             program by Joseph Weizenbaum. It is written in GAWK and\
             uses an HTML GUI."
    } else if (MENU[2] == "StartELIZA") {
        gsub(/\+/, " ", GETARG["YouSay"])
        # Here we also have to substitute coded special characters
        Document    = "<form method=GET>" \
             "<h3>" ElizaSays(GETARG["YouSay"]) "</h3>\
             <p><input type=text name=YouSay value=\"\" size=60>\
             <br><input type=submit value=\"Tell her about it\"></p></form>"
    }
}
```

Now we are down to the heart of ELIZA, so you can see how it works. Initially the user does not say anything; then ELIZA resets its money counter and asks the user to tell what comes to mind open heartedly. The subsequent answers are converted to uppercase characters and stored for later comparison. ELIZA presents the bill when being confronted with a sentence that contains the phrase "shut up." Otherwise, it looks for keywords in the sentence, conjugates the rest of the sentence, remembers the keyword for later use, and finally selects an answer from the set of possible answers:

```
function ElizaSays(YouSay) {
    if (YouSay == "") {
        cost = 0
        answer = "HI, IM ELIZA, TELL ME YOUR PROBLEM"
    } else {
        q = toupper(YouSay)
        gsub("'", "", q)
        if (q == qold) {
            answer = "PLEASE DONT REPEAT YOURSELF !"
        } else {
            if (index(q, "SHUT UP") > 0) {
                answer = "WELL, PLEASE PAY YOUR BILL. ITS EXACTLY ... $"\
                    int(100*rand()+30+cost/100)
            } else {
                qold = q
                w = "-"                      # no keyword recognized yet
                for (i in k) {               # search for keywords
                    if (index(q, i) > 0) {
                        w = i
                        break
                    }
                }
```

```
                if (w == "-") {          # no keyword, take old subject
                    w    = wold
                    subj = subjold
                } else {                  # find subject
                    subj = substr(q, index(q, w) + length(w)+1)
                    wold = w
                    subjold = subj       # remember keyword and subject
                }
                for (i in conj)
                    gsub(i, conj[i], q) # conjugation
                # from all answers to this keyword, select one randomly
                answer = r[indices[int(split(k[w], indices) * rand()) + 1]]
                # insert subject into answer
                gsub("_", subj, answer)
            }
        }
    }
    cost += length(answer) # for later payment : 1 cent per character
    return answer
}
```

In the long but simple function SetUpEliza, you can see tables for conjugation, keywords, and answers.* The associative array k contains indices into the array of answers r. To choose an answer, ELIZA just picks an index randomly:

```
function SetUpEliza() {
    srand()
    wold = "-"
    subjold = " "

    # table for conjugation
    conj[" ARE "     ] = " AM "
    conj["WERE "     ] = "WAS "
    conj[" YOU "     ] = " I "
    conj["YOUR "     ] = "MY "
    conj[" IVE "     ] =\
    conj[" I HAVE "  ] = " YOU HAVE "
    conj[" YOUVE "   ] =\
    conj[" YOU HAVE "] = " I HAVE "
    conj[" IM "      ] =\
    conj[" I AM "    ] = " YOU ARE "
    conj[" YOURE "   ] =\
    conj[" YOU ARE " ] = " I AM "

    # table of all answers
    r[1]    = "DONT YOU BELIEVE THAT I CAN  _"
    r[2]    = "PERHAPS YOU WOULD LIKE TO BE ABLE TO _ ?"
    ...
```

---

* The version shown here is abbreviated. The full version comes with the *gawk* distribution.

```
# table for looking up answers that fit to a certain keyword
k["CAN YOU"]       = "1 2 3"
k["CAN I"]         = "4 5"
k["YOU ARE"]       =\
k["YOURE"]         = "6 7 8 9"
...
}
```

Some interesting remarks and details (including the original source code of ELIZA) are found on Mark Humphry's home page. Yahoo! also has a page with a collection of ELIZA-like programs. Many of them are written in Java, some of them disclosing the Java source code, and a few even explain how to modify the Java source code.

Network Programming Caveats

By now it should be clear that debugging a networked application is more complicated than debugging a single-process single-hosted application. The behavior of a networked application sometimes looks noncausal because it is not reproducible in a strong sense. Whether a network application works or not sometimes depends on the following.

- How crowded the underlying network is
- Whether the party at the other end is running
- The state of the party at the other end

The most difficult problems for a beginner arise from the hidden states of the underlying network. After closing a TCP connection, it's often necessary to wait a short while before reopening the connection. Even more difficult is the establishment of a connection that previously ended with a "broken pipe." Those connections have to "time out" for a minute or so before they can reopen. Check this with the command netstat -a, which provides a list of still "active" connections.

Some Applications and Techniques

In this section, we look at a number of self-contained scripts, with an emphasis on concise networking. Along the way, we work towards creating building blocks that encapsulate often needed functions of the networking world, show new techniques that broaden the scope of problems that can be solved with *gawk*, and explore leading edge technology that may shape the future of networking.

We often refer to the site-independent core of the server that we built in the section "A Simple Web Server" earlier in this chapter. When building new and nontrivial servers, we always copy this building block and append new instances of the two functions SetUpServer and HandleGET.

This makes a lot of sense, since this scheme of event-driven execution provides *gawk* with an interface to the most widely accepted standard for GUIs: the web browser. Now, *gawk* can rival even Tcl/Tk.

Tcl and *gawk* have much in common. Both are simple scripting languages that allow us to quickly solve problems with short programs. But Tcl has Tk on top of it, and *gawk* had nothing comparable up to now. While Tcl needs a large and ever-changing library (Tk, which was bound to the X Window System until recently), *gawk* needs just the networking interface and some kind of browser on the client's side. Besides better portability, the most important advantage of this approach (embracing well-established standards such HTTP and HTML) is that *we do not need to change the language*. We let others do the work of fighting over protocols and standards. We can use HTML, JavaScript, VRML, or whatever else comes along to do our work.

PANIC: An Emergency Web Server

At first glance, the `"Hello, world"` example in the section "A Primitive Web Service" earlier in this chapter, seems useless. By adding just a few lines, we can turn it into something useful.

The PANIC program tells everyone who connects that the local site is not working. When a web server breaks down, it makes a difference if customers get a strange "network unreachable" message, or a short message telling them that the server has a problem. In such an emergency, the hard disk and everything on it (including the regular web service) may be unavailable. Rebooting the web server off a diskette makes sense in this setting.

To use the PANIC program as an emergency web server, all you need are the *gawk* executable and the program below on a diskette. By default, it connects to port 8080. A different value may be supplied on the command line:

```
BEGIN {
    RS = ORS = "\r\n"
    if (MyPort ==  0) MyPort = 8080
    HttpService = "/inet/tcp/" MyPort "/0/0"
    Hello = "<HTML><HEAD><TITLE>Out Of Service</TITLE>" \
        "</HEAD><BODY><H1>" \
        "This site is temporarily out of service." \
        "</H1></BODY></HTML>"
    Len = length(Hello) + length(ORS)
```

```
        while ("awk" != "complex") {
            print "HTTP/1.0 200 OK"              |& HttpService
            print "Content-Length: " Len ORS     |& HttpService
            print Hello                          |& HttpService
            while ((HttpService |& getline) > 0)
                continue
            close(HttpService)
        }
    }
```

GETURL: Retrieving Web Pages

GETURL is a versatile building block for shell scripts that need to retrieve files from the Internet. It takes a web address as a command-line parameter and tries to retrieve the contents of this address. The contents are printed to standard output, while the header is printed to */dev/stderr*. A surrounding shell script could analyze the contents and extract the text or the links. An ASCII browser could be written around GETURL. But more interestingly, web robots are straightforward to write on top of GETURL. On the Internet, you can find several programs of the same name that do the same job. They are usually much more complex internally and at least 10 times longer.

At first, GETURL checks if it was called with exactly one web address. Then, it checks if the user chose to use a special proxy server whose name is handed over in a variable. By default, it is assumed that the local machine serves as proxy. GETURL uses the GET method by default to access the web page. By handing over the name of a different method (such as HEAD), it is possible to choose a different behavior. With the HEAD method, the user does not receive the body of the page content, but does receive the header:

```
BEGIN {
    if (ARGC != 2) {
        print "GETURL - retrieve Web page via HTTP 1.0"
        print "IN:\n    the URL as a command-line parameter"
        print "PARAM(S):\n    -v Proxy=MyProxy"
        print "OUT:\n    the page content on stdout"
        print "    the page header on stderr"
        print "JK 16.05.1997"
        print "ADR 13.08.2000"
        exit
    }
    URL = ARGV[1]; ARGV[1] = ""
    if (Proxy     == "")  Proxy      = "127.0.0.1"
    if (ProxyPort == 0)   ProxyPort = 80
    if (Method    == "")  Method     = "GET"
    HttpService = "/inet/tcp/0/" Proxy "/" ProxyPort
    ORS = RS = "\r\n\r\n"
    print Method " " URL " HTTP/1.0" |& HttpService
    HttpService                      |& getline Header
    print Header > "/dev/stderr"
```

```
        while ((HttpService |& getline) > 0)
            printf "%s", $0
        close(HttpService)
    }
```

This program can be changed as needed, but be careful with the last lines. Make sure transmission of binary data is not corrupted by additional line breaks. Even as it is now, the byte sequence "\r\n\r\n" would disappear if it were contained in binary data. Don't get caught in a trap when trying a quick fix on this one.

REMCONF: Remote Configuration of Embedded Systems

Today, you often find powerful processors in embedded systems. Dedicated network routers and controllers for all kinds of machinery are examples of embedded systems. Processors like the Intel 80x86 or the AMD Elan are able to run multitasking operating systems, such as XINU or GNU/Linux in embedded PCs. These systems are small and usually do not have a keyboard or a display. Therefore, it is difficult to set up their configuration. There are several widespread ways to set them up:

- DIP switches

- Read Only Memories such as EPROMs

- Serial lines or some kind of keyboard

- Network connections via *telnet* or SNMP

- HTTP connections with HTML GUIs

In this section, we look at a solution that uses HTTP connections to control variables of an embedded system that are stored in a file. Since embedded systems have tight limits on resources like memory, it is difficult to employ advanced techniques such as SNMP and HTTP servers. *gawk* fits in quite nicely with its single executable which needs just a short script to start working. The following program stores the variables in a file, and a concurrent process in the embedded system may read the file. The program uses the site-independent part of the simple web server that we developed in the section "A Web Service with Interaction" earlier in this chapter. As mentioned there, all we have to do is to write two new procedures, `SetUpServer` and `HandleGET`:

```
function SetUpServer() {
  TopHeader = "<HTML><title>Remote Configuration</title>"
  TopDoc = "<BODY>\
    <h2>Please choose one of the following actions:</h2>\
    <UL>\
    <LI><A HREF=" MyPrefix "/AboutServer>About this server</A></LI>\
    <LI><A HREF=" MyPrefix "/ReadConfig>Read Configuration</A></LI>\
```

```
      <LI><A HREF=" MyPrefix "/CheckConfig>Check Configuration</A></LI>\
      <LI><A HREF=" MyPrefix "/ChangeConfig>Change Configuration</A></LI>\
      <LI><A HREF=" MyPrefix "/SaveConfig>Save Configuration</A></LI>\
      </UL>"
   TopFooter  = "</BODY></HTML>"
   if (ConfigFile == "") ConfigFile = "config.asc"
}
```

The function SetUpServer initializes the top-level HTML texts as usual. It also initializes the name of the file that contains the configuration parameters and their values. In case the user supplies a name from the command line, that name is used. The file is expected to contain one parameter per line, with the name of the parameter in column one and the value in column two.

The function HandleGET reflects the structure of the menu tree as usual. The first menu choice tells the user what this is all about. The second choice reads the configuration file line by line and stores the parameters and their values. Notice that the record separator for this file is "\n", in contrast to the record separator for HTTP. The third menu choice builds an HTML table to show the contents of the configuration file just read. The fourth choice does the real work of changing parameters, and the last one just saves the configuration into a file:

```
function HandleGET() {
    if (MENU[2] == "AboutServer") {
        Document  = "This is a GUI for remote configuration of an\
           embedded system. It is is implemented as one GAWK script."
    } else if (MENU[2] == "ReadConfig") {
        RS = "\n"
        while ((getline < ConfigFile) > 0)
            config[$1] = $2
        close(ConfigFile)
        RS = "\r\n"
        Document = "Configuration has been read."
    } else if (MENU[2] == "CheckConfig") {
        Document = "<TABLE BORDER=1 CELLPADDING=5>"
        for (i in config)
            Document = Document "<TR><TD>" i "</TD>" \
                "<TD>" config[i] "</TD></TR>"
        Document = Document "</TABLE>"
    } else if (MENU[2] == "ChangeConfig") {
        if ("Param" in GETARG) {              # any parameter to set?
            if (GETARG["Param"] in config) {  # is  parameter valid?
                config[GETARG["Param"]] = GETARG["Value"]
                Document = (GETARG["Param"] " = " GETARG["Value"] ".")
            } else {
                Document = "Parameter <b>" GETARG["Param"] "</b> is invalid."
            }
```

```
        } else {
            Document = "<FORM method=GET><h4>Change one parameter</h4>\
                <TABLE BORDER CELLPADDING=5>\
                <TR><TD>Parameter</TD><TD>Value</TD></TR>\
                <TR><TD><input type=text name=Param value=\"\" size=20></TD>\
                <TD><input type=text name=Value value=\"\" size=40></TD>\
                </TR></TABLE><input type=submit value=\"Set\"></FORM>"
        }
    } else if (MENU[2] == "SaveConfig") {
        for (i in config)
            printf("%s %s\n", i, config[i]) > ConfigFile
        close(ConfigFile)
        Document = "Configuration has been saved."
    }
}
```

We could also view the configuration file as a database. From this point of view, the previous program acts like a primitive database server. Real SQL database systems also make a service available by providing a TCP port that clients can connect to. But the application level protocols they use are usually proprietary and also change from time to time. This is also true for the protocol that MiniSQL uses.

URLCHK: Look for Changed Web Pages

Most people who make heavy use of Internet resources have a large bookmark file with pointers to interesting web sites. It is impossible to regularly check by hand if any of these sites have changed. A program is needed to automatically look at the headers of web pages and tell which ones have changed. URLCHK does the comparison after using GETURL with the HEAD method to retrieve the header.

Like GETURL, this program first checks that it is called with exactly one command-line parameter. URLCHK also takes the same command-line variables Proxy and ProxyPort as GETURL, because these variables are handed over to GETURL for each URL that gets checked. The one and only parameter is the name of a file that contains one line for each URL. In the first column, we find the URL, and the second and third columns hold the length of the URL's body when checked for the two last times. Now, we follow this plan:

1. Read the URLs from the file and remember their most recent lengths.

2. Delete the contents of the file.

3. For each URL, check its new length and write it into the file.

4. If the most recent and the new length differ, tell the user.

It may seem a bit peculiar to read the URLs from a file together with their two most recent lengths, but this approach has several advantages. You can call the program again and again with the same file. After running the program, you can regenerate the changed URLs by extracting those lines that differ in their second and third columns:

```
BEGIN {
    if (ARGC != 2) {
        print "URLCHK - check if URLs have changed"
        print "IN:\n    the file with URLs as a command-line parameter"
        print "    file contains URL, old length, new length"
        print "PARAMS:\n    -v Proxy=MyProxy -v ProxyPort=8080"
        print "OUT:\n    same as file with URLs"
        print "JK 02.03.1998"
        exit
    }
    URLfile = ARGV[1]; ARGV[1] = ""
    if (Proxy     != "") Proxy     = " -v Proxy="     Proxy
    if (ProxyPort != "") ProxyPort = " -v ProxyPort=" ProxyPort
    while ((getline < URLfile) > 0)
        Length[$1] = $3 + 0
    close(URLfile)      # now, URLfile is read in and can be updated
    GetHeader = "gawk " Proxy ProxyPort \
                " -v Method=\"HEAD\" -f geturl.awk "
    for (i in Length) {
        GetThisHeader = GetHeader i " 2>&1"
        while ((GetThisHeader | getline) > 0)
            if (toupper($0) ~ /CONTENT-LENGTH/)
                NewLength = $2 + 0
        close(GetThisHeader)
        print i, Length[i], NewLength > URLfile
        if (Length[i] != NewLength)  # report only changed URLs
            print i, Length[i], NewLength
    }
    close(URLfile)
}
```

Another thing that may look strange is the way GETURL is called. Before calling GETURL, we have to check if the proxy variables need to be passed on. If so, we prepare strings that will become part of the command line later. In `GetHeader`, we store these strings together with the longest part of the command line. Later, in the loop over the URLs, `GetHeader` is appended with the URL and a redirection operator to form the command that reads the URL's header over the Internet. GETURL always produces the headers over */dev/stderr*. That is the reason why we need the redirection operator to have the header piped in.

This program is not perfect because it assumes that changing URLs results in changed lengths, which is not necessarily true. A more advanced approach is to look at some other header line that holds time information. But, as always when things get a bit more complicated, this is left as an exercise to the reader.

WEBGRAB: Extract Links from a Page

Sometimes it is necessary to extract links from web pages. Browsers do it, web robots do it, and sometimes even humans do it. Since we have a tool like GETURL at hand, we can solve this problem with some help from the Bourne shell:

```
BEGIN { RS = "http://[#%&\\+\\-\\./0-9\\:;\\?A-Z_a-z\\~]*" }
RT != "" {
    command = ("gawk -v Proxy=MyProxy -f geturl.awk " RT \
        " > doc" NR ".html")
    print command
}
```

Notice that the regular expression for URLs is rather crude. A precise regular expression is much more complex. But this one works rather well. One problem is that it is unable to find internal links of an HTML document. Another problem is that ftp, telnet, news, mailto, and other kinds of links are missing in the regular expression. However, it is straightforward to add them, if doing so is necessary for other tasks.

This program reads an HTML file and prints all the HTTP links that it finds. It relies on *gawk*'s ability to use regular expressions as record separators. With RS set to a regular expression that matches links, the second action is executed each time a nonempty link is found. We can find the matching link itself in RT.

The action could use the system function to let another GETURL retrieve the page, but here we use a different approach. This simple program prints shell commands that can be piped into *sh* for execution. This way it is possible to first extract the links, wrap shell commands around them, and pipe all the shell commands into a file. After editing the file, execution of the file retrieves exactly those files that we really need. In case we do not want to edit, we can retrieve all the pages like this:

```
gawk -f geturl.awk http://www.suse.de | gawk -f webgrab.awk | sh
```

After this, you will find the contents of all referenced documents in files named *doc*.html* even if they do not contain HTML code. The most annoying thing is that we always have to pass the proxy to GETURL. If you do not like to see the headers of the web pages appear on the screen, you can redirect them to */dev/null*. Watching the headers appear can be quite interesting, because it reveals interesting details such as which web server the companies use. Now, it is clear how the clever marketing people use web robots to determine the market shares of Microsoft and Netscape in the web server market.

Port 80 of any web server is like a small hole in a repellent firewall. After attaching a browser to port 80, we usually catch a glimpse of the bright side of the server (its home page). With a tool like GETURL at hand, we are able to discover some of the more concealed or even "indecent" services (i.e., lacking conformity to standards of quality). It can be exciting to see the fancy CGI scripts that lie there, revealing the inner workings of the server, ready to be called:

- With a command such as:

```
gawk -f geturl.awk http://any.host.on.the.net/cgi-bin/
```

some servers give you a directory listing of the CGI files. Knowing the names, you can try to call some of them and watch for useful results. Sometimes there are executables in such directories (such as Perl interpreters) that you may call remotely. If there are subdirectories with configuration data of the web server, this can also be quite interesting to read.

- The well-known Apache web server usually has its CGI files in the directory */cgi-bin*. There you can often find the scripts *test-cgi* and *printenv*. Both tell you some things about the current connection and the installation of the web server. Just call:

```
gawk -f geturl.awk http://any.host.on.the.net/cgi-bin/test-cgi
gawk -f geturl.awk http://any.host.on.the.net/cgi-bin/printenv
```

- Sometimes it is even possible to retrieve system files like the web server's log file—possibly containing customer data—or even the file */etc/passwd*. (We don't recommend this!)

 Although this may sound funny or simply irrelevant, we are talking about severe security holes. Try to explore your own system this way and make sure that none of the above reveals too much information about your system.

STATIST: Graphing a Statistical Distribution

In the HTTP server examples we've shown thus far, we never present an image to the browser and its user. Presenting images is one task. Generating images that reflect some user input and presenting these dynamically generated images is another. In this section, we use GNUPlot for generating *.png*, *.ps*, or *.gif* files.*

---

* Due to licensing problems, the default installation of GNUPlot disables the generation of *.gif* files. If your installed version does not accept set term gif, just download and install the most recent version of GNUPlot and the GD library (*http://www.Boutell.com/gd/*) by Thomas Boutell. Otherwise, you still have the chance to generate some ASCII-art-style images with GNUPlot by using set term dumb. (We tried it and it worked.)

The program we develop takes the statistical parameters of two samples and computes the t-test statistics. As a result, we get the probabilities that the means and the variances of both samples are the same. In order to let the user check plausibility, the program presents an image of the distributions. The statistical computation follows *Numerical Recipes in C: The Art of Scientific Computing* by William H. Press, Saul A. Teukolsky, William T. Vetterling, and Brian P. Flannery (Cambridge University Press). Since *gawk* does not have a built-in function for the computation of the beta function, we use the ibeta function of GNUPlot. As a side effect, we learn how to use GNUPlot as a sophisticated calculator. The comparison of means is done as in tutest, paragraph 14.2, page 613, and the comparison of variances is done as in ftest, page 611 in *Numerical Recipes*.

As usual, we take the site-independent code for servers and append our own functions SetUpServer and HandleGET:

```
function SetUpServer() {
  TopHeader = "<HTML><title>Statistics with GAWK</title>"
  TopDoc = "<BODY>\
    <h2>Please choose one of the following actions:</h2>\
    <UL>\
    <LI><A HREF=" MyPrefix "/AboutServer>About this server</A></LI>\
    <LI><A HREF=" MyPrefix "/EnterParameters>Enter Parameters</A></LI>\
    </UL>"
  TopFooter  = "</BODY></HTML>"
  GnuPlot    = "gnuplot 2>&1"
  m1=m2=0;    v1=v2=1;    n1=n2=10
}
```

Here, you see the menu structure that the user sees. Later, we will see how the program structure of the HandleGET function reflects the menu structure. What is missing here is the link for the image we generate. In an event-driven environment, request, generation, and delivery of images are separated.

Notice the way we initialize the GnuPlot command string for the pipe. By default, GNUPlot outputs the generated image via standard output, as well as the results of printed calculations via standard error. The redirection causes standard error to be mixed into standard output, enabling us to read results of calculations with get-line. By initializing the statistical parameters with some meaningful defaults, we make sure the user gets an image the first time he uses the program.

Following is the rather long function HandleGET, which implements the contents of this service by reacting to the different kinds of requests from the browser. Before you start playing with this script, make sure that your browser supports JavaScript and that it also has this option switched on. The script uses a short snippet of JavaScript code for delayed opening of a window with an image. A more detailed explanation follows:

```
function HandleGET() {
  if (MENU[2] == "AboutServer") {
    Document   = "This is a GUI for a statistical computation.\
       It compares means and variances of two distributions.\
       It is implemented as one GAWK script and uses GNUPLOT."
  } else if (MENU[2] == "EnterParameters") {
    Document = ""
    if ("m1" in GETARG) {    # are there parameters to compare?
      Document = Document "<SCRIPT LANGUAGE=\"JavaScript\">\
        setTimeout(\"window.open(\\\"" MyPrefix "/Image" systime()\
        "\\\",\\\"dist\\\", \\\"status=no\\\");\", 1000); </SCRIPT>"
      m1 = GETARG["m1"]; v1 = GETARG["v1"]; n1 = GETARG["n1"]
      m2 = GETARG["m2"]; v2 = GETARG["v2"]; n2 = GETARG["n2"]
      t = (m1-m2)/sqrt(v1/n1+v2/n2)
      df = (v1/n1+v2/n2)*(v1/n1+v2/n2)/((v1/n1)*(v1/n1)/(n1-1) \
          + (v2/n2)*(v2/n2) /(n2-1))
      if (v1 > v2) {
        f = v1 / v2
        df1 = n1 - 1
        df2 = n2 - 1
      } else {
        f = v2 / v1
        df1 = n2 - 1
        df2 = n1 - 1
      }
      print "pt=ibeta(" df/2 ",0.5," df/(df+t*t) ")"  |& GnuPlot
      print "pF=2.0*ibeta(" df2/2 "," \
            df1/2 "," df2/(df2+df1*f) ")"            |& GnuPlot
      print "print pt, pF"                          |& GnuPlot
      RS="\n"; GnuPlot |& getline; RS="\r\n"  # $1 is pt, $2 is pF
      print "invsqrt2pi=1.0/sqrt(2.0*pi)"          |& GnuPlot
      print "nd(x)=invsqrt2pi/sd*exp(-0.5*((x-mu)/sd)**2)"   |& GnuPlot
      print "set term png small color"             |& GnuPlot
      #print "set term postscript color"           |& GnuPlot
      #print "set term gif medium size 320,240"    |& GnuPlot
      print "set yrange[-0.3:]"                     |& GnuPlot
      print "set label 'p(m1=m2) =" $1 "' at 0,-0.1 left"  |& GnuPlot
      print "set label 'p(v1=v2) =" $2 "' at 0,-0.2 left"  |& GnuPlot
      print "plot mu=" m1 ",sd=" sqrt(v1) ", nd(x) title 'sample 1',\
            mu=" m2 ",sd=" sqrt(v2) ", nd(x) title 'sample 2'" |& GnuPlot
      print "quit"                                  |& GnuPlot
      GnuPlot |& getline Image
      while ((GnuPlot |& getline) > 0)
        Image = Image RS $0
      close(GnuPlot)
    }
```

```
        Document = Document "\
          <h3>Do these samples have the same Gaussian distribution?</h3>\
          <FORM METHOD=GET> <TABLE BORDER CELLPADDING=5>\
          <TR>\
          <TD>1. Mean   </TD>\
          <TD><input type=text name=m1 value=" m1 " size=8></TD>\
          <TD>1. Variance</TD>\
          <TD><input type=text name=v1 value=" v1 " size=8></TD>\
          <TD>1. Count   </TD>\
          <TD><input type=text name=n1 value=" n1 " size=8></TD>\
          </TR><TR>\
          <TD>2. Mean   </TD>\
          <TD><input type=text name=m2 value=" m2 " size=8></TD>\
          <TD>2. Variance</TD>\
          <TD><input type=text name=v2 value=" v2 " size=8></TD>\
          <TD>2. Count   </TD>\
          <TD><input type=text name=n2 value=" n2 " size=8></TD>\
          </TR>            <input type=submit value=\"Compute\">\
          </TABLE></FORM><BR>"
    } else if (MENU[2] ~ "Image") {
      Reason = "OK" ORS "Content-type: image/png"
      #Reason = "OK" ORS "Content-type: application/x-postscript"
      #Reason = "OK" ORS "Content-type: image/gif"
      Header = Footer = ""
      Document = Image
    }
  }
```

As usual, we give a short description of the service in the first menu choice. The third menu choice shows us that generation and presentation of an image are two separate actions. While the latter takes place quite instantly in the third menu choice, the former takes place in the much longer second choice. Image data passes from the generating action to the presenting action via the variable `Image` that contains a complete *.png* image, which is otherwise stored in a file. If you prefer *.ps* or *.gif* images over the default *.png* images, you may select these options by uncommenting the appropriate lines. But remember to do so in two places: when telling GNUPlot which kind of images to generate and when transmitting the image at the end of the program.

Looking at the end of the program, the way we pass the `Content-type` to the browser is a bit unusual. It is appended to the `OK` of the first header line to make sure the type information becomes part of the header. The other variables that get transmitted across the network are made empty, because in this case we do not have an HTML document to transmit, but rather raw image data to contain in the body.

Most of the work is done in the second menu choice. It starts with a strange JavaScript code snippet. When first implementing this server, we used a short `"<IMG SRC=" MyPrefix "/Image>"` here. But then browsers got smarter and tried to improve on speed by requesting the image and the HTML code at the same time.

When doing this, the browser tries to build up a connection for the image request while the request for the HTML text is not yet completed. The browser tries to connect to the *gawk* server on port 8080 while port 8080 is still in use for transmission of the HTML text. The connection for the image cannot be built up, so the image appears as "broken" in the browser window. We solved this problem by telling the browser to open a separate window for the image, but only after a delay of 1,000 milliseconds. By this time, the server should be ready for serving the next request.

But there is one more subtlety in the JavaScript code. Each time the JavaScript code opens a window for the image, the name of the image is appended with a timestamp (`systime`). Why this constant change of name for the image? Initially, we always named the image `Image`, but then the Netscape browser noticed the name had *not* changed since the previous request and displayed the previous image (caching behavior). The server core is implemented so that browsers are told *not* to cache anything. Obviously HTTP requests do not always work as expected. One way to circumvent the cache of such overly smart browsers is to change the name of the image with each request. Those three lines of JavaScript caused us a lot of trouble.

The rest can be broken down into two phases. At first, we check if there are statistical parameters. When the program is first started, there usually are no parameters because it enters the page coming from the top menu. Then, we only have to present the user a form that he can use to change statistical parameters and submit them. Subsequently, the submission of the form causes the execution of the first phase because *now* there *are* parameters to handle.

Now that we have parameters, we know there will be an image available. Therefore, we insert the JavaScript code here to initiate the opening of the image in a separate window. Then, we prepare some variables that will be passed to GNU-Plot for calculation of the probabilities. Prior to reading the results, we must temporarily change `RS` because GNUPlot separates lines with newlines. After instructing GNUPlot to generate a *.png* (or *.ps* or *.gif*) image, we initiate the insertion of some text, explaining the resulting probabilities. The final `plot` command actually generates the image data. This raw binary has to be read in carefully without adding, changing, or deleting a single byte. Hence the unusual initialization of `Image` and completion with a `while` loop.

When using this server, it soon becomes clear that it is far from being perfect. It mixes source code of six scripting languages or protocols:

- GNU *awk* implements a server for the protocol

- HTTP, which transmits

- HTML text, which contains a short piece of

- JavaScript code opening a separate window

- A Bourne shell script is used for piping commands into

- GNUPlot to generate the image to be opened

After all this work, the GNUPlot image opens in the JavaScript window where it can be viewed by the user.

It is probably better not to mix up so many different languages. The result is very hard to read. Furthermore, the statistical part of the server does not take care of invalid input. Among others, using negative variances will cause invalid results.

MOBAGWHO: A Simple Mobile Agent

A *mobile agent* is a program that can be dispatched from a computer and transported to a remote server for execution. This is called *migration*, which means that a process on another system is started that is independent from its originator. Ideally, it wanders through a network while working for its creator or owner. In places like the UMBC Agent Web, people are quite confident that (mobile) agents are a software engineering paradigm that enables us to significantly increase the efficiency of our work. Mobile agents could become the mediators between users and the networking world. For an unbiased view at this technology, see David Chass, Colin Harrison, and Aaron Kershenbaum's remarkable paper "Mobile Agents: Are They a Good Idea?"[*]

When trying to migrate a process from one system to another, a server process is needed on the receiving side. Depending on the kind of server process, several ways of implementation come to mind. How the process is implemented depends upon the kind of server process:

- HTTP can be used as the protocol for delivery of the migrating process. In this case, we use a common web server as the receiving server process. A universal CGI script mediates between migrating process and web server. Each server willing to accept migrating agents makes this universal service available. HTTP supplies the POST method to transfer some data to a file on the web server. When a CGI script is called remotely with the POST method to transfer

---

[*] See *http://www.research.ibm.com/massive/mdoag.ps.*

some data to a file on the web server. When a CGI script is called remotely with the GET method, data is transmitted from the client process to the standard input of the server's CGI script. So, to implement a mobile agent, we must not only write the agent program to start on the client side, but also the CGI script to receive the agent on the server side.

- The PUT method can also be used for migration. HTTP does not require a CGI script for migration via PUT. However, with common web servers there is no advantage to this solution, because web servers such as Apache require explicit activation of a special PUT script.

- *Agent Tcl* pursues a different course; it relies on a dedicated server process with a dedicated protocol specialized for receiving mobile agents.

Our agent example abuses a common web server as a migration tool. So, it needs a universal CGI script on the receiving side (the web server). The receiving script is activated with a POST request when placed into a location like */httpd/cgi-bin/PostAgent.sh*. Make sure that the server system uses a version of *gawk* that supports network access (Version 3.1 or later; verify with gawk --version):

```
#!/bin/sh
MobAg=/tmp/MobileAgent.$$
# direct script to mobile agent file
cat > $MobAg
gawk -f $MobAg $MobAg > /dev/null &   # execute agent concurrently
# HTTP header, terminator and body
gawk 'BEGIN { print "\r\nAgent started" }'
rm $MobAg                             # delete script file of agent
```

By making its process id ($$) part of the unique filename, the script avoids conflicts between concurrent instances of the script. First, all lines from standard input (the mobile agent's source code) are copied into this unique file. Then, the agent is started as a concurrent process and a short message reporting this fact is sent to the submitting client. Finally, the script file of the mobile agent is removed because it is no longer needed. Although it is a short script, there are several noteworthy points:

Security

There is none. In fact, the CGI script should never be made available on a server that is part of the Internet because everyone would be allowed to execute arbitrary commands with it. This behavior is acceptable only when performing rapid prototyping.

Self-reference

Each migrating instance of an agent is started in a way that enables it to read its own source code from standard input and use the code for subsequent migrations. This is necessary because it needs to treat the agent's code as data to transmit. *gawk* is not the ideal language for such a job. Lisp and Tcl are more suitable because they do not make a distinction between program code and data.

Independence

After migration, the agent is not linked to its former home in any way. By reporting `Agent started`, it waves "Goodbye" to its origin. The originator may choose to terminate or not.

The originating agent itself is started just like any other command-line script, and reports the results on standard output. By letting the name of the original host migrate with the agent, the agent that migrates to a host far away from its origin can report the result back home. Having arrived at the end of the journey, the agent establishes a connection and reports the results. This is the reason for determining the name of the host with `uname -n` and storing it in `MyOrigin` for later use. We may also set variables with the $-v$ option from the command line. This interactivity is only of importance in the context of starting a mobile agent; therefore, this `BEGIN` pattern and its action do not take part in migration:

```
BEGIN {
    if (ARGC != 2) {
        print "MOBAG - a simple mobile agent"
        print "CALL:\n    gawk -f mobag.awk mobag.awk"
        print "IN:\n    the name of this script", \
                        "as a command-line parameter"
        print "PARAM:\n    -v MyOrigin=myhost.com"
        print "OUT:\n    the result on stdout"
        print "JK 29.03.1998 01.04.1998"
        exit
    }
    if (MyOrigin == "") {
        "uname -n" | getline MyOrigin
        close("uname -n")
    }
}
```

Since *gawk* cannot manipulate and transmit parts of the program directly, the source code is read and stored in strings. Therefore, the program scans itself for the beginning and the ending of functions. Each line in between is appended to the code string until the end of the function has been reached. A special case is this part of the program itself. It is not a function. Placing a similar framework around it causes it to be treated like a function. Notice that this mechanism works for all the functions of the source code, but it cannot guarantee that the order of the functions is preserved during migration:

```
#ReadMySelf
/^function /                        { FUNC = $2 }
/^END/ || /^#ReadMySelf/            { FUNC = $1 }
FUNC != ""                         { MOBFUN[FUNC] = MOBFUN[FUNC] RS $0 }
(FUNC != "") && (/^}/ || /^#EndOfMySelf/) \
                                   { FUNC = "" }
#EndOfMySelf
```

The web server code in the section "A Web Service with Interaction" earlier in this chapter was first developed as a site-independent core. Likewise, the *gawk*-based mobile agent starts with an agent-independent core, to which can be appended application-dependent functions. What follows is the only application-independent function needed for the mobile agent:

```
function migrate(Destination, MobCode, Label) {
    MOBVAR["Label"] = Label
    MOBVAR["Destination"] = Destination
    RS = ORS = "\r\n"
    HttpService = "/inet/tcp/0/" Destination
    for (i in MOBFUN)
        MobCode = (MobCode "\n" MOBFUN[i])
    MobCode = MobCode  "\n\nBEGIN {"
    for (i in MOBVAR)
        MobCode = (MobCode "\n  MOBVAR[\"" i "\"] = \"" MOBVAR[i] "\"")
    MobCode = MobCode "\n}\n"
    print "POST /cgi-bin/PostAgent.sh HTTP/1.0"  |& HttpService
    print "Content-length:", length(MobCode) ORS |& HttpService
    printf "%s", MobCode                         |& HttpService
    while ((HttpService |& getline) > 0)
        print $0
    close(HttpService)
}
```

The migrate function prepares the aforementioned strings containing the program code and transmits them to a server. A consequence of this modular approach is that the migrate function takes some parameters that aren't needed in this application, but that will be in future ones. Its mandatory parameter Destination holds the name (or IP address) of the server that the agent wants as a host for its code. The optional parameter MobCode may contain some *gawk* code that is inserted during migration in front of all other code. The optional parameter Label may contain a string that tells the agent what to do in program execution after arrival at its new home site. One of the serious obstacles in implementing a framework for mobile agents is that it does not suffice to migrate the code. It is also necessary to migrate the state of execution of the agent. In contrast to *Agent Tcl*, this program does not try to migrate the complete set of variables. The following conventions are used:

- Each variable in an agent program is local to the current host and does *not* migrate.

- The array MOBFUN shown above is an exception. It is handled by the function migrate and does migrate with the application.

- The other exception is the array MOBVAR. Each variable that takes part in migration has to be an element of this array. migrate also takes care of this.

Now it's clear what happens to the Label parameter of the function migrate. It is copied into MOBVAR["Label"] and travels alongside the other data. Since traveling takes place via HTTP, records must be separated with "\r\n" in RS and ORS as usual. The code assembly for migration takes place in three steps:

1. Iterate over MOBFUN to collect all functions verbatim.

2. Prepare a BEGIN pattern and put assignments to mobile variables into the action part.

3. Transmission itself resembles GETURL: the header with the request and the Content-length is followed by the body. In case there is any reply over the network, it is read completely and echoed to standard output to avoid irritating the server.

The application-independent framework is now almost complete. What follows is the END pattern that is executed when the mobile agent has finished reading its own code. First, it checks whether it is already running on a remote host or not. In case initialization has not yet taken place, it starts MyInit. Otherwise (later, on a remote host), it starts MyJob:

```
END {
    if (ARGC != 2) exit     # stop when called with wrong parameters
    if (MyOrigin != "")     # is this the originating host?
        MyInit()            # if so, initialize the application
    else                    # we are on a host with migrated data
        MyJob()             # so we do our job
}
```

All that's left to extend the framework into a complete application is to write two application-specific functions: MyInit and MyJob. Keep in mind that the former is executed once on the originating host, while the latter is executed after each migration:

```
function MyInit() {
    MOBVAR["MyOrigin"] = MyOrigin
    MOBVAR["Machines"] = "localhost/80 max/80 moritz/80 castor/80"
    split(MOBVAR["Machines"], Machines)     # which host is the first?
    migrate(Machines[1], "", "")            # go to the first host
    # wait for result
    while (("/inet/tcp/8080/0/0" |& getline) > 0)
        print $0                            # print result
    close("/inet/tcp/8080/0/0")
}
```

As mentioned earlier, this agent takes the name of its origin (MyOrigin) with it. Then, it takes the name of its first destination and goes there for further work. Notice that this name has the port number of the web server appended to the name of the server, because the function migrate needs it this way to create the HttpService variable. Finally, it waits for the result to arrive. The MyJob function runs on the remote host:

```
function MyJob() {
    # forget this host
    sub(MOBVAR["Destination"], "", MOBVAR["Machines"])
    MOBVAR["Result"] = MOBVAR["Result"] SUBSEP \
                        SUBSEP MOBVAR["Destination"] ":"
    while (("who" | getline) > 0)              # who is logged in?
        MOBVAR["Result"] = MOBVAR["Result"] SUBSEP $0
    close("who")
    # any more machines to visit?
    if (index(MOBVAR["Machines"], "/") > 0) {
        split(MOBVAR["Machines"], Machines)    # which host is next?
        migrate(Machines[1], "", "")           # go there
    } else {                                    # no more machines
        gsub(SUBSEP, "\n", MOBVAR["Result"])   # send result to origin
        print MOBVAR["Result"] |& "/inet/tcp/0/" \
                MOBVAR["MyOrigin"] "/8080"
        close("/inet/tcp/0/" MOBVAR["MyOrigin"] "/8080")
    }
}
```

After migrating, the first thing to do in MyJob is to delete the name of the current host from the list of hosts to visit. Now, it is time to start the real work by appending the host's name to the result string, and reading line by line who is logged in on this host. A very annoying circumstance is the fact that the elements of MOBVAR cannot hold the newline character ("\n"). If they did, migration of this string did not work because the string didn't obey the syntax rule for a string in *gawk*. SUBSEP is used as a temporary replacement. If the list of hosts to visit holds at least one more entry, the agent migrates to that place to go on working there. Otherwise, we replace the SUBSEPs with a newline character in the resulting string and report it to the originating host, whose name is stored in MOBVAR["MyOrigin"].

Related Links

This section lists the URLs for various items discussed in this chapter. They are presented in the order in which they occur:

Richard Stevens's home page and books
  http://www.kohala.com/~rstevens

The SPAK home page
  http://www.userfriendly.net/linux/RPM/contrib/libc6/i386/
  spak-0.6b-1.i386.html

Volume III of Internetworking with TCP, by Comer and Stevens
  http://www.cs.purdue.edu/homes/dec/tcpip3s.cont.html

XBM graphics file format
  http://www.wotsit.org/download.asp?f=xbm

Mark Humphry's ELIZA page
  http://www.compapp.dcu.ie/~humphrys/eliza.html

Yahoo! ELIZA information
  http://dir.yahoo.com/Recreation/Games/Computer_Games/Internet_Games/
  Web_Games/Artificial_Intelligence

Java versions of ELIZA
  http://www.tjhsst.edu/Psych/ch1/eliza.html

Java versions of ELIZA with source code
  http://home.adelphia.net/~lifeisgood/eliza/eliza.htm

ELIZA programs with explanations
  http://chayden.net/chayden/eliza/Eliza.shtml

Tcl/Tk information
  http://www.scriptics.com

XINU
  http://willow.canberra.edu.au/~chrisc/xinu.html

MiniSQL
  http://www.hughes.com.au/library/

Numerical Recipes in C: The Art of Scientific Computing
  http://www.nr.com

The UMBC Agent Web
  http://www.cs.umbc.edu/agents

III

Appendixes

Part III contains the appendixes (including the two licenses that cover the *gawk* source code and this book, respectively) and the Glossary:

- Appendix A, *The Evolution of the awk Language*
- Appendix B, *Installing gawk*
- Appendix C, *Implementation Notes*
- Appendix D, *Basic Programming Concepts*
- Appendix E, *GNU General Public License*
- Appendix F, *GNU Free Documentation License*
- Glossary

The Evolution of the awk Language

This book describes the GNU implementation of *awk*, which follows the POSIX specification. Many long-time *awk* users learned *awk* programming with the original *awk* implementation in Version 7 Unix. (This implementation was the basis for *awk* in Berkeley Unix, through 4.3-Reno. Subsequent versions of Berkeley Unix, and systems derived from 4.4BSD-Lite, use various versions of *gawk* for their *awk*.) This chapter briefly describes the evolution of the *awk* language, with cross-references to other parts of the book where you can find more information.

Major Changes Between V7 and SVR3.1

The *awk* language evolved considerably between the release of Version 7 Unix (1978) and the new version that was first made generally available in System V Release 3.1 (1987). This section summarizes the changes, with cross-references to further details:

- The requirement for ; to separate rules on a line (see the section "awk Statements Versus Lines" in Chapter 1, *Getting Started with awk*).

- User-defined functions and the `return` statement (see the section "User-Defined Functions" in Chapter 8, *Functions*).

- The `delete` statement (see the section "The delete Statement" in Chapter 7, *Arrays in awk*).

- The `do-while` statement (see the section "The do-while Statement" in Chapter 6, *Patterns, Actions, and Variables*).

- The built-in functions `atan2`, `cos`, `sin`, `rand`, and `srand` (see the section "Numeric Functions" in Chapter 8).

- The built-in functions gsub, sub, and match (see the section "String-Manipulation Functions" in Chapter 8).

- The built-in functions close and system (see the section "Input/Output Functions" in Chapter 8).

- The ARGC, ARGV, FNR, RLENGTH, RSTART, and SUBSEP built-in variables (see the section "Built-in Variables" in Chapter 6).

- The conditional expression using the ternary operator ?: (see the section "Conditional Expressions" in Chapter 5, *Expressions*).

- The exponentiation operator ^ (see the section "Arithmetic Operators" in Chapter 5) and its assignment operator form ^= (see the section "Assignment Expressions" in Chapter 5).

- C-compatible operator precedence, which breaks some old *awk* programs (see the section "Operator Precedence (How Operators Nest)" in Chapter 5).

- Regexps as the value of FS (see the section "Specifying How Fields Are Separated" in Chapter 3, *Reading Input Files*) and as the third argument to the split function (see the section "String-Manipulation Functions" in Chapter 8).

- Dynamic regexps as operands of the ~ and !~ operators (see the section "How to Use Regular Expressions" in Chapter 2, *Regular Expressions*).

- The escape sequences \b, \f, and \r (see the section "Escape Sequences" in Chapter 2). (Some vendors have updated their old versions of *awk* to recognize \b, \f, and \r, but this is not something you can rely on.)

- Redirection of input for the getline function (see the section "Explicit Input with getline" in Chapter 3).

- Multiple BEGIN and END rules (see the section "The BEGIN and END Special Patterns" in Chapter 6).

- Multidimensional arrays (see the section "Multidimensional Arrays" in Chapter 7).

Changes Between SVR3.1 and SVR4

The System V Release 4 (1989) version of Unix *awk* added these features (some of which originated in *gawk*):

- The ENVIRON variable (see the section "Built-in Variables" in Chapter 6).

- Multiple *−f* options on the command line (see the section "Command-Line Options" in Chapter 11, *Running awk and gawk*).

- The *−v* option for assigning variables before program execution begins (see the section "Command-Line Options" in Chapter 11).

- The *−−* option for terminating command-line options.

- The \a, \v, and \x escape sequences (see the section "Escape Sequences" in Chapter 2).

- A defined return value for the srand built-in function (see the section "Numeric Functions" in Chapter 8).

- The toupper and tolower built-in string functions for case translation (see the section "String-Manipulation Functions" in Chapter 8).

- A cleaner specification for the %c format-control letter in the printf function (see the section "Format-Control Letters" in Chapter 4, *Printing Output*).

- The ability to dynamically pass the field width and precision ("%*.*d") in the argument list of the printf function (see the section "Format-Control Letters" in Chapter 4).

- The use of regexp constants, such as /foo/, as expressions, where they are equivalent to using the matching operator, as in $0 ~ /foo/ (see the section "Using Regular Expression Constants" in Chapter 5).

- Processing of escape sequences inside command-line variable assignments (see the section "Assigning Variables on the Command Line" in Chapter 5).

Changes Between SVR4 and POSIX awk

The POSIX Command Language and Utilities standard for *awk* (1992) introduced the following changes into the language:

- The use of *−W* for implementation-specific options (see the section "Command-Line Options" in Chapter 11).

- The use of CONVFMT for controlling the conversion of numbers to strings (see the section "Conversion of Strings and Numbers" in Chapter 5).

- The concept of a numeric string and tighter comparison rules to go with it (see the section "Variable Typing and Comparison Expressions" in Chapter 5).

- More complete documentation of many of the previously undocumented features of the language.

The following common extensions are not permitted by the POSIX standard:

- \x escape sequences are not recognized (see the section "Escape Sequences" in Chapter 2).

- Newlines do not act as whitespace to separate fields when FS is equal to a single space (see the section "Examining Fields" in Chapter 3).

- Newlines are not allowed after ? or : (see the section "Conditional Expressions" in Chapter 5).

- The synonym func for the keyword function is not recognized (see the section "Function Definition Syntax" in Chapter 8).

- The operators ** and **= cannot be used in place of ^ and ^= (see the section "Arithmetic Operators" and section "Assignment Expressions" in Chapter 5).

- Specifying –Ft on the command line does not set the value of FS to be a single tab character (see the section "Specifying How Fields Are Separated" in Chapter 3).

- The fflush built-in function is not supported (see the section "Input/Output Functions" in Chapter 8).

Extensions in the Bell Laboratories awk

Brian Kernighan, one of the original designers of Unix *awk*, has made his version available via his home page (see the section "Other Freely Available awk Implementations" in Appendix B, *Installing gawk*). This section describes extensions in his version of *awk* that are not in POSIX *awk*:

- The –mf *N* and –mr *N* command-line options to set the maximum number of fields and the maximum record size, respectively (see the section "Command-Line Options" in Chapter 11). As a side note, his *awk* no longer needs these options; it continues to accept them to avoid breaking old programs.

- The fflush built-in function for flushing buffered output (see the section "Input/Output Functions" in Chapter 8).

- The ** and **= operators (see the section "Arithmetic Operators" and section "Assignment Expressions" in Chapter 5).

- The use of func as an abbreviation for function (see the section "Function Definition Syntax" in Chapter 8).

The Bell Laboratories *awk* also incorporates the following extensions, originally developed for *gawk*:

- The \x escape sequence (see the section "Escape Sequences" in Chapter 2).

- The */dev/stdin*, */dev/stdout*, and */dev/stderr* special files (see the section "Special Filenames in gawk" in Chapter 4).

- The ability for FS and for the third argument to split to be null strings (see the section "Making Each Character a Separate Field" in Chapter 3).

- The nextfile statement (see the section "Using gawk's nextfile Statement" in Chapter 6).

- The ability to delete all of an array at once with delete *array* (see the section "The delete Statement" in Chapter 7).

Extensions in gawk Not in POSIX awk

The GNU implementation, *gawk*, adds a large number of features. This section lists them in the order they were added to *gawk*. They can all be disabled with either the --*traditional* or --*posix* options (see the section "Command-Line Options" in Chapter 11).

Version 2.10 of *gawk* introduced the following features:

- The AWKPATH environment variable for specifying a path search for the –*f* command-line option (see the section "Command-Line Options" in Chapter 11).

- The IGNORECASE variable and its effects (see the section "Case Sensitivity in Matching" in Chapter 2).

- The */dev/stdin*, */dev/stdout*, */dev/stderr*, and */dev/fd/N* special filenames (see the section "Special Filenames in gawk" in Chapter 4).

Version 2.13 of *gawk* introduced the following features:

- The FIELDWIDTHS variable and its effects (see the section "Reading Fixed-Width Data" in Chapter 3).

- The systime and strftime built-in functions for obtaining and printing timestamps (see the section "Using gawk's Timestamp Functions" in Chapter 8).

- The –*W lint* option to provide error and portability checking for both the source code and at runtime (see the section "Command-Line Options" in Chapter 11).

- The –*W compat* option to turn off the GNU extensions (see the section "Command-Line Options" in Chapter 11).

- The –*W posix* option for full POSIX compliance (see the section "Command-Line Options" in Chapter 11).

Version 2.14 of *gawk* introduced the following feature:

- The `next file` statement for skipping to the next datafile (see the section "Using gawk's nextfile Statement" in Chapter 6).

Version 2.15 of *gawk* introduced the following features:

- The `ARGIND` variable, which tracks the movement of `FILENAME` through `ARGV` (see the section "Built-in Variables" in Chapter 6).

- The `ERRNO` variable, which contains the system error message when `getline` returns −1 or `close` fails (see the section "Built-in Variables" in Chapter 6).

- The */dev/pid*, */dev/ppid*, */dev/pgrpid*, and */dev/user* filename interpretation (see the section "Special Filenames in gawk" in Chapter 4).

- The ability to delete all of an array at once with `delete array` (see the section "The delete Statement" in Chapter 7).

- The ability to use GNU-style long-named options that start with −− (see the section "Command-Line Options" in Chapter 11).

- The −−*source* option for mixing command-line and library-file source code (see the section "Command-Line Options" in Chapter 11).

Version 3.0 of *gawk* introduced the following features:

- `IGNORECASE` changed, now applying to string comparison as well as regexp operations (see the section "Case Sensitivity in Matching" in Chapter 2).

- The `RT` variable that contains the input text that matched `RS` (see the section "How Input Is Split into Records" in Chapter 3).

- Full support for both POSIX and GNU regexps (see Chapter 2).

- The `gensub` function for more powerful text manipulation (see the section "String-Manipulation Functions" in Chapter 8).

- The `strftime` function acquired a default time format, allowing it to be called with no arguments (see the section "Using gawk's Timestamp Functions" in Chapter 8).

- The ability for `FS` and for the third argument to `split` to be null strings (see the section "Making Each Character a Separate Field" in Chapter 3).

- The ability for `RS` to be a regexp (see the section "How Input Is Split into Records" in Chapter 3).

- The `next file` statement became `nextfile` (see the section "Using gawk's nextfile Statement" in Chapter 6).

- The *—lint–old* option to warn about constructs that are not available in the original Version 7 Unix version of *awk* (see the section "Major Changes Between V7 and SVR3.1" earlier in this appendix).

- The *–m* option and the fflush function from the Bell Laboratories research version of *awk* (see the section "Command-Line Options" in Chapter 11; also see the section "Input/Output Functions" in Chapter 8).

- The *—re–interval* option to provide interval expressions in regexps (see the section "Regular Expression Operators" in Chapter 2).

- The *—traditional* option was added as a better name for *—compat* (see the section "Command-Line Options" in Chapter 11).

- The use of GNU Autoconf to control the configuration process (see the section "Compiling gawk for Unix" in Appendix B).

- Amiga support.

Version 3.1 of *gawk* introduced the following features:

- The BINMODE special variable for non-POSIX systems, which allows binary I/O for input and/or output files (see the section "Using gawk on PC Operating Systems" in Appendix B).

- The LINT special variable, which dynamically controls lint warnings (see the section "Built-in Variables" in Chapter 6).

- The PROCINFO array for providing process-related information (see the section "Built-in Variables" in Chapter 6).

- The TEXTDOMAIN special variable for setting an application's internationalization text domain (see the section "Built-in Variables" in Chapter 6, and Chapter 9, *Internationalization with gawk*).

- The ability to use octal and hexadecimal constants in *awk* program source code (see the section "Octal and Hexadecimal Numbers" in Chapter 5).

- The |& operator for two-way I/O to a coprocess (see the section "Two-Way Communications with Another Process" in Chapter 10, *Advanced Features of gawk*).

- The */inet* special files for TCP/IP networking using |& (see the section "Using gawk for Network Programming" in Chapter 10).

- The optional second argument to close that allows closing one end of a two-way pipe to a coprocess (see the section "Two-Way Communications with Another Process" in Chapter 10).

- The optional third argument to the match function for capturing text-matching subexpressions within a regexp (see the section "String-Manipulation Functions" in Chapter 8).

- Positional specifiers in `printf` formats for making translations easier (see the section "Rearranging printf Arguments" in Chapter 9).

- The `asort` function for sorting arrays (see the section "Sorting Array Values and Indices with gawk" in Chapter 7).

- The `bindtextdomain` and `dcgettext` functions for internationalization (see the section "Internationalizing awk Programs" in Chapter 9).

- The `extension` built-in function and the ability to add new built-in functions dynamically (see the section "Adding New Built-in Functions to gawk" in Appendix C, *Implementation Notes*).

- The `mktime` built-in function for creating timestamps (see the section "Using gawk's Timestamp Functions" in Chapter 8).

- The `and`, `or`, `xor`, `compl`, `lshift`, `rshift`, and `strtonum` built-in functions (see the section "Bit-Manipulation Functions of gawk" in Chapter 8).

- The support for `next file` as two words was removed completely (see the section "Using gawk's nextfile Statement" in Chapter 6).

- The *--dump-variables* option to print a list of all global variables (see the section "Command-Line Options" in Chapter 11).

- The *--gen-po* command-line option and the use of a leading underscore to mark strings that should be translated (see the section "Extracting Marked Strings" in Chapter 9).

- The *--non-decimal-data* option to allow nondecimal input data (see the section "Allowing Nondecimal Input Data" in Chapter 10).

- The *--profile* option and *pgawk*, the profiling version of *gawk*, for producing execution profiles of *awk* programs (see the section "Profiling Your awk Programs" in Chapter 10).

- The *--enable-portals* configuration option to enable special treatment of pathnames that begin with */p* as BSD portals (see the section "Using gawk with BSD Portals" in Chapter 10).

- The use of GNU Automake to help in standardizing the configuration process (see the section "Compiling gawk for Unix" in Appendix B).

- The use of GNU `gettext` for *gawk*'s own message output (see the section "gawk Can Speak Your Language" in Chapter 9).

- BeOS support.

- Tandem support.

- The Atari port became officially unsupported.

- The source code now uses new-style function definitions, with *ansi2knr* to convert the code on systems with old compilers.

Major Contributors to gawk

This section names the major contributors to *gawk* and/or this book, in approximate chronological order:

- Dr. Alfred V. Aho, Dr. Peter J. Weinberger, and Dr. Brian W. Kernighan, all of Bell Laboratories, designed and implemented Unix *awk*, from which *gawk* gets the majority of its feature set.

- Paul Rubin did the initial design and implementation in 1986, and wrote the first draft (around 40 pages) of this book.

- Jay Fenlason finished the initial implementation.

- Diane Close revised the first draft of this book, bringing it to around 90 pages.

- Richard Stallman helped finish the implementation and the initial draft of this book. He is also the founder of the FSF and the GNU project.

- John Woods contributed parts of the code (mostly fixes) in the initial version of *gawk*.

- In 1988, David Trueman took over primary maintenance of *gawk*, making it compatible with "new" *awk*, and greatly improving its performance.

- Pat Rankin provided the VMS port and its documentation.

- Conrad Kwok, Scott Garfinkle, and Kent Williams did the initial ports to MS-DOS with various versions of MSC.

- Hal Peterson provided help in porting *gawk* to Cray systems.

- Kai Uwe Rommel provided the port to OS/2 and its documentation.

- Michal Jaegermann provided the port to Atari systems and its documentation. He continues to provide portability checking with DEC Alpha systems, and has done a lot of work to make sure *gawk* works on non-32-bit systems.

- Fred Fish provided the port to Amiga systems and its documentation.

- Scott Deifik currently maintains the MS-DOS port.

- Juan Grigera maintains the port to Win32 systems.

- Dr. Darrel Hankerson acts as coordinator for the various ports to different PC platforms and creates binary distributions for various PC operating systems. He is also instrumental in keeping the documentation up to date for the various PC platforms.

- Christos Zoulas provided the `extension` built-in function for dynamically adding new modules.

- Jürgen Kahrs contributed the initial version of the TCP/IP networking code and documentation, and motivated the inclusion of the `|&` operator.

- Stephen Davies provided the port to Tandem systems and its documentation.

- Martin Brown provided the port to BeOS and its documentation.

- Arno Peters did the initial work to convert *gawk* to use GNU Automake and `gettext`.

- Alan J. Broder provided the initial version of the `asort` function as well as the code for the new optional third argument to the `match` function.

- Arnold Robbins has been working on *gawk* since 1988, at first helping David Trueman, and as the primary maintainer since around 1994.

B

Installing gawk

This appendix provides instructions for installing *gawk* on Unix-like systems and on PC operating systems.* The primary developer supports GNU/Linux (and Unix), whereas the other ports are contributed. See the section "Reporting Problems and Bugs" later in this chapter for the electronic mail addresses of the people who maintain the respective ports.

The gawk Distribution

This section describes how to get the *gawk* distribution, how to extract it, and then what is in the various files and subdirectories.

Getting the gawk Distribution

There are three ways to get GNU software:

- Copy it from someone else who already has it.

- Order *gawk* directly from the Free Software Foundation. Software distributions are available for Unix, MS-DOS, and VMS, on tape and CD-ROM. Their address is:

  Free Software Foundation
  59 Temple Place, Suite 330
  Boston, MA 02111-1307 USA
  Phone: (617) 542-5942
  Fax (including Japan): (617) 542-2652
  Email: *gnu@gnu.org*
  URL: *http://www.gnu.org*

---

* See the online Texinfo or Info versions of this book for information about other operating systems. VMS, Amiga, and BeOS have supported ports. Atari and Tandem have unsupported ports.

Ordering from the FSF directly contributes to the support of the foundation and to the production of more free software.

- Retrieve *gawk* by using anonymous *ftp* to the Internet host `gnudist.gnu.org`, in the directory */gnu/gawk*.

The GNU software archive is mirrored around the world. The up-to-date list of mirror sites is available at the main FSF web site *http://www.gnu.org/order/ftp.html*. Try to use one of the mirrors; they will be less busy, and you can usually find one closer to your site.

Extracting the Distribution

gawk is distributed as a `tar` file compressed with the GNU Zip program, `gzip`.

Once you have the distribution (for example, *gawk-3.1.0.tar.gz*), use `gzip` to expand the file and then use `tar` to extract it. You can use the following pipeline to produce the *gawk* distribution:

```
# Under System V, add 'o' to the tar options
gzip -d -c gawk-3.1.0.tar.gz | tar -xvpf -
```

This creates a directory named *gawk-3.1.0* in the current directory.

The distribution filename is of the form *gawk-V.R.P.tar.gz*. The *V* represents the major version of *gawk*, the *R* represents the current release of version *V*, and the *P* represents a *patch level*, meaning that minor bugs have been fixed in the release. The current patch level is 0, but when retrieving distributions, you should get the version with the highest version, release, and patch level. (Note, however, that patch levels greater than or equal to 80 denote "beta" or nonproduction software; you might not want to retrieve such a version unless you don't mind experimenting.) If you are not on a Unix system, you need to make other arrangements for getting and extracting the *gawk* distribution. You should consult a local expert.

Contents of the gawk Distribution

The *gawk* distribution has a number of C source files, documentation files, subdirectories, and files related to the configuration process (see the section "Compiling and Installing gawk on Unix" later in this appendix), as well as several subdirectories related to different non-Unix operating systems:

Various .c, .y, and .h files
> The actual *gawk* source code.

README
README_d/README.*
> Descriptive files: *README* for *gawk* under Unix and the rest for the various hardware and software combinations.

INSTALL
> A file providing an overview of the configuration and installation process.

ChangeLog
> A detailed list of source code changes as bugs are fixed or improvements made.

NEWS
> A list of changes to *gawk* since the last release or patch.

COPYING
> The GNU General Public License.

FUTURES
> A brief list of features and changes being contemplated for future releases, with some indication of the time frame for the feature, based on its difficulty.

LIMITATIONS
> A list of those factors that limit *gawk*'s performance. Most of these depend on the hardware or operating system software and are not limits in *gawk* itself.

POSIX.STD
> A description of one area in which the POSIX standard for *awk* is incorrect as well as how *gawk* handles the problem.

doc/awkforai.txt
> A short article describing why *gawk* is a good language for AI (Artificial Intelligence) programming.

doc/README.card, doc/ad.block, doc/awkcard.in, doc/cardfonts, doc/colors,
doc/macros, doc/no.colors, doc/setter.outline
> The *troff* source for a five-color *awk* reference card. A modern version of *troff* such as GNU *troff* (*groff*) is needed to produce the color version. See the file *README.card* for instructions if you have an older *troff.*

doc/gawk.1
> The *troff* source for a manual page describing *gawk*. This is distributed for the convenience of Unix users.

doc/gawk.texi

The Texinfo source file for this book. It should be processed with TEX to produce a printed document, and with *makeinfo* to produce an Info or HTML file.

doc/gawk.info

The generated Info file for this book.

doc/gawkinet.texi

The Texinfo source file for *TCP/IP Internetworking with gawk*. It should be processed with TEX to produce a printed document and with *makeinfo* to produce an Info or HTML file. (This document has been condensed into Chapter 14, *Internetworking with gawk*, for the O'Reilly & Associates edition.)

doc/gawkinet.info

The generated Info file for *TCP/IP Internetworking with gawk*.

doc/igawk.1

The *troff* source for a manual page describing the *igawk* program presented in the section "An Easy Way to Use Library Functions" in Chapter 13, *Practical awk Programs*.

doc/Makefile.in

The input file used during the configuration process to generate the actual *Makefile* for creating the documentation.

Makefile.am
*/Makefile.am

Files used by the GNU *automake* software for generating the *Makefile.in* files used by *autoconf* and *configure*.

Makefile.in, acconfig.h, acinclude.m4, aclocal.m4, configh.in, configure.in, configure, custom.h, missing_d/*, m4/*

These files and subdirectories are used when configuring *gawk* for various Unix systems. They are explained in the section "Compiling and Installing gawk on Unix" later in this chapter.

intl/*
po/*

The *intl* directory provides the GNU gettext library, which implements *gawk*'s internationalization features, while the *po* library contains message translations.

awklib/extract.awk, awklib/Makefile.am, awklib/Makefile.in, awklib/eg/*

The *awklib* directory contains a copy of *extract.awk* (see the section "Extracting Programs from Texinfo Source Files" in Chapter 13), which can be used to extract the sample programs from the Texinfo source file for this book. It also contains a *Makefile.in* file, which *configure* uses to generate a *Makefile*. *Makefile.am* is used by GNU Automake to create *Makefile.in*. The library functions from Chapter 12, *A Library of awk Functions*, and the *igawk* program from the section "An Easy Way to Use Library Functions" in Chapter 13, are included as ready-to-use files in the *gawk* distribution. They are installed as part of the installation process. The rest of the programs in this book are available in appropriate subdirectories of *awklib/eg*.

unsupported/atari/*

Files needed for building *gawk* on an Atari ST (see the online *gawk.info* and *gawk.texi* files in the *gawk* distribution for details).

unsupported/tandem/*

Files needed for building *gawk* on a Tandem (see the online *gawk.info* and *gawk.texi* files in the *gawk* distribution for details).

posix/*

Files needed for building *gawk* on POSIX-compliant systems.

pc/*

Files needed for building *gawk* under MS-DOS, MS Windows and OS/2 (see the section "Installation on PC Operating Systems" later in this appendix, for details).

vms/*

Files needed for building *gawk* under VMS (see the online *gawk.info* and *gawk.texi* files in the *gawk* distribution for details).

test/*

A test suite for *gawk*. You can use `make check` from the top-level *gawk* directory to run your version of *gawk* against the test suite. If *gawk* successfully passes `make check`, then you can be confident of a successful port.

Compiling and Installing gawk on Unix

Usually, you can compile and install *gawk* by typing only two commands. However, if you use an unusual system, you may need to configure *gawk* for your system yourself.

Compiling gawk for Unix

After you have extracted the *gawk* distribution, *cd* to *gawk-3.1.0*. Like most GNU software, *gawk* is configured automatically for your Unix system by running the *configure* program. This program is a Bourne shell script that is generated automatically using GNU *autoconf*. (The *autoconf* software is described fully in *Autoconf—Generating Automatic Configuration Scripts*, which is available from the Free Software Foundation.)

To configure *gawk*, simply run *configure*:

```
sh ./configure
```

This produces a *Makefile* and *config.h* tailored to your system. The *config.h* file describes various facts about your system. You might want to edit the *Makefile* to change the CFLAGS variable, which controls the command-line options that are passed to the C compiler (such as optimization levels or compiling for debugging).

Alternatively, you can add your own values for most *make* variables on the command line, such as CC and CFLAGS, when running *configure*:

```
CC=cc CFLAGS=-g sh ./configure
```

See the file *INSTALL* in the *gawk* distribution for all the details.

After you have run *configure* and possibly edited the *Makefile*, type:

```
make
```

Shortly thereafter, you should have an executable version of *gawk*. That's all there is to it! To verify that *gawk* is working properly, run make check. All of the tests should succeed. If these steps do not work, or if any of the tests fail, check the files in the *README_d* directory to see if you've found a known problem. If the failure is not described there, please send in a bug report (see the section "Reporting Problems and Bugs" later in this appendix.)

Additional Configuration Options

There are several additional options you may use on the *configure* command line when compiling *gawk* from scratch, including:

--enable-portals
> Treat pathnames that begin with */p* as BSD portal files when doing two-way I/O with the |& operator (see the section "Using gawk with BSD Portals" in Chapter 10, *Advanced Features of gawk*).

--with-included-gettext
> Use the version of the gettext library that comes with *gawk*. This option should be used on systems that do *not* use Version 2 (or later) of the GNU C library. All known modern GNU/Linux systems use Glibc 2. Use this option on any other system.

--disable-nls
> Disable all message-translation facilities. This is usually not desirable, but it may bring you some slight performance improvement. You should also use this option if *--with-included-gettext* doesn't work on your system.

The Configuration Process

This section is of interest only if you know something about using the C language and the Unix operating system.

The source code for *gawk* generally attempts to adhere to formal standards wherever possible. This means that *gawk* uses library routines that are specified by the ISO C standard and by the POSIX operating system interface standard. When using an ISO C compiler, function prototypes are used to help improve the compile-time checking.

Many Unix systems do not support all of either the ISO or the POSIX standards. The *missing_d* subdirectory in the *gawk* distribution contains replacement versions of those functions that are most likely to be missing.

The *config.h* file that *configure* creates contains definitions that describe features of the particular operating system where you are attempting to compile *gawk*. The three things described by this file are: what header files are available, so that they can be correctly included, what (supposedly) standard functions are actually available in your C libraries, and various miscellaneous facts about your variant of Unix. For example, there may not be an st_blksize element in the stat structure. In this case, HAVE_ST_BLKSIZE is undefined.

It is possible for your C compiler to lie to *configure*. It may do so by not exiting with an error when a library function is not available. To get around this, edit the file *custom.h*. Use an #ifdef that is appropriate for your system, and either #define any constants that *configure* should have defined but didn't, or #undef any constants that *configure* defined and should not have. *custom.h* is automatically included by *config.h*.

It is also possible that the *configure* program generated by *autoconf* will not work on your system in some other fashion. If you do have a problem, the file *configure.in* is the input for *autoconf*. You may be able to change this file and generate a new version of *configure* that works on your system (see the section "Reporting Problems and Bugs" later in this appendix, for information on how to report problems in configuring *gawk*). The same mechanism may be used to send in updates to *configure.in* and/or *custom.h*.

Installation on PC Operating Systems

This section covers installation and usage of *gawk* on x86 machines running DOS, any version of Windows, or OS/2. In this section, the term "Win32" refers to any of Windows-95/98/ME/NT/2000.

The limitations of DOS (and DOS shells under Windows or OS/2) has meant that various "DOS extenders" are often used with programs such as *gawk*. The varying capabilities of Microsoft Windows 3.1 and Win32 can add to the confusion. For an overview of the considerations, please refer to *README_d/README.pc* in the distribution.

Installing a Prepared Distribution for PC Systems

If you have received a binary distribution prepared by the DOS maintainers, then *gawk* and the necessary support files appear under the *gnu* directory, with executables in *gnu/bin*, libraries in *gnu/lib/awk*, and manual pages under *gnu/man*. This is designed for easy installation to a */gnu* directory on your drive—however, the files can be installed anywhere provided AWKPATH is set properly. Regardless of the installation directory, the first line of *igawk.cmd* and *igawk.bat* (in *gnu/bin*) may need to be edited.

The binary distribution contains a separate file describing the contents. In particular, it may include more than one version of the *gawk* executable. OS/2 binary distributions may have a different arrangement, but installation is similar.

Compiling gawk for PC Operating Systems

gawk can be compiled for MS-DOS, Win32, and OS/2 using the GNU development tools from DJ Delorie (DJGPP; MS-DOS only) or Eberhard Mattes (EMX; MS-DOS, Win32 and OS/2). Microsoft Visual C/C++ can be used to build a Win32 version, and Microsoft C/C++ can be used to build 16-bit versions for MS-DOS and OS/2. The file *README_d/README.pc* in the *gawk* distribution contains additional notes, and *pc/Makefile* contains important information on compilation options.

To build *gawk*, copy the files in the *pc* directory (*except* for *ChangeLog*) to the directory with the rest of the *gawk* sources. The *Makefile* contains a configuration section with comments and may need to be edited in order to work with your *make* utility.

The *Makefile* contains a number of targets for building various MS-DOS, Win32, and OS/2 versions. A list of targets is printed if the *make* command is given without a target. As an example, to build *gawk* using the DJGPP tools, enter `make djgpp`.

Using *make* to run the standard tests and to install *gawk* requires additional Unix-like tools, including *sh*, *sed*, and *cp*. In order to run the tests, the *test/*.ok* files may need to be converted so that they have the usual DOS-style end-of-line markers. Most of the tests work properly with Stewartson's shell along with the companion utilities or appropriate GNU utilities. However, some editing of *test/Makefile* is required. It is recommended that you copy the file *pc/Makefile.tst* over the file *test/Makefile* as a replacement. Details can be found in *README_d/README.pc* and in the file *pc/Makefile.tst*.

Using gawk on PC Operating Systems

The OS/2 and MS-DOS versions of *gawk* search for program files as described in the section "The AWKPATH Environment Variable" in Chapter 11, *Running awk and gawk*. However, semicolons (rather than colons) separate elements in the AWKPATH variable. If AWKPATH is not set or is empty, then the default search path is `".;c:/lib/awk;c:/gnu/lib/awk"`.

An *sh*-like shell (as opposed to *command.com* under MS-DOS or *cmd.exe* under OS/2) may be useful for *awk* programming. Ian Stewartson has written an excellent shell for MS-DOS and OS/2, Daisuke Aoyama has ported GNU bash to MS-DOS using the DJGPP tools, and several shells are available for OS/2, including *ksh*. The file *README_d/README.pc* in the *gawk* distribution contains information on these shells. Users of Stewartson's shell on DOS should examine its documentation for handling command lines; in particular, the setting for *gawk* in the shell configuration may need to be changed and the `ignoretype` option may also be of interest.

Under OS/2 and DOS, *gawk* (and many other text programs) silently translate end-of-line `"\r\n"` to `"\n"` on input and `"\n"` to `"\r\n"` on output. A special BINMODE variable allows control over these translations and is interpreted as follows:

- If BINMODE is `"r"`, or (BINMODE & 1) is nonzero, then binary mode is set on read (i.e., no translations on reads).

- If BINMODE is `"w"`, or (BINMODE & 2) is nonzero, then binary mode is set on write (i.e., no translations on writes).

- If BINMODE is `"rw"` or `"wr"`, binary mode is set for both read and write (same as (BINMODE & 3)).

- BINMODE=*non-null-string* is the same as BINMODE=3 (i.e., no translations on reads or writes). However, *gawk* issues a warning message if the string is not one of `"rw"` or `"wr"`.

The modes for standard input and standard output are set one time only (after the command line is read, but before processing any of the *awk* program). Setting BINMODE for standard input or standard output is accomplished by using an appropriate -v BINMODE=*N* option on the command line. BINMODE is set at the time a file or pipe is opened and cannot be changed mid-stream.

The name BINMODE was chosen to match *mawk* (see the section "Other Freely Available awk Implementations" later in this appendix). Both *mawk* and *gawk* handle BINMODE similarly; however, *mawk* adds a -W BINMODE=*N* option and an environment variable that can set BINMODE, RS, and ORS. The files *binmode[1-3].awk* (under *gnu/lib/awk* in some of the prepared distributions) have been chosen to match *mawk*'s -W BINMODE=*N* option. These can be changed or discarded; in particular, the setting of RS giving the fewest "surprises" is open to debate. *mawk* uses RS = "\r\n" if binary mode is set on read, which is appropriate for files with the DOS-style end-of-line.

To illustrate, the following examples set binary mode on writes for standard output and other files, and set ORS as the "usual" DOS-style end-of-line:

```
gawk -v BINMODE=2 -v ORS="\r\n" ...
```

or:

```
gawk -v BINMODE=w -f binmode2.awk ...
```

These give the same result as the -W BINMODE=2 option in *mawk*. The following changes the record separator to "\r\n" and sets binary mode on reads, but does not affect the mode on standard input:

```
gawk -v RS="\r\n" --source "BEGIN { BINMODE = 1 }" ...
```

or:

```
gawk -f binmode1.awk ...
```

With proper quoting, in the first example the setting of RS can be moved into the BEGIN rule.

Reporting Problems and Bugs

If you have problems with *gawk* or think that you have found a bug, please report it to the developers; we cannot promise to do anything but we might well want to fix it.

Before reporting a bug, make sure you have actually found a real bug. Carefully reread the documentation and see if it really says you can do what you're trying to do. If it's not clear whether you should be able to do something or not, report that too; it's a bug in the documentation!

Before reporting a bug or trying to fix it yourself, try to isolate it to the smallest possible *awk* program and input datafile that reproduces the problem. Then send us the program and datafile, some idea of what kind of Unix system you're using, the compiler you used to compile *gawk*, and the exact results *gawk* gave you. Also say what you expected to occur; this helps us decide whether the problem is really in the documentation.

Once you have a precise problem, send email to *bug-gawk@gnu.org*.

Please include the version number of *gawk* you are using. You can get this information with the command gawk --version. Using this address automatically sends a carbon copy of your mail to me. If necessary, I can be reached directly at *arnold@gnu.org.* The bug reporting address is preferred since the email list is archived at the GNU Project. *All email should be in English, since that is my native language.*

 Do *not* try to report bugs in *gawk* by posting to the Usenet/Internet newsgroup comp.lang.awk. While the *gawk* developers do occasionally read this newsgroup, there is no guarantee that we will see your posting. The steps described above are the official recognized ways for reporting bugs.

Non-bug suggestions are always welcome as well. If you have questions about things that are unclear in the documentation or are just obscure features, ask me; I will try to help you out, although I may not have the time to fix the problem. You can send me electronic mail at the Internet address noted previously.

If you find bugs in one of the non-Unix ports of *gawk*, please send an electronic mail message to the person who maintains that port. They are named in the following list, as well as in the *README* file in the *gawk* distribution. Information in the *README* file should be considered authoritative if it conflicts with this book.

The people maintaining the non-Unix ports of *gawk* are as follows:

Amiga
Fred Fish, *fnf@ninemoons.com.*

BeOS
Martin Brown, *mc@whoever.com.*

MS-DOS
Scott Deifik, *scottd@amgen.com,* and Darrel Hankerson, *hankedr@mail.auburn.edu.*

MS-Windows
Juan Grigera, *juan@biophnet.unlp.edu.ar.*

OS/2
Kai Uwe Rommel, *rommel@ars.de.*

Tandem
Stephen Davies, *scldad@sdc.com.au.*

VMS
Pat Rankin, *rankin@eql.caltech.edu.*

If your bug is also reproducible under Unix, please send a copy of your report to the *bug-gawk@gnu.org* email list as well.

Other Freely Available awk Implementations

There are three other freely available *awk* implementations. This section briefly describes where to get them:

Unix awk

Brian Kernighan has made his implementation of *awk* freely available. You can retrieve this version via the World Wide Web from his home page.* It is available in several archive formats:

Shell archive

    http://cm.bell-labs.com/who/bwk/awk.shar

Compressed tar file

    http://cm.bell-labs.com/who/bwk/awk.tar.gz

Zip file

    http://cm.bell-labs.com/who/bwk/awk.zip

This version requires an ISO C (1990 standard) compiler; the C compiler from GCC (the GNU Compiler Collection) works quite nicely.

See the section "Extensions in the Bell Laboratories awk" in Appendix A, *The Evolution of the awk Language*, for a list of extensions in this *awk* that are not in POSIX *awk*.

mawk

Michael Brennan has written an independent implementation of *awk*, called *mawk*. It is available under the GPL (see Appendix E, *GNU General Public License*), just as *gawk* is.

You can get it via anonymous *ftp* to the host `ftp.whidbey.net`. Change directory to */pub/brennan*. Use "binary" or "image" mode, and retrieve *mawk1.3.3.tar.gz* (or the latest version that is there).

gunzip may be used to decompress this file. Installation is similar to *gawk*'s (see the section "Compiling and Installing gawk on Unix" earlier in this appendix).

---

* *http://cm.bell-labs.com/who/bwk/.*

mawk has the following extensions that are not in POSIX *awk*:

- The `fflush` built-in function for flushing buffered output (see the section "Input/Output Functions" in Chapter 8, *Functions*).

- The `**` and `**=` operators (see the section "Arithmetic Operators" and section "Assignment Expressions" in Chapter 5, *Expressions*).

- The use of `func` as an abbreviation for `function` (see the section "Function Definition Syntax" in Chapter 8).

- The `\x` escape sequence (see the section "Escape Sequences" in Chapter 2, *Regular Expressions*).

- The */dev/stdout*, and */dev/stderr* special files (see the section "Special File-names in gawk" in Chapter 4, *Printing Output*). Use `"-"` instead of `"/dev/stdin"` with *mawk*.

- The ability for `FS` and for the third argument to `split` to be null strings (see the section "Making Each Character a Separate Field" in Chapter 3, *Reading Input Files*).

- The ability to delete all of an array at once with `delete array` (see the section "The delete Statement" in Chapter 7, *Arrays in awk*).

- The ability for `RS` to be a regexp (see the section "How Input Is Split into Records" in Chapter 3).

- The `BINMODE` special variable for non-Unix operating systems (see the section "Using gawk on PC Operating Systems" earlier in this appendix).

The next version of *mawk* will support `nextfile`.

awka

Written by Andrew Sumner, *awka* translates *awk* programs into C, compiles them, and links them with a library of functions that provides the core *awk* functionality. It also has a number of extensions.

The *awk* translator is released under the GPL, and the library is under the LGPL.

To get *awka*, go to its home page at *http://awka.sourceforge.net*. You can reach Andrew Sumner at *andrew_sumner@bigfoot.com*.

C

Implementation Notes

This appendix contains information mainly of interest to implementors and maintainers of *gawk*. Everything in it applies specifically to *gawk* and not to other implementations.

Downward Compatibility and Debugging

See the section "Extensions in gawk Not in POSIX awk" in Appendix A, *The Evolution of the awk Language*, for a summary of the GNU extensions to the *awk* language and program. All of these features can be turned off by invoking *gawk* with the *--traditional* option or with the *--posix* option.

If *gawk* is compiled for debugging with -DDEBUG, then there is one more option available on the command line:

```
-W parsedebug
--parsedebug
```
Prints out the parse stack information as the program is being parsed.

This option is intended only for serious *gawk* developers and not for the casual user. It probably has not even been compiled into your version of *gawk*, since it slows down execution.

Making Additions to gawk

If you find that you want to enhance *gawk* in a significant fashion, you are perfectly free to do so. That is the point of having free software; the source code is available and you are free to change it as you want (see Appendix E, *GNU General Public License*).

This section discusses the ways you might want to change *gawk* as well as any considerations you should bear in mind.

Adding New Features

You are free to add any new features you like to *gawk*. However, if you want your changes to be incorporated into the *gawk* distribution, there are several steps that you need to take in order to make it possible for me to include your changes:

1. Before building the new feature into *gawk* itself, consider writing it as an extension module (see the section "Adding New Built-in Functions to gawk" later in this appendix). If that's not possible, continue with the rest of the steps in this list.

2. Get the latest version. It is much easier for me to integrate changes if they are relative to the most recent distributed version of *gawk*. If your version of *gawk* is very old, I may not be able to integrate them at all. (See the section "Getting the gawk Distribution" in Appendix B, *Installing gawk*, for information on getting the latest version of *gawk*.)

3. Follow the *GNU Coding Standards*. This document describes how GNU software should be written. If you haven't read it, please do so, preferably *before* starting to modify *gawk*. (The *GNU Coding Standards* are available from the GNU Project's FTP site, at *ftp://gnudist.gnu.org/gnu/GNUInfo/standards.text*. Texinfo, Info, and DVI versions are also available.)

4. Use the *gawk* coding style. The C code for *gawk* follows the instructions in the *GNU Coding Standards*, with minor exceptions. The code is formatted using the traditional "K&R" style, particularly as regards to the placement of braces and the use of tabs. In brief, the coding rules for *gawk* are as follows:

   - Use ANSI/ISO style (prototype) function headers when defining functions.

   - Put the name of the function at the beginning of its own line.

   - Put the return type of the function, even if it is int, on the line above the line with the name and arguments of the function.

   - Put spaces around parentheses used in control structures (if, while, for, do, switch, and return).

- Do not put spaces in front of parentheses used in function calls.

- Put spaces around all C operators and after commas in function calls.

- Do not use the comma operator to produce multiple side effects, except in `for` loop initialization and increment parts, and in macro bodies.

- Use real tabs for indenting, not spaces.

- Use the "K&R" brace layout style.

- Use comparisons against `NULL` and `'\0'` in the conditions of `if`, `while`, and `for` statements, as well as in the `cases` of `switch` statements, instead of just the plain pointer or character value.

- Use the `TRUE`, `FALSE` and `NULL` symbolic constants and the character constant `'\0'` where appropriate, instead of 1 and 0.

- Use the `ISALPHA`, `ISDIGIT`, etc. macros, instead of the traditional lowercase versions; these macros are better behaved for non-ASCII character sets.

- Provide one-line descriptive comments for each function.

- Do not use `#elif`. Many older Unix C compilers cannot handle it.

- Do not use the `alloca` function for allocating memory off the stack. Its use causes more portability trouble than is worth the minor benefit of not having to free the storage. Instead, use `malloc` and `free`.

 If I have to reformat your code to follow the coding style used in *gawk*, I may not bother to integrate your changes at all.

---

5. Be prepared to sign the appropriate paperwork. In order for the FSF to distribute your changes, you must either place those changes in the public domain and submit a signed statement to that effect, or assign the copyright in your changes to the FSF. Both of these actions are easy to do and *many* people have done so already. If you have questions, please contact me (see the section "Reporting Problems and Bugs" in Appendix B), or *gnu@gnu.org*.

6. Update the documentation. Along with your new code, please supply new sections and/or chapters for this book. If at all possible, please use real Texinfo, instead of just supplying unformatted ASCII text (although even that is better than no documentation at all). Conventions to be followed in *Effective awk Programming* are provided after the `@bye` at the end of the Texinfo source file. If possible, please update the manpage as well.

    You will also have to sign paperwork for your documentation changes.

7. Submit changes as context diffs or unified diffs. Use `diff -c -r -N` or `diff -u -r -N` to compare the original *gawk* source tree with your version. (I find context diffs to be more readable but unified diffs are more compact.) I recommend using the GNU version of *diff.* Send the output produced by either run of *diff* to me when you submit your changes. (See the section "Reporting Problems and Bugs" in Appendix B, for the electronic mail information.)

   Using this format makes it easy for me to apply your changes to the master version of the *gawk* source code (using `patch`). If I have to apply the changes manually, using a text editor, I may not do so, particularly if there are lots of changes.

8. Include an entry for the *ChangeLog* file with your submission. This helps further minimize the amount of work I have to do, making it easier for me to accept patches.

Although this sounds like a lot of work, please remember that while you may write the new code, I have to maintain it and support it. If it isn't possible for me to do that with a minimum of extra work, then I probably will not.

Porting gawk to a New Operating System

If you want to port *gawk* to a new operating system, there are several steps:

1. Follow the guidelines in the previous section concerning coding style, submission of diffs, and so on.

2. When doing a port, bear in mind that your code must coexist peacefully with the rest of *gawk* and the other ports. Avoid gratuitous changes to the system-independent parts of the code. If at all possible, avoid sprinkling `#ifdefs` just for your port throughout the code.

   If the changes needed for a particular system affect too much of the code, I probably will not accept them. In such a case, you can, of course, distribute your changes on your own, as long as you comply with the GPL (see Appendix E).

3. A number of the files that come with *gawk* are maintained by other people at the Free Software Foundation. Thus, you should not change them unless it is for a very good reason; i.e., changes are not out of the question, but changes to these files are scrutinized extra carefully. The files are *getopt.h*, *getopt.c*, *getopt1.c*, *regex.h*, *regex.c*, *dfa.h*, *dfa.c*, *install-sh*, and *mkinstalldirs*.

4. Be willing to continue to maintain the port. Non-Unix operating systems are supported by volunteers who maintain the code needed to compile and run *gawk* on their systems. If noone volunteers to maintain a port, it becomes unsupported and it may be necessary to remove it from the distribution.

5. Supply an appropriate *gawkmisc.???* file. Each port has its own *gawkmisc.???* that implements certain operating system specific functions. This is cleaner than a plethora of #ifdefs scattered throughout the code. The *gawkmisc.c* in the main source directory includes the appropriate *gawkmisc.???* file from each subdirectory. Be sure to update it as well. Each port's *gawkmisc.???* file has a suffix reminiscent of the machine or operating system for the port—for example, *pc/gawkmisc.pc* and *vms/gawkmisc.vms*. The use of separate suffixes, instead of plain *gawkmisc.c*, makes it possible to move files from a port's subdirectory into the main subdirectory, without accidentally destroying the real *gawkmisc.c* file. (Currently, this is only an issue for the PC operating system ports.)

6. Supply a *Makefile* as well as any other C source and header files that are necessary for your operating system. All your code should be in a separate subdirectory, with a name that is the same as, or reminiscent of, either your operating system or the computer system. If possible, try to structure things so that it is not necessary to move files out of the subdirectory into the main source directory. If that is not possible, then be sure to avoid using names for your files that duplicate the names of files in the main source directory.

7. Update the documentation. Please write a section (or sections) for this book describing the installation and compilation steps needed to compile and/or install *gawk* for your system.

8. Be prepared to sign the appropriate paperwork. In order for the FSF to distribute your code, you must either place your code in the public domain and submit a signed statement to that effect, or assign the copyright in your code to the FSF.

Following these steps makes it much easier to integrate your changes into *gawk* and have them coexist happily with other operating systems' code that is already there.

In the code that you supply and maintain, feel free to use a coding style and brace layout that suits your taste.

Adding New Built-in Functions to gawk

Beginning with *gawk* 3.1, it is possible to add new built-in functions to *gawk* using dynamically loaded libraries. This facility is available on systems (such as GNU/Linux) that support the dlopen and dlsym functions. This section describes how to write and use dynamically loaded extentions for *gawk*. Experience with programming in C or C++ is necessary when reading this section.

The facilities described in this section are very much subject to change in the next *gawk* release. Be aware that you may have to re-do everything, perhaps from scratch, upon the next release.

A Minimal Introduction to gawk Internals

The truth is that *gawk* was not designed for simple extensibility. The facilities for adding functions using shared libraries work, but are something of a "bag on the side." Thus, this tour is brief and simplistic; would-be *gawk* hackers are encouraged to spend some time reading the source code before trying to write extensions based on the material presented here. Of particular note are the files *awk.h*, *builtin.c*, and *eval.c*. Reading *awk.y* in order to see how the parse tree is built would also be of use.

With the disclaimers out of the way, the following types, structure members, functions, and macros are declared in *awk.h* and are of use when writing extensions. The next section shows how they are used:

AWKNUM

> An AWKNUM is the internal type of *awk* floating-point numbers. Typically, it is a C double.

NODE

> Just about everything is done using objects of type NODE. These contain both strings and numbers, as well as variables and arrays.

AWKNUM force_number(NODE *n)

> This macro forces a value to be numeric. It returns the actual numeric value contained in the node. It may end up calling an internal *gawk* function.

void force_string(NODE *n)

> This macro guarantees that a NODE's string value is current. It may end up calling an internal *gawk* function. It also guarantees that the string is zero-terminated.

n->param_cnt

> The number of parameters actually passed in a function call at runtime.

n->stptr
n->stlen

> The data and length of a NODE's string value, respectively. The string is *not* guaranteed to be zero-terminated. If you need to pass the string value to a C library function, save the value in n->stptr[n->stlen], assign '\0' to it, call the routine, and then restore the value.

`n->type`

> The type of the NODE. This is a C enum. Values should be either Node_var or Node_var_array for function parameters.

`n->vname`

> The "variable name" of a node. This is not of much use inside externally written extensions.

`void assoc_clear(NODE *n)`

> Clears the associative array pointed to by n. Make sure that n->type == Node_var_array first.

`NODE **assoc_lookup(NODE *symbol, NODE *subs, int reference)`

> Finds, and installs if necessary, array elements. symbol is the array, subs is the subscript. This is usually a value created with tmp_string (see below). reference should be TRUE if it is an error to use the value before it is created. Typically, FALSE is the correct value to use from extension functions.

`NODE *make_string(char *s, size_t len)`

> Take a C string and turn it into a pointer to a NODE that can be stored appropriately. This is permanent storage; understanding of *gawk* memory management is helpful.

`NODE *make_number(AWKNUM val)`

> Take an AWKNUM and turn it into a pointer to a NODE that can be stored appropriately. This is permanent storage; understanding of *gawk* memory management is helpful.

`NODE *tmp_string(char *s, size_t len);`

> Take a C string and turn it into a pointer to a NODE that can be stored appropriately. This is temporary storage; understanding of *gawk* memory management is helpful.

`NODE *tmp_number(AWKNUM val)`

> Take an AWKNUM and turn it into a pointer to a NODE that can be stored appropriately. This is temporary storage; understanding of *gawk* memory management is helpful.

`NODE *dupnode(NODE *n)`

> Duplicate a node. In most cases, this increments an internal reference count instead of actually duplicating the entire NODE; understanding of *gawk* memory management is helpful.

`void free_temp(NODE *n)`

> This macro releases the memory associated with a NODE allocated with tmp_string or tmp_number. Understanding of *gawk* memory management is helpful.

```
void make_builtin(char *name, NODE *(*func)(NODE *), int count)
```
Register a C function pointed to by func as new built-in function name. name is a regular C string. count is the maximum number of arguments that the function takes. The function should be written in the following manner:

```
/* do_xxx --- do xxx function for gawk */

NODE *
do_xxx(NODE *tree)
{
    ...
}
```

```
NODE *get_argument(NODE *tree, int i)
```
This function is called from within a C extension function to get the i-th argument from the function call. The first argument is argument zero.

```
void set_value(NODE *tree)
```
This function is called from within a C extension function to set the return value from the extension function. This value is what the *awk* program sees as the return value from the new *awk* function.

```
void update_ERRNO(void)
```
This function is called from within a C extension function to set the value of *gawk*'s ERRNO variable, based on the current value of the C errno variable. It is provided as a convenience.

An argument that is supposed to be an array needs to be handled with some extra code, in case the array being passed in is actually from a function parameter. The following boilerplate code shows how to do this:

```
NODE *the_arg;

the_arg = get_argument(tree, 2); /* assume need 3rd arg, 0-based */

/* if a parameter, get it off the stack */
if (the_arg->type == Node_param_list)
    the_arg = stack_ptr[the_arg->param_cnt];

/* parameter referenced an array, get it */
if (the_arg->type == Node_array_ref)
    the_arg = the_arg->orig_array;

/* check type */
if (the_arg->type != Node_var && the_arg->type != Node_var_array)
    fatal("newfunc: third argument is not an array");

/* force it to be an array, if necessary, clear it */
the_arg->type = Node_var_array;
assoc_clear(the_arg);
```

Again, you should spend time studying the *gawk* internals; don't just blindly copy this code.

Directory and File Operation Built-ins

Two useful functions that are not in *awk* are `chdir` (so that an *awk* program can change its directory) and `stat` (so that an *awk* program can gather information about a file). This section implements these functions for *gawk* in an external extension library.

Using chdir and stat

This section shows how to use the new functions at the *awk* level once they've been integrated into the running *gawk* interpreter. Using `chdir` is very straightforward. It takes one argument, the new directory to change to:

```
...
newdir = "/home/arnold/funstuff"
ret = chdir(newdir)
if (ret < 0) {
    printf("could not change to %s: %s\n",
                   newdir, ERRNO) > "/dev/stderr"
    exit 1
}
...
```

The return value is negative if the `chdir` failed, and ERRNO (see the section "Built-in Variables" in Chapter 6, *Patterns, Actions, and Variables*) is set to a string indicating the error.

Using `stat` is a bit more complicated. The C `stat` function fills in a structure that has a fair amount of information. The right way to model this in *awk* is to fill in an associative array with the appropriate information:

```
file = "/home/arnold/.profile"
fdata[1] = "x"      # force 'fdata' to be an array
ret = stat(file, fdata)
if (ret < 0) {
    printf("could not stat %s: %s\n", file, ERRNO) > "/dev/stderr"
    exit 1
}
printf("size of %s is %d bytes\n", file, fdata["size"])
```

The `stat` function always clears the data array, even if the `stat` fails. It fills in the following elements:

`"name"`

> The name of the file that was stat'ed.

`"dev"`
`"ino"`

> The file's device and inode numbers, respectively.

`"mode"`

> The file's mode, as a numeric value. This includes both the file's type and its permissions.

`"nlink"`

> The number of hard links (directory entries) the file has.

`"uid"`
`"gid"`

> The numeric user and group ID numbers of the file's owner.

`"size"`

> The size in bytes of the file.

`"blocks"`

> The number of disk blocks the file actually occupies. This may not be a function of the file's size if the file has holes.

`"atime"`, `"mtime"`, `"ctime"`

> The file's last access, modification, and inode update times, respectively. These are numeric timestamps, suitable for formatting with `strftime` (see the section "Built-in Functions" in Chapter 8, *Functions*).

`"pmode"`

> The file's "printable mode." This is a string representation of the file's type and permissions, such as what is produced by `ls -l`—for example, `"drwxr-xr-x"`.

`"type"`

> A printable string representation of the file's type. The value is one of the following:

`"blockdev"`
`"chardev"`

> The file is a block or character device ("special file").

`"directory"`

> The file is a directory.

`"fifo"`

> The file is a named-pipe (also known as a FIFO).

`"file"`
> The file is just a regular file.

`"socket"`
> The file is an AF_UNIX ("Unix domain") socket in the filesystem.

`"symlink"`
> The file is a symbolic link.

Several additional elements may be present depending upon the operating system and the type of the file. You can test for them in your *awk* program by using the in operator (see the section "Referring to an Array Element" in Chapter 7, *Arrays in awk*):

`"blksize"`
> The preferred block size for I/O to the file. This field is not present on all POSIX-like systems in the C stat structure.

`"linkval"`
> If the file is a symbolic link, this element is the name of the file the link points to (i.e., the value of the link).

`"rdev"`, `"major"`, `"minor"`
> If the file is a block or character device file, then these values represent the numeric device number and the major and minor components of that number, respectively.

C code for chdir and stat

Here is the C code for these extensions. They were written for GNU/Linux. The code needs some more work for complete portability to other POSIX-compliant systems:*

```
#include "awk.h"

#include <sys/sysmacros.h>

/*  do_chdir --- provide dynamically loaded chdir() builtin for gawk */

static NODE *
do_chdir(tree)
NODE *tree;
{
    NODE *newdir;
    int ret = -1;

    newdir = get_argument(tree, 0);
```

---

* This version is edited slightly for presentation. The complete version can be found in *extension/filefuncs.c* in the *gawk* distribution.

The file includes the `"awk.h"` header file for definitions for the *gawk* internals. It includes `<sys/sysmacros.h>` for access to the `major` and `minor` macros.

By convention, for an *awk* function `foo`, the function that implements it is called `do_foo`. The function should take a `NODE *` argument, usually called `tree`, that represents the argument list to the function. The `newdir` variable represents the new directory to change to, retrieved with `get_argument`. Note that the first argument is numbered zero.

This code actually accomplishes the `chdir`. It first forces the argument to be a string and passes the string value to the `chdir` system call. If the `chdir` fails, `ERRNO` is updated. The result of `force_string` has to be freed with `free_temp`:

```
if (newdir != NULL) {
    (void) force_string(newdir);
    ret = chdir(newdir->stptr);
    if (ret < 0)
        update_ERRNO();

    free_temp(newdir);
}
```

Finally, the function returns the return value to the *awk* level, using `set_value`. Then it must return a value from the call to the new built-in (this value ignored by the interpreter):

```
/* Set the return value */
set_value(tmp_number((AWKNUM) ret));

/* Just to make the interpreter happy */
return tmp_number((AWKNUM) 0);
}
```

The `stat` built-in is more involved. First comes a function that turns a numeric mode into a printable representation (e.g., 644 becomes –rw-r–r–). This is omitted here for brevity:

```
/* format_mode --- turn a stat mode field into something readable */

static char *
format_mode(fmode)
unsigned long fmode;
{
    ...
}
```

Next comes the actual do_stat function itself. First come the variable declarations and argument checking:

```
/* do_stat --- provide a stat() function for gawk */

static NODE *
do_stat(tree)
NODE *tree;
{
    NODE *file, *array;
    struct stat sbuf;
    int ret;
    char *msg;
    NODE **aptr;
    char *pmode;      /* printable mode */
    char *type = "unknown";

    /* check arg count */
    if (tree->param_cnt != 2)
        fatal(
    "stat: called with incorrect number of arguments (%d), should be 2",
            tree->param_cnt);
```

Then comes the actual work. First, we get the arguments. Then, we always clear the array. To get the file information, we use lstat, in case the file is a symbolic link. If there's an error, we set ERRNO and return:

```
    /* directory is first arg, array to hold results is second */
    file = get_argument(tree, 0);
    array = get_argument(tree, 1);

    /* empty out the array */
    assoc_clear(array);

    /* lstat the file, if error, set ERRNO and return */
    (void) force_string(file);
    ret = lstat(file->stptr, & sbuf);
    if (ret < 0) {
        update_ERRNO();

        set_value(tmp_number((AWKNUM) ret));

        free_temp(file);
        return tmp_number((AWKNUM) 0);
    }
```

Now comes the tedious part: filling in the array. Only a few of the calls are shown here, since they all follow the same pattern:

```
            /* fill in the array */
            aptr = assoc_lookup(array, tmp_string("name", 4), FALSE);
            *aptr = dupnode(file);

            aptr = assoc_lookup(array, tmp_string("mode", 4), FALSE);
            *aptr = make_number((AWKNUM) sbuf.st_mode);

            aptr = assoc_lookup(array, tmp_string("pmode", 5), FALSE);
            pmode = format_mode(sbuf.st_mode);
            *aptr = make_string(pmode, strlen(pmode));
```

When done, we free the temporary value containing the filename, set the return value, and return:

```
            free_temp(file);

            /* Set the return value */
            set_value(tmp_number((AWKNUM) ret));

            /* Just to make the interpreter happy */
            return tmp_number((AWKNUM) 0);
        }
```

Finally, it's necessary to provide the "glue" that loads the new function(s) into *gawk*. By convention, each library has a routine named dlload that does the job:

```
        /* dlload --- load new builtins in this library */

        NODE *
        dlload(tree, dl)
        NODE *tree;
        void *dl;
        {
            make_builtin("chdir", do_chdir, 1);
            make_builtin("stat", do_stat, 2);
            return tmp_number((AWKNUM) 0);
        }
```

And that's it! As an exercise, consider adding functions to implement system calls such as chown, chmod, and umask.

Integrating the extensions

Now that the code is written, it must be possible to add it at runtime to the running *gawk* interpreter. First, the code must be compiled. Assuming that the functions are in a file named *filefuncs.c*, and *idir* is the location of the *gawk* include files, the following steps create a GNU/Linux shared library:

```
$ gcc -shared -DHAVE_CONFIG_H -c -O -g -Iidir filefuncs.c
$ ld -o filefuncs.so -shared filefuncs.o
```

Once the library exists, it is loaded by calling the `extension` built-in function. This function takes two arguments: the name of the library to load and the name of a function to call when the library is first loaded. This function adds the new functions to *gawk*. It returns the value returned by the initialization function within the shared library:

```
# file testff.awk
BEGIN {
    extension("./filefuncs.so", "dlload")

    chdir(".")   # no-op

    data[1] = 1 # force 'data' to be an array
    print "Info for testff.awk"
    ret = stat("testff.awk", data)
    print "ret =", ret
    for (i in data)
        printf "data[\"%s\"] = %s\n", i, data[i]
    print "testff.awk modified:",
        strftime("%m %d %y %H:%M:%S", data["mtime"])
}
```

Here are the results of running the program:

```
$ gawk -f testff.awk
Info for testff.awk
ret = 0
data["blksize"] = 4096
data["mtime"] = 932361936
data["mode"] = 33188
data["type"] = file
data["dev"] = 2065
data["gid"] = 10
data["ino"] = 878597
data["ctime"] = 971431797
data["blocks"] = 2
data["nlink"] = 1
data["name"] = testff.awk
data["atime"] = 971608519
data["pmode"] = -rw-r--r--
data["size"] = 607
data["uid"] = 2076
testff.awk modified: 07 19 99 08:25:36
```

Probable Future Extensions

This section briefly lists extensions and possible improvements that indicate the directions we are currently considering for *gawk*. The file *FUTURES* in the *gawk* distribution lists these extensions as well.

Following is a list of probable future changes visible at the *awk* language level:

Loadable module interface

It is not clear that the *awk*-level interface to the modules facility is as good as it should be. The interface needs to be redesigned, particularly taking name-space issues into account, as well as possibly including issues such as library search path order and versioning.

RECLEN *variable for fixed-length records*

Along with FIELDWIDTHS, this would speed up the processing of fixed-length records. PROCINFO["RS"] would be "RS" or "RECLEN", depending upon which kind of record processing is in effect.

Additional printf *specifiers*

The 1999 ISO C standard added a number of additional printf format speci-fiers. These should be evaluated for possible inclusion in *gawk*.

Databases

It may be possible to map a GDBM/NDBM/SDBM file into an *awk* array.

Large character sets

It would be nice if *gawk* could handle UTF-8 and other character sets that are larger than eight bits.

More lint *warnings*

There are more things that could be checked for portability.

Following is a list of probable improvements that will make *gawk*'s source code easier to work with:

Loadable module mechanics

The current extension mechanism works (see the earlier section "Adding New Built-in Functions to gawk)", but is rather primitive. It requires a fair amount of manual work to create and integrate a loadable module. Nor is the current mechanism as portable as might be desired. The GNU *libtool* package pro-vides a number of features that would make using loadable modules much easier. *gawk* should be changed to use *libtool*.

Loadable module internals

The API to its internals that *gawk* "exports" should be revised. Too many things are needlessly exposed. A new API should be designed and imple-mented to make module writing easier.

Better array subscript management

gawk's management of array subscript storage could use revamping, so that using the same value to index multiple arrays only stores one copy of the index value.

Integrating the DBUG library

    Integrating Fred Fish's DBUG library would be helpful during development, but it's a lot of work to do.

Following is a list of probable improvements that will make *gawk* perform better:

An improved version of dfa

    The dfa pattern matcher from GNU *grep* has some problems. Either a new version or a fixed one will deal with some important regexp matching issues.

Compilation of awk programs

    gawk uses a Bison (YACC-like) parser to convert the script given it into a syntax tree; the syntax tree is then executed by a simple recursive evaluator. This method incurs a lot of overhead, since the recursive evaluator performs many procedure calls to do even the simplest things.

    It should be possible for *gawk* to convert the script's parse tree into a C program which the user would then compile, using the normal C compiler and a special *gawk* library to provide all the needed functions (regexps, fields, associative arrays, type coercion, and so on).

    An easier possibility might be for an intermediate phase of *gawk* to convert the parse tree into a linear byte code form like the one used in GNU Emacs Lisp. The recursive evaluator would then be replaced by a straight line byte code interpreter that would be intermediate in speed between running a compiled program and doing what *gawk* does now.

Finally, the programs in the test suite could use documenting in this book.

See the earlier section "Making Additions to gawk" if you are interested in tackling any of these projects.

D

Basic Programming Concepts

This appendix attempts to define some of the basic concepts and terms that are used throughout the rest of this book. As this book is specifically about *awk*, and not about computer programming in general, the coverage here is by necessity fairly cursory and simplistic. (If you need more background, there are many other introductory texts that you should refer to instead.)

What a Program Does

At the most basic level, the job of a program is to process some input data and produce results. This is shown graphically in Figure D-1.

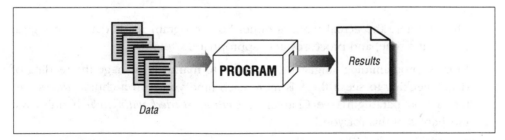

Figure D-1. The basic job of a program

The "program" in the figure can be either a compiled program* (such as *ls*), or it may be *interpreted*. In the latter case, a machine-executable program such as *awk* reads your program, and then uses the instructions in your program to process the data.

---

* Compiled programs are typically written in lower-level languages such as C, C++, Fortran, or Ada, and then translated, or *compiled*, into a form that the computer can execute directly.

When you write a program, it usually consists of the following, very basic set of steps, as shown in Figure D-2:

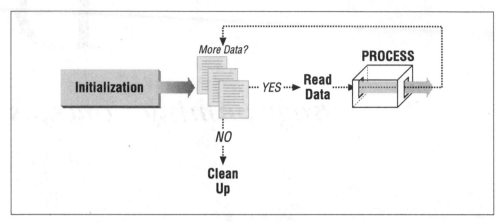

Figure D-2. The basic outline of a program

Initialization

These are the things you do before actually starting to process data, such as checking arguments, initializing any data you need to work with, and so on. This step corresponds to *awk*'s BEGIN rule (see the section "The BEGIN and END Special Patterns" in Chapter 6, *Patterns, Actions, and Variables*).

If you were baking a cake, this might consist of laying out all the mixing bowls and the baking pan, and making sure you have all the ingredients that you need.

Processing

This is where the actual work is done. Your program reads data, one logical chunk at a time, and processes it as appropriate.

In most programming languages, you have to manually manage the reading of data, checking to see if there is more each time you read a chunk. *awk*'s pattern-action paradigm (see Chapter 1, *Getting Started with awk*) handles the mechanics of this for you.

In baking a cake, the processing corresponds to the actual labor: breaking eggs, mixing the flour, water, and other ingredients, and then putting the cake into the oven.

Clean Up

Once you've processed all the data, you may have things you need to do before exiting. This step corresponds to *awk*'s END rule (see the section "The BEGIN and END Special Patterns" in Chapter 6).

> After the cake comes out of the oven, you still have to wrap it in plastic wrap to keep anyone from tasting it, as well as wash the mixing bowls and utensils.

An *algorithm* is a detailed set of instructions necessary to accomplish a task, or process data. It is much the same as a recipe for baking a cake. Programs implement algorithms. Often, it is up to you to design the algorithm and implement it, simultaneously.

The "logical chunks" we talked about previously are called *records*, similar to the records a company keeps on employees, a school keeps for students, or a doctor keeps for patients. Each record has many component parts, such as first and last names, date of birth, address, and so on. The component parts are referred to as the *fields* of the record.

The act of reading data is termed *input*, and that of generating results, not too surprisingly, is termed *output*. They are often referred to together as "input/output," and even more often, as "I/O" for short. (You will also see "input" and "output" used as verbs.)

awk manages the reading of data for you, as well as the breaking it up into records and fields. Your program's job is to tell *awk* what to with the data. You do this by describing *patterns* in the data to look for, and *actions* to execute when those patterns are seen. This *data-driven* nature of *awk* programs usually makes them both easier to write and easier to read.

Data Values in a Computer

In a program, you keep track of information and values in things called *variables*. A variable is just a name for a given value, such as first_name, last_name, address, and so on. *awk* has several predefined variables, and it has special names to refer to the current input record and the fields of the record. You may also group multiple associated values under one name, as an array.

Data, particularly in *awk*, consists of either numeric values, such as 42 or 3.1415927, or string values. String values are essentially anything that's not a number, such as a name. Strings are sometimes referred to as *character data*, since they store the individual characters that comprise them. Individual variables, as well as numeric and string variables, are referred to as *scalar* values. Groups of values, such as arrays, are not scalars.

Within computers, there are two kinds of numeric values: *integers* and *floating-point*. In school, integer values were referred to as "whole" numbers—that is, numbers without any fractional part, such as 1, 42, or −17. The advantage to integer numbers is that they represent values exactly. The disadvantage is that their range is limited. On most modern systems, this range is −2,147,483,648 to

2,147,483,647.

Integer values come in two flavors: *signed* and *unsigned.* Signed values may be negative or positive, with the range of values just described. Unsigned values are always positive. On most modern systems, the range is from 0 to 4,294,967,295.

Floating-point numbers represent what are called "real" numbers; i.e., those that do have a fractional part, such as 3.1415927. The advantage to floating-point numbers is that they can represent a much larger range of values. The disadvantage is that there are numbers that they cannot represent exactly. *awk* uses *double-precision* floating-point numbers, which can hold more digits than *single-precision* floating-point numbers. Floating-point issues are discussed more fully in the section "Floating-Point Number Caveats" later in this appendix.

At the very lowest level, computers store values as groups of binary digits, or *bits.* Modern computers group bits into groups of eight, called *bytes.* Advanced applications sometimes have to manipulate bits directly, and *gawk* provides functions for doing so.

While you are probably used to the idea of a number without a value (i.e., zero), it takes a bit more getting used to the idea of zero-length character data. Nevertheless, such a thing exists. It is called the *null string.* The null string is character data that has no value. In other words, it is empty. It is written in *awk* programs like this: `""`.

Humans are used to working in decimal; i.e., base 10. In base 10, numbers go from 0 to 9, and then "roll over" into the next column. (Remember grade school? 42 is 4 times 10 plus 2.)

There are other number bases though. Computers commonly use base 2 or *binary,* base 8 or *octal,* and base 16 or *hexadecimal.* In binary, each column represents two times the value in the column to its right. Each column may contain either a 0 or a 1. Thus, binary 1010 represents 1 times 8, plus 0 times 4, plus 1 times 2, plus 0 times 1, or decimal 10. Octal and hexadecimal are discussed more in the section "Octal and Hexadecimal Numbers" in Chapter 5, *Expressions.*

Programs are written in programming languages. Hundreds, if not thousands, of programming languages exist. One of the most popular is the C programming language. The C language had a very strong influence on the design of the *awk* language.

There have been several versions of C. The first is often referred to as "K&R" C, after the initials of Brian Kernighan and Dennis Ritchie, the authors of the first book on C. (Dennis Ritchie created the language, and Brian Kernighan was one of the creators of *awk.*)

In the mid-1980s, an effort began to produce an international standard for C. This work culminated in 1989, with the production of the ANSI standard for C. This standard became an ISO standard in 1990. Where it makes sense, POSIX *awk* is compatible with 1990 ISO C.

In 1999, a revised ISO C standard was approved and released. Future versions of *gawk* will be as compatible as possible with this standard.

Floating-Point Number Caveats

As mentioned earlier, floating-point numbers represent what are called "real" numbers, i.e., those that have a fractional part. *awk* uses double-precision floating-point numbers to represent all numeric values. This section describes some of the issues involved in using floating-point numbers.

There is a very nice paper on floating-point arithmetic by David Goldberg, "What Every Computer Scientist Should Know About Floating-point Arithmetic," *ACM Computing Surveys* **23**, 1 (1991-03), 5-48.* This is worth reading if you are interested in the details, but it does require a background in computer science.

Internally, *awk* keeps both the numeric value (double-precision floating-point) and the string value for a variable. Separately, *awk* keeps track of what type the variable has (see the section "Variable Typing and Comparison Expressions" in Chapter 5), which plays a role in how variables are used in comparisons.

It is important to note that the string value for a number may not reflect the full value (all the digits) that the numeric value actually contains. The following program (*values.awk*) illustrates this:

```
{
    $1 = $2 + $3
    # see it for what it is
    printf("$1 = %.12g\n", $1)
    # use CONVFMT
    a = "<" $1 ">"
    print "a =", a
    # use OFMT
    print "$1 =", $1
}
```

This program shows the full value of the sum of $2 and $3 using `printf`, and then prints the string values obtained from both automatic conversion (via CONVFMT) and from printing (via OFMT).

---

* *http://www.validgh.com/goldberg/paper.ps.*

Here is what happens when the program is run:

```
$ echo 2 3.654321 1.2345678 | awk -f values.awk
$1 = 4.8888888
a = <4.88889>
$1 = 4.88889
```

This makes it clear that the full numeric value is different from what the default string representations show.

CONVFMT's default value is `"%.6g"`, which yields a value with at least six significant digits. For some applications, you might want to change it to specify more precision. On most modern machines, most of the time, 17 digits is enough to capture a floating-point number's value exactly.*

Unlike numbers in the abstract sense (such as what you studied in high school or college math), numbers stored in computers are limited in certain ways. They cannot represent an infinite number of digits, nor can they always represent things exactly. In particular, floating-point numbers cannot always represent values exactly. Here is an example:

```
$ awk '{ printf("%010d\n", $1 * 100) }'
515.79
0000051579
515.80
0000051579
515.81
0000051580
515.82
0000051582
Ctrl-d
```

This shows that some values can be represented exactly, whereas others are only approximated. This is not a "bug" in *awk*, but simply an artifact of how computers represent numbers.

Another peculiarity of floating-point numbers on modern systems is that they often have more than one representation for the number zero! In particular, it is possible to represent "minus zero" as well as regular, or "positive" zero.

This example shows that negative and positive zero are distinct values when stored internally, but that they are in fact equal to each other, as well as to "regular" zero:

---

* Pathological cases can require up to 752 digits (!), but we doubt that you need to worry about this.

```
$ gawk 'BEGIN { mz = -0 ; pz = 0
> printf "-0 = %g, +0 = %g, (-0 == +0) -> %d\n", mz, pz, mz == pz
> printf "mz == 0 -> %d, pz == 0 -> %d\n", mz == 0, pz == 0
> }'
-0 = -0, +0 = 0, (-0 == +0) -> 1
mz == 0 -> 1, pz == 0 -> 1
```

It helps to keep this in mind should you process numeric data that contains negative zero values; the fact that the zero is negative is noted and can affect comparisons.

E

GNU General Public License

Version 2, June 1991

Copyright © 1989, 1991 Free Software Foundation, Inc.
59 Temple Place, Suite 330, Boston, MA 02111, USA

Everyone is permitted to copy and distribute verbatim copies
of this license document, but changing it is not allowed.

Preamble

The licenses for most software are designed to take away your freedom to share and change it. By contrast, the GNU General Public License is intended to guarantee your freedom to share and change free software—to make sure the software is free for all its users. This General Public License applies to most of the Free Software Foundation's software and to any other program whose authors commit to using it. (Some other Free Software Foundation software is covered by the GNU Library General Public License instead.) You can apply it to your programs, too.

When we speak of free software, we are referring to freedom, not price. Our General Public Licenses are designed to make sure that you have the freedom to distribute copies of free software (and charge for this service if you wish), that you receive source code or can get it if you want it, that you can change the software or use pieces of it in new free programs; and that you know you can do these things.

To protect your rights, we need to make restrictions that forbid anyone to deny you these rights or to ask you to surrender the rights. These restrictions translate to certain responsibilities for you if you distribute copies of the software, or if you modify it.

For example, if you distribute copies of such a program, whether gratis or for a fee, you must give the recipients all the rights that you have. You must make sure that they, too, receive or can get the source code. And you must show them these terms so they know their rights.

We protect your rights with two steps: (1) copyright the software, and (2) offer you this license which gives you legal permission to copy, distribute and/or modify the software.

Also, for each author's protection and ours, we want to make certain that everyone understands that there is no warranty for this free software. If the software is modified by someone else and passed on, we want its recipients to know that what they have is not the original, so that any problems introduced by others will not reflect on the original authors' reputations.

Finally, any free program is threatened constantly by software patents. We wish to avoid the danger that redistributors of a free program will individually obtain patent licenses, in effect making the program proprietary. To prevent this, we have made it clear that any patent must be licensed for everyone's free use or not licensed at all.

The precise terms and conditions for copying, distribution, and modification follow.

Terms and Conditions for Copying, Distribution, and Modification

0. This License applies to any program or other work which contains a notice placed by the copyright holder saying it may be distributed under the terms of this General Public License. The "Program," below, refers to any such program or work, and a "work based on the Program" means either the Program or any derivative work under copyright law: that is to say, a work containing the Program or a portion of it, either verbatim or with modifications and/or translated into another language. (Hereinafter, translation is included without limitation in the term "modification.") Each licensee is addressed as "you."

    Activities other than copying, distribution and modification are not covered by this License; they are outside its scope. The act of running the Program is not restricted, and the output from the Program is covered only if its contents constitute a work based on the Program (independent of having been made by running the Program). Whether that is true depends on what the Program does.

1. You may copy and distribute verbatim copies of the Program's source code as you receive it, in any medium, provided that you conspicuously and appropriately publish on each copy an appropriate copyright notice and disclaimer of warranty; keep intact all the notices that refer to this License and to the absence of any warranty; and give any other recipients of the Program a copy of this License along with the Program.

    You may charge a fee for the physical act of transferring a copy, and you may at your option offer warranty protection in exchange for a fee.

2. You may modify your copy or copies of the Program or any portion of it, thus forming a work based on the Program, and copy and distribute such modifications or work under the terms of Section 1 above, provided that you also meet all of these conditions:

    a. You must cause the modified files to carry prominent notices stating that you changed the files and the date of any change.

    b. You must cause any work that you distribute or publish, that in whole or in part contains or is derived from the Program or any part thereof, to be licensed as a whole at no charge to all third parties under the terms of this License.

    c. If the modified program normally reads commands interactively when run, you must cause it, when started running for such interactive use in the most ordinary way, to print or display an announcement including an appropriate copyright notice and a notice that there is no warranty (or else, saying that you provide a warranty) and that users may redistribute the program under these conditions, and telling the user how to view a copy of this License. (Exception: if the Program itself is interactive but does not normally print such an announcement, your work based on the Program is not required to print an announcement.)

    These requirements apply to the modified work as a whole. If identifiable sections of that work are not derived from the Program, and can be reasonably considered independent and separate works in themselves, then this License, and its terms, do not apply to those sections when you distribute them as separate works. But when you distribute the same sections as part of a whole which is a work based on the Program, the distribution of the whole must be on the terms of this License, whose permissions for other licensees extend to the entire whole, and thus to each and every part regardless of who wrote it.

    Thus, it is not the intent of this section to claim rights or contest your rights to work written entirely by you; rather, the intent is to exercise the right to control the distribution of derivative or collective works based on the Program.

In addition, mere aggregation of another work not based on the Program with the Program (or with a work based on the Program) on a volume of a storage or distribution medium does not bring the other work under the scope of this License.

3. You may copy and distribute the Program (or a work based on it, under section 2) in object code or executable form under the terms of sections 1 and 2 above provided that you also do one of the following:

    a. Accompany it with the complete corresponding machine-readable source code, which must be distributed under the terms of sections 1 and 2 above on a medium customarily used for software interchange; or,

    b. Accompany it with a written offer, valid for at least three years, to give any third party, for a charge no more than your cost of physically performing source distribution, a complete machine-readable copy of the corresponding source code, to be distributed under the terms of Sections 1 and 2 above on a medium customarily used for software interchange; or,

    c. Accompany it with the information you received as to the offer to distribute corresponding source code. (This alternative is allowed only for noncommercial distribution and only if you received the program in object code or executable form with such an offer, in accord with Subsection b above.)

    The source code for a work means the preferred form of the work for making modifications to it. For an executable work, complete source code means all the source code for all modules it contains, plus any associated interface definition files, plus the scripts used to control compilation and installation of the executable. However, as a special exception, the source code distributed need not include anything that is normally distributed (in either source or binary form) with the major components (compiler, kernel, and so on) of the operating system on which the executable runs, unless that component itself accompanies the executable.

    If distribution of executable or object code is made by offering access to copy from a designated place, then offering equivalent access to copy the source code from the same place counts as distribution of the source code, even though third parties are not compelled to copy the source along with the object code.

4. You may not copy, modify, sublicense, or distribute the Program except as expressly provided under this License. Any attempt otherwise to copy, modify, sublicense or distribute the Program is void, and will automatically terminate your rights under this License. However, parties who have received copies, or rights, from you under this License will not have their licenses terminated so long as such parties remain in full compliance.

5. You are not required to accept this License, since you have not signed it. However, nothing else grants you permission to modify or distribute the Program or its derivative works. These actions are prohibited by law if you do not accept this License. Therefore, by modifying or distributing the Program (or any work based on the Program), you indicate your acceptance of this License to do so, and all its terms and conditions for copying, distributing or modifying the Program or works based on it.

6. Each time you redistribute the Program (or any work based on the Program), the recipient automatically receives a license from the original licensor to copy, distribute or modify the Program subject to these terms and conditions. You may not impose any further restrictions on the recipients' exercise of the rights granted herein. You are not responsible for enforcing compliance by third parties to this License.

7. If, as a consequence of a court judgment or allegation of patent infringement or for any other reason (not limited to patent issues), conditions are imposed on you (whether by court order, agreement or otherwise) that contradict the conditions of this License, they do not excuse you from the conditions of this License. If you cannot distribute so as to satisfy simultaneously your obligations under this License and any other pertinent obligations, then as a consequence you may not distribute the Program at all. For example, if a patent license would not permit royalty-free redistribution of the Program by all those who receive copies directly or indirectly through you, then the only way you could satisfy both it and this License would be to refrain entirely from distribution of the Program.

   If any portion of this section is held invalid or unenforceable under any particular circumstance, the balance of the section is intended to apply and the section as a whole is intended to apply in other circumstances.

   It is not the purpose of this section to induce you to infringe any patents or other property right claims or to contest validity of any such claims; this section has the sole purpose of protecting the integrity of the free software distribution system, which is implemented by public license practices. Many people have made generous contributions to the wide range of software distributed through that system in reliance on consistent application of that system; it is up to the author/donor to decide if he or she is willing to distribute software through any other system and a licensee cannot impose that choice.

   This section is intended to make thoroughly clear what is believed to be a consequence of the rest of this License.

8. If the distribution and/or use of the Program is restricted in certain countries either by patents or by copyrighted interfaces, the original copyright holder who places the Program under this License may add an explicit geographical

distribution limitation excluding those countries, so that distribution is permitted only in or among countries not thus excluded. In such case, this License incorporates the limitation as if written in the body of this License.

9. The Free Software Foundation may publish revised and/or new versions of the General Public License from time to time. Such new versions will be similar in spirit to the present version, but may differ in detail to address new problems or concerns.

   Each version is given a distinguishing version number. If the Program specifies a version number of this License which applies to it and "any later version," you have the option of following the terms and conditions either of that version or of any later version published by the Free Software Foundation. If the Program does not specify a version number of this License, you may choose any version ever published by the Free Software Foundation.

10. If you wish to incorporate parts of the Program into other free programs whose distribution conditions are different, write to the author to ask for permission. For software which is copyrighted by the Free Software Foundation, write to the Free Software Foundation; we sometimes make exceptions for this. Our decision will be guided by the two goals of preserving the free status of all derivatives of our free software and of promoting the sharing and reuse of software generally.

NO WARRANTY

11. BECAUSE THE PROGRAM IS LICENSED FREE OF CHARGE, THERE IS NO WARRANTY FOR THE PROGRAM, TO THE EXTENT PERMITTED BY APPLICABLE LAW. EXCEPT WHEN OTHERWISE STATED IN WRITING THE COPYRIGHT HOLDERS AND/OR OTHER PARTIES PROVIDE THE PROGRAM "AS IS" WITHOUT WARRANTY OF ANY KIND, EITHER EXPRESSED OR IMPLIED, INCLUDING, BUT NOT LIMITED TO, THE IMPLIED WARRANTIES OF MERCHANTABILITY AND FITNESS FOR A PARTICULAR PURPOSE. THE ENTIRE RISK AS TO THE QUALITY AND PERFORMANCE OF THE PROGRAM IS WITH YOU. SHOULD THE PROGRAM PROVE DEFECTIVE, YOU ASSUME THE COST OF ALL NECESSARY SERVICING, REPAIR OR CORRECTION.

12. IN NO EVENT UNLESS REQUIRED BY APPLICABLE LAW OR AGREED TO IN WRITING WILL ANY COPYRIGHT HOLDER, OR ANY OTHER PARTY WHO MAY MODIFY AND/OR REDISTRIBUTE THE PROGRAM AS PERMITTED ABOVE, BE LIABLE TO YOU FOR DAMAGES, INCLUDING ANY GENERAL, SPECIAL, INCIDENTAL OR CONSEQUENTIAL DAMAGES ARISING OUT OF THE USE OR INABILITY TO USE THE PROGRAM (INCLUDING BUT NOT LIMITED TO LOSS OF DATA OR DATA BEING RENDERED INACCURATE OR LOSSES SUSTAINED BY YOU OR THIRD PARTIES OR A FAILURE OF THE

PROGRAM TO OPERATE WITH ANY OTHER PROGRAMS), EVEN IF SUCH HOLDER OR OTHER PARTY HAS BEEN ADVISED OF THE POSSIBILITY OF SUCH DAMAGES.

END OF TERMS AND CONDITIONS

How to Apply These Terms to Your New Programs

If you develop a new program, and you want it to be of the greatest possible use to the public, the best way to achieve this is to make it free software which everyone can redistribute and change under these terms.

To do so, attach the following notices to the program. It is safest to attach them to the start of each source file to most effectively convey the exclusion of warranty; and each file should have at least the "copyright" line and a pointer to where the full notice is found:

```
one line to give the program's name and an idea of what it does.
Copyright (C) year  name of author

This program is free software; you can redistribute it and/or
modify it under the terms of the GNU General Public License
as published by the Free Software Foundation; either version 2
of the License, or (at your option) any later version.

This program is distributed in the hope that it will be useful,
but WITHOUT ANY WARRANTY; without even the implied warranty of
MERCHANTABILITY or FITNESS FOR A PARTICULAR PURPOSE. See the
GNU General Public License for more details.

You should have received a copy of the GNU General Public License
along with this program; if not, write to the Free Software
Foundation, Inc., 59 Temple Place, Suite 330, Boston, MA 02111, USA.
```

Also add information on how to contact you by electronic and paper mail.

If the program is interactive, make it output a short notice like this when it starts in an interactive mode:

```
Gnomovision version 69, Copyright (C) year name of author
Gnomovision comes with ABSOLUTELY NO WARRANTY; for details
type 'show w'. This is free software, and you are welcome
to redistribute it under certain conditions; type 'show c'
for details.
```

The hypothetical commands show w and show c should show the appropriate parts of the General Public License. Of course, the commands you use may be called something other than show w and show c; they could even be mouse-clicks or menu items—whatever suits your program.

You should also get your employer (if you work as a programmer) or your school, if any, to sign a "copyright disclaimer" for the program, if necessary. Here is a sample; alter the names:

```
Yoyodyne, Inc., hereby disclaims all copyright
interest in the program 'Gnomovision'
(which makes passes at compilers) written
by James Hacker.

signature of Ty Coon, 1 April 1989
Ty Coon, President of Vice
```

This General Public License does not permit incorporating your program into proprietary programs. If your program is a subroutine library, you may consider it more useful to permit linking proprietary applications with the library. If this is what you want to do, use the GNU Lesser General Public License instead of this License.

GNU Free Documentation License

Version 1.1, March 2000

Copyright © 2000 Free Software Foundation, Inc.
59 Temple Place, Suite 330, Boston, MA 02111-1307 USA

Everyone is permitted to copy and distribute verbatim copies
of this license document, but changing it is not allowed.

0. PREAMBLE

The purpose of this License is to make a manual, textbook, or other written document "free" in the sense of freedom: to assure everyone the effective freedom to copy and redistribute it, with or without modifying it, either commercially or noncommercially. Secondarily, this License preserves for the author and publisher a way to get credit for their work, while not being considered responsible for modifications made by others.

This License is a kind of "copyleft", which means that derivative works of the document must themselves be free in the same sense. It complements the GNU General Public License, which is a copyleft license designed for free software.

We have designed this License in order to use it for manuals for free software, because free software needs free documentation: a free program should come with manuals providing the same freedoms that the software does. But this License is not limited to software manuals; it can be used for any textual work, regardless of subject matter or whether it is published as a printed book. We recommend this License principally for works whose purpose is instruction or reference.

1. APPLICABILITY AND DEFINITIONS

This License applies to any manual or other work that contains a notice placed by the copyright holder saying it can be distributed under the terms of this License. The "Document," below, refers to any such manual or work. Any member of the public is a licensee, and is addressed as "you."

A "Modified Version" of the Document means any work containing the Document or a portion of it, either copied verbatim, or with modifications and/or translated into another language.

A "Secondary Section" is a named appendix or a front-matter section of the Document that deals exclusively with the relationship of the publishers or authors of the Document to the Document's overall subject (or to related matters) and contains nothing that could fall directly within that overall subject. (For example, if the Document is in part a textbook of mathematics, a Secondary Section may not explain any mathematics.) The relationship could be a matter of historical connection with the subject or with related matters, or of legal, commercial, philosophical, ethical or political position regarding them.

The "Invariant Sections" are certain Secondary Sections whose titles are designated, as being those of Invariant Sections, in the notice that says that the Document is released under this License.

The "Cover Texts" are certain short passages of text that are listed, as Front-Cover Texts or Back-Cover Texts, in the notice that says that the Document is released under this License.

A "Transparent" copy of the Document means a machine-readable copy, represented in a format whose specification is available to the general public, whose contents can be viewed and edited directly and straightforwardly with generic text editors or (for images composed of pixels) generic paint programs or (for drawings) some widely available drawing editor, and that is suitable for input to text formatters or for automatic translation to a variety of formats suitable for input to text formatters. A copy made in an otherwise Transparent file format whose markup has been designed to thwart or discourage subsequent modification by readers is not Transparent. A copy that is not "Transparent" is called "Opaque."

Examples of suitable formats for Transparent copies include plain ASCII without markup, Texinfo input format, LaTeX input format, SGML or XML using a publicly available DTD, and standard-conforming simple HTML designed for human modification. Opaque formats include PostScript, PDF, proprietary formats that can be read and edited only by proprietary word processors, SGML or XML for which the DTD and/or processing tools are not generally available, and the machine-generated HTML produced by some word processors for output purposes only.

The "Title Page" means, for a printed book, the title page itself, plus such following pages as are needed to hold, legibly, the material this License requires to appear in the title page. For works in formats which do not have any title page as such, "Title Page" means the text near the most prominent appearance of the work's title, preceding the beginning of the body of the text.

2. VERBATIM COPYING

You may copy and distribute the Document in any medium, either commercially or noncommercially, provided that this License, the copyright notices, and the license notice saying this License applies to the Document are reproduced in all copies, and that you add no other conditions whatsoever to those of this License. You may not use technical measures to obstruct or control the reading or further copying of the copies you make or distribute. However, you may accept compensation in exchange for copies. If you distribute a large enough number of copies you must also follow the conditions in section 3.

You may also lend copies, under the same conditions stated above, and you may publicly display copies.

3. COPYING IN QUANTITY

If you publish printed copies of the Document numbering more than 100, and the Document's license notice requires Cover Texts, you must enclose the copies in covers that carry, clearly and legibly, all these Cover Texts: Front-Cover Texts on the front cover, and Back-Cover Texts on the back cover. Both covers must also clearly and legibly identify you as the publisher of these copies. The front cover must present the full title with all words of the title equally prominent and visible. You may add other material on the covers in addition. Copying with changes limited to the covers, as long as they preserve the title of the Document and satisfy these conditions, can be treated as verbatim copying in other respects.

If the required texts for either cover are too voluminous to fit legibly, you should put the first ones listed (as many as fit reasonably) on the actual cover, and continue the rest onto adjacent pages.

If you publish or distribute Opaque copies of the Document numbering more than 100, you must either include a machine-readable Transparent copy along with each Opaque copy, or state in or with each Opaque copy a publicly-accessible computer-network location containing a complete Transparent copy of the Document, free of added material, which the general network-using public has access to download anonymously at no charge using public-standard network protocols. If you use the latter option, you must take reasonably prudent steps, when you begin distribution of Opaque copies in quantity, to ensure that this Transparent copy will remain thus accessible at the stated location until at least one year after the last time you distribute an Opaque copy (directly or through your agents or retailers) of that edition to the public.

It is requested, but not required, that you contact the authors of the Document well before redistributing any large number of copies, to give them a chance to provide you with an updated version of the Document.

4. MODIFICATIONS

You may copy and distribute a Modified Version of the Document under the conditions of sections 2 and 3 above, provided that you release the Modified Version under precisely this License, with the Modified Version filling the role of the Document, thus licensing distribution and modification of the Modified Version to whoever possesses a copy of it. In addition, you must do these things in the Modified Version:

A. Use in the Title Page (and on the covers, if any) a title distinct from that of the Document, and from those of previous versions (which should, if there were any, be listed in the History section of the Document). You may use the same title as a previous version if the original publisher of that version gives permission.

B. List on the Title Page, as authors, one or more persons or entities responsible for authorship of the modifications in the Modified Version, together with at least five of the principal authors of the Document (all of its principal authors, if it has less than five).

C. State on the Title page the name of the publisher of the Modified Version, as the publisher.

D. Preserve all the copyright notices of the Document.

E. Add an appropriate copyright notice for your modifications adjacent to the other copyright notices.

F. Include, immediately after the copyright notices, a license notice giving the public permission to use the Modified Version under the terms of this License, in the form shown in the Addendum below.

G. Preserve in that license notice the full lists of Invariant Sections and required Cover Texts given in the Document's license notice.

H. Include an unaltered copy of this License.

I. Preserve the section entitled "History," and its title, and add to it an item stating at least the title, year, new authors, and publisher of the Modified Version as given on the Title Page. If there is no section entitled "History" in the Document, create one stating the title, year, authors, and publisher of the Document as given on its Title Page, then add an item describing the Modified Version as stated in the previous sentence.

J. Preserve the network location, if any, given in the Document for public access to a Transparent copy of the Document, and likewise the network locations given in the Document for previous versions it was based on. These may be placed in the "History" section. You may omit a network location for a work that was published at least four years before the Document itself, or if the original publisher of the version it refers to gives permission.

K. In any section entitled "Acknowledgements" or "Dedications," preserve the section's title, and preserve in the section all the substance and tone of each of the contributor acknowledgements and/or dedications given therein.

L. Preserve all the Invariant Sections of the Document, unaltered in their text and in their titles. Section numbers or the equivalent are not considered part of the section titles.

M. Delete any section entitled "Endorsements." Such a section may not be included in the Modified Version.

N. Do not retitle any existing section as "Endorsements" or to conflict in title with any Invariant Section.

If the Modified Version includes new front-matter sections or appendices that qualify as Secondary Sections and contain no material copied from the Document, you may at your option designate some or all of these sections as invariant. To do this, add their titles to the list of Invariant Sections in the Modified Version's license notice. These titles must be distinct from any other section titles.

You may add a section entitled "Endorsements," provided it contains nothing but endorsements of your Modified Version by various parties—for example, statements of peer review or that the text has been approved by an organization as the authoritative definition of a standard.

You may add a passage of up to five words as a Front-Cover Text, and a passage of up to 25 words as a Back-Cover Text, to the end of the list of Cover Texts in the Modified Version. Only one passage of Front-Cover Text and one of Back-Cover Text may be added by (or through arrangements made by) any one entity. If the Document already includes a cover text for the same cover, previously added by you or by arrangement made by the same entity you are acting on behalf of, you may not add another; but you may replace the old one, on explicit permission from the previous publisher that added the old one.

The author(s) and publisher(s) of the Document do not by this License give permission to use their names for publicity for or to assert or imply endorsement of any Modified Version.

5. COMBINING DOCUMENTS

    You may combine the Document with other documents released under this License, under the terms defined in section 4 above for modified versions, provided that you include in the combination all of the Invariant Sections of all of the original documents, unmodified, and list them all as Invariant Sections of your combined work in its license notice.

    The combined work need only contain one copy of this License, and multiple identical Invariant Sections may be replaced with a single copy. If there are multiple Invariant Sections with the same name but different contents, make the title of each such section unique by adding at the end of it, in parentheses, the name of the original author or publisher of that section if known, or else a unique number. Make the same adjustment to the section titles in the list of Invariant Sections in the license notice of the combined work.

    In the combination, you must combine any sections entitled "History" in the various original documents, forming one section entitled "History"; likewise combine any sections entitled "Acknowledgements," and any sections entitled "Dedications." You must delete all sections entitled "Endorsements."

6. COLLECTIONS OF DOCUMENTS

    You may make a collection consisting of the Document and other documents released under this License, and replace the individual copies of this License in the various documents with a single copy that is included in the collection, provided that you follow the rules of this License for verbatim copying of each of the documents in all other respects.

    You may extract a single document from such a collection, and distribute it individually under this License, provided you insert a copy of this License into the extracted document, and follow this License in all other respects regarding verbatim copying of that document.

7. AGGREGATION WITH INDEPENDENT WORKS

    A compilation of the Document or its derivatives with other separate and independent documents or works, in or on a volume of a storage or distribution medium, does not as a whole count as a Modified Version of the Document, provided no compilation copyright is claimed for the compilation. Such a compilation is called an "aggregate," and this License does not apply to the other self-contained works thus compiled with the Document, on account of their being thus compiled, if they are not themselves derivative works of the Document.

If the Cover Text requirement of section 3 is applicable to these copies of the Document, then if the Document is less than one quarter of the entire aggregate, the Document's Cover Texts may be placed on covers that surround only the Document within the aggregate. Otherwise they must appear on covers around the whole aggregate.

8. TRANSLATION

Translation is considered a kind of modification, so you may distribute translations of the Document under the terms of section 4. Replacing Invariant Sections with translations requires special permission from their copyright holders, but you may include translations of some or all Invariant Sections in addition to the original versions of these Invariant Sections. You may include a translation of this License provided that you also include the original English version of this License. In case of a disagreement between the translation and the original English version of this License, the original English version will prevail.

9. TERMINATION

You may not copy, modify, sublicense, or distribute the Document except as expressly provided for under this License. Any other attempt to copy, modify, sublicense or distribute the Document is void, and will automatically terminate your rights under this License. However, parties who have received copies, or rights, from you under this License will not have their licenses terminated so long as such parties remain in full compliance.

10. FUTURE REVISIONS OF THIS LICENSE

The Free Software Foundation may publish new, revised versions of the GNU Free Documentation License from time to time. Such new versions will be similar in spirit to the present version, but may differ in detail to address new problems or concerns. See *http://www.gnu.org/copyleft/*.

Each version of the License is given a distinguishing version number. If the Document specifies that a particular numbered version of this License "or any later version" applies to it, you have the option of following the terms and conditions either of that specified version or of any later version that has been published (not as a draft) by the Free Software Foundation. If the Document does not specify a version number of this License, you may choose any version ever published (not as a draft) by the Free Software Foundation.

ADDENDUM: How to Use This License for Your Documents

To use this License in a document you have written, include a copy of the License in the document and put the following copyright and license notices just after the title page:

```
Copyright (C)  year  your name.
Permission is granted to copy, distribute and/or modify this document
under the terms of the GNU Free Documentation License, Version 1.1
or any later version published by the Free Software Foundation;
with the Invariant Sections being list their titles, with the
Front-Cover Texts being list, and with the Back-Cover Texts being list.
A copy of the license is included in the section entitled "GNU
Free Documentation License".
```

If you have no Invariant Sections, write "with no Invariant Sections" instead of saying which ones are invariant. If you have no Front-Cover Texts, write "no Front-Cover Texts" instead of "Front-Cover Texts being *list*"; likewise for Back-Cover Texts.

If your document contains nontrivial examples of program code, we recommend releasing these examples in parallel under your choice of free software license, such as the GNU General Public License, to permit their use in free software.

Glossary

Action

A series of *awk* statements attached to a rule. If the rule's pattern matches an input record, *awk* executes the rule's action. Actions are always enclosed in curly braces. (See the section "Actions" in Chapter 6, *Patterns, Actions, and Variables*.)

Amazing awk Assembler

Henry Spencer at the University of Toronto wrote a retargetable assembler completely as *sed* and *awk* scripts. It is thousands of lines long, including machine descriptions for several eight-bit microcomputers. It is a good example of a program that would have been better written in another language. It is available over the Internet from *ftp://ftp.freefriends.org/arnold/Awkstuff/aaa.tgz*.

Amazingly Workable Formatter (awf)

Henry Spencer at the University of Toronto wrote a formatter that accepts a large subset of the `nroff -ms` and `nroff -man` formatting commands, using *awk* and *sh*. It is available over the Internet from *ftp://ftp.freefriends.org/arnold/Awkstuff/awf.tgz*.

Anchor

The regexp metacharacters ^ and $, which force the match to the beginning or end of the string, respectively.

ANSI

The American National Standards Institute. This organization produces many standards, among them the standards for the C and C++ programming languages. These standards often become international standards as well. See also "ISO."

Array

A grouping of multiple values under the same name. Most languages provide just sequential arrays. *awk* provides associative arrays (see "Associative Array").

Assertion

A statement in a program that a condition is true at this point in the program. Useful for reasoning about how a program is supposed to behave.

Assignment

An *awk* expression that changes the value of some *awk* variable or data object. An object that you can assign to is called an *lvalue*. The assigned values are called *rvalues*. See the section "Assignment Expressions" in Chapter 5, *Expressions*.

Associative Array

Arrays in which the indices may be numbers or strings, not just sequential integers in a fixed range.

awk Language

The language in which *awk* programs are written.

awk Program

An *awk* program consists of a series of *patterns* and *actions*, collectively known as *rules*. For each input record given to the program, the program's rules are all processed in turn. *awk* programs may also contain function definitions.

awk Script

Another name for an *awk* program.

Bash

The GNU version of the standard shell (the Bourne-again shell). See also "Bourne Shell."

BBS

See "Bulletin Board System."

Bit Short for "Binary Digit." All values in computer memory ultimately reduce to binary digits: values that are either zero or one. Groups of bits may be interpreted differently—as integers, floating-point numbers, character data, addresses of other memory objects, or other data. *awk* lets you work with floating-point numbers and strings. *gawk* lets you manipulate bit values with the built-in functions described in the section "Bit-Manipulation Functions of gawk" in Chapter 8, *Functions*.

Computers are often defined by how many bits they use to represent integer values. Typical systems are 32-bit systems, but 64-bit systems are becoming increasingly popular, while 16-bit systems are waning in popularity.

Boolean Expression

Named after the English mathematician Boole. See also "Logical Expression."

Bourne Shell

The standard shell (*/bin/sh*) on Unix and Unix-like systems, originally written by Steven R. Bourne. Many shells (Bash, *ksh*, *pdksh*, *zsh*) are generally upwardly compatible with the Bourne shell.

Built-in Function

The *awk* language provides built-in functions that perform various numerical, I/O-related, and string computations. Examples are sqrt (for the square root of a number) and substr (for a substring of a string). *gawk* provides functions for timestamp management, bit manipulation, and runtime string translation. (See the section "Built-in Functions" in Chapter 8.)

Built-in Variable

ARGC, ARGV, CONVFMT, ENVIRON, FILENAME, FNR, FS, NF, NR, OFMT, OFS, ORS, RLENGTH, RSTART, RS, and SUBSEP are the variables that have special meaning to *awk*. In addition, ARGIND, BINMODE, ERRNO, FIELDWIDTHS, IGNORECASE, LINT, PROCINFO, RT, and TEXTDOMAIN are the variables that have special meaning to *gawk*. Changing some of them affects *awk*'s running environment. (See the section "Built-in Variables" in Chapter 6.)

Braces

See "Curly Braces."

Bulletin Board System

A computer system allowing users to log in and read and/or leave messages for other users of the system, much like leaving paper notes on a bulletin board.

C The system programming language that most GNU software is written in. The *awk* programming language has C-like syntax, and this book points out similarities between *awk* and C when appropriate.

In general, *gawk* attempts to be as similar to the 1990 version of ISO C as makes sense. Future versions of *gawk* may adopt features from the newer 1999 standard, as appropriate.

C++

A popular object-oriented programming language derived from C.

Character Set

The set of numeric codes used by a computer system to represent the characters (letters, numbers, punctuation, etc.) of a particular country or place. The most common character set in use today is ASCII (American Standard Code for Information Interchange). Many European countries use an extension of ASCII known as ISO-8859-1 (ISO Latin-1).

CHEM

A preprocessor for *pic* that reads descriptions of molecules and produces *pic* input for drawing them. It was written in *awk* by Brian Kernighan and Jon Bentley, and is available from *http://cm.bell-labs.com/netlib/typesetting/ chem.gz.*

Coprocess

A subordinate program with which two-way communication is possible.

Compiler

A program that translates human-readable source code into machine-executable object code. The object code is then executed directly by the computer. See also "Interpreter."

Compound Statement

A series of *awk* statements, enclosed in curly braces. Compound statements may be nested. (See the section "Control Statements in Actions" in Chapter 6.)

Concatenation

Concatenating two strings means sticking them together, one after another, producing a new string. For example, the string foo concatenated with the string bar gives the string foobar. (See the section "String Concatenation" in Chapter 5.)

Conditional Expression

An expression using the ?: ternary operator, such as *expr1 ? expr2 : expr3*. The expression *expr1* is evaluated; if the result is true, the value of the whole expression is the value of *expr2*; otherwise, the value is *expr3*. In either case, only one of *expr2* and *expr3* is evaluated. (See the section "Conditional Expressions" in Chapter 5.)

Comparison Expression

A relation that is either true or false, such as (a < b). Comparison expressions are used in if, while, do, and for statements, and in patterns to select which input records to process. (See the section "Variable Typing and Comparison Expressions" in Chapter 5.)

Curly Braces

The characters { and }. Curly braces are used in *awk* for delimiting actions, compound statements, and function bodies.

Dark Corner

An area in the language in which specifications often were (or still are) not clear, leading to unexpected or undesirable behavior. Such areas are marked with "(d.c.)" in the text and are indexed under the heading "dark corner."

Data Driven

A description of *awk* programs, in which you specify the data you are interested in processing and what to do when that data is seen.

Data Objects

Numbers and strings of characters. Numbers are converted into strings and vice versa, as needed. (See the section "Conversion of Strings and Numbers" in Chapter 5.)

Deadlock

The situation in which two communicating processes are each waiting for the other to perform an action.

Double-Precision

An internal representation of numbers that can have fractional parts. Double-precision numbers keep track of more digits than do single-precision numbers, but operations on them are sometimes more expensive. This is the way *awk* stores numeric values. It is the C type double.

Dynamic Regular Expression

A dynamic regular expression is a regular expression written as an ordinary expression. It could be a string constant, such as "foo", but it may also be an expression whose value can vary. (See the section "Using Dynamic Regexps" in Chapter 2, *Regular Expressions*.)

Environment

A collection of strings, of the form *name=val*, that each program has available to it. Users generally place values into the environment in order to provide information to various programs. Typical examples are the environment variables HOME and PATH.

Empty String

See "Null String."

Epoch

The date used as the "beginning of time" for timestamps. Time values in Unix systems are represented as seconds since the epoch, with library functions available for converting these values into standard date and time formats.

The epoch on Unix and POSIX systems is 1970-01-01 00:00:00 UTC. See also "GMT" and "UTC."

Escape Sequences

A special sequence of characters used for describing nonprinting characters, such as \n for newline or \033 for the ASCII ESC (Escape) character. (See the section "Escape Sequences" in Chapter 2.)

FDL

See "Free Documentation License."

Field

When *awk* reads an input record, it splits the record into pieces separated by whitespace (or by a separator regexp that you can change by setting the built-in variable FS). Such pieces are called fields. If the pieces are of fixed length, you can use the built-in variable FIELDWIDTHS to describe their lengths. (See the section "Specifying How Fields Are Separated" and the section "Reading Fixed-Width Data" in Chapter 3, *Reading Input Files.*)

Flag

A variable whose truth value indicates the existence or nonexistence of some condition.

Floating-Point Number

Often referred to in mathematical terms as a "rational" or real number, this is just a number that can have a fractional part. See also "Double-Precision" and "Single-Precision."

Format

Format strings are used to control the appearance of output in the strftime and sprintf functions, and are used in the printf statement as well. Also, data conversions from numbers to strings are controlled by the format string contained in the built-in variable CONVFMT. (See the section "Format-Control Letters" in Chapter 4, *Printing Output.*)

Free Documentation License

This document describes the terms under which this book is published and may be copied. (See Appendix F, *GNU Free Documentation License.*)

Function

A specialized group of statements used to encapsulate general or program-specific tasks. *awk* has a number of built-in functions, and also allows you to define your own. (See Chapter 8.)

FSF

See "Free Software Foundation."

Free Software Foundation

A nonprofit organization dedicated to the production and distribution of freely distributable software. It was founded by Richard M. Stallman, the author of the original Emacs editor. GNU Emacs is the most widely used version of Emacs today.

gawk

The GNU implementation of *awk*.

General Public License

This document describes the terms under which *gawk* and its source code may be distributed. (See Appendix E, *GNU General Public License*.)

GMT

"Greenwich Mean Time." This is the old term for UTC. It is the time of day used as the epoch for Unix and POSIX systems. See also "Epoch" and "UTC."

GNU

"GNU's not Unix." An ongoing project of the Free Software Foundation to create a complete, freely distributable, POSIX-compliant computing environment.

GNU/Linux

A variant of the GNU system using the Linux kernel, instead of the Free Software Foundation's Hurd kernel. Linux is a stable, efficient, full-featured clone of Unix that has been ported to a variety of architectures. It is most popular on PC-class systems, but runs well on a variety of other systems too. The Linux kernel source code is available under the terms of the GNU General Public License, which is perhaps its most important aspect.

GPL

See "General Public License."

Hexadecimal

Base 16 notation, in which the digits are 0–9 and A–F, with A representing 10, B representing 11, and so on, up to F for 15. Hexadecimal numbers are written in C using a leading 0x, to indicate their base. Thus, 0x12 is 18 (1 times 16 plus 2).

I/O

Abbreviation for "input/output," the act of moving data into and/or out of a running program.

Input Record

A single chunk of data that is read in by *awk*. Usually, an *awk* input record consists of one line of text. (See the section "How Input Is Split into Records" in Chapter 3.)

Integer

A whole number, i.e., a number that does not have a fractional part.

Internationalization

The process of writing or modifying a program so that it can use multiple languages without requiring further source code changes.

Interpreter

A program that reads human-readable source code directly, and uses the instructions in it to process data and produce results. *awk* is typically (but not always) implemented as an interpreter. See also "Compiler."

Interval Expression

A component of a regular expression that lets you specify repeated matches of some part of the regexp. Interval expressions were not traditionally available in *awk* programs.

ISO

The International Standards Organization. This organization produces international standards for many things, including programming languages, such as C and C++. In the computer arena, important standards like those for C, C++, and POSIX become both American national and ISO international standards simultaneously. This book refers to Standard C as "ISO C" throughout.

Keyword

In the *awk* language, a keyword is a word that has special meaning. Keywords are reserved and may not be used as variable names.

gawk's keywords are: `BEGIN`, `END`, `if`, `else`, `while`, `do...while`, `for`, `for...in`, `break`, `continue`, `delete`, `next`, `nextfile`, `function`, `func`, and `exit`.

Lesser General Public License (LGPL)

This document describes the terms under which binary library archives or shared objects, and whether their source code may be distributed.

Linux

See "GNU/Linux."

Localization

The process of providing the data necessary for an internationalized program to work in a particular language.

Logical Expression

An expression using the operators for logic, AND, OR, and NOT, written `&&`, `||`, and `!` in *awk*. Often called Boolean expressions, after the mathematician who pioneered this kind of mathematical logic.

Lvalue

An expression that can appear on the left side of an assignment operator. In most languages, *lvalues* can be variables or array elements. In *awk*, a field designator can also be used as an *lvalue*.

Matching

The act of testing a string against a regular expression. If the regexp describes the contents of the string, it is said to *match* it.

Metacharacters

Characters used within a regexp that do not stand for themselves. Instead, they denote regular expression operations, such as repetition, grouping, or alternation.

Null String

A string with no characters in it. It is represented explicitly in *awk* programs by placing two double quote characters next to each other (`""`). It can appear in input data by having two successive occurrences of the field separator appear next to each other.

Number

A numeric-valued data object. Modern *awk* implementations use double-precision floating-point to represent numbers. Very old *awk* implementations use single-precision floating-point.

Octal

Base-8 notation, in which the digits are 0–7. Octal numbers are written in C using a leading 0, to indicate their base. Thus, 013 is 11 (1 times 8 plus 3).

P1003.2

See "POSIX."

Pattern

Patterns tell *awk* which input records are interesting to which rules.

A pattern is an arbitrary conditional expression against which input is tested. If the condition is satisfied, the pattern is said to *match* the input record. A typical pattern might compare the input record against a regular expression. (See the section "Pattern Elements" in Chapter 6.)

POSIX

The name for a series of standards that specify a Portable Operating System interface. The "IX" denotes the Unix heritage of these standards. The main standard of interest for *awk* users is *IEEE Standard for Information Technology, Standard 1003.2-1992, Portable Operating System Interface (POSIX) Part 2: Shell and Utilities.* Informally, this standard is often referred to as simply "P1003.2."

Precedence

The order in which operations are performed when operators are used without explicit parentheses.

Private

Variables and/or functions that are meant for use exclusively by library functions and not for the main *awk* program. Special care must be taken when naming such variables and functions. (See the section "Naming Library Function Global Variables" in Chapter 12, *A Library of awk Functions.*)

Range (of input lines)

A sequence of consecutive lines from the input file(s). A pattern can specify ranges of input lines for *awk* to process or it can specify single lines. (See the section "Pattern Elements" in Chapter 6.)

Recursion

When a function calls itself, either directly or indirectly. If this isn't clear, refer to the entry for "redirection."

Redirection

Redirection means performing input from something other than the standard input stream, or performing output to something other than the standard output stream.

You can redirect the output of the `print` and `printf` statements to a file or a system command, using the >, >>, |, and |& operators. You can redirect input to the `getline` statement using the <, |, and |& operators. (See the section "Redirecting Output of print and printf" in Chapter 4, and the section "Explicit Input with getline" in Chapter 3.)

Regexp

Short for *regular expression*. A regexp is a pattern that denotes a set of strings, possibly an infinite set. For example, the regexp R.*xp matches any string starting with the letter R and ending with the letters xp. In *awk*, regexps are used in patterns and in conditional expressions. Regexps may contain escape sequences. (See Chapter 2.)

Regular Expression

See "Regexp."

Regular Expression Constant

A regular expression constant is a regular expression written within slashes, such as /foo/. This regular expression is chosen when you write the *awk* program and cannot be changed during its execution. (See the section "How to Use Regular Expressions" in Chapter 2.)

Rule

A segment of an *awk* program that specifies how to process single-input records. A rule consists of a *pattern* and an *action*. *awk* reads an input record; then, for each rule, if the input record satisfies the rule's pattern, *awk* executes the rule's action. Otherwise, the rule does nothing for that input record.

Rvalue

A value that can appear on the right side of an assignment operator. In *awk*, essentially every expression has a value. These values are *rvalues*.

Scalar

A single value, be it a number or a string. Regular variables are scalars; arrays and functions are not.

Search Path

In *gawk*, a list of directories to search for *awk* program source files. In the shell, a list of directories to search for executable programs.

Seed

The initial value, or starting point, for a sequence of random numbers.

sed

See "Stream Editor."

Shell

The command interpreter for Unix and POSIX-compliant systems. The shell works both interactively, and as a programming language for batch files or shell scripts.

Short-Circuit

The nature of the *awk* logical operators && and ||. If the value of the entire expression is determinable from evaluating just the lefthand side of these operators, the righthand side is not evaluated. (See the section "Boolean Expressions" in Chapter 5.)

Side Effect

A side effect occurs when an expression has an effect aside from merely producing a value. Assignment expressions, increment and decrement expressions, and function calls have side effects. (See the section "Assignment Expressions" in Chapter 5.)

Single-Precision

An internal representation of numbers that can have fractional parts. Single-precision numbers keep track of fewer digits than do double-precision numbers, but operations on them are sometimes less expensive in terms of CPU time. This is the type used by some very old versions of *awk* to store numeric values. It is the C type `float`.

Space

The character generated by hitting the space bar on the keyboard.

Special File

A filename interpreted internally by *gawk*, instead of being handed directly to the underlying operating system—for example, */dev/stderr*. (See the section "Special Filenames in gawk" in Chapter 4.)

Stream Editor

A program that reads records from an input stream and processes them one or more at a time. This is in contrast with batch programs, which may expect to read their input files in entirety before starting to do anything, as well as with interactive programs that require input from the user.

String

A datum consisting of a sequence of characters, such as `I am a string`. Constant strings are written with double quotes in the *awk* language and may contain escape sequences. (See the section "Escape Sequences" in Chapter 2.)

Tab

The character generated by hitting the Tab key on the keyboard. It usually expands to up to eight spaces upon output.

Text Domain

A unique name that identifies an application. Used for grouping messages that are translated at runtime into the local language.

Timestamp

A value in the "seconds since the epoch" format used by Unix and POSIX systems. Used for the *gawk* functions `mktime`, `strftime`, and `systime`. See also "Epoch" and "UTC."

Unix

A computer operating system originally developed in the early 1970s at AT&T Bell Laboratories. It initially became popular in universities around the world and later moved into commercial environments as a software-development system and network-server system. There are many commercial versions of Unix, as well as several work-alike systems whose source code is freely available (such as GNU/Linux, NetBSD, FreeBSD, and OpenBSD).

UTC

The accepted abbreviation for "Universal Coordinated Time." This is standard time in Greenwich, England, which is used as a reference time for day and date calculations. See also "Epoch" and "GMT."

Whitespace

A sequence of space, tab, or newline characters occurring inside an input record or a string.

Index

We'd like to hear your suggestions for improving our indexes. Send email to *index@oreilly.com*.

About the Author

Arnold Robbins, a native of Atlanta, Georgia, is a professional programmer and a technical author. He is also a happy husband, the father of four very cute children, and an amateur Talmudist (Babylonian and Jerusalem). Since late 1997, he and his family have been living happily in Israel.

Arnold has been working with Unix systems since 1980, when he was introduced to a PDP-11 running a version of Sixth Edition Unix. He has been a heavy *awk* user since 1987, when he became involved with *gawk*, the GNU project's version of *awk*. As a member of the POSIX 1003.2 balloting group, he helped shape the POSIX standard for *awk*. He currently maintains *gawk* and its documentation (i.e., this book). The documentation is also available from the Free Software Foundation (*http://www.gnu.org*).

In previous incarnations, Arnold was a systems administrator and taught continuing education classes in Unix and networking. He has also had more than one poor experience with startup software companies, about which he prefers not to think anymore.

O'Reilly & Associates has been keeping him busy. In addition to this book, Arnold is the author of *Unix in a Nutshell*, Third Edition, and the *sed & awk Pocket Reference*; he is the coauthor of *sed & awk*, Second Edition, and *Learning the vi Editor*, Sixth Edition.

Colophon

Our look is the result of reader comments, our own experimentation, and feedback from distribution channels. Distinctive covers complement our distinctive approach to technical topics, breathing personality and life into potentially dry subjects.

The animal on the cover of *Effective awk Programming*, Third Edition, is a great auk, a powerful symbol of nineteenth-century European and American arrogance toward nature. In using great auks as food and for their oil, and later collecting specimen for the kind of trivial display so popular with the inhabitants of mansions in Victorian England, mankind showed no mercy; mankind did not take care to effectively manage the few delicate populations as sustainable resources, much less treat the great auk as a living species worthy of respect. In 1844, sailors working for a British collector killed the last two great auks and stole their incubating egg on an island off the coast of Iceland.

The original penguin, great auks were large, black and white, flightless seabirds with pronounced, bent, orange beaks. The auks nested for three to four weeks each spring on craggy islands in the North Atlantic. When not nesting with their lifelong mates, great auks swam the seas in extended-family groups, occasionally deep-sea diving for large fish. Sixteenth-century sailors who exploited nesting populations for food during long voyages called the birds penguins, a name they also gave to the smaller-beaked seabirds of the Southern Hemisphere that still exist today.

Jeffrey Holcomb was the production editor for *Effective awk Programming*, Third Edition. Claire Cloutier was the production manager. Mary Brady was the copyeditor, and Maureen Dempsey was the proofreader. Rachel Wheeler, Matt Hutchinson, and Claire Cloutier provided quality control. Kimo Carter and Matt Hutchinson provided production support. Arnold Robbins and Nancy Crumpton wrote the index.

Hanna Dyer designed the cover of this book, based on a series design by Edie Freedman. The cover image is a 19th-century engraving from *Century Illustrated Monthly Magazine*. Emma Colby produced the cover layout with QuarkXPress 4.1 using Adobe's ITC Garamond font.

David Futato designed the interior layout based on a series design by Nancy Priest. Using a version of *makeinfo* modified by Phillippe Martin to create DocBook and enhanced by the author, the book was converted by the author from the Texinfo source into DocBook XML. Arnold then post-processed the generated DocBook with no less than six *awk* scripts (of course!), finally tuning the DocBook source files by hand. The print version of this book was created by translating the DocBook XML markup of its source files into a set of *groff* macros using a filter developed at O'Reilly & Associates by Norman Walsh. Steve Talbott designed and wrote the underlying macro set on the basis of the GNU *troff –mgs* macros; Lenny Muellner adapted them to XML and implemented the book design. The GNU *groff* text formatter Version 1.11.1 was used to generate PostScript output. The text and heading fonts are ITC Garamond Light and Garamond Book; the code font is Constant Willison. The illustrations that appear in the book were produced by Robert Romano and Jessamyn Read using Macromedia FreeHand 9 and Adobe Photoshop 6. This colophon was written by Sarah Jane Shangraw.

Whenever possible, our books use a durable and flexible lay-flat binding. If the page count exceeds this binding's limit, perfect binding is used.

More Titles from O'Reilly

UNIX Tools

The UNIX CD Bookshelf, 2nd Edition

By O'Reilly & Associates, Inc.
2nd Edition February 2000
624 pages, Features CD-ROM
ISBN 0-596-00000-6

The second edition of *The UNIX CD Bookshelf* contains six books from O'Reilly, plus the software from *UNIX Power Tools* – all on a convenient CD-ROM. Buyers also get a bonus hard-copy book, *UNIX in a Nutshell 3rd Edition*. The CD-ROM contains *UNIX in a Nutshell, 3rd Edition*; *UNIX Power Tools, 2nd Edition* (with software); *Learning the UNIX Operating System, 4th Edition*; *Learning the vi Editor, 6th Edition*; *sed & awk, 2nd Edition*; and *Learning the Korn Shell*.

sed & awk, 2nd Edition

By Dale Dougherty & Arnold Robbins
2nd Edition March 1997
432 pages, ISBN 1-56592-225-5

sed & awk describes two text manipulation programs that are mainstays of the UNIX programmer's toolbox. This edition covers the sed and awk programs as they are mandated by the POSIX standard and includes discussion of the GNU versions of these programs.

lex & yacc, 2nd Edition

By John Levine, Tony Mason & Doug Brown
2nd Edition October 1992
366 pages, ISBN 1-56592-000-7

Shows programmers how to use two UNIX utilities, lex and yacc, in program development. You'll find tutorial sections for novice users, reference sections for advanced users, and a detailed index. Major MS-DOS and UNIX versions of lex and yacc are explored in depth. Also covers Bison and Flex.

Managing Projects with make, 2nd Edition

By Andrew Oram & Steve Talbott
2nd Edition October 1991
152 pages, ISBN 0-937175-90-0

make is one of UNIX's greatest contributions to software development, and this book is the clearest description of make ever written. It describes all the basic features and provides guidelines on meeting the needs of large, modern projects. Also contains a description of free products that contain major enhancements to make.

Writing GNU Emacs Extensions

By Bob Glickstein
1st Edition April 1997
236 pages, ISBN 1-56592-261-1

This book introduces Emacs Lisp and tells you how to make the editor do whatever you want, whether it's altering the way text scrolls or inventing a whole new "major mode." Topics progress from simple to complex, from lists, symbols, and keyboard commands to syntax tables, macro templates, and error recovery.

UNIX Power Tools, 2nd Edition

By Jerry Peek, Tim O'Reilly & Mike Loukides
2nd Edition August 1997
1120 pages, Includes CD-ROM
ISBN 1-56592-260-3

Loaded with practical advice about almost every aspect of UNIX, this second edition of *UNIX Power Tools* addresses the technology that UNIX users face today. You'll find thorough coverage of POSIX utilities, including GNU versions, detailed bash and tcsh shell coverage, a strong emphasis on Perl, and a CD-ROM that contains the best freeware available.

UNIX Tools

sed & awk Pocket Reference

By Arnold Robbins
1st Edition January 2000
50 pages, ISBN 1-56592-729-X

The *sed & awk Pocket Reference* is a
companion volume to *sed & awk, 2nd
Edition*, and *Unix in a Nutshell, 3rd Edition*.
This small book is a handy reference guide
to the information presented in the larger
volumes, presenting a concise summary of
regular expressions and pattern matching,
and summaries of sed and awk.

Learning the bash Shell, 2nd Edition

By Cameron Newham & Bill Rosenblatt
2nd Edition January 1998
336 pages, ISBN 1-56592-347-2

This second edition covers all of the
features of bash Version 2.0, while still
applying to bash Version 1.x. It includes
one-dimensional arrays, parameter expansion,
more pattern-matching operations, new
commands, security improvements, additions
to ReadLine, improved configuration and installation, and an
additional programming aid, the bash shell debugger.

Applying RCS and SCCS

By Don Bolinger & Tan Bronson
1st Edition September 1995
528 pages, ISBN 1-56592-117-8

Applying RCS and SCCS is a thorough
introduction to these two systems, viewed
as tools for project management. This book
takes the reader from basic source control
of a single file, through working with multiple
releases of a software project, to coordinating
multiple developers. It also presents TCCS, a representative
"front-end" that addresses problems RCS and SCCS can't handle
alone, such as managing groups of files, developing for multiple
platforms, and linking public and private development areas.

Programming with GNU Software

By Mike Loukides & Andy Oram
1st Edition December 1996
260 pages, Includes CD-ROM
ISBN 1-56592-112-7

This book and CD combination is a complete
package for programmers who are new to
UNIX or who would like to make better use
of the system. The tools come from Cygnus
Support, Inc., and Cyclic Software, companies
that provide support for free software. Contents include GNU Emacs,
gcc, C and C++ libraries, gdb, RCS, and make. The book provides
an introduction to all these tools for a C programmer.

MySQL & mSQL

By Randy Jay Yarger, George Reese & Tim King
1st Edition July 1999
506 pages, ISBN 1-56592-434-7

This book teaches you how to use MySQL
and mSQL, two popular and robust database
products that support key subsets of SQL
on both Linux and UNIX systems. Anyone
who knows basic C, Java, Perl, or Python can
write a program to interact with a database,
either as a stand-alone application or through a Web page. This
book takes you through the whole process, from installation and
configuration to programming interfaces and basic administration.
Includes ample tutorial material.

Practical Internet Groupware

By Jon Udell
1st Edition October 1999
524 pages, ISBN 1-56592-537-8

This revolutionary book tells users,
programmers, IS managers, and system
administrators how to build Internet
groupware applications that organize the
casual and chaotic transmission of online
information into useful, disciplined, and
documented data.

How to stay in touch with O'Reilly

1. Visit Our Award-Winning Web Site

http://www.oreilly.com/

★ "Top 100 Sites on the Web" —*PC Magazine*
★ "Top 5% Web sites" —*Point Communications*
★ "3-Star site" —*The McKinley Group*

Our web site contains a library of comprehensive product information (including book excerpts and tables of contents), downloadable software, background articles, interviews with technology leaders, links to relevant sites, book cover art, and more. File us in your Bookmarks or Hotlist!

2. Join Our Email Mailing Lists

New Product Releases

To receive automatic email with brief descriptions of all new O'Reilly products as they are released, send email to:
ora-news-subscribe@lists.oreilly.com
Put the following information in the first line of your message (*not* in the Subject field):
subscribe ora-news

O'Reilly Events

If you'd also like us to send information about trade show events, special promotions, and other O'Reilly events, send email to:
ora-news-subscribe@lists.oreilly.com
Put the following information in the first line of your message (*not* in the Subject field):
subscribe ora-events

3. Get Examples from Our Books via FTP

There are two ways to access an archive of example files from our books:

Regular FTP

- ftp to:
  ftp.oreilly.com
  (login: anonymous
  password: your email address)
- Point your web browser to:
  ftp://ftp.oreilly.com/

FTPMAIL

- Send an email message to:
  ftpmail@online.oreilly.com
  (Write "help" in the message body)

4. Contact Us via Email

order@oreilly.com
To place a book or software order online. Good for North American and international customers.

subscriptions@oreilly.com
To place an order for any of our newsletters or periodicals.

books@oreilly.com
General questions about any of our books.

software@oreilly.com
For general questions and product information about our software. Check out O'Reilly Software Online at **http://software.oreilly.com/** for software and technical support information. Registered O'Reilly software users send your questions to: **website-support@oreilly.com**

cs@oreilly.com
For answers to problems regarding your order or our products.

booktech@oreilly.com
For book content technical questions or corrections.

proposals@oreilly.com
To submit new book or software proposals to our editors and product managers.

international@oreilly.com
For information about our international distributors or translation queries. For a list of our distributors outside of North America check out:
http://www.oreilly.com/distributors.html

5. Work with Us

Check out our website for current employment opportunites:
http://jobs.oreilly.com/

O'Reilly & Associates, Inc.
101 Morris Street, Sebastopol, CA 95472 USA
TEL   707-829-0515 or 800-998-9938
        (6am to 5pm PST)
FAX   707-829-0104

International Distributors

UK, EUROPE, MIDDLE EAST AND AFRICA (EXCEPT FRANCE, GERMANY, AUSTRIA, SWITZERLAND, LUXEMBOURG, AND LIECHTENSTEIN)

INQUIRIES

O'Reilly UK Limited
4 Castle Street
Farnham
Surrey, GU9 7HS
United Kingdom
Telephone: 44-1252-711776
Fax: 44-1252-734211
Email: information@oreilly.co.uk

ORDERS

Wiley Distribution Services Ltd.
1 Oldlands Way
Bognor Regis
West Sussex PO22 9SA
United Kingdom
Telephone: 44-1243-843294
UK Freephone: 0800-243207
Fax: 44-1243-843302 (Europe/EU orders)
or 44-1243-843274 (Middle East/Africa)
Email: cs-books@wiley.co.uk

FRANCE

INQUIRIES & ORDERS

Éditions O'Reilly
18 rue Séguier
75006 Paris, France
Tel: 1-40-51-71-89
Fax: 1-40-51-72-26
Email: france@oreilly.fr

GERMANY, SWITZERLAND, AUSTRIA, LUXEMBOURG, AND LIECHTENSTEIN

INQUIRIES & ORDERS

O'Reilly Verlag
Balthasarstr. 81
D-50670 Köln, Germany
Telephone: 49-221-973160-91
Fax: 49-221-973160-8
Email: anfragen@oreilly.de (inquiries)
Email: order@oreilly.de (orders)

CANADA (FRENCH LANGUAGE BOOKS)

Les Éditions Flammarion ltée
375, Avenue Laurier Ouest
Montréal (Québec) H2V 2K3
Tel: 00-1-514-277-8807
Fax: 00-1-514-278-2085
Email: info@flammarion.qc.ca

HONG KONG

City Discount Subscription Service, Ltd.
Unit A, 6th Floor, Yan's Tower
27 Wong Chuk Hang Road
Aberdeen, Hong Kong
Tel: 852-2580-3539
Fax: 852-2580-6463
Email: citydis@ppn.com.hk

KOREA

Hanbit Media, Inc.
Chungmu Bldg. 210
Yonnam-dong 568-33
Mapo-gu
Seoul, Korea
Tel: 822-325-0397
Fax: 822-325-9697
Email: hant93@chollian.dacom.co.kr

PHILIPPINES

Global Publishing
G/F Benavides Garden
1186 Benavides Street
Manila, Philippines
Tel: 632-254-8949/632-252-2582
Fax: 632-734-5060/632-252-2733
Email: globalp@pacific.net.ph

TAIWAN

O'Reilly Taiwan
1st Floor, No. 21, Lane 295
Section 1, Fu-Shing South Road
Taipei, 106 Taiwan
Tel: 886-2-27099669
Fax: 886-2-27038802
Email: mori@oreilly.com

INDIA

Shroff Publishers & Distributors Pvt. Ltd.
12, "Roseland", 2nd Floor
180, Waterfield Road, Bandra (West)
Mumbai 400 050
Tel: 91-22-641-1800/643-9910
Fax: 91-22-643-2422
Email: spd@vsnl.com

CHINA

O'Reilly Beijing
SIGMA Building, Suite B809
No. 49 Zhichun Road
Haidian District
Beijing, China PR 100080
Tel: 86-10-8809-7475
Fax: 86-10-8809-7463
Email: beijing@oreilly.com

JAPAN

O'Reilly Japan, Inc.
Yotsuya Y's Building
7 Banch 6, Honshio-cho
Shinjuku-ku
Tokyo 160-0003 Japan
Tel: 81-3-3356-5227
Fax: 81-3-3356-5261
Email: japan@oreilly.com

SINGAPORE, INDONESIA, MALAYSIA AND THAILAND

TransQuest Publishers Pte Ltd
30 Old Toh Tuck Road #05-02
Sembawang Kimtrans Logistics Centre
Singapore 597654
Tel: 65-4623112
Fax: 65-4625761
Email: wendiw@transquest.com.sg

ALL OTHER ASIAN COUNTRIES

O'Reilly & Associates, Inc.
101 Morris Street
Sebastopol, CA 95472 USA
Tel: 707-829-0515
Fax: 707-829-0104
Email: order@oreilly.com

AUSTRALIA

Woodslane Pty., Ltd.
7/5 Vuko Place
Warriewood NSW 2102
Australia
Tel: 61-2-9970-5111
Fax: 61-2-9970-5002
Email: info@woodslane.com.au

NEW ZEALAND

Woodslane New Zealand, Ltd.
21 Cooks Street (P.O. Box 575)
Waganui, New Zealand
Tel: 64-6-347-6543
Fax: 64-6-345-4840
Email: info@woodslane.com.au

ARGENTINA

Distribuidora Cuspide
Suipacha 764
1008 Buenos Aires
Argentina
Phone: 5411-4322-8868
Fax: 5411-4322-3456
Email: libros@cuspide.com

O'REILLY®